Granddad's Mondays

85 More Stories for My Grandchildren about the Reiss Family and Farm which dates from 1838 in St. Clair County, Illinois. Stories span to 1830s to 1930s

by Stephen W. Reiss

Granddad's Mondays
Copyright © 2024 by Stephen W. Reiss

ISBN: 979-8894790497 (hc)
ISBN: 979-8894790473 (sc)
ISBN: 979-8894790480 (e)

The Reading Glass Books
(888) 420-3050
www.readingglassbooks.com
fulfillment@readingglassbooks.com

Dedication to the Past

Three wonderful women married into the Reiss family and quickly became dynamic matriarchs for the family, the farm, and their respective generations. Read stories about:

Margaret Basler Reiss Ebert on page 96

Anna Sybilla Feder Reiss on page 184

Catherine Luetzelschwab Reiss on page 302

Dedication to the Future

We are blessed with four terrific grandchildren, ages 1 to 6. Two are in Chicago and two are in Springfield. Our home near Peoria is almost midway between them. My wife's name is Diane but our grandchildren call her Grand DD. They call me Granddad.

William Stephen Reiss

Kayla Marie Reiss

Ava Brooke Reiss

Blake Saber Reiss

Book Cover

This aerial photo was taken in 1980 looking northwest. Those roads are square with the world. The old farmstead is in the center with the 1920 barn in red, the 1889 house beyond it, and the 1940 house to the left.

Inspiration

Tradition means giving votes to the most obscure of all classes, our ancestors. It is the democracy of the dead. Tradition refuses to submit to the self-important living who merely happen to be walking around.

G. K. Chesterton
British author, philosopher

In family and faith, a knowledge of roots older than yourself is the key to fruit that will outlast you.

Rev. Bob Phillips
First Methodist Church of Peoria, IL

Before you knock over an ancient landmark, learn why it was put there.

Proverbs 22:28

Ask now about the former days, long before your time.

Deuteronomy 4:32

To forget one's ancestors is to be a brook without a source, a tree without a root.

Chinese proverb

Why waste your money looking up your family tree, just go into politics and your opponents will do it for you.

Mark Twain

Introduction – 85 Stories

April 1, 2012 was Palm Sunday. I was in the balcony at the First United Methodist Church of Peoria, Illinois. My mind wandered during several hymns. It struck me that I was more than 65 years older than our two grandchildren born in 2010 and 2011. Sadly I concluded that I would probably never have comprehensive adult conversations with our grandchildren about important family history, significant experiences, family vacation travels, and heavy philosophical subjects. Consequently, I resolved that Sunday morning to write two stories on such subjects to our grandchildren every Monday. They would be called Granddad's Mondays (GMs) and they would go as email attachments to their parents who are our two sons and their wives. My wife would get a copy and there would occasional blind copies to special relatives and friends. A third grandchild arrived in December 2013 and a fourth in January 2015. Now I'm more than 70 years older than the last two grandchildren.

Initially I found these stories very easy to write in less than an hour as one page including a photo. Within a month however my stories lengthened to two or three pages with more photos which required two or more hours to complete. I was having fun and often downloaded a paragraph from the Internet and an occasional aerial photo. That extra researching taught me more about those GM subjects. I was having great fun and took pride in each story being self-explanatory, informative, and entertaining. I have privately published annual volumes of stories at PIP Printing here in Peoria as Granddad's Mondays for 2012, then 2013, 2014, and 2015. The grandchildren and I appear on each book cover. Each grandchild and their parents receive an autographed book for Christmas. Even though our grandchildren might not read these books for another 20 years or more, at least my stories are in weekly emails and annual print such that they will outlast me. There have been 457 stories through 2015.

I have 780 family letters which my great great grandmother Margaret saved from her siblings, children, grandchildren, and friends from 1852 to 1888. That's 36 years including the Civil War and parts of three generations. Most were written in "old" German and had to be translated. The fun ones were written in phonetic English with thousands of misspellings. All of these letters were published in 2009 by Author House in a book titled It Takes A Matriarch. This was such a fun and fact-filled exercise that I'm looking forward to meeting those people in heaven, if that's the way it works!!!

I have 1,000 daily letters that my parents exchanged for 1.5 years during World War II. Dad was in Burma and India. Mom was in California with newborn me. In transcribing those letters, I got to meet and appreciate my parents when they were in their mid-twenties which is otherwise impossible. Those letters were published by Author House in a book titled From Burma With Love. My wife and I visited Burma, now called Myanmar, for ten days in 2013. That was very special.

I have two of my Grandmother Katie's five-year daily diaries beginning in 1944 and 1949 while my grandparents owned and operated the family farm south of Belleville, Illinois in St. Clair County. I transcribed those diaries, added a few explanatory paragraphs in italics, added lots of old photographs, and published them with Author House as Quilter, Granger, Grandma, Matriarch and as Granger, Quilter, Grandma, Matriarch.

I have 150 stories which my dad wrote for the *Sullivan Daily Times* in Sullivan, Indiana from 1984 to 2004. I also have a dozen professional speeches he made on the subject of reclaiming strip-mined coal lands back into productive farming. He was president of the farming subsidiary for a large Midwestern coal company. All of his writings are in another book by Author House called Family, Farming and Freedom.

I have 85 poems and almost that many milk bottles from the Reiss Dairy in Sikeston, Missouri. Those poems were composed by local citizen/customers from 1938 to about 1952, printed on new orders of milk bottles, and are now popular items on eBay. All that history is in another book by Author House called Reiss Dairy, Famous for Milk Bottles with Poems.

I have 40 years of my Uncle Frank's daily diaries. He was a professor in the Agriculture Department at the University of Illinois for 43 years. I read all 4.2 million of his words and transcribed 96,000 of them into a book titled Highlights of 40 Years of Frank Reiss Diaries. It was published by PIP Printing in Peoria and distributed only to family members. Frank was born and raised on the family farm and helped his parents manage it for another 20 years.

I digitized 26,000 old family slides from 1943 onward. That project took over 100 hours in 40 sittings using a magic electronic black box. Those photos and the flexibility to Photoshop are now a major resource for more stories.

All of my seven non-GM books involved compiling, editing, and developing transitions so everything flowed well with 1.22 million words on 2,584 total pages. Now all those books, old photos, my 40 years working for Caterpillar in Peoria and Asia, and thousands of my personal memories are very fertile resource soil for planting and cultivating special stories for our special grandchildren. There have been 457 GM stories through 2015. Some 172 of them appear in this and a companion book published by Pip Printing. First title is 85 Stories for My Grandchildren About the Reiss Family and Farm in St. Clair County, Illinois – 1830 to 1930. The second title is 88 More Stories for My Grandchildren About the Reiss Family and Farm in St. Clair County, Illinois – 1930 to Present.

Most of my GM stories are about other people but with my spin on who they were and what transpired. Even though I'm officially writing to our four young grandchildren, I'm really writing to our sons, Adam and Grant, and to their wives, Heather and Hany, with occasional bcc's to relatives. I can and do discretely plant seeds, coach, educate, encourage, and document history for the future benefit of all generations. If I forget to send stories on an occasional Monday, my sons call with a reminder. That's a compliment.

I'm having an absolute ball because all these books and stories will survive my cremation!!!

Stephen W. Reiss
Dunlap, Illinois

Table of Contents

1830 – 1839

1830 Population of St. Clair County is 7,078.

1830 States total 24, national population is 12.86 million. Arkansas is added in 1836 and Michigan in 1837.

1830 President is Andrew Jackson. Martin Van Buren is inaugurated in 1837.

1835 P. T. Barnum begins first circus tour of the US.

1836 Remember the Alamo.

1837 City of Chicago granted a charter by Illinois.

1837 Illinois capital moved from Vandalia to Springfield.

1838 Telegraph and Morse Code demonstrated.

1839 Charles Goodyear invents vulcanization of rubber.

The German Heritage Area of Southwestern Illinois
Clinton, Monroe, and St. Clair Counties

Dear Will, Kayla, Ava,   December 16, 2013

==Happy Birthday, Ava.== You were born yesterday at 3:45 in the afternoon. Welcome to your first of many Granddad's Mondays stories.

As you know, your mom/aunt Hany was born in Malaysia so her first language is Malay. She gradually learned English in school and from family and friends before moving to the US where English is the primary language. Your mom/aunt is totally bilingual. Now both of your parents, Kayla, are working hard to teach you both Malay and English. I'm very impressed by their plans and am confident you will eventually be bilingual as well.

Now let me tell you about another language, German, and how it fits with our heritage. My dad, your great grandfather Irv Reiss, grew up on the family farm in St. Clair County, Illinois. Both his parents spoke German in the household so that was his first language. He later learned English in school and from family and friends just like your mom/aunt Hany did. But that's kinda where it ended within our immediate family. My siblings and I learned maybe 50 German words but that was about it. German was not offered in the public schools or college that I attended so I remain mono-lingual.

Maybe I can make up for that a little bit by passing along the general German history that follows (in English) for southwestern Illinois where our German ancestors have been farmers since 1834. Some of this is from the history of St. Michael's Catholic Church in Paderborn, some is from a brochure published by the Southwestern Illinois Tourism Bureau, and some is from the Internet.

From the Tourism Bureau – The influx of immigrants from Germany in the early 1830's and again in the late 1840's created a lasting impression upon the typical and cultural landscape of Clinton, Monroe, and St. Clair Counties. Throughout the region, today's residents have retained and preserved an especially high level of their German heritage. German is still spoken in several places. Many of the homes, businesses, and churches built by German settlers still exist. German immigrants established the Belleville Public Library in 1836. They founded, in 1866, the Belleville Philharmonic Society, which is the second oldest orchestra in terms of continuous performance, in the United States.

Towns and places have names which reflect the significance of German settlement. The community of Hecker is named for the leader of the 1848 German revolution, Frederick Hecker, who is buried in the nearby town of Summerfield. Wartburg is named after the Castle of Wartburg where Martin Luther translated the Bible into German. Other places with German roots include Darmstadt, Freeburg, Germantown, Lenzburg, Millstadt, Saxtown, New Gaden, New Hanover, Paderborn, and Rentchler. The village of Maeystown is listed on the National Register of Historic Places because many of the original buildings, flagstone gutters, stone church and bridge have been preserved in nearly the same condition as when they were built by German settlers in the mid to late nineteenth century.

The retention of German heritage is manifested in architecture of the region and in the religious traditions, social activities, and customs of the people. Visitors from Germany should feel comfortable here amid the many familiar things which will remind them of home.

Civic organizations and churches hold festivals throughout the year to celebrate the heritage and ethnic traditions of their German ancestry. Three communities have Sister Cities in Germany: Belleville – Paderborn, Waterloo – Porta Westfalica, and Columbia – Gedern. The Belleville organization sponsors a banquet called "Taste of Germany" in early October which coincides with German – American Day. Waterloo's Porta Westfalica German Sister City Festival is in June. Columbia hosts the Sister City Bavarian Dinner Dance and Auction in March. Millstadt is in the process of organizing a Sister Cities exchange program. Other festivals and celebrations include Bierfest, Deutschfest, Fastnacht, Fruehlingsfest, Fruehlingstantz, Kirchenfest, Maifest, Oktoberfest, Rauchenfest, Schlachfest, Spassfest, and Wurstmarkt. The German Waterloo Band performs at many of these festivities where fine music is accompanied by lots of good, hearty German food, barrels of beer, arts and craft shows, antique fairs, quilt bingo, fun, and games.

The preservation and retention of German heritage is clearly evident in churches and religious traditions of the area. Holy Cross Lutheran Church in Wartburg was built in 1863 and the congregation has been observing Good Friday services in German for nearly 150 years. The Cathedral of St. Peter in Belleville is the largest Catholic cathedral in Illinois and served as the German-speaking parish for the entire community. Immaculate Conception Church in Madonnaville, built in 1856 using local limestone, is an excellent example of the craftsmanship of German stonemasons. Zoar United Church of Christ in New Hanover is another stone church and the cemetery contains graves of many of the early German settlers of the area. St. John Evangelical Church of the United Church of Christ in Maeystown was built by German stonemasons in 1865-67 and is the focal point of the village's historic district. Substantial, well-constructed churches throughout the area remain today as a testament to the faithfulness of the people and talent of the builders.

From St. Michael's Church history – The migration that took place in the 1830's was not so much a wanderlust or perhaps the idea of get rich quick, but rather, an avenue of escape.

We will briefly review the history starting with the eventful years of 1830-31. The revolution in France rekindled the smoldering fires of German patriotism and freedom. A movement of rebellion against oppression was gaining momentum. In 1832 the Bavarian government became alarmed and started to suppress or forbid the movement. However, the populace disregarded the order. Enthusiasm for reform was unbound. This was answered by military surveillance. All movements were suppressed by the government.

Disappointed, the German populace despaired and was ready to leave the fatherland for a land where one could live in freedom. Thus began the so-called Latin Immigration of the 1830's.

Prior to this time, the German press carried articles discussing the feasibility of creating a German State in Brazil or the United States. About the same time a certain Gottfried Deiden gave a report on his journey to the western states of North America. This report was in book form, and became a top seller in Europe. This book, even though idealistic, gave a rather accurate description of the general conditions of the land, climate, soil conditions, and commercial facilities. He favored Missouri rather than Illinois. To him the prairies did not appear productive. His contention was that the prairie land was too poor for even trees to grow. He also pointed out that the stagnant ponds in the prairies, like the swamp land in the bottoms, were mosquito breeders, with resultant typhoid and malaria.

The Germans placed great confidence in Deiden's writings. Therefore, the early settlers did not settle in the prairies, but rather on the hilly and rolling timber lands. Those who came later took the fertile prairie land where no clearing of timber was required, but simply some drainage to get rid of the water "in the ponds" as Deiden called them.

At the same time there was hunger in Germany. There was one crop failure after another. To this was added the overcrowded population. All of this gave cause for rebellion. It seems at Giesen, there was a college. This became a sort of melting pot for ideas. At any rate, it was there that the so called "Geisener Geselschaft" (Geisen Organization) started. However, as good as their plans may have been, they only served to get the ball rolling. For soon after their departure, the organization more or less lost itself due to several reasons: (1) not all could leave at the same time, (2) many stopped at various points after arriving in this country and thus lost contact with each other or (3) many died on the journey.

Another migration group was the Hesse group, made up of mostly Bavarian residents. Both migration groups existed about 1833-34. By 1834 active operations were in full swing. There was no more postponing. Migration was definitely planned and nothing would stop it. There were instances where mothers with newborn infants only a few weeks old were in these immigration groups.

There were two divisions as to the port of immigration. One group decided to go by way of New Orleans, the other by way of Baltimore. All started from Havre, France. Many of those who went by way of New Orleans died from cholera, smallpox, or yellow fever. The departure was not at all smooth since there were so many. There never was enough room on the ships and many had to remain behind to wait for another ship.

From the Internet – From the 1830s to the 1860s, more than 1.5 million Germans immigrated to United States of America. German immigrants to America were typically struggling farmers, political refugees, religious refugees, or men avoiding conscription in the German military. These German immigrants settled throughout the United States, in both urban and rural communities; however, the majority settled in the Midwestern states. German immigrants acquired a reputation for being hardworking, thrifty, and law-abiding people. Germans made numerous contributions to American culture, including inventions, traditions, sports, and food. The flooding of German immigrants to America was the result of long-term social, religious, and economic changes occurring throughout the German states.

Many of the farmers who came to America were troubled by the collapse of the Industrial Revolution in Germany, agricultural reform, overpopulation, crop failure, and lack of land in

Germany. During the time period of 1830 – 1860, most German immigrants came from the southwestern states of Germany where many were farmers.

Although the German immigrants dispersed themselves across the United States, the Midwest was the most popular region for the Germans to settle in. Germans migrated to the limestone floored valleys, such as the Mississippi Valley and the Ohio Valley. Cities, such as Cincinnati, St. Louis, and Milwaukee became urban centers for German immigrants. German immigrants who lived in these cities were mostly skilled artisans and craftsmen. Also, Wisconsin, Iowa, Michigan, and Ohio had similar climates and geographical conditions to that of Central Europe, therefore making these states appealing to the German farmers.

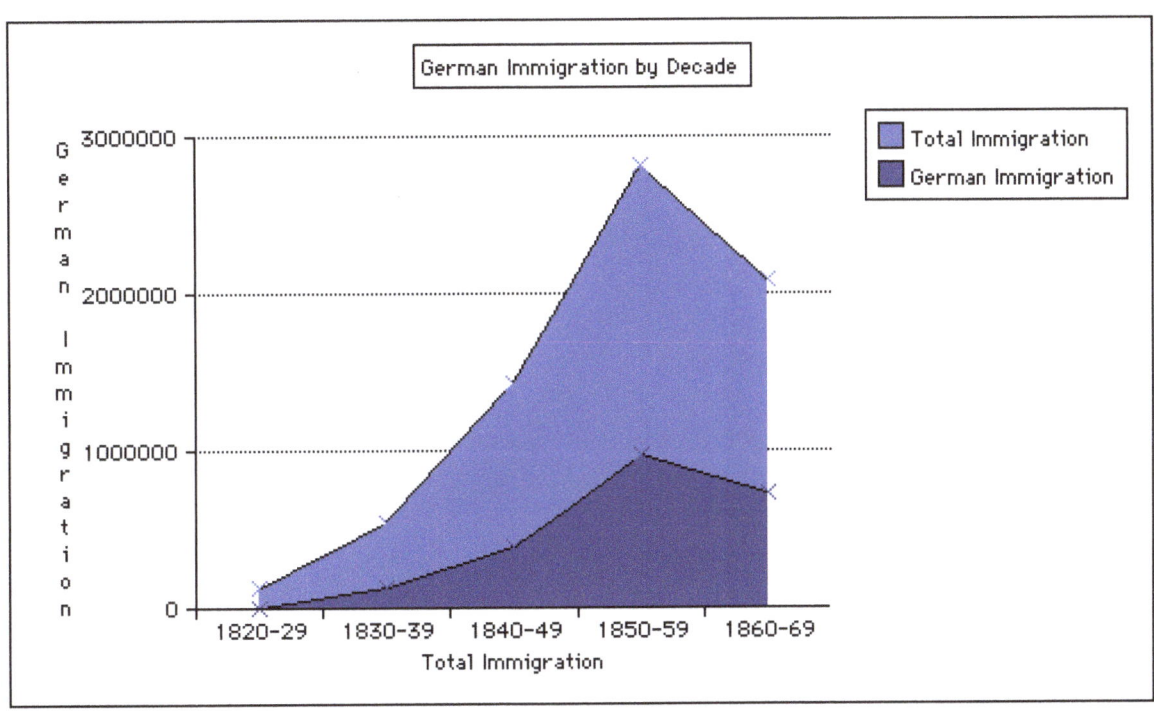

German immigrants introduced and brought to America valuable ideas and important products. Both the Conestoga wagon and the Kentucky rifle were invented by German-Americans.

Germans were also strong supporters of public education. In 1853, Kindergarten, was introduced to the public schools by German immigrants. When Americans saw the superior schools being established by the Germans, it made the Americans raise their educational standards. Germans also started the first paper mill in the United States, made important contributions in printing, and were the first people to work with iron and glass in America. German farmers were among the first American farmers to preserve their land by rotating their crops. Germans also formed labor unions in America as early as 1850.

Germans also made immense contributions to music and sports in America. The first American symphony organization was the Germania Orchestra, started in New York, in 1848. Songfests, inspired by Germans, have become popular throughout the United States as well. Germans also are credited as being the first people to found gymnastic societies. At one point, these societies grew so elaborate that competitions included parades, pageants, concerts, public addresses, and theatrical performances, in addition to bowling matches and competitions on the parallel bars and tumbling mats. German gymnastic societies led to the incorporation of physical education into the schooling system.

Many German customs evolved into American customs by the large number of Germans who came to America. Germans drank bier (beer) in large quantities on Sundays to celebrate the Sabbath. They also enjoyed swimming, target shooting, and bowling, all of which went on to be associated with American culture. Germans also contributed many different foods to America. Cole slaw, deli meats, oatmeal, frankfurters, and hamburgers all came to America through the German immigrants.

Will, Kayla, and Ava, you three will soon be going to kindergarten but now you know it's a German educational concept for young children. It's a German loanword without an English equivalent. Another German loanword is sauerkraut. I like it best in a Reuben sandwich which also includes Swiss cheese and Russian dressing. That heated sandwich is almost as international as the three of you. One report says it was created in 1914 by Arnold Reuben, the German owner of the once-famous Reuben's Delicatessen in New York City. Even the noun "delicatessen" is a German loanword. Enjoy and appreciate your German heritage.

Love, Granddad

Chapter 64 on St. Clair County in <u>The History of Southern Illinois</u> by George Washington Smith in 1912

There are many ways in which St. Clair stands at the head of the list. First it was the first county organized within the present state of Illinois. To be sure the legislature of Virginia created the county of Illinois which should include all settlers north and west of the Ohio River. This was in October, 1778.

General St. Clair Creates the County – In March, 1790, when General St. Clair came to Kaskaskia he created by proclamation the county of St. Clair. This county included all the territory between a line drawn from where Pekin is to Old Fort Massac, and the Illinois, Mississippi and the Ohio. Cahokia was made the capital of the county and a court house was constructed which still stands in a park in Chicago. As told elsewhere, the territory included in St. Clair was divided in 1795, October 5, the south half being called Randolph. The boundary lines of these two counties were changed several times. By 1812 when Madison County was created, St. Clair was reduced almost to its present limits. It was later enlarged to include most of Clinton and all of Washington. In 1825 it was reduced to its present boundary.

County Seat Transferred from Cahokia to Belleville – The capital or county seat was first at Cahokia, but in 1813 it was located in Belleville. The site at that time was a cornfield belonging to George Blair. The court house was built by Etienne Personeau in 1814 and about the same time George Blair built a hotel, Joseph Kerr opened a store and the town began to grow.

German Immigration – Belleville is now composed quite largely of Germans. But the Germans were latecomers. In 1825 there were only two Germans in Belleville, Conrad Bornman and Jacob Mauer. In 1825 Governor Ninian Edwards bought out Personeau and the site was resurveyed and lots were sold and new settlers come from Virginia bringing their slaves.

Among the Germans that came to St. Clair County in the 30's was Gustavus Koerner. He became a very active public spirited citizen. He was elected lieutenant governor with Governor Matteson in 1852. He was identified with the Republican Party and held many appointive offices. He died in Belleville in 1896, at the age of 87 years.

John Reynolds and John M. Peck – Governor John Reynolds lived in the earlier part of the Nineteenth Century at Cahokia but later made his home in Belleville. He built a railroad from the bluffs across the low lands to the present site of East St. Louis in 1837 for the transportation of coal to the Mississippi River. This was the first road which was actually finished and used. The motive power was horses.

Nothing in connection with the story of St. Louis County is so interesting as the life work of John M. Peck, who lived at Rock Spring some two miles west of the present city of Lebanon. Here he established Rock Spring Seminary which afterwards became Shurtleff College. This story has been told in connection with the chapter on education. No less interesting is the story and early struggles of McKendree College at Lebanon. These two schools and Illinois College, Jacksonville, were the first colleges west of the Alleghany Mountains.

Cahokia and Prairie du Pont – Cahokia was an Indian village at the time the Kaskaskia Indians migrated from near Starved Rock to Old Kaskaskia just above Chester. But without doubt the French soon made this Indian village into a mission station. At any rate the French Government very early in the Nineteenth Century made a grant of several thousands of acres to the village as Commons and as Commonfield. These common lands reached from the bluffs to the river. The city of East St. Louis occupies the northwest corner of these grants. Nearly all of this land is now owned by individuals and corporations, but there is yet a quantity that has never been alienated by the village. The income from these village lands sustains the schools and probably cares for the village interests. There is little left of the once prosperous town. The old cemetery may still be seen and the old church stands as a reminder of a forgotten age.

Prairie du Pont was a French village just south of and adjacent to Cahokia. To this old village was also given a grant of commons and common lands. The Prairie du Pont river or creek rises just a couple of miles west of Belleville, flows west through the bluffs and makes its way across the alluvial plain occupying a new bed every few years. It was on this stream where it flows into the river that the village grew up.

The Present County and County Seat – St. Clair County has a population of 119,870. It is dotted with villages and many of the farmers are engaged in truck gardening and occupy small farms. The Germans who are numerous in the population, are very thrifty indeed. It is an interesting sight to drive from East St. Louis to Belleville early in the morning and meet hundreds of wagons and carts going into the Twin Cities with their farm produce. The old rock road has been completely worn out with travel and the paving of the road from Belleville to East

St. Louis is underway. It is a distance of fourteen or fifteen miles, and it is estimated that it will take 19,000,000 paving blocks to pave this highway.

Belleville, the county seat, is a substantial city of 21,122 people. Its interests are mining, manufacturing, and commercial. There are a number of coal mines in the immediate vicinity of Belleville. This makes manufacturing inexpensive as far as the fuel question is concerned. Several lines of manufacturing are carried on. As early as the opening of the Civil war the old "Belleville Separator" for threshing wheat was common in the wheat producing counties in southern and central Illinois. Glass and bottle factories have flourished, foundries are substantial and remunerative forms of industry. The large population produces a demand for large and varied assortments of merchandise. The schools have always had the reputation of being abreast of the times, while religious and social life does not lag.

Charles Dickens and Son – An interesting bit of history connected with St. Clair County is the coming of Charles Dickens, the great English author, to see a real prairie. In 1842 Charles Dickens visited America. He came into the west via Pittsburgh and the Ohio River. He lectured in St. Louis. While here some literary friends to gratify a wish Dickens expressed to see a real prairie, got up a jaunting party to visit Looking Glass Prairie. Friday, April 15, 1842, a party of four teams, about fourteen people, crossed the river and drove through what was eventually to be the city of East St. Louis and seven or eight miles across the American Bottom and over the clay uplands to Belleville where they arrived about noon. Court was in session and at dinner time the judge and the lawyers and the guests from St. Louis mingled freely in the hotel, the old Mansion House on the northeast corner of Main and High streets. After dinner the jaunting party proceeded to Lebanon where they arrived about 4 o'clock. From here they passed over the road east from town about a mile and stopped near an abandoned cabin. Here they ate their lunch, and from this point they could get a fine view of Looking Glass Prairie and also of Emerald Mound. They returned to Lebanon where they remained over night at the Mermaid Tavern. The next day the party returned to St. Louis by way of Monk's Mound in the American Bottom. Only two St. Louis men are named of those who accompanied Dickens on this jaunt John Anderson, a banker, and George Knapp, of the St. Louis Republican.

Sixty-nine years after Charles Dickens made the above jaunt, his son, Alfred Tennyson Dickens, went over practically the same road. He crossed the Father of Waters over the Eads Bridge in an automobile, and rode in a palace electric car to Lebanon. From here an auto ride to the edge of Looking Glass Prairie gave him the same trip his father took. From Lebanon the party went to Belleville where Mr. Dickens inspected the Mansion House, after which a reception was held in the Court House. Mr. Dickens was greatly delighted with his reception. He died suddenly in New York January 9, 1912.

East St. Louis – East St. Louis is the third largest city in the state, with a population of 58,547. Its interests are varied. It is a real city. Meat packing is a great industry. Railroading absorbs the interests of thousands. The greatest mule market in the world is here. The school system is modern and the church and social life is upon a high plane. There are three bridges across the great river and a fourth one nearing completion. St. Clair has a number of other flourishing towns among which are Lebanon, O'Fallen, Freeburg, New Athens, and still smaller villages.

Adam Reiss Arrives in Illinois

Dear Will, Kayla, Ava, and Blake,   July 27, 2015

Your great great great great grandfather, Johann Adam Reiss, emigrated from Germany to the US, arriving in New Orleans, Louisiana in late 1833. He was born on May 7, 1804 so he was 29 years old when he arrived. He went by his middle name of Adam.

Despite repeated searches of ship passenger lists, I've been unable to find Adam's entry data regardless of how his name may have been misspelled. Family lore has it that he worked his way north along the Mississippi River, spending the winter of 1833/34 in Natchez, Mississippi before eventually buying his first 40-acre farm in St. Clair County, Illinois on April 1, 1834.

Here is Adam's family home in Obernau, Bavaria, Germany. Looks like it has been significantly modified to create several apartment units with off-street parking in the back yard. These two photos were provided by my fifth cousin Marianne Walter who lives in the area. She is also a professional genealogist. I visited Obernau in 1962, 1986, and 1991 so a re-visit is overdue for more exploring and research.

The rear view is on the next page along with a map of what the US looked like in 1833 when Adam arrived. There were only 24 states, less than half of the 50 states we have now. Arkansas joined the Union on 6/15/1836 as the 25th state. Illinois had joined the Union on 12/3/1818 as the 21st state.

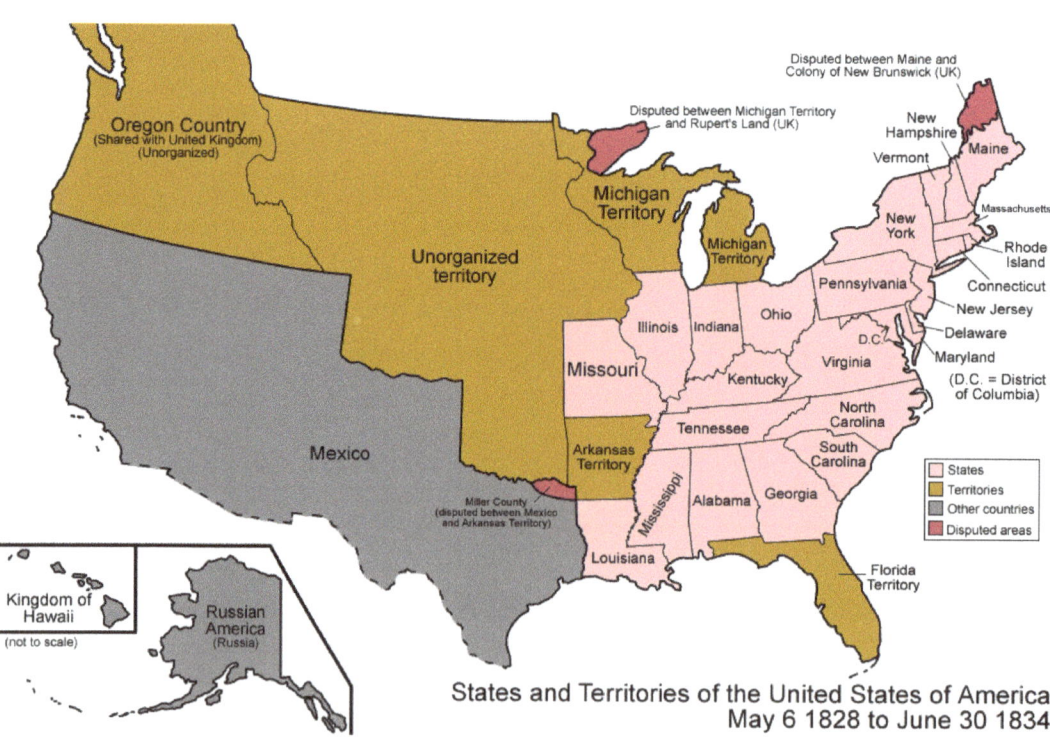

States and Territories of the United States of America
May 6 1828 to June 30 1834

10

Will, Kayla, Ava, and Blake, the pink area totals 52,581 square miles which is just 22.5% of the total area of the US today. Adam and your later ancestors have witnessed a more than four-fold increase in the area of the US in the last 182 years. Missouri, Georgia, and Illinois went from the three largest states in 1834 to the 21st, 24th, and 25th largest states today. I'll bet you can't wait to further study all this history in school.

Love, Granddad

Anna Maria Schuessler

Dear Will, Kayla, Ava, and Blake,   July 27, 2015

We have finally found more basic information about the first wife of my great great grandfather Adam Reiss. For over 75 years we had thought her name was Mary Schuessler and that she was from the same village of Obernau, near Aschaffenburg, Germany that Adam Reiss was from. We did not know her full name, when she was born, or when she came to America. We didn't know her parents or siblings. We thought she and Adam were sweethearts in Obernau and that their plan was for him to come to America, get established on a farm, and then send for her.

I wrote to the Katholische Kirche St. Peter und Paul in Obernau – Aschaffenburg, Germany asking what history they might have on Mary Schuessler from the early 1800s. A reply arrived in two weeks saying that Anna Maria Schuessler was born on December 20, 1808 in Obernau, Bavaria. She was the daughter of Ulrich Schuessler and Barbara Hoessbacher Schuessler. Her godmother was Anna Maria Hoessbacher whose husband was Martin so he was the brother of Barbara.

Going back in history, Ulrich Schuessler was born about 1757 and died on November 18, 1813. He married Barbara Hoessbacher before 1801. She was born about 1770 and died on April 10, 1834 in Obernau. They had three children:

Martin Schuessler was born January 20, 1801 in Obernau and died on September 12, 1834 at age 33, never married, and was a soldier in the Royal Regiment Wrede of Landau in Spitnen. His death certificate was sent by the Royal military administration and the Catholic priest Geissler to the local church for entry and returned to the local county court.

Johann Schuessler was born on March 18, 1804 in Obernau.

Anna Maria Schuessler was born on December 20, 1808 in Obernau and immigrated to America in 1836. Check out the scans on the next page. Anna Maria and Adam got their marriage license on Monday May 7, 1838. Both of their names were misspelled. They were married a week later on Tuesday May 15, 1838 by Charles Meyer. It may have been a very small wedding service.

The "Illinois Catholic Historical Review" shows Reverend Charles Meyer assigned to scattered German settlements in southwest St. Clair County in 1838-39. At the same time he was assigned to St. Thomas near Columbia in 1838-40.

Sadly, Anna Maria died in the birth of their first child on December 11, 1838 at the Reiss family farm in St. Clair County, Illinois. Their son John survived so we have to assume that he was close to full term. That means that Anna Maria would have gotten pregnant in February 1838 before their formal wedding. So my guess is that they had a common law wedding some time in late 1836 or in 1837 while they were getting established in America.

State of Illinois, Sct.
St. Clair County,

TO ALL TO WHOM THESE PRESENTS SHALL COME, Greeting:

KNOW YE, that License is hereby granted to any Minister of the Gospel authorized to marry by the Church or Society to which he belongs, any Justice of the Supreme Court, Judge, or Justice of the Peace, to join together in the holy banns of Wedlock *Adam Rice* and *Mary Shesler* of the said County, and for so doing this shall be your sufficient warrant, and certify the same at my Office according to Law.

Given under my hand and seal at Belleville, the 7th day of May A.D. 1838.

James M. Charles c. c. c. c, St. Clair co.

State of Illinois
St. Clair County

This is to certify that on the 15th day of May I joined in wedlock Adam Rice and Mary Shesler

Carles Meyer, Curl

I was trying to get lucky on another Schuessler connection. John and Mary Schuessler bought 40 acres from Thomas Houghan for $155 on August 13, 1841. It was half a mile south of the Adam Reiss farm. It was the southeast quarter of the northeast quarter of Section 18. It was adjacent to the 40 acres that Frantz Stauder bought in 1840. So my question was whether Adam's wife Anna Maria was related to John Schuessler? Well, it doesn't look like it, or at least not a very close relationship. We do know the Adam Reiss children were friends with the Schuessler children for over 25 years. We also know this Schuessler family was related to the Neff brothers who married the Ebert daughters by the second marriage of my great great grandmother Margaret Basler Reiss to Conrad Ebert.

Will, Kayla, Ava, and Blake, it's so exciting that we finally have a lot more history on Anna Maria Schuessler Reiss. You can call her your great great great great step-grandmother. She and Adam had a strong commitment to each other with him immigrating about three years ahead of her, buying and selling his first 40-acre farm, buying another 40-acre farm together, building a log home and log granary, and trying to start a family. We are truly blessed to have such incredible people in our family tree.

Love, Granddad

Adam Reiss Buys Four 40-Acre Farms in St. Clair County

Dear Will, Kayla, Ava, and Blake,   April 28, 2014

Your great great great great grandfather Adam Reiss bought his first 40-acre farm 180 years ago this Wednesday on April 30, 1834. That was a huge event in the history of our extended family which now includes six generations of Adam's descendents. That purchase was the start of the Reiss Family Farm (RFF) in St. Clair County, Illinois. . . . . . or was it? Isn't 1834 the year which half a dozen family reunions celebrated over the last 180 years? Is that date not correct? What exactly have we been celebrating? The RFF consists of three 40-acre parcels which Adam bought. What is this fourth parcel all about and where is it?

My Uncle Frank Reiss was the keeper of all the RFF land documents, except for one which was missing – the deed for the first 40-acre farm that Adam Reiss purchased. When Uncle Frank died in 2002, Aunt Gerry gave me those 32 documents for study and safekeeping. That library included three deeds for the three 40-acre parcels in Section 7 of Prairie du Long Township, aka Town 2 South, ==Range 8 West==. Those 120 acres defined the Adam Reiss farm which was the beginning of the RFF. The first RFF deed on the next page was dated 9/1/1838 for the northeast quarter of the southwest quarter. The second deed was dated 4/26/1839 for the southeast quarter of the northwest quarter. The third deed was dated 9/29/1842 for the southwest quarter of the northeast quarter. The seller for all three parcels was a big time land speculator named Thomas Houghan who will be the subject of a separate Granddad's Mondays story.

The satellite photo on page 4 shows how these three purchases nested together to create the Adam Reiss Farm. So our oldest document is 1838. How are we going to get to 1834 which family lore says is when Adam Reiss founded his farm? Uncle Frank had also noted this date "discrepancy" but could not explain it.

The Illinois Public Domain Land Records in the Illinois State Archives show two men both named Adam Reis buying land in this area in the 1830s. One man bought six parcels in and near the village of Waterloo in Monroe County and the other man bought a single 40-acre parcel in New Athens Township of St. Clair County. Don't worry about that missing "s" in the last names. That happened frequently in going from German to English spellings. In fact our Adam Reiss' tombstone is spelled Reisz which is yet another spelling.

The Adam Reis near Waterloo sold his properties in the early 1840s and public documents show that his wife Philippina signed away her dower rights on each parcel sale. So that man was not our Adam Reiss because we have no Philippina in our family tree.

Let's look at the 40 acres in New Athens Township which was purchased by Adam Reis on April 30, 1834. That purchase was recorded but the original deed has been lost. Hummm, the name works and the date gets us to 1834. Could this be our man? But this Adam sold his 40 acres in 1837 to John Messinger. There is no public document showing where an Adam Reis wife signed away her dower rights with that sale. That also fits because our Adam didn't marry Mary Schuessler until May 15, 1838.

This Indenture made this first day of September in the year of our Lord one thousand Eight hundred & thirty eight between Thomas Houghan of the Town of Springfield & State of Illinois of the one part & Adam Ries of the other part Witnesseth That the said Thomas Houghan for & in consideration of the sum of one hundred dollars to him in hand paid by the said Adam Ries the receipt whereof is hereby acknowledged, hath bargained & sold, & by these presents doth bargain & sell unto the said Adam Ries his heirs & assigns forever the North East quarter of the South West quarter of Section seven Town two South of range eight west, situated in the County of St Clair. To have & to hold the said tract of land with all the appurtenances thereunto belonging unto him the said Adam Ries his heirs & assigns forever. and the said Thomas Houghan for himself his heirs & assigns doth warrant & defend the title to the aforesaid lands free from the claims of all persons whomsoever. In Testimony whereof I have hereunto set my hand and seal the day and year above written.

Thomas Houghan (seal)
J. Mitchell att: in fact.

State of Illinois ss.

Be it remembered that on this twentieth day of October A.D. one thousand eight hundred & thirty eight personally appeared before me John Hay Clerk of the Circuit Court for the County of St Clair & State aforesaid Jas Mitchell in his capacity of att. in fact of Thomas Houghan whose name is subscribed to the foregoing instrument of writing & personally known to me to be the same person who executed the same & acknowledged to have signed sealed & delivered the same as his free act & deed & for the purposes therein expressed.

In Testimony whereof I have hereunto set my hand & affixed the seal of the said Court at my office in Belleville the day & year above written.

(Seal)

John Hay

Recorded this twentieth October Eighteen hundred & thirty eight

John Hay Recorder

This 40 acres purchased in 1834 is in Section 7 of New Athens Township, aka Town 2 South, Range 7 West. It is the northeast quarter of the southeast quarter. In other words, this 40 acres is in exactly the same location in New Athens Township that the 40 acres Adam purchased in 1838 is in Prairie du Long Township. These two 40-acre parcels are exactly six miles apart because most townships in the Midwest are exactly six miles square. This Section 7 coincidence is interesting but it does nothing to further identify the 1834 Adam Reis.

Nine months ago I retained Diane Walsh, a Board-certified Genealogist in Belleville, to help with learning more about the two men named Adam Reis and hopefully lots of other cool stuff. Diane even has some Schuesslers in her family tree so we may be distant cousins. She has done a terrific job researching leads, finding documents when available, raising questions, and explaining how land and people history happened in the 1830s. One of her suggestions was to look for signatures. Here are three she found on Adam Reis, the last of which is our Adam Reiss. Material in the next paragraphs is taken from her reports, quoted with permission.

Adam Reis signature on a petition for a new road – "In order to sign the petition in 1835, voters being white males above age 21 who *"resided in the state six months next preceding the election"* [i] needed to apply for a new road and if not residing in the same district as the road, would be required to labor on that road (if approved) or else be fined $1.00. One might expect those who used the road and lived nearby would sign the road petition. That said, at its signing in 1835, your Adam may have lived in the Centreville precinct[ii] in which Seibert's Road was located until such time as the future Reiss Family Farm and homestead of 1838 was bought and erected. In 1839, however, your Adam's homestead, his residence, was in Richland Precinct bordering Centreville Precinct on the east." Ignore the inclined lines at the end of the first name and halfway through the last name. They belong to the signature above.

"Here's what the letter "A" looked like in German Gothic handwriting. Our Adam's "A" is a little more plain, omitting the top left loop, but the basic form is there."

Adam Reis signature on land sale – Another example of Adam Reis's signature was found in the 1839 deed record for the sale of his 40-acres in New Athens Township in 1837 to John M. Messinger. "Both men were of St. Clair County which again distinguishes your Adam from the like-named man in adjoining Monroe County near Waterloo. Generally, signatures reflect the Recorder's handwriting as he copied the deed, however, some St. Clair County deed books show what appear to be authentic signatures of the seller which appears to be the case here when the Recorder's handwriting is compared to Adam's signature."

Adam Reis signature on his last will and testament[iii] – In the spring of 1849 our patriarch knew he was near death from cholera. He signed his will shortly before he died at the age of 45 on May 23, 1849. That document and the subsequent probate of his estate will be the subject of a separate Granddad's Mondays story next month. He died in the log cabin that he had built a decade earlier for his young family of wife Margaret and five children under age 11.

"One can see the change from German Gothic style in 1835 to more Americanized lettering. Similar letter forms include the *d* and *ss* in 1835 and 1839; the *R* in *Reiss* is similar in 1839 and 1849."

Will, Kayla, and Ava, I believe these three signatures over 14 years are by the same man. I also believe that the other data we have like no wife in 1837 and the traditional family lore farm start date of 1834 mean that our mystery has been solved. So I'm very confident in saying it was indeed our Adam Reiss who bought his first farm from the Federal Government land office in

Kaskaskia, Illinois on April 30, 1834. Actual farm size was 39.61 acres. He paid $1.25 per acre or $49.51 for his first farm. You can't even buy a tank of gas for your car for that price these days!!! That purchase appears on page 029 of volume 031 of The Illinois Public Domain Land Records.

Grand DD and I visited Adam's Farm #1 on 4/1/2014. Here is a picture from the southeast corner looking northwest. On the next page is an aerial photo showing all four of Adam's 40-acre parcels. It was really neat to see and walk on the exact land where our Reiss family farm history started 180 years ago (less 29 days). It's very obvious that Adam built no buildings or fences in the three years that he owned his first 40 acres. There are/were simply no trees nearby which he could cut and hew into timbers for log buildings as a home for himself and shelter for horses. Here are related questions:

1. Adam's first farm would have been prairie grass which was extremely difficult to plow because its roots were so deep and the vegetative matter so thick. John Deere didn't invent his first commercially successful steel plow until 1837 so Adam would have been greatly hindered by early plow technology.

2. Will, you and I visited this draft horse plowing demonstration north of Springfield last year so you know it takes two big horses to pull a single-bottom plow. Those horses need shelter and a fenced pasture. The first patent for barbed wire was 1867, so Adam would have needed a barn and a heavy duty split rail fence for his horses.

3. Where did Adam live from April 1834 until he could have started the log cabin on his second 40 acres in September 1838? Where did Adam work if farming his first farm was not a full time job? Freeburg was about three miles north and New Athens was about three miles southeast but neither was laid out until 1836. Smithton was laid out in 1853, Floraville in 1857, and Paderborn in 1863. These "laid out" dates refer to formal plats. There would have been settlers and several dozen homes already in place at each village.

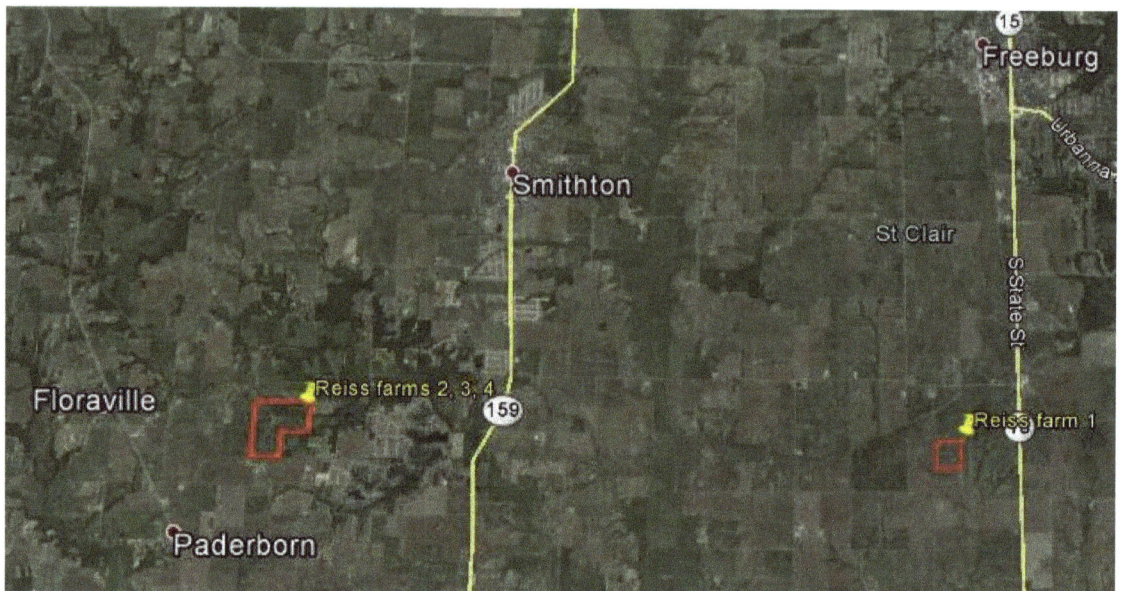

4. If there were no buildings on Adam's first farm, maybe he rented the land to neighbors who already had buildings, equipment, and horses. Maybe Adam even lived with those neighbors and was his own crop share tenant.

5. Adam married marry Mary Schuessler on May 15, 1838 which is 3.5 months before he bought his second 40 acres on September 1, 1838. Did they live with her parents? There was a Schuessler farm half a mile southwest of the RFF but it didn't start until 1842. Nevertheless, Mary's family may have been in the area such that she and Adam were able to meet and marry in the first place. We still don't know when/how Mary arrived in St. Clair County or when/where she was born.

6. Mary was pregnant with their first child for at least the last half of 1838. Their son John was born on December 11, 1838 but sadly Mary died during that childbirth. She was probably buried in the Paderborn Cemetery. We have to assume they were living with her parents. Not being a landowner again until September 1838 Adam would have been busy with his job, whatever it was. He could not have built his log cabin and moved there all in late 1838.

7. Adam probably built his log cabin and log granary in 1839. We know that Catholic church services were held on his farm in that timeframe before St. Michael's Church was completed in Paderborn in 1842. The Basler family arrived in New Orleans on November 28, 1839 and quickly made their way to St. Clair County. I believe the

18

Baslers began worshiping on Adam's farm and that's where their daughter Margaret met and fell in love with Adam Reiss and his infant son John. She became Adam's second wife on September 10, 1840.

8. So that's my 1834 to 1840 scenario about Adam's first two marriages and first two farm locations and I'm stickin' to it!!!

Will, Kayla, Ava, and Blake, we announced at our 2009 Reiss Family Reunion which supposedly celebrated 175 years of the Reiss Family Farm, that our next reunion would be in 2034 to celebrate the bicentennial of that founding. Well, now we know we were off by four years if it is indeed the "founding" that we're celebrating. Instead we should say we're celebrating the 1834 anniversary of Adam Reiss becoming an American farmer.

You want to know something else that's really wild and crazy. That same 40 acres that Adam Reiss bought and sold in New Athens Township was later bought by Conrad Dintelmann on November 11, 1882. Conrad paid $39.50 per acre where Adam paid $1.25 some 48 years earlier. Conrad's sister Eva married Adam Reiss' son Charles and Conrad's son George married Adam's granddaughter Margaret. There were two more Dintelmann-Reiss weddings in later years. So the Dintelmann and Reiss families have both blood and dirt connections!!!

Love, Granddad

Adam Reiss Buys 40 Acres in Monroe County

Dear Will, Kayla, Ava, and Blake,   February 2, 2015

It was 176 years ago this coming Thursday on February 5, 1839 that your great great great great grandfather Adam Reiss bought his third 40-acre farm. It was in Monroe County. His two previous farms and his two later farms were all in St. Clair County. For the last 130 years, everyone in our extended family knew only about the 120 acres Adam bought in Prairie du Long Township. Then my Granddad's Mondays story of 4/28/2014 told you about 40 acres Adam bought in New Athens Township. This story today is telling you about yet another 40 acres Adam bought in adjoining Monroe County. So when Adam Reiss died in 1849, he had bought 200 acres in two counties, sold 40 acres in New Athens Township, had the core 120 acres as his homestead, and had this 40 acres in Monroe County.

The purchase record in Waterloo shows Adam Reiss as Adam Ris. That's why we haven't found this record in recent searches. I've never seen our last name spelled that way in any other historical documents. Anyway, Adam bought the northwest quarter of the southwest quarter of Section 23, Township 2 South, Range 9 West.

Adam's 40 acres is the red square. You may recognize the red triangle from my Granddad's Mondays story of 12/29/2014 where Adam's grandson (my grandfather) George Reiss bought that tract on 12/30/1914 from the Crook family. Those two farms are two miles apart.

Fast forward to 2/19/1875. The deed on the next page shows where Margaret and Conrad Ebert and her son Frank Reiss and his wife Anna sold the south half of these 40 acres in Monroe County to John Helfrich for $407.50.

This 1875 atlas still shows all 40 acres under J. F. Ries when it should have been F. J. Reiss, et. al. Frank had inherited his share when his father Adam Reiss died in 1849. His siblings and his mother Margaret (later Ebert) got the rest.

20

The deed image (a Warranty Deed) reads, as best as can be made out:

322

WARRANTY DEED.—Culver, Page & Hoyne, Stationers and Blank Book Manufacturers, 118 and 120 Monroe Street, Chicago.

This Indenture, Made this Ninth /9th/ day of February in the year of our Lord One Thousand Eight Hundred and seventy five BETWEEN Frank J. Reiss and Anna A. Reiss his wife and Margaret a widow and Conrad Ebert her husband heirs at Law of of the first part Adam Reiss deceased of the County of St Clair Illinois of the first part and John Helfrich of the County of St Clair State of Illinois of the second part WITNESSETH, That the said party of the first part, for and in consideration of the sum of Four Hundred and fifty Dollars in hand paid by the said party of the second part, the receipt whereof is hereby acknowledged, have GRANTED, BARGAINED AND SOLD, and by these presents do GRANT, BARGAIN AND SELL, unto the said party of the second part, his heirs and assigns, all the following described lot piece, or parcel of land, situated in the County of Monroe and State of Illinois, to wit:

The South Half of the North West quarter of the South West Quarter of section No Twenty three /23/ in Township No two /2/ South of Range No Nine /9/ West of the third principal meridian containing Twenty /20/ acres. Also the right of way for a cart road on the West side of the North Half of the North West quarter of the South West quarter of the same section township and Range, to be twelve /12/ feet wide and forty /40/ rods long, running parallel with the West line of said tract.

I have a quit claim deed made 4-13-1875 and filed 9-9-1875 where Charles M. and Catharina Reiss Wittig sold her share of the full 40 acres to her brother Frank J. Reiss for $950. She did very well on her sale at $950 which could have been as small as a 1/8th interest. Frank and his mother got $407.50 for the south half above and $575 for the north half below.

Fast forward to 8/7/1882. The deed on the next page shows where Adam Reiss' widow Margaret, his son Frank, and Frank's wife Anna sold the north half of these 40 acres in Monroe County to Henry Brinkman who already owned adjoining land to the north. All three sellers' last names are spelled as Reis. I have this original sales document which is how we identified this particular farm in the first place. My professional genealogist Diane Walsh in Belleville did the rest of the legwork finding Adam's original purchase details and what later happened to the south half of this farm. None of these 40 acres is in our family now.

Will, Kayla, Ava, and Blake, isn't it great fun to "find two farms" that our patriarch, Adam Reiss, bought in 1834 and 1839 that have been lost to family awareness for over 130 years. I'm kinda proud of what we accomplished. Now I wonder if there are even more missing Reiss farms out there waiting to be discovered. Whaduyathink?

Love, Granddad

F.J. Reis
Etal.

Deed

TO

Henry
Brinkmann

The Grantors Franz J. Reis, Anna V Reis his wife and Margaretha Ebert of the County of St Clair and State of Illinois for and in Consideration of Five hundred and Seventy five Dollars in hand paid Convey and warrant to Henry Brinkmann of the County of Monroe and State of Illinois the following described Real Estate The North half of the North West quarter of the South West quarter of Section Twenty three (23) Township two (2) South, Range, Nine (9) West, excepting a strip of land Fifteen feet wide of the West line used as a roadway Situated in the County of Monroe and State of Illinois, hereby releasing and waiving all rights under and by virtue of the homestead exemption laws of this state —

Dated this Seventh day of August AD 1882. —

Franz J. Reis (Seal)
Anna V Reis (Seal)
Margaretha Reis (Seal)

State of Illinois }
St Clair County } ss I George J Eimer a Justice of the Peace in and for the said St Clair County, in the State aforesaid, do hereby Certify that Franz J. Reis, Anna V Reis, and Margaretha Ebert personally known to me as the same persons whose names are subscribed to the forgoing instrument, appeared before me this day in person, and acknowledged that they Signed Sealed and delivered the said instrument in writing as their free and

Thomas Houghan

Dear Will, Kayla, Ava, and Grant Jr.,   June 23, 2014

Your great great great great grandfather Adam Reiss established the family farm by buying three 40-acre tracts on 9/1/1838, 1/1/1839, and 9/28/1842 from a prominent land speculator named Thomas Houghan. It turns out that Thomas Houghan was much more than a land speculator, much more!!! Here's the skinny.

- Thomas Houghan's real last name was Hughan. He had changed the spelling after serving a term in debtors' prison in New York State. In 1817 or 1818 Houghan abandoned his wife and child in New York.

- Following his disappearance, Hughan/Houghan reportedly spent time in Central or South America. He then moved to St. Louis where he became a partner in a bookselling business. His partner died soon thereafter and Houghan bigamously married his widow.

- Thomas Houghan then moved to Springfield as one of that city's first 10 physicians. He played a prominent role in local affairs, serving on the city health board, as a bank and railroad director, and as a founding trustee of the University of Illinois.

- Thomas Houghan built a mansion in Springfield, Illinois in 1833. It was in a 14-acre grove of elm, walnut, and maple trees on the northern edge of town. Today it's a mile north of the old state capitol and is home to the Springfield Art Association. It is the oldest house in Springfield still on its original foundation. Houghan sold it in 1843 to Benjamin Edwards whose father Ninian was Illinois' first territorial governor and whose older brother also named Ninian married Abraham Lincoln's sister-in-law Elizabeth Todd.

- Although Houghan's New York relatives located him about 1835, according to a deposition filed as part of the later lawsuit, they "religiously kept the secret of his identity" until after his death in St. Louis in 1862.

- On 3/3/1837 Thomas Houghan was appointed one of three commissioners to superintend the construction of the new state capitol. But Houghan declined shortly thereafter and was replaced by William Herndon, a relative of Lincoln's future law partner.

- Houghan engaged heavily in land speculation in eight counties from Tazewell County southward to Monroe County and owned 57,747 acres altogether over a period of about ten years. Some he resold in a few months while other tracts took up to three years. In most cases he doubled his money from $1.25 per acre to $2.50 or $3.00 per acre.

- Each of Houghan's three sale documents to Adam Reiss and others had a phrase like: To have and to hold the said tract of land with all the appurtenances thereunto belonging with him the said Adam Reis, his heirs, and assigns forever. And the said Thomas Houghan for himself, his heirs, and assigns doth warrant and defend the title to the aforesaid lands free from the claims of all present whomsoever. In testimony whereof I have hereunto set my hand and seal this day and year above written. Signed Thomas Houghan

This respected doctor and financier amassed a great fortune in central Illinois land. After his death in St. Louis in 1862, a headline-making lawsuit in New York revealed that Houghan had lived a double life. His first wife sued over 400 people for her dower rights, including my great great grandparents Conrad and Margaret Ebert who had inherited part of the Reiss Family Farm after Adam Reiss' death in 1849. Because the first Houghan marriage was never formally dissolved by divorce, and because his first wife had never signed away her dower rights to those 57,747 acres, she and her children were entitled to one-third of Houghan's estate.

Mrs. Hughan and her son-in-law filed claims against all those landowners asking for her one-third interest. That subpoena appears below on pages 5 through 7 and commands those named to appear in Springfield. It is dated Thursday 6/15/1865 and requires all defendants to appear before Monday 8/7/1865. You can see that Adam Reiss' widow Margaret Reiss and her second husband Conrad Ebert were named half way through that subpoena. It turns out that any of the owners who came forward as required by the lawsuit were excused from the case with no further consequences. Those that did not come forward were apparently still on the hook, the outcome of which we do not know. Since there are no more documents saved by Margaret or Conrad on this subject, we can assume that one or both made the trip to Springfield and were thus excused from the suit. Ironically five or ten years after this law suit was filed, Mrs. Houghan's son-in-law had her committed to an insane asylum. It's apparent to me that the son-in-law was really the instigator in all this and was blinded by dollar signs.

Here is the lawsuit as reported in the 𝕿𝖍𝖊 𝕹𝖊𝖜 𝖄𝖔𝖗𝖐 𝕿𝖎𝖒𝖊𝖘 on June 5, 1864 and the St. Louis Republican on June 2, 1864. The related subpoena to some 400 owners was dated 8/7/1865.

Romance in Real Life: A Delinquent Husband Sued for the Board of His Wife
Deposition by Hon. D. S. Dickinson

Yesterday, a case was submitted to Judge Reber, the details of which have all the interest of a romance. The style of the action is as follows: Aushurn Birdsall vs. Wm. T. Essex, executor of the estate of Thomas Houghan, alias Thomas Hughan, deceased. The plaintiff resides in the State of New York. This petition sets forth that Dr. Thos. Houghan, otherwise called Thomas B. Hughan, deceased, departed this life in the city of St. Louis, in August, 1862, and that by his last will, he appointed William T. Essex executor of his estate. The plaintiff further states that the said Thomas Houghan, in the year 1813 or 1814, was lawfully married to Sophia L. Knapp, who survives the said Thomas, and who now resides in the State of New York; that for the period of twenty years, he (the plaintiff) has boarded the wife of the said Thomas Houghan, and he asks that judgment in the sum of $5,000 be awarded to him as compensation therefore. The court, after hearing the deposition in the case, rendered judgment for the plaintiff in the sum of $580.

A lengthy deposition from Hon. Daniel S. Dickinson, Binghamton, Broome County, N.Y., was read, of which we give the following synopsis: Mr. Dickinson states that he was brought up in the same neighborhood with Thomas B. Hughan, that they were schoolfellows together, and intimate friends; that in the same neighborhood also resided Dr. Knapp, who had several daughters, one of whom (Sophia L. Knapp) Hughan married in 1813. Another was married to, and is now the wife of Hon. Mr. Dickinson, the witness. Mr. Dickinson's deposition then continues as follows:

Thomas B. Hughan was a young man of peculiar talent, genius, and learning. He had been unused to business, and he became (after his marriage and subsequent settlement in Unadilla, near Guilford, as a physician,) embarrassed with debts. Imprisonment for debt then existed and Dr. Knapp (Hughan's father-in-law) was an old-fashioned, rigid man, and after helping him a while, declined to help him further, and Hughan was put upon the jail limits for debt. He was a proud-spirited man, of great sensibility, and when he got released from the jail limits he suddenly left the country and went away. Before leaving, (the date of which I do not remember accurately) his wife, Sophia, had given birth to two children, the first of which did not survive its birth. The other, a daughter, grew up to womanhood. He had always lived happily in his family, and no cause is known in the family for his leaving, except his embarrassments. As I remember, he left in 1817 or 1818. I never saw him after, till about the year 1835. He was said to have returned once, privately, to see his mother, wife and child, but that his wife being absent in Connecticut, he only saw his mother and child. With that exception he never returned to that section of the country nor to his family, as far as I know or believe. His wife divided her time between her father's family and my family and her mother's friends in Connecticut. About 1823 letters came from Dr. Hughan, dated at Baltimore, to his wife and mother. That to his mother I read. It stated he had been abroad in a tropical clime for years, and requested his wife to forgive his absence, and if she was now living for her and his child to join him. Letters were sent advising him to return, but nothing more was heard of him until sometime afterwards, when a letter came to his mother saying that he remained in Baltimore some time, but hearing nothing from his wife or the family, he was going to return south again. Nothing was heard of him again for some years. From subsequent information we learned that he spent his time in South or Central America during the wars then going on there. Mrs. Dickinson and myself adopted his daughter, and she was married to Ausburn Birdsall (the plaintiff) in 1836, and she died in 1860. In 1830 or 1831, while I yet remained, in Guilford, I had subscribed to a periodical publication, published at St. Louis, or in that region, in which a friend of mine had some connection. He was then acting as missionary in the Mississippi Valley. Not far from the year 1831 I saw some notice in the publication of Dr. Thos. Hughan. I wrote to my clergyman friend, desiring him to make some inquiry if it was the same Hughan. I also wrote to the Postmaster at St. Louis, asking him to inform me who Dr. Hughan was. I received answers to both letters, the contents of which I do not remember accurately. I also received one or two letters from Dr. Hughan himself. All this correspondence was burned when my office was destroyed by fire in 1838. I remember Dr. Hughan's letter. He stated he had been informed about any inquiries for his "identity" that he had recently settled in St. Louis, a stranger, and that I was aware it was very unpleasant to be inquired for with a view to identification; that he was not the gentleman I suspected, and he knew nothing about him; that if would appoint to meet him in the City of New York, he would meet me there and satisfy me beyond question that he was not the person I suspected him to be. I had been, familiar with his hand writing all my days, up to the time our correspondence ceased, and I recognized that letter as being his handwriting, although elaborately disguised. The West then had become developed pretty rapidly, and we learned the gentleman had removed to Springfield, Illinois. About the same time family relatives moved into the neighborhood of Springfield. They were furnished with an accurate description and likeness of Thomas Hughan, and were requested to see if the gentleman at Springfield was the same. They were satisfied he was the man, and called to see him and charged him with it. He denied it, but upon being pressed, and the facts and circumstances stated to him, he confessed he was Dr. Hughan, of Guilford, but desired them to keep the matter secret, as he had married in St. Louis, and was a member of a church there, and maintained other relations in society. I sent him word through them, both by letter and verbally, that his daughter Louisa was about to be married, and I received through them, (said to come from him,) about $200 for his daughter, which I appropriated for her use. From the time his identity became thus known, his family, as far as I know, have religiously kept the secret of his identity. From the time of Mr. Birdsall's marriage, or shortly after, Mr. Birdsall has cared for and supported Mrs. Sophia Hughan, his wife's mother. About the year 1855, I met Mr. Hughan at the Astor House, in New York City. He had then, as I understood from him and others, moved back to St. Louis, having remained in Springfield but a short time. I identified him at once as the husband of Sophia Hughan. We had a long conversation, in full detail, of family history and affairs. He inquired, with some particularity, for Mrs. Dickinson, his wife Sophia, Dr. Knapp, Mrs. Birdsall and others, and thanked me very kindly and warmly for the assistance I had rendered his wife and children.

The above is the substance of Mr. Dickinson's deposition. The court rendered judgment as above stated.

Will, Kayla, Ava, and Grant Jr., can you imagine receiving a letter from a Federal Court saying you do not have clear title to the farm your late husband purchased 27 years earlier? That has to be really scary. I wonder how many sleepless nights that caused!!! Margaret and Conrad probably recognized a dozen or more other names on that subpoena as their neighbors who owned nearby farms. Maybe they traveled together to Springfield to appear before the court. That trip is 110 miles which would have taken several days each direction by coach and train. Maybe they visited the tomb of President Abraham Lincoln whose funeral was on 5/1/1865 in Springfield.

Isn't this a strange bump in the road in the ongoing history of the Reiss Family Farm? This all happened after the passing of both Thomas Houghan and our Adam Reiss. Maybe those guys met in heaven and Adam said to Thomas, "What do you mean you didn't have clear title to the land you sold me? What about this warranty deed and land patent and my decade of sweat equity? My descendants and I cannot be victims!!!"

Love, Granddad

26

2,238.

CIRCUIT COURT UNITED STATES,

SOUTHERN DISTRICT OF ILLINOIS.

AUSBURN BIRDSALL,

Conservator of Sophia L. Houghan,

vs.

LEIGH R. KIMBALL ET AL.

Subpœna in Chancery.

SUBPŒNA IN CHANCERY.

Returnable to rule day, first Monday in August, A. D. 1865.

P. P. ENOS, Clerk.

STUART, EDWARDS & BROWN,
HAY & CULLOM,

Comp'ts Solicitors.

COPY.

MEMORANDUM.—The within named defendants are notified that unless they be and appear as within commanded, enter their appearance in the Clerk's Office of said Court, at Springfield aforesaid, on or before the day to which this writ is returnable, the Complainant's Bill will be taken *pro confesso*, as against them, and decree entered accordingly.

P. P. ENOS, Clerk.

UNITED STATES OF AMERICA. }
SOUTHERN DISTRICT OF ILLINOIS. } ss.

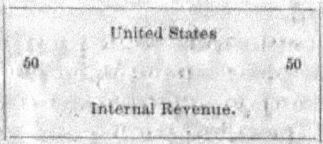

THE UNITED STATES OF AMERICA:

To the Marshal of the Southern District of Illinois---GREETING:

WE COMMAND YOU THAT YOU SUBPŒNA

Frank Siebert, Andre Bien, Nicholas Legendre, Joseph Stolze, William Siebert, George Siebert, George Bauer, Isaac Francis, Joseph Veile, Peter Barthelot, Joseph Becherer, Philip A. Gauch, Rigdon Quick, Henry Bewig, Philip Schmidt first, George Weinel, Hyacinth Munier, Gregor Hermann, Conrad Etling, Mrs. Wm. J. Wilderman, Henry Drew, Louis Holcomb, Isaac Phillips, Peter Hill, Henry Phillips, William B. Phillips, John N. Daab, Michael Schmidt, George Klotz, George Heinrich, Mrs. Louisa Althaus, Peter Brandenburger, Joseph Degenhardt, Amos Phillips, Benjamin Higgins, Jacob Miller, Robert Higgins, Ferdinand Fischer, Henry Putzbach, George Brenner, Philip Benedick, Richard Becherer, Stephen Cortner, Michael Germain, Henry Lippert junr., George Lippert, junr., Henry Lippert, Joseph Whitacker, Balthasar Haeussler, John Funk, Adam Kaestel, Bernard Wessel, Samuel Roach, Andrew Harsche, John Hecktor, Valentine Biehl, Jacob Hammel, George Hammel, Anne Margaret Bohley, Jacob Mauterle, Theobald Lang, Christ. Henecke, Nicholas Eckert, George Dehn, Charles Grossman, Adam Krupp, George Lindauer, Fredrick Ahrens, Adam Kempff, Jacob Schmahlenberger, John Pieper, Frank M. Heer, Thomas Quinlin, G. J Fischer, Fredrick Fischer, Mrs. James Laughlin, Frederick Eckert, Mrs. Mary Schuchard, John G. Neubarth, Gottfreid Probst, Peter Petric, John C. Probst, Louis Metzler, William Holcomb, George Storzum, Fredrick Fiedler, Philip Ettling, Fredrick Querin, George Klotz, junr., Christ. Schwengel, Conrad Daesch, Charles Hamill, Josiah P. Hill, Nathan Robertson, O. J. Clampitt, James Woods, Louis Forcade, John Grommet, Joseph Woods, Robert J. Smith, Fredrick Berkel, George Schmerbauch, John Wissell, George Quirin, George Ritter, Nicholas Klein, Andrew Rapp, John Roth, Regina Fleckenstein & Co., Caspar Mueth,

John George, Conrad Ebert, Margaret Reiss, Jacob Schaefer, Christian Hintermann, Jacob Muren, Bartholome Goldmann, Margaret Reitz, Louis Hagen, Christain Hagen, Joseph Herold, Fredrick Grohmann, George Weigand, Ignatius Neff, Elizabeth Rapp, Joseph Fleckenstein, Anton Kayser, Christain Wachtel, Philip Hoerniss, Michael Wolf, Max. Klingler, Michael Schoenborn, Ennerich Kreher, Philip Schwarz, Mrs. J. T. Holcomb, Nelson Barker, Christopher Hagen, Conrad Roth, Peter Woods, William Brickey, Mrs. Nathan F. Carr, Henry Pfeffer, Joseph Grossheim, Joseph Thompson, A. P. Rittinghouse, Mrs. Perry E. Carr, Joseph McMurtrey, Washington Vaughan, Thomas J. Vaughan, Perry Carr, Henry Wilderman, Anna Wakefield, Mrs. William Preston, Robert Keightley, E. C. Kelting, Benjamin Vaughan, J. R. Dunlap, Mrs. S. W. Stookey, Peter Frank, Mrs. Frederick Schwartz, Michael Miller, Nath. McKie, Thomas Bamber, Richard Parker, Samuel Winn, Michael P. Stubbs, Jacob Spalt, August Stehfest, F. C. Dewey, C. H. Rapp, John Rapp, William Horn, Philip Etling, John Stortzum, George Stortzum, George Stortzum, Senr.; Rosalie Lehner, John G. Just, George Kesselring, Conrad Rosenberger, John P. Keim, Catherine Kinkel, Adam Probst, Catherine Radmacher, William Methier, Peter Methier, Conrad Weil, Andrew Herbert, Mrs. Ernst Kamper, Jacob Ruppenthal, John N. Funk, Peter Wedel, Jacob Honecker, John Becker, Charles Hesse, John Vogel, Christian Biele, Henry Sensel, Peter Etling, Frederick Horn, George Philip Skaer, William Skaer, Frederick C. Horn, Wilhelmina Widewill, Ennerich Kreher, Senr.; Frank Reinhardt, George Remspecher, Nicholas Miller, Leo Reinhard, Valentine Berg, Adalbert Kaburek, John Metzger, Paul Jaeckle, John Lehr, John Sensel, William Kettler, Alexander Crook, George Sturtzum, Caspar Kruse, Andre Hoffman, William Ritzel, Valentine Saul, Conrad Fuerstenberg, Michael Reheis, Nicholas H. Ridgely, Lorenz Kohlenberg, Wm. Zimbelmann, Charles Yatho, junr.; Michael Ringeisen, Henry Oestreich, Henry Goddel, Adam Goddel, Wm. Hilzinger, John Wall, Peter Metzenbacher, Peter Waring, William Otto, Franz Degenhard, James Miller, John Koechel, Thomas Drinkall, Samuel Schilling, Mrs. Thomas Ervin, James Mitchell, Valentine Degenhard, Thomas Blackburn, Charles J. Brandt, E. C. Coffey, E. B. Marshall, Amos Watts, John Wightman, John T. Preston, Samuel Y. Henry, Jesse Liveley, W. E. Anderson, John Akins, Wm. H. M. Wright, Henry Darter, Absalom Shinall, Henry H. Robinson, Henry Lander, Andrew White, Miles Stewart, James B. Sawyer, Mrs. Z. H. Vernor, George W. Vernor, Francis M. Vernor, Richard E. Vernor, William A. Hoffman, Gillum Shelton, Lucinda Watts, Pinckney K. Watts, Finley P. Watts, Abram L. Watts, Maria J. Watts, Richard I. Watts, Josephine Watts, if they be found in your District, to be and appear before our Judges of our Circuit Court of the United States of America for the Southern District of Illinois, at Springfield, in said District on the first Monday of August next, to answer the bill of complaint of Ausburn Birdsall, filed in the Clerks Office of said Court on the eighteenth day of April, A. D., 1865, in said City of Springfield, and the amended bill of complaint of said Ausburn Birdsall, committee of Sophia L. Houghan, also filed in said Clerk's office in said City of Springfield, this day, then and there to receive and abide by such judgment and decree, as shall then or thereafter be made, upon pain of judgment being pronounced against them by default.

WITNESS, The Hon. SALMON P. CHASE, Chief Justice of the Supreme Court of the United States of America, at Springfield aforesaid, this fifteenth day of June, in the year of our Lord, one thousand eight hundred and sixty-five, and of the Independence of the United States the eighty-ninth year.

[L. S.]

P. P. ENOS, Clerk.

Thomas Houghan in St. Clair County

Dear Will, Kayla, Ava, and Grant Jr.,   June 23, 2014

Thomas Houghan is the subject of both of my other Granddad's Mondays stories today. The story below is primarily about just what he did in St. Clair County where the Reiss Family Farm is located in Section 7 of Prairie du Long Township. But first let's review how the personal ownership of private property developed in the United States over the last 400 years.

History of land patents in the United States – Land in the US was acquired by purchase, war, or treaty from the United Kingdom, France, Spain, Mexico, Russia, the Kingdom of Hawaii, and the Native American peoples.

As Great Britain began to colonize colonial America, the Crown made large grants of territory to individuals and companies. In turn, those companies and colonial governors later made smaller grants of land based on actual surveys of the land. Thus, in colonial America on the Atlantic seaboard, a connection was made between the surveying of a land tract and its "patenting" as private property.

Many original colonies' land patents came from the corresponding country of control (e.g., the United Kingdom). Most such patents were permanently granted. Those patents are still in force; the US government honors those patents by treaty law, and, as with all such land patents, they cannot be changed.

After the American Revolution and the ratification of the Constitution of the United States, the US Treasury Department was placed in charge of managing all public lands. In 1812, the General Land Office was created to assume that duty.

In accord with specific Acts of Congress, and under the hand and seal of the President of the United States of America, the General Land Office issued more than 2 million land grants made patent (land patents), passing the title of specific parcels of public land from the nation to private parties (individuals or private companies). Some of the land so granted had survey or other costs associated with it. Some patentees paid those fees for their land in cash, others homesteaded a claim, and still others came into ownership via one of the many donation acts that Congress passed to transfer public lands to private ownership. Whatever the method, the General Land Office followed a two-step procedure in granting a patent.

First, the private claimant went to the land office in the land district where the public land was located. The claimant filled out entry papers to select the public land, and the land office register (clerk) checked the local registrar records to make sure the claimed land was still available. The receiver (bursar) took the claimant's payment, because even homesteaders had to pay administrative fees.

Next, the district land office register and receiver sent the paperwork to the General Land Office in Washington. That office double-checked the accuracy of the claim, its availability, and the form of payment. **Finally**, the General Land Office issued a land patent for the claimed public land and sent it on to the President for his signature.

The first United States land patent was issued on March 4, 1788, to John Martin. That patent reserves to the United States one-third of all gold, silver, lead, and copper within the claimed land.

Usage restrictions (e.g., oil and mineral rights, roadways, ditches and canals) placed on the land are spelled out in the patent. Such private property rights can also be thereafter negotiated in accord with the terms of private contracts. The rights inherent in patented land are carried from heir to heir, heir to assignee, or assignee to assignee, and cannot be changed except by private contract (warranty deed, quitclaim deed, etc.). In most cases, the law of a particular piece of patented land will be governed by the Congressional Act or treaty under which it was acquired, or by terms spelled out in the patent. For example, in the United States the laws governing the land may involve the Homestead Act or reservations placed on the face of the patent, or the Treaty of Guadalupe Hidalgo, which governs certain jurisdictional dicta relating to large amounts of land in California and adjoining territories.

Because most people become familiar with land rights only when they acquire real estate either by inheritance or through the process of a purchase contract, they never learn the difference between land and the property appurtenant to it. Accordingly, their familiarity with land law remains virtually non-existent; and, they only become accustomed to State statutory regulations relative to the property appurtenant to the land, that is to say: property taxing, zoning, and building codes, etc.

On 8/15/1836 Thomas Houghan bought 16,270 acres in St. Clair County from the US General Land Office in Kaskaskia, Illinois at their base price of $1.25/acre. Those tracts of 40 acres and larger were scattered among several townships. All that documentation and payment was then sent to the GLO in Washington, DC for the patenting process and presidential signature.

Houghan's purchases in just Prairie du Long Township totaled 5,513.89 acres. The legal description for that township is "Town 2 South, Range 8 West." It is 6 miles square and contains 23,040 acres so Houghan bought 23.9% of that township. On pages 5 and 6 below are the GLO patent for Thomas Houghan's purchases in just Prairie du Long Township. It is dated 7/20/1844 and signed by President John Tyler or one of his surrogate signers. That 8-year gap between purchase and patent is unusually long. Below is the Section 7 part of that patent.
Here's the map I made of Section 7 showing the original tract buyers and purchase dates. You

can see that Thomas Houghan bought ten 40-acre tracts in 1836. I don't know why he didn't also buy the two tracts which Mitchell bought two years later. The three salmon tracts were sold by Houghan to Adam Reiss in 1838, 1839, and 1842. The green tracts were bought by Conrad and Margaret Reiss Ebert from others in 1854 and 1868. The grey tracts were bought by George and Katie Reiss in 1917 who also bought more land to the right that year in Section 8.

MITCHELL 1838	HOUGHAN 1836	HOUGHAN 1836	RAPP 1835
	K L E I N R O A D		
RICHARDS 1834	HOUGHAN 1836	HOUGHAN 1836	MITCHELL 1838
RICHARDS 1834	HOUGHAN 1836	HOUGHAN 1836	HOUGHAN 1836
HOUGHAN 1836	BATES 1833	HOUGHAN 1836	HOUGHAN 1836

Thomas Houghan probably never saw or walked over any of the land he purchased. He simply walked into the land office in Kaskaskia, paid cash to the local Receiver for the tracts he wanted, and walked out with a receipt and deed. Those Receiver books are now stored in Springfield and can be viewed via the Illinois Public Doman Land Tract Sales Database which contains initial sales of public domain lands made through federal land district offices. The Kaskaskia office was later moved to Edwardsville as land for sale around the Kaskaskia office was depleted.

The Receiver at Kaskaskia issued a receipt and deed to Houghan and then forwarded the purchase information to the Government Land Office in Washington, DC. The GLO also issued a receipt and eventually a land patent to each first-time owner. But the GLO was so inundated and behind that patents were often issued several years after the original land purchase. The GLO was later renamed as the Bureau of Land Management or BLM.

The two following pages show Houghan's land patent for Prairie du Long Township. It's kinda hard to read which is why I enlarged just Section 7 on page 2 above where our family farm is located. You can see President John Tyler's signature at the bottom.

Look back at my Granddad's Mondays of 1/13/2014 and you'll see that Thomas Houghan also sold 40 acres to Robert and Nancy Tate on 5/13/1839 who in turn sold it to your great great great great great grandfather Johann Basler on 12/13/1841. Coming up in my Granddad's Mondays of 6/30/2014 you'll see that Thomas Houghan also sold two 40-acre tracts to your great great great great great uncle Franz Stauder on 10/5/1840 and 1/3/1844. Franz married Margaret Basler Reiss' sister Sophia on 3/19/1842 and lived a mile south of the Reiss Family Farm.

Altogether Thomas Houghan bought 57,747 acres in eight Illinois counties at $1.25/acre from the Federal Government's Land Office in Kaskaskia between 6/8/1832 and 4/15/1843. His major years were 1836 through 1839. He sold (flipped) essentially all of his land within five years of purchase at a minimum profit of 100%. His eight counties were St. Clair, Monroe, and Washington to the south, Tazewell and Logan to the north, and Sangamon, Christian, and Macoupin in the middle. All of his purchases were within 100 miles of Springfield because that's where he lived.

Here's the house Houghan built in Springfield in 1833 about a mile straight north of the first state capitol building. He lived there for ten years before selling it in 1843 to Benjamin Edwards whose father Ninian was Illinois' first territorial governor and whose older brother, also named Ninian, married Abraham Lincoln's sister-in-law Elizabeth Todd.

Will, Kayla, Ava, and Grant Jr., now you know lots of history about Thomas Houghan and how he was directly connected to the Reiss and Stauder family farms and indirectly to the Basler family farm. I chose not to due lengthy chain of title searches on family farms of other relatives including Dintelmann, Feder, Lang, Luetzelschwab, Neff, and Charles Reiss but it wouldn't surprise me that many more Houghan connections would be revealed. Let's plan on touring the Thomas Houghan home in Springfield which now belongs to the Springfield Art Association. You can share footsteps with Abraham Lincoln and hundreds of other famous visitors.

Love, Granddad

Certificate
No. 3090

To all to whom these Presents shall come, Greeting:

Whereas, Thomas Houghan of Springfield, ~~County of~~ State of Illinois, has deposited in the General Land Office of the United States a Certificate of the Register of the Land Office at Kaskaskia, whereby it appears that full payment has been made by the said Thomas Houghan, according to the provisions of the Act of Congress of the 24th of April 1820, entitled "An Act making further provision for the Sale of the Public Lands" for the West half of the North West quarter, containing eighty Acres, the West half of the South West quarter containing eighty Acres; the South West quarter of the South East quarter containing forty Acres, of Section Thirty three; the North half containing three hundred and twenty Acres, and the East half of the South West quarter containing eighty Acres; the East half of the South East quarter containing eighty Acres of Section Thirty two; the North West quarter containing one hundred and forty seven Acres and sixty hundredths of an Acre, and the East half of the South West quarter containing seventy four Acres and sixty two hundredths of an Acre of Section thirty one; the North half containing three hundred and twenty Acres; the East half of the South East quarter containing eighty Acres, and the West half of the South West quarter containing eighty Acres of Section twenty eight; the East half of the South East quarter containing eighty Acres of Section twenty nine; the South East quarter of the North East quarter containing forty Acres, and the South West quarter of the South West quarter containing forty Acres of Section twenty nine; the West half containing three hundred and two Acres and seventy four hundredths of an Acre and the West half of the North East quarter containing eighty Acres of Section thirty; the North West quarter containing one hundred and fifty nine Acres and the West half of the North East quarter containing eighty Acres of Section nineteen; the West half of the North West quarter containing eighty Acres; the North West and the South East quarters of the North East quarter containing eighty Acres, and the North West quarter of the South West quarter containing forty Acres of Section twenty; the South half containing three hundred and twenty Acres and the South West quarter of the North West quarter containing forty Acres of Section twenty one; the South half of the South West quarter containing eighty Acres; the West half of the South East quarter containing eighty Acres; the East half of the North West quarter containing eighty Acres and the West half of the North East quarter containing eighty Acres of Section seventeen; the South East quarter containing one hundred and sixty Acres; the East half of the North East quarter containing eighty Acres; the West half of the North West quarter containing eighty Acres, and the East half of the South West quarter containing eighty Acres of Section eighteen; the South East quarter containing one hundred and sixty Acres; the West half of the North East quarter containing eighty Acres; the East half of the North West quarter containing seventy six Acres and ninety hundredths of an Acre; the North East quarter of the South West quarter containing forty Acres and twelve hundredths of an Acre and the South West quarter of the South West quarter containing forty Acres and twelve hundredths of an Acre of Section seven; the East half of the South East quarter containing eighty Acres, and the East half of the North West quarter containing seventy five Acres and sixty seven hundredths of an Acre of Section one; the North West quarter containing one hundred and forty five Acres and forty nine hundredths of an Acre, and the West half of the South West quarter containing eighty Acres of Section three; the South West quarter containing one hundred and sixty Acres and the East half of the South East quarter containing eighty Acres of Section four; the South half of the North East quarter, containing ninety six Acres and eight hundredths of an Acre; the East half of the North West quarter containing seventy one Acres and eighty seven hundredths of an Acre and the West half of the south West quarter containing eighty Acres of Section five; the south half of the South East quarter containing eighty Acres, the North West quarter containing one hundred and forty six Acres and forty one hundredths of an Acre, the West half of the North East quarter containing ninety five acres and fifty two hundredths of an Acre, and the East half of the South West quarter containing eighty one Acres and twenty hundredths of an Acre of Section five, the West half containing three hundred and twenty Acres and the West half of the South East quarter containing eighty Acres of Section eight All in Township two South, of Range eight West, in the District of Lands subject to sale at Kaskaskia, Illinois, containing in all, Five Thousand Five Hundred and Thirteen Acres, and Eighty nine hundredths of an Acre, according to the Official plat of the Survey of the said Lands, returned to the General Land Office by the Surveyor General which said tracts have been purchased by the said Thomas Houghan. Now Know Ye that the United States of America in consideration of the Premises, and in conformity with the several acts of Congress, in such case made and provided Have Given And Granted and by these presents Do Give And Grant unto the said Thomas Houghan, and to his heirs the said tracts above described To Have And To Hold the same together with all the rights privileges, immunities and appurtenances of whatsoever nature thereunto belonging unto the said Thomas Houghan and to his heirs and assigns forever.

In Testimony Whereof, I, John Tyler

President of the United States of America have caused these Letters to be made Patent and the Seal of the General Land Office to be hereunto affixed.

Given under my hand at the City of Washington the tenth day of July in the Year of our Lord one thousand eight hundred and forty four and of the Independence of the United States the sixty Ninth.

By The President, John Tyler

By John Tyler Jr Secy.

R. M. Whitney P. W. Williamson Recorder of the General Land Office

Signed by Recorder 10. Dec 1844

Log Cabin and Log Granary Built in 1838

Dear Will and Kayla,   April 23, 2012

This is a picture of the log cabin built on the Reiss Family Farm south of Belleville, Illinois in 1838 by your great great great great grandfather, Johann Adam Reiss. He is your grandfather's grandfather's grandfather. He went by Adam instead of by Johann.

Adam was born on May 7, 1804 in Obernau, Bavaria, Germany which today is a suburb of the much larger city of Aschaffenburg. He sailed for America in 1833 and landed in New Orleans. Economic and political times were difficult in Germany so he was striking out on his own for farming opportunities in the new world. He worked his way north along the Mississippi River and may have spent his first winter in Natchez, Mississippi. In April 1834 (178 years ago this month) he arrived in St. Clair County, Illinois and bought his first 40 acres of land from a famous speculator named Thomas Houghan, but that's the subject of another of Granddad's Mondays.

Adam built this log cabin for himself. Note the brick chimney above the roof which means there was a fireplace inside for heat. The cabin was about 15 by 18 feet so it was very small compared to modern homes. Adam married Mary Schuessler on May 15, 1838. She may have also been from Obernau so perhaps they were sweethearts back in Germany such that his coming to America to establish a farm and home (with her to follow when it was ready) was their joint master plan. But sadly Mary died in this cabin during the birth of their first child, John, on December 11, 1838. The baby survived despite having no mother to nurse him and the onset of winter.

Well, God provided another very nice woman who became Adam's second wife. Her name was Margaritha Basler, but she went by her Americanized name of Margaret. She was born in Zeihen, Switzerland near the Germany border on October 22, 1818 and immigrated to St. Clair County with her parents and siblings in 1839. Margaret married Adam on September 10, 1840. They both spoke German in this, their log home. Adam and Margaret had five children in the cabin but the last one died in infancy. Adam died in this cabin on May 23, 1849 of cholera which was an epidemic in the area.

On April 2, 1850 Margaret then married Conrad Ebert who may have also been a childhood friend of Adam's from Obernau who had also immigrated to St. Clair County and lived near the Reiss farm. Margaret and Conrad were probably already good friends because they married less than a year after Adam died and here was Margaret with five children under age eleven. Conrad must have been a real saint of a guy to take on an instant family and a farm which by then consisted of 120 acres.

To kinda wrap up the cabin history, Adam's and Margaret's oldest son Frank Reiss married Anna Syvilla Feder in a double wedding ceremony with his sister on April 9, 1866 (146 years and two weeks ago). Frank and Anna are the two oval pictures in my den. Margaret and Conrad built a new log cabin for themselves half a mile southeast so that Frank and Anna could have this older one. Here is where ten of their eleven children were born and here is also where four of them died of disease. Frank and Anna built a new house right next door in 1889 and that is where their eleventh child was born. His name was William Martin Reiss, almost like yours, Will. That new home is also where your great grandfather (my dad), Irwin Henry Reiss, was born on September 18, 1917.

Sadly this cabin was demolished in 1957 to make room for a new three-stall concrete block garage. Removing that historic cabin was a huge mistake in my opinion. On the good side, however, the log granary which was also built nearby in 1838 survives to this day. Maintaining that structure and its memories is now a major family priority.

Will and Kayla, I see major similarities between our original Adam Reiss and your mom/aunt Hany. Both left their native countries, families, language, friends, and comfort zone to strike out for America. Both had lots of energy, self-confidence, and determination to make things work in

a new country over 8,000 miles from where they were born. And both were or are continuing to be very successful. Your mom/aunt is a pioneer and her husband Grant is a fifth generation descendant of one. I'm very impressed. You should be doubly proud. But, dear grandchildren, please don't take all this story as authority to leave Illinois and strike out for yet another country on your own!!!

Love, Granddad

Here's my aunt Katie Petri at the log cabin door about 1948. You can see some of the construction. Two more photos appear on the next page. The first one from 1950 shows the cabin at the far left. Farm tenants are living in that part of the homestead at that time so that's their child.

Original Log Cabin on Reiss Farm probably built in the mid 1830's

Catholic Church on the Reiss Farm

Dear Will, Kayla, Ava, and Grant Jr.,   November 10, 2014

Your great great great great grandfather Adam Reiss built two log buildings on the farm he established in 1838 in St. Clair County, Illinois. One was his personal cabin with a wood-burning stove. The other was a granary to store grain, farm supplies, and equipment that he needed. Both were about the same size of 15 feet by 18 feet. One or both of these buildings were used for Catholic church services according to a history of St. Michael's Catholic Church in Paderborn written in 1962 by Dominic Reinhardt. Here are excerpts from Reinhardt's history of St. Michael's Church which is two miles southwest of our home farm:

"The first masses offered on the soil of Prairie du Long Township were between 1834 and 1842. Catholic services were offered on the Adam Reiss farm, presently owned by George W. Reiss, a grandson of the aforementioned. Until 1957, that original dwelling was preserved and still in use. Catholic services also occurred on the John Roth farm, presently owned by Gustave Metzger. The foundation of the original log cabin in which mass was said still stands."

We know that the first wife of Adam Reiss died in childbirth on December 11, 1838 and that the child, a son named John, survived. Adam married Margaretha Basler on September 10, 1940. She was the second child and oldest daughter of Johann and Katharina Basler.

Here's more written history – "It was not until the latter part of 1841 that Johann Basler obtained or purchased a portion of the land which today is the farm owned by Michael Mueth. Mr. Basler, apparently as immediate relative to the aforementioned Adam Reiss' wife *(her father)*, on January 24, 1843, sold two acres of land for one cent for the purpose of building a church thereon. This transaction is recorded in the St. Clair County recorder's office Book N, page 165, and again on page 488. This second entry is a warranty deed to the Rt. Rev. Peter Kenrick, Bishop of St. Louis. This same year, November 1843, it is recorded that Mr. Basler conveyed his farm with exception of two acres upon which a Catholic Church is built. This gives evidence that the first Church was built in the Year of Our Lord Eighteen Hundred and Forty-Three (1843). This church was known as the Church of St. Thomas the Apostle."

"It is believed that Father J. F. R. Loisel was the founder of this parish. The log church, which is a proven fact, stood on the original two acres. It was a one-room structure built of logs and clap board roof. The altar most likely was a table. There were no pews or benches. Tradition tells us that the people brought chairs or seats from home. These were also used to sit on while en route to and from church. It was a custom in those days in many places, instead of pew rent, there was a rental for the space on which one placed his chair."

"There is a mistaken belief that the Church of St. Thomas stood on the Louis Hagen farm, presently owned by John Mueth south of Paderborn. The fact is that after the present stone church was built, Mr. Hagen bought the log church and moved it to his farm to be used as a farm building. Thus old timers used to refer to the building as the old church, not mentioning that it was no longer on its original site." See the John Mueth farm in the 1980 plat book below.

Cholera – "A cholera epidemic swept this area somewhere along the year 1849. It is claimed that fifty-two persons died and were buried in the old cemetery. Most of the graves were never marked, but the location was along the extreme west end of the old cemetery. This may be the reason that some family names recorded in the early church records are no longer here. The "Belleville" cholera epidemic claimed 236 lives from May 18 to July 31, 1849." One of those was our Adam Reiss who died on May 23, 1849. He is buried in St. Augustine Catholic Cemetery in Hecker.

Johann Basler's wife Katharina was born in Switzerland on December 27, 1793. She died March 5, 1841 in Prairie du Long Township. We do not know her gravesite but perhaps it is here near the original log church in Paderborn. Their second daughter Sophie Basler married Frantz Stauder in the log church on March 19, 1842. Perhaps these are reasons why Johann Basler formally donated these two acres of land on January 24, 1843. Little did anyone realize that Sophie Basler Stauder would die young at age 42 and be buried here on July 25, 1865. Her tombstone is the second one from the northeast corner in the old cemetery.

Cemetery – "The first cemetery is part of the church grounds. One of the ancient tombstones in this old cemetery marks the burial place of an individual born in 1777. During the course of years, many of the stones have deteriorated. Today only fifty-five monuments are left to mark the graves of the early settlers of the area."

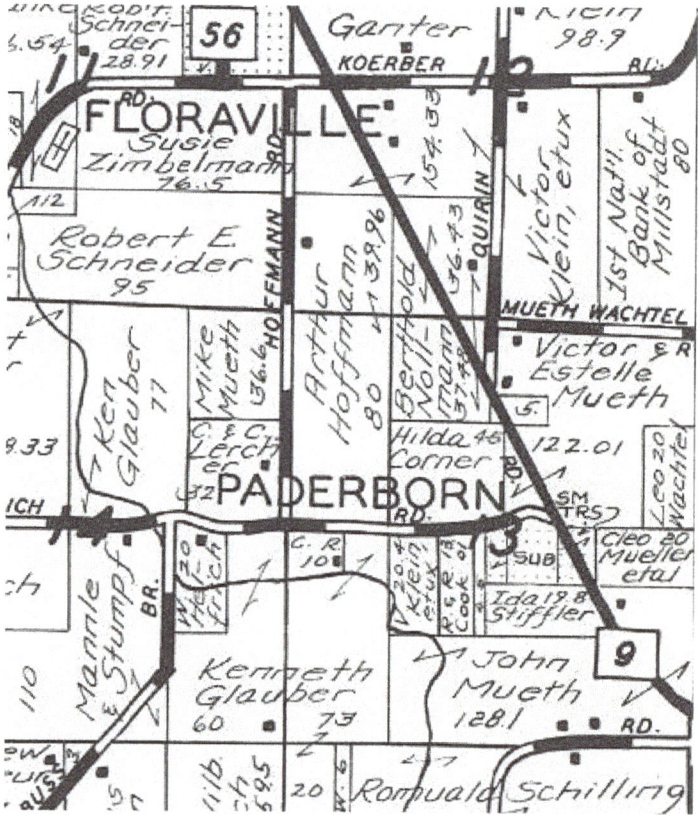

"In 1876 a new cemetery was laid out a short distance to the west of the parish grounds. Two former pastors have been buried in the priest's section of this cemetery in front of the crucifix. They are Father John T. Sonnen who died in 1932 and Father Francis Wiskamp who died in 1943. May they, and all who are buried in these cemeteries, rest in peace."

Will, Kayla, Ava, and Grant Jr., isn't it absolutely awesome that your great great great great grandfather Adam Reiss hosted Catholic church services in his home? Isn't it equally absolutely awesome that Adam's father-in-law, your great great great great great grandfather Johann Basler, donated two acres of his farm for the purposes of building a Catholic church and cemetery? Adam arrived from Germany in 1833 and Johann arrived from Switzerland in 1839. I'll bet you a nickel that Adam met his future wife Margaret at Catholic church in his own home!!!!!!!!!!!!!

Love, Granddad

The Basler Family Arrives on November 28, 1839

Dear Will, Kayla, and Ava,   January 13, 2014

Last Wednesday, January 8, was the 198th wedding anniversary of your great great great great great grandparents <mark>Johann (John) and Katharina Basler</mark>. They almost didn't get married, however, because they were first cousins and had to get dispensation from the Catholic Church in Switzerland. It probably helped a lot that Johann's brother Joseph was a priest and actually performed the marriage ceremony on January 8, 1816.

The Baslers and eight of their nine living children left Switzerland in mid-1839 to immigrate to the United States. The children were ages 3 to 21. They arrived in New Orleans on 11/28/1839 and soon moved north to Prairie du Long Township of St. Clair County, Illinois. Their oldest child, Nicholaus Johann Basler age 23, had already immigrated to the US arriving in New Orleans on 12/3/1836. He was living in Louisville, Kentucky but moved to St. Clair County to be with his parents.

We don't know where the Baslers lived but my guess it was a house in Paderborn about 1.5 miles southwest of the Adam Reiss farm. We know from the published history of St. Michael's Catholic Church in Paderborn that earlier church services were held on the Adam Reiss farm before that church was built. My guess is that the entire Basler family got to know (and be impressed by) Adam by going to church in his log cabin and/or his log granary depending on what season it was. They got to see how tenderly Adam cared for his 13-month old son John who had survived when his mother Mary died in childbirth. Adam no doubt got to appreciate weekly hugging, feeding, and diaper changing of young John by John Basler's oldest daughter, Margaret. <mark>Adam and Margaret were married on September 10, 1840, probably on the Adam Reiss farm.</mark> He was 14.5 years her senior.

Tragically Katharina Basler died the following year on 5/5/1841 and was buried in the old cemetery in Paderborn but her grave can no longer be identified. Margaret wrote the German details below on the left which I had translated to English on the right. All of that may have been on her missing tombstone but it would have taken up a lot of space. Perhaps her marker was made of wood which would have offered more space but also have disappeared over the years.

Hier liegt in Christ	Here lies in Christ
Katherina Basler von Niederzeihen	Katherina Basler from Niederzeihen
Bzk. Lunfensburg	District Laufenburg
Canton Aargau Schweiz	Canton Aargau Switzerland
Geb. D. 5 27 Dec 1793	Born 27 December 1793
Gest. D 5 May 1841	Died 5 May 1841
Alter 47 J. 2M. 9T	Age 47 years, 2 months, 9 days
Born in Bazil, Switzerland	Born in Basil, Switzerland

The following poem only in English was written on the same piece of paper where Margaret wrote the German information above. It was written with excellent penmanship probably by someone else.

> Dearest mother, thou hast left us,
> Here thy loss we deeply feel,
> But 'tis God that hath bereft us,
> He can all our sorrows heal.
> Yet again we hope to meet thee,
> Where no farewell tear is shed,
> And in heaven with joy to greet thee,
> Where our joys unmixed with thee.

There are three more major events in the St. Clair County life of the Basler family which will be covered in separate "Granddad's Mondays" stories:

- John Basler's 1841 purchase and 1843 sale of a 40-acre farm northeast of Paderborn.

- John Basler's 1843 donation of two acres from the southeast corner of that farm to the congregation St. Michael's Catholic Church so they could build their first church building.

- Margaret's younger sister Sophia marrying Franz Stauder on March 28, 1842 in Belleville. Franz also had a farm just south of the Adam Reiss farm. Sadly Sophia died young at age 42 on July 25, 1865 and is buried in St. Michael's Cemetery. I have seen her grave.

Will, Kayla, and Ava, isn't it great that you three are related to so many wonderful people especially to three outstanding guys all named Adam Reiss -- Johann Adam Reiss (5/7/1804 – 5/23/1849), his grandson Adam Joseph Reiss (9/25/1869 – 11/5/1874), and our current Adam Stephen Reiss (8/8/1976 --). Our ancestors survived incredible hardships compared to the standard of living we all enjoy today. We are all so very fortunate.

Love, Granddad

Basler Homes in Switzerland

Dear Will, Kayla, and Ava,   January 6, 2014

Let's go back over 200 years and summarize what we know about your relatives whose last name is Basler. It was Margaretha Basler who was the second wife of Adam Reiss who established the family farm. I'm sure you've heard of her because she is on the cover of our family history book, It Takes A Matriarch. She is the one who saved 780 letters between 1852 and 1888 which were all translated and transcribed into that book by author and in date order. She is the reason we know so much about our family history.

Your great great great great great great great grandparents

These relatives were all born in Switzerland between 1750 and 1770. Simon and Johann Basler were brothers. Simon was a Catholic priest.

Brother Simon Basler married Julina (or Justine) Schwander and were the parents of Johann Basler. There are going to be too many "Johanns" so try to keep them straight.

Brother Johann Basler married Margarita Meyer and they were the parents of Katharina Basler.

Since Simon and Johann were brothers, their children Johann and Katharina are first cousins.

Your great great great great great grandparents

Johann Basler married his first cousin Katharina Basler on January 8, 1816 which is 198 years from this coming Wednesday. Katharina was already a Basler so she didn't have to change her name when she married Johann. His family lived in Herznach. Her family lived three miles away in Zeihen. After marrying, Johann and Katharina lived in Zeihen, probably with her parents. They had ten children but sadly the eighth one died in infancy. This family of parents and nine children emigrated to America in 1839.

Johann Basler (1/7/1791 – late 1854) died at age 63. Birth source is Swiss baptism record. Death source is Letters #429 and #398 in our Matriarch book. He was mayor of Zeihen in 1815. His brother Joseph was a priest and who baptized Johann's son George Anselm Basler in 1831.

Katharina Basler (12/27/1793 – 3/5/1841) died at age 47. She was related to her husband as a first cousin such that they had to get a dispensation from the church before they were allowed to marry on 1/8/1816.

Grand DD and I spent two days in Switzerland in 2008 researching the Basler family, their homes, and current relatives. Here are two pages my notes from **Friday September 26, 2008** – We reached Zeihen and Herznach where my Basler ancestors emigrated from in 1839. Checked into Hotel Roessli in Zeihen which was owned by my great great great great uncle about 1820. It is three guest rooms above a restaurant below where we will host dinner tonight for my fifth cousin Kaspar Basler and for Frantz Wuelser who is the town clerk for this village of 950 souls.

We had invited Matthias Ackle, the town clerk for nearby Herznach, but he was unable to attend. Kaspar was mayor (gemeindeammann or burgermeister) of Zeihen for twelve years starting about 1994. My great great great grandfather Johann Basler was also mayor of Zeihen in 1815.

Our hotel room has twin beds and overlooks the street below. There is a feather comforter but no top sheet. Dinner was at 7:00 where we met Kaspar and Roseli Basler and village clerk Franz Wuelser. English was somewhat limited but it was not a problem. The Baslers showed us their family tree from 1533 to 1670 so now somehow we need to connect that to 1791 where mine starts. Dinner was weinerschnitzel, pom frits, and red wine which were all good. The Baslers gave us a bottle of their pear brandy which was distilled from their own pears and is 42% alcohol by volume.

After dinner Franz Wuelser took all of us across the street to his office in the village hall. We made copies of the Basler family tree and looked in the village record books back to 1810. We found where my great great great grandfather had been mayor of Zeihen in 1815. We had a quick tour of the village museum which included lots of old wooden farm tools and several 300-year-old alpine horns. It was a great evening of food, conversation, and connecting. The Baslers invited us for a late breakfast tomorrow at their farmstead. We adjourned at 10:00.

Here's a Swiss aerial photo showing the villages of Zeihen and Herznach from where our ancestors came and the farm of my cousin, Kasper Basler where we went for breakfast.

September 27 Saturday – Up at 7:00 at an attempted light breakfast of zwei eire ungefar drei minuten (two eggs soft boiled for three minutes) which turned out too runny. Roseli Basler picked us up at 8:30 to visit their farm of about 100 acres about 1.5 miles away. We breakfasted with the entire family outlined below except Jacqueline who lives two hours away.

Kaspar Basler (9/10/1941 --) married Roseli ?? (7/2/1952 --) on ??

    Colette Basler (10/26/1973 --) married Markus Plattner (now Basler) (2/4/ 1973 -) on ??

        Laurin Basler (8/28/2002 --)

        Pascale Basler (12/19/2003 --)

    Patricia Basler (5/10/1976 --) Her email is patti_on_tour@hotmail.com

    Jacqueline Basler (3/26/1981 --)

We enjoyed homemade bread and butter, white coffee made with whole milk. All three generations live in one large semi-duplex house with the community rooms in the center and individual family bedrooms and bathrooms on the right and left sides. Most meals are shared. Kaspar and his son-in-law operate the dairy, pasture, and fruit businesses as a family partnership.

Kaspar and Roseli have sold their farm at a discounted price to Colette and Markus, but retained a life estate for themselves. They also gave similar funds to their other two daughters who were not interested in becoming farmers. Swiss laws allow such tax-reduced transfers but with the stipulation that the son-in-law changes his last name to that of his wife's parents. So now Markus' last name is Basler so that name continues for another generation.

We toured the dairy barn where some 50 cows are milked twice a day and where young steers are raised and sold for meat. Milk is stored in a 2,000 liter tank at 4.5 degrees Celsius. Milk production records are kept by cow using numbers on their ear tags. Cows are fed a mixture of silage and pasture grass. Best milk producers are Holsteins, then red Holsteins, and then brown Swiss. The Baslers subcontract hay bailing and buy cut firewood for heating their home. They also take fermented orchard fruit to a local distiller for conversion into brandy. A new calf was born this morning but they were hand feeding it from a large bottle to give it various meds and to also keep the mother's milk from their business.

Roseli took us on a driving tour of the area where we saw vineyards where she will help pick grapes next week and saw the home farm of her son-in-law Markus. We stopped at the former underground iron mine in Herznach where its above ground storage ore silo has been converted to a bed and breakfast. The terrain is quite hilly such that most farms are pastures. Fields with row crops are relatively small.

We found the old Basler homes in Zeihen and Herznach which appear below. These villages and the countryside between are absolutely beautiful. In fact all this is so beautiful that if it weren't for severe political and economic unrest back in the mid-1830s, I'm sure my ancestors would never have left.

Apple trees were heavily loaded with fruit. There were cows with cow bells, some running loose and some in pastures. About 10% of the fields were corn but most of that was being cut as silage for cows. There we no soy beans. Wheat had been in some fields. There were a few vineyards. Most of the village homes had window flowerboxes.

Back to the Basler house for lunch of cheese fondue with the entire family except for Jacqueline who was away. We enjoyed conversations on many more subjects. Patricia lives about two hours away but has a job there teaching English so language was not a limitation around the table. We talked about how to fill the gap in our family trees between 1670 and 1791. We said our goodbyes and then Roseli drove us back to our hotel. This was a fun morning.

Here is a photo of Zeihen. The Kasper Basler farm is that yellow wheat field in the top center. They have awesome views in all directions. Their three children and now their grandchildren enjoy sleeping outside on the upper balcony overlooking the farm. It is totally awesome.

Here are emails for the Roessli hotel where we stayed in Zeihen and the two village clerks.

rogger-roessli@bluewin.ch, franz.wuelser@zeihen.ch, matthias.ackle@herznach.ch.

Will, Kayla, and Ava, above is the original Basler home in Herznach. Looks like there have been two additions over the years. Below is the original Basler home in Zeihen. Grand DD and I are fortunate that we are retired, can spend time with you three, and that we have time and resources to travel and discover more about our family heritage. Someday we'll all visit Zeihen and Herznach in Switzerland.

Love, Granddad

1840 – 1849

1840 Population of St. Clair County is 13,631.

1840 States total 26, national population is 17.07 million. Florida and Texas are added in 1845, Iowa in 1846, and Wisconsin in 1848.

1840 President is Martin Van Buren. William Henry Harrison is inaugurated in 1841 and dies in his first month. John Tyler is inaugurated in 1841, James Polk in 1845, and Zachary Taylor in 1849.

1841 First wagon train from Missouri to California, took 188 days.

1845 The game of baseball is developed.

1846 The boundary between Canada and the US west of the Rocky Mountains is fixed at the 49th parallel.

1847 First US postage stamps with adhesive.

1848 Mexican War is settled with the Treaty of Guadalupe Hidalgo.

1848 Gold discovered at Sutter's Mill in California.

1849 Regular steamship service established between east and west coasts via Cape Horn, takes 4.5 months.

John Basler Buys a 40-Acre Farm on 12/13/1841

Dear Will, Kayla, Ava, and Blake,   January 13, 2014

This story is pretty complicated so bear with me. In red is the 40-acre farm which Robert and Nancy Tate bought on 5/13/1839 from big-time land speculator Thomas Houghan who had bought it from the Federal Government on 8/15/1836. Houghan is the same guy that Adam Reiss bought three of his forty-acre parcels from on 9/1/1838, 1/1/1839, and 9/28/1842. All three of the 1838 and 1839 purchases were $100 each and Adam's 1842 purchase was $120 or $3.00 per acre.

Five months after John Basler's daughter Margaret married Adam Reiss on 9/10/1840, his wife Katharina died on 3/5/1841 and was buried in the old cemetery in Paderborn. John now had to make plans for his remaining family consisting of Johann Nicholaus 24, Johann Jakob 20, Sophia 18, Martin 15, Ferdinand 13, George Anselm 10, Katharina 6, and Maria Aloisia (Louisa) 5. Tragically Katharina died on her youngest daughter's fifth birthday.

John Basler decided to buy 40 acres from the Tates for $240 on 12/13/1841 exactly 19 months after they had bought it for $100. Even though this $240 is double what Adam Reiss paid a year later for his third forty acres, John's parcel was 85% tillable versus Adam's at 50%. Plus, if the Baslers were indeed living in Paderborn as I suspect, this new farm was in easy walking distance.

The next event for the Basler family was the marriage of daughter Sophia to Frantz Stauder on 3/28/1842 in Belleville. My guess is that Frantz and Sophia also met at Catholic Church services on the Adam Reiss farm just like Adam and Margaret probably did. Frantz had also lost his first wife and was raising a son and daughter both under age five. Frantz had bought forty acres on 10/5/1840 half a mile south of the Reiss farm and may have been living there in a log cabin he built or in a house in Paderborn. Both Basler sisters and both widowed men would have made shared nurturing of their respective children or step-children-to-be part of their courtships.

John Basler Indenture on 6/14/1842

For reasons I do not understand, John Basler sold his 40 acres to five of his children per the indenture below for $360 which was drafted on June 14, 1842 but not recorded until thirteen months later on 7/22/1843. An indenture is any deed, contract, or sealed agreement between two or more parties. His five children in this agreement are Johann 25, Margaret Reiss 23, George 11, Katharina 7, and Maria Aloisia 6. Where were those five offspring, three of whom are children, going to find $360 and why? Here's the indenture. See if it makes any sense.

This Indenture made and entered into this fourteenth day of June, A.D. one thousand eight hundred and forty-two between John Basler of Saint Clair County, and, State of Illinois, party of the first part, and John N. Balser, Margaretha Basler, George A. Basler, Catherine Basler, Maria Aloisia Basler; all of Saint Clair County and State of Illinois, parties of the second part, witnesseth: That the said John Basler for and in consideration of three hundred and sixty dollars, to him in hand paid by the said parties of the second part, the receipt where of is hereby acknowledged, hath granted, bargained, and sold and by these presents doth grant, bargain, sell, alien, and confirm unto the said parties of the second part and to their heirs and assigns forever all that tract or parcel of land, situate in the County of Saint Clair and State of Illinois, being the southwest quarter of the northeast quarter of Section Thirteen, Township Two South of Range Nine West, with all and singular the rights and appurtenances thereunto belonging, or in anywise appertaining, also all the chattels, household stuff, and furniture, hereinafter more particularly expressed, that is to say: one horse and harness, one cow and calf, one heifer, bedsteads & bedding, furniture, hogs and chickens; all now remaining and being in the County of Saint Clair and State of Illinois. To have and to hold the premises aforesaid with all the privileges and appurtenances thereunto belonging or in anywise appertaining with them the said parties of the second part, their heirs, and assigns forever. Provided always, that these presents are upon this express condition, that if the said John Basler shall pay or cause to be paid to the said parties of the second part, their heirs, executors, administrators or assigns the sum of three hundred and sixty dollars on or before the fourteenth day of June A. D. one thousand eight hundred and forty-six, together with the interest that may accrue thereon, in a manner particularly specified in nine separate notes or allegations, bearing even date herewith, executed by the said John Basler, to the said parties of the second part each separately, thence and from thenceforth these presents and everything herein contained shall cease and be void anything herein contained to the contrary notwithstanding. In witness whereof the said party of the first part hath hereunto set his hand and seal this day and year first herein written.

Signed, sealed, and delivered

Johan Basler (seal)

In the presence of Wm. Grief, witness. I Bernard Dingwerth, a Justice of the Peace of said county of St. Clair County certify that John Basler whose signature appears to the foregoing deed and who is personally known to me to be the person described in and who executed the same did acknowledge the same to be his free and voluntary act and Deed for the use and purposes therein mentioned. Given under my hand and seal this 22nd day of July 1843.

(signed) Bernard Dingwerth, J.P. Granted this twenty-second day of July, Eighteen Hundred and Forty-Three.

Will, Kayla, and Ava, I saw where Bernard Dingwerth does appear in the 1840 Census as living in St. Clair County, Illinois. This looks like a routine document. John may have advanced his own money to these five children who then paid him right back. This action made these five children the legal owners of his farm. Maybe he feared bankruptcy or a lawsuit and needed to legally separate himself from his farm.

John Basler Donates Two Acres to St. Michael's Church in Paderborn on 1/24/1843 and 9/8/1843

Are you confused yet? John wanted to give two acres from his southeast corner to the St. Michael's Church congregation so they could build a church on the northeast corner of Paderborn. This whole St. Michael's history lesson is the subject of a future Granddad's Mondays story but I'll summarize it here. The cleanest way for a donation was actually a deed of sale with a price of $.01. But it turned out church property ownership must be held at the bishop level rather than at the local congregation level. That meant a second deed of sale, this time to the bishop in St. Louis and this time with a price of $1.00. Now John Basler's remaining farm is 38 acres.

John Basler Sells 38 Acres to Nicholas Biebel on 11/2/1843

Slightly over three months after recording his indenture with his children, John Basler sold his remaining 38 acres to Nicholaus Biebel for $330. I don't know how he was able to sell something that five of his children owned rather than himself. Here's that sale indenture. See if anything looks fishy:

This Indenture is made this second day of November in the year of our Lord one thousand eight hundred and forty-three between John Basler of the first part and Nicholas Biebel of the second part all of the County of St. Clair and State of Illinois. Witness that the said party of the first part for and in consideration of the sum of three hundred and thirty dollars to him in hand paid the receipt thereof is hereby acknowledged hath granted, bargained, and sold and by these presents doth grant bargain unto the said Nicholas Biebel the party of the second part his heirs and assigns forever the southwest quarter of the northwest quarter of Section thirteen in Township two south of Range nine west situate and being in the County of St. Clair and Sate of Illinois to have and to hold the said lot of land with the (exception of two acres off of the south side of the above described lot of land on which the Catholic church is built) and said party of the first part for themselves and their heirs the said land doth warrant and forever defense free from all claims of every person whomsoever they may be. Testimony whereof the said party of the first part hereunto set his hand and seal the day and year first above written.

Witnesses: N. J. Basler   Johan Basler (Seal)
                 Adam Reiss
                 Franz Stauder

Will, Kayla, Ava, and Blake, notice that three witnesses are John Basler's oldest son and his two sons-in-law. It looks like whatever impact the 6/14/1842 indenture sale by John Basler to his five children might/should have had on this transfer was ignored. It is probably significant that two of the adult owners (including Adam via Margaret) are in agreement with all this since they signed off as witnesses.

Soon after selling his farm, John Basler and his family move to Louisville, Kentucky. Nicholaus gets married there in 1844 probably to a lady he knew from before and starts a family. Johann Jakob and Ferdinand appear next in 1847 operating a confectionary in Galena, Illinois. Johann gets married in Galena in 1849 and starts a family. Ferdinand moves to my hometown of Sullivan, Indiana in 1849, marries, and starts a family. Martin marries in 1849 in St. Louis and then in 1852 he, his wife, and two-month old son take a covered wagon to Sacramento. George and Katharina appear in the 1850 Census living in Louisville with the Sacksteder family. George next appears in San Francisco in 1853 via steamships from New York to Panama and from there to California. Kate and Louisa eventually marry and raise families in St. Louis. Sadly John Basler dies in Louisville in late 1854.

Will, Kate, and Ava, I want you to realize that there are extraordinary people in your heritage. I hope you were able to follow all those farm ownership changes and the eventual scattering of the Basler family. Not much is lost however because your great great great great grandmother Margaret Basler Reiss saved 780 letters she received from 1852 to 1888 from her Basler siblings and her own Reiss children. Those letters are all in your home right now in a thick book appropriately titled, <mark>It Takes A Matriarch</mark>.

Love, Granddad

John Basler Donates Two Acres to St. Michael's Church

Dear Will, Kayla, and Ava,   October 13, 2014

This story is kinda complicated but it underscores the generosity of your great great great great great grandfather, Johann (John) Basler. Let me set the stage. In late summer 1839 John, his wife, and eight children left Switzerland to immigrate to the United States. They arrived in New Orleans on 11/28/1839 and moved north to St. Clair County, Illinois. On 12/13/1841 John bought 40 acres of farmland northeast of the village of Paderborn. It is outlined here in red as part of Section 13 which comprises this map. Then on January 24, 1843 John sold two of those forty acres to the Catholic congregation of St. Michael's who wanted to build a church. Those two acres are in solid red. Price for the sale was just one penny.

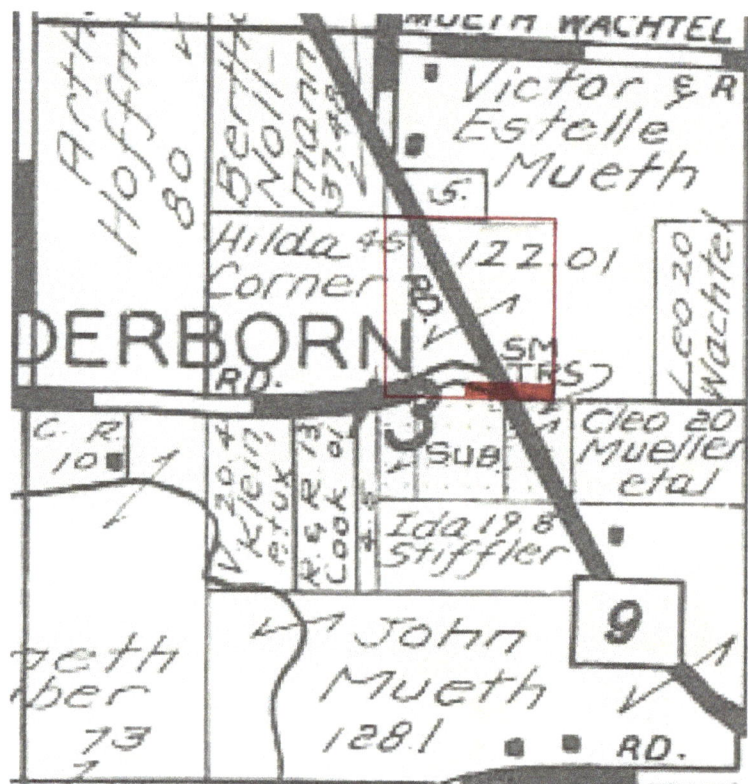

Eight months later on September 8, 1843 John sold those two acres all over again except this time the price was one dollar, 100 times his first sale price. The second sale was to the Catholic Bishop of St. Louis, the Right Reverend Peter Kenrick. I think this second almost identical sale was necessary because the Catholics just like the Methodists hold church property ownership at the district level rather than within individual churches.

Maybe John should have sold his two acres a third time to the Pope in Rome for another 100-fold price increase to $100. Pretty soon we're talking about real money 170 years ago!

Here is the legal document for the first sale – This Deed, made and entered into this twenty-fourth day of January eighteen hundred and forty-three by and between John Basler of Saint Clair County and State of Illinois, of the first part, and the members of Saint Michael Church of the county and State aforesaid, of the second part, witnesseth: That the said party of the first part for and in consideration of the sum of one cent to him kindly hand paid, by the said party of the second part, the receipt whereof is hereby received and acknowledged, has granted, bargained and sold, and by these presents does grant, bargain and sell, convey and confirm, unto the said party of the second part, their heirs and assigns forever, two acres of land, for the use of a church building in the southwest quarter of the northeast quarter of Section thirteen, township two south of range nine west, situated and being in the county of Saint Clair, and State of Illinois, commencing at the southeast corner running north forty yards, thence west two hundred and twenty, thence south forty, thence east two hundred and twenty to the place of the beginning, to have and to hold the same with all the rights, privileges, and appurtenances thereunto belonging, or in anywise appertaining, unto there, the said party of the second part, their heirs and assigns forever, the said John Basler, party of the first part, hereby covenanting that his heirs, executors and administrators who warrant and defend the title to the said premises and every part thereof to the party of the second part, their heirs and assigns, a guarantee which claim or claims of all and every person or persons whatsoever claiming or to claim the same or any part thereof. In witness whereof the said party of the first part, has hereunto set his hand and seal, the day and year first therein written.

Johann Basler (seal)

In the presence of Bernard Dingwerth, Wm Grieff. I, William C. Kinney, Clerk of the St. Clair Circuit Court, do hereby certify that Johann Basler, who is personally known to me to be the person, whose name is signed to the foregoing instrument of writing, as having executed the same, came before me and acknowledged the said instrument to be his act and deed for the purposes therein mentioned. In testimony whereof I have hereunto signed my name and affixed the Seal of said Court at Office in Belleville, the 25th day of January A.D. 1843. Recorded this 25th day of January Eighteen Hundred and Forty-Three.

W. C. Kinney, Clerk

Here is the legal document for the second sale – This Deed made and entered into this eighth day of September of the year of our Lord one thousand eight hundred and forty-three, between John Basler of Saint Clair County and State of Illinois of the first part and the Right Rev. Peter R. Kenrick, Bishop of St. Louis, State of Missouri of the second part for the use of a Catholic Church and in trust for the Congregation of St. Michael in Prairie du Long, St. Clair 'County, Illinois. Witnesseth that the said party of the first part for and in consideration of the sum of one dollar to him in hand paid by the said party. The receipt whereof is hereby confessed and acknowledged has granted, bargained and sold and by these presents does grant, bargain and sell, convey and confirm unto the said party of the second part, his heirs, and assigns, and successors in office forever two acres of land for the use of a church being in the southwest quarter of the northeast quarter of Section thirteen, Township two south of Range nine west situated and being in the County of St. Clair and State of Illinois commencing at the southeast corner and running forty yards, thense west two hundred and twenty yards, thence south for forty yards, thence east two hundred and twenty yards to the place of the beginning to have and to hold the same with all the rights, privileges, and appurtenances thereunto belonging or in anywise appertaining unto him the said party of the second part his heirs, and assigns, and successor forever the said John Basler party of the first part hereby covenanting that his heirs, executors, and administrators will forever warrant and defend the title and possession to the said premises and every part thereof to them the said party of the second part his heirs and assigns against the lawful claims of all and every persons whosoever claiming or to claim the same or any part thereof in witness whereof the said party of the first part has hereunto set his hand and seal the day and year herein written in the presence of Bernard Dingwerth, interlined at the sixth line from the top, State of Illinois, St. Clair County.

Johan Basler (seal)

I, Bernard Dingwerth, a justice of the peace of the said county, do hereby certify that John Basler who is personally known to me to be the person whose name is signed to the foregoing deed as having executed the same before me and acknowledged the said deed to be his act and deed for the purposes therein mentioned. In testimony whereof I have hereunto signed my name and seal this 8th day of September A.D. 1843.

Bernard Dingwerth, J.P

Recorded this eighth day of September Eighteen Hundred and Forty-Three.

Richard Hay, Recorder

The first log church stood on the original two acres. It was a one-room structure built of logs and clap board roof. The altar most likely was a table. There were no pews or benches. There is a mistaken belief that this first church stood on the Louis Hagen farm, presently owned by John Mueth south of Paderborn. The fact is that after the present stone church at right was built in 1862, Mr. Hagen bought the log church and moved it to his farm for use as a storage building.

You can see the John Mueth farm in the map above. I wrote to Estelle Mueth who currently owns both of the Mueth farms in Section 13. I wanted to know if that log church was still there and whether she had land abstracts that might tell us more about the original Basler farm. There was no reply.

Will, Kayla, and Ava, I forgot to mention that this church land actually measured 40 yards by 220 yards, which figures out to 1.812 acres rather than 2.000 acres. So your great great great great great grandfather John Basler was twice overpaid by about 10%. Nevertheless, he was still a very generous man. Born on 1/7/1791, he is the oldest of any of our relatives to immigrate to America. You should be proud.

Love, Granddad

PS: On a clear day you can see this beautiful 1862 church from our Reiss family farm. It's about two miles to the southwest. If we're all in that area for the 6/6/2015 Luetzelschwab family reunion, I'll show it to you. Hopefully it would be open that Saturday for a tour.

Francis Stauder Arrives on October 19, 1836

Dear Will, Kayla, and Ava,   June 30, 2014

You saw the next paragraph in my Granddad's Mondays of 1/13/2014 titled "The Basler Farm in St. Clair County." This story today is the promised sequel to that earlier story.

The next event for the Basler family was the marriage of daughter Sophia to Frantz Stauder on 3/28/1842 in Belleville. My guess is that Frantz (Francis) and Sophia also met at Catholic Church services on the Adam Reiss farm just like Adam and his wife Margaret probably did. Sophia and Margaret were sisters. Francis had also lost his first wife and was raising a son and daughter both under age five. Francis had bought 40 acres on 10/5/1840 in Section 18 of Prairie du Long Township half a mile south of the Reiss farm. Both Basler sisters and both widowed men would have made shared nurturing of their respective children or step-children-to-be part of their courtships. Francis and Sophia also bought the adjoining 40 acres to the south on 1/3/1844. He may have been living there in a log cabin he built or in a house in Paderborn before and/or after he married Sophia Basler. The seller of both 40-acre tracts was Thomas Houghan.

So who is Francis Stauder? Well, he was born on 6/8/1811 in Fechenbach, Bavaria, Germany. He was a hunter by profession. He departed the German port of Bremen at age 24 on a ship named Gustave to arrive in New York on 10/19/1836. On board with Francis were Jacobine Henning of Reitsenhausen who would become his wife and a friend, Bernard Wolff, who was also from Fechenbach.

Francis married Jacobine soon after their arrival. They had two children but then Jacobine died sometime before the 1840 census because she is not mentioned.

- Theresia Stauder (1/4/1838 -- >1910)

- Joseph Stauder (6/21/1839 – 11/5/1896)

Francis married Sophia Basler on 3/19/1842 in a civil service in Belleville and again on 3/28/1842 in a Catholic ceremony by a visiting priest, Father Charles Meyer. The couple settled in Paderborn or on the farm Francis owned a half mile south of the Reiss farm. Sophia and Francis had five more children.

- Frederick "Fritz" Stauder (2/28/1843 – 10/22/1887)

- John Stauder (1/16/1845 – 2/22/1922)

- Catharine Stauder (3/7/1847 – 12/26/1849)

- Barbara Stauder (3/25/1849 – 2/19/1872)

- Charles Stauder (9/12/1860 – 9/20/1937)

Their son, John Stauder, has by far the most descendents of the seven children. They include Francis and Sophia's great granddaughter Mary Genevieve Stauder (4/7/1911 -- ??) who professed her first vows on 8/7/1933 to become a Catholic nun as Sister Borgia. She celebrated her 70th year jubilee at the motherhouse in St. Louis on 8/10/2003. In Belleville she served as a math professor at LeClerc College and as a school principal and superintendent in Aviston.

Great grandson William V. Stauder (4/23/1922 – 9/29/2002) served as a priest, faculty member, and administrator at Saint Louis University in St. Louis from 1959 to 1999. He became academic vice-president in 1989. He had a bachelor's degree in Latin, a master's degree in physics, a licentiate in sacred theology all from SLU, and a doctorate in geophysics from the University of California at Berkley. He was an authority on plate tectonics and earthquakes.

Our patriarch Adam Reiss died on 5/23/1849. Francis Stauder was a witness to Adam's last will and testament written the day he died. Francis was also co-administrator with Margaret of Adam's estate and compiled an inventory of Adam's personal property. That will was the subject of another Granddad's Mondays story on 5/19/2014. It's fascinating and confirms that Francis and Adam were good buddies and good neighbors.

Sadly, Sophia Basler Stauder died young at age 42 on 7/25/1865. She is buried at St. Michael's Cemetery in Paderborn where her stone is visible in the northeast corner. It appears below on page 4. Remember that it was her father Johann Basler who donated two acres of his farm on 1/24/1843 for what became St. Michael's Church and that cemetery.

There are six letters by Francis Stauder and one by his daughter Barbara in our family history book, It Takes A Matriarch, starting on page 171. Three were written shortly after Sophia's passing and are quite emotional.

Here's more on the Stauder family in Germany. Professor Dr. Karl Stauder of Nurnberg wrote a book in 1931 titled, Aus der Geschichte Family Stauder (Of the History Family Stauder). It gives the history of ancestors dating back to 1590 from Urspringen, an area on the Main River. It includes charts showing Francis Stauder born 8/6/1811 and his sister Margaretha born 3/8/1816 going to America. Their parents were Joseph Anton Stauder and Genovefa Brand.

Francis Stauder sold his 80-acre farm in 1866 and moved to Trenton, Illinois to be near his daughter Barbara. He next appears in the 1870 census living with his son Fritz in Nokomis, Illinois about 50 miles southeast of Springfield. They are farmers and are also joined there by other Stauder relatives. There are about 50 of them buried in the Nokomis Cemetery. This small town is also where our Aunt Gerry Hulet Reiss grew up and graduated from the high school where her father was principal.

Francis Stauder's farm appears in Section 18 just south of the Reiss farm in Sections 7 and 8. The red 40 acres near Paderborn is what Francis' father-in-law Johann Basler bought on 12/13/1841. Johann Basler is also your great great great great great grandfather.

Maybe you recognize this map from my Granddad's Mondays on 4/21/2014 titled "The Dintelmann Farms." The 80-acre Wachtel farm just west of the 80-acre Stauder farm was the "Dint 80" farm bought by Conrad and Henry Dintelmann on 6/29/1863. They paid $36 per acre which is 4.8 times the $7.50 per acre that Francis paid just 23 years earlier.

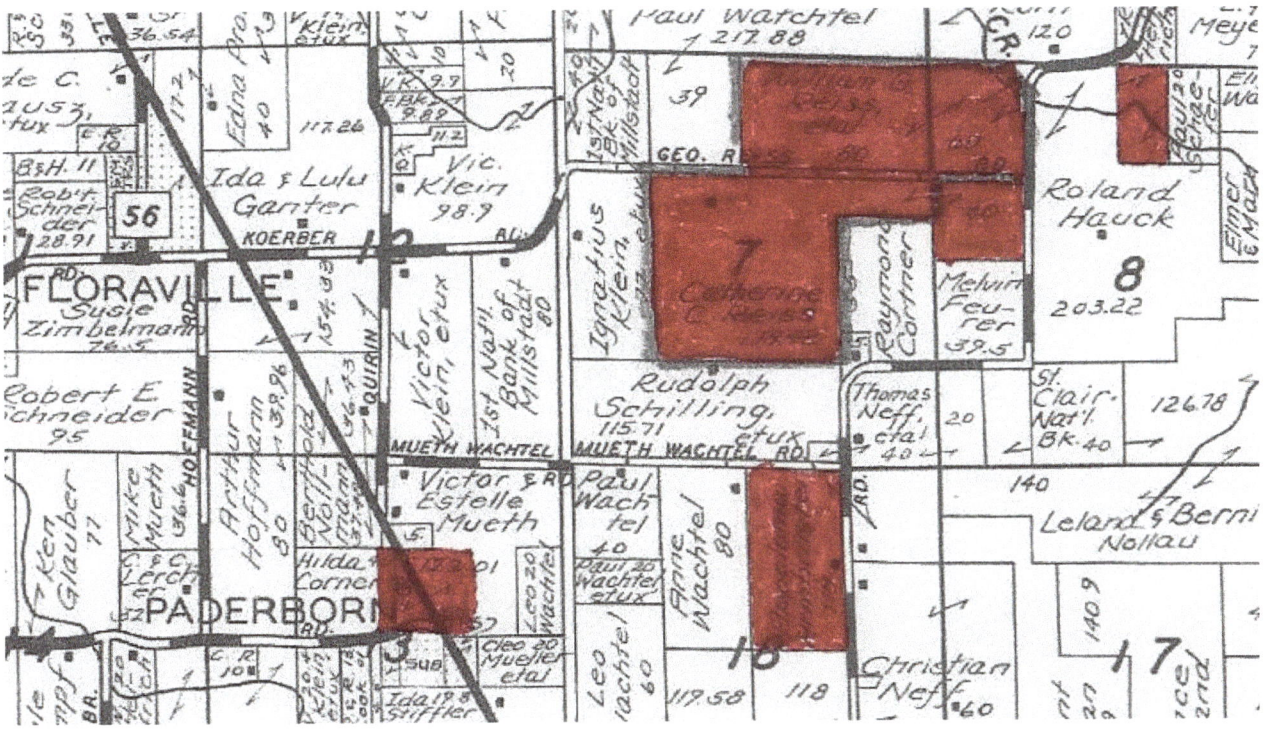

Will, Kayla, and Ava, it's sad to summarize that your great great great great great uncle Francis Stauder outlived two wives, two daughters, a son, a daughter-in-law, a son-in-law, and many of his 39 grandchildren. Two of his grandchildren died on the same day right after Christmas on 12/28/1872. The grieving took a toll on his health. He was yearning to travel to the cemeteries where his lost family members were buried but had to wait until his health improved and the smallpox era was over. Francis died 11/27/1888 at age 77.

Love, Granddad

"If you want to be an uncle when you grow up, you gotta marry an aunt."

The Feder Family Arrives on October 28, 1845

Dear Will, Kayla, and Ava,   October 28, 2013

Your great great great grandmother Anna Sybilla Feder (below) was born September 26, 1844 in Popendorf Landgericht, Bordenstein Koenigreig Bavaria, Germany which is about 100 miles north of Munich. She arrived in New Orleans 168 years ago today on October 28, 1845. She was 13 months old when she arrived with her parents, George Feder (born in December 1817) and Sybilla Rau Feder (born in June 1821). Her parents were married on August 25, 1845 so Anna Sybilla was probably adopted since her birth date is almost a year before her parents were married. The name of the ship was Rajah and it sailed from Bremen, Germany near the North Sea, taking well over 40 days to make the trip by just the power of the wind.

The Feders settled on a farm in Ridge Prairie just west of O'Fallon, Illinois about 18 miles north of the Reiss Family Farm in St. Clair County. They had nine more children there with the overall total being five girls and five boys. The last one was born in 1865. There was one death in 1900 and the next one in 1912 so they all lived long productive lives.

Anna Sybilla married Frank Reiss (above) on April 9, 1866 in a double wedding ceremony with Frank's younger sister Kate marrying Charles Max Wittig. The ceremony was conducted by Justice of the Peace, Theod. I. Krafft, but I don't know the location. The Reiss marriage lasted 55.5 years and the Wittig marriage lasted two weeks short of 50 years. Must be something lucky about double weddings. It was almost a triple wedding but brother Charles Reiss delayed his marriage to Eva Dintelmann until November 15, 1866.

Here are two letters which Sybilla's father George wrote to the newlyweds a few months later. The letters were in German but I had them translated to English so there may be a few errors on names. By the time of the second letter Anna Sybilla was expecting their first child, Charles Martin Reiss, who was born on October 17, 1867. Doesn't look like she has told her dad yet.

#269 – German

Belleville,
the 18th of January 1867

Beloved Franz and Sybilla,

I have received your letter on the 18th of this month with my own hand, when I was in Belleville again for the first time. I thank you for your worries you had for me. Thank God everything is better again, for ten days I had suffered great pain. But not of Bier, where many suffer, because it comes every day from 9 o'clock in the morning until 3 o'clock in the afternoon, who takes it again.

In your letter I have seen that you like to see Nani to hear the news from here. She intended to be at your house on Sunday the 20th of January, Jonn Hennig and Anna. But the weather is too cold and it is too cold for the trip. We have bought the old Schinos farm at the "Rieschbrem" (*Rich Prairie?*) 140 acres for $15,250. 50 acres are rented out I get $6 per acre. 50 acres I get immediately for planting. The table is set for noon the 23rd of January, then I must pay $8000, the rest over one year at 6% interest. We don't have the quarters yet, but I think we'll get it soon.

I cannot write you yet when we will move. I hope we will see each other soon so I can describe the matter in detail. Thank God we are all healthy what I also wish of you, with all my heart. I close my letter and hope that these lines will find you healthy. Many greetings to all, Father, Mother, Frank, Sybilla, Karl and wife.

from Georg Feder, Mother and
another portion of greetings from
Ionn, Arno (?), Henry, Kath, Mari
and Liesset.

#247 – German

O'Fallon
the 21st of February 1867

Dear Sybilla and Frank,

We have received your letter on the 10th of February and saw that you are still healthy. As far as we are concerned, thank God, we are also healthy. We went on Tuesday, the 12th of February to the Rieschbrem, at the old Schinoth land, half a mile from Cousin Hans' old place west towards St. Louis, on the large road next to Seibel's. We can see Karl's (*Charles Reiss's*) house every day, it is only about half a mile from here, but now we still see the tag because the rats have undercut so much that it sank down halfway, the young boys were there and killed more than 60, but of the young ones a 10th of them ran away.

We have seen from your letter that you would like to see Naani, she would also like that, and she is already sorry that she can't be there for the fest. But we all hope that when Karl moves that you will spend the night here, we have enough room especially when Tschoh (?) moves, what he wants to do every day.

And don't forget when you bring Karl's family out here, that you bring me a few grapevine plants. We have heard that Frank and Karl were in Belleville on the 7th and that they came only about 1/ 2 mile by our house, we were so sorry that they didn't come by.

I hope that these few lines find you in the best of health.

Greetings to all of you,

Georg Feder

Frank Reiss was born on September 27, 1841 so he was one day short of being three years older than Anna Sybilla. They had eleven children between October 1867 to September 1890. All but the youngest were born in the log cabin built in 1834 by Frank's father Adam Reiss. The last child, Will Reiss, was born in a "new" house which Anna and Frank built 50 feet away in 1889. We now refer to it as the "old" house on the Reiss Family Farm. Of their eleven children only seven of them reached adulthood with the oldest being your great great grandfather George Reiss. Here's his photo with wife Katie Luetzelschwab Reiss. Their marriage was also long at 53 years even though George got a late start by not marrying until age 38.

The census taken on April 25, 1910 shows Anna Sybilla, Frank, and their oldest surviving son George living in the 1889 house. Also enumerated with them is Katie C. Luietcelschwab working as a domestic servant. The census taker butchered the spelling of her name which should have been Luetzelschwab. Katie's employment there is how she and George met. They were married a year later on April 16, 1911. Katie had over a year to impress George with her cooking, cleaning, laundry, darning, quilting, and sewing skills. George had that same year to impress Katie as a very hard working and prosperous farmer. How cool is that!!!

Here is a 1915 photo of the "old new" house built which was built in 1889. That date appears on the southeast foundation cornerstone and is visible by sliding the front wooden step off to the side. From left to right are Charles Reiss (brother of Frank), Frank Reiss, Anna Sybilla Reiss, plus Katie and George Reiss with their son William between them. He was born on May 5, 1912. Behind the group is the horse and buggy that brought Charles from his farm near O'Fallon to the Reiss Family Farm.

L-R. Unknown, Frank Reiss, Anna Reiss, Catherine Reiss, William Reiss, George Reiss about 1915 on Reiss farm

Anna Sybilla and Frank lived in this 1889 house from the day it was built until they passed away – him on November 21, 1921 and her on May 14, 1930. They are buried together in Section 2W3-2 in Franklin Cemetery in Smithton.

Will, Kayla, and Ava, Anna Sybilla Feder Reiss is my great grandmother or your great great great grandmother. You've seen those oval photographs (above) of her and husband Frank in my den. Here is the entire Feder family with all ten children from about 1880. Anna Syvilla is on the left. But Anna Sybilla is not our only Feder connection. Anna Sybilla's next younger brother John (back right) had a granddaughter named Willette "Toddy" Feder who married Edgar John Jacob Luetzelschwab who was a nephew of my grandmother Katie Luetzelschwab Reiss. That's a little tough to follow so let's just leave it that Toddy and Edgar's four children are both second cousins to me through the Reiss connection and third cousins to me through the Luetzelschwab connection. How cool is that!!!

Love, Granddad

George Feder family, about 1880

The Feder Family Farm

Dear Will, Kayla, and Ava,   May 12, 2014

You've seen the two oval photographs in my den of my great grandparents, Frank and Anna Sybilla Feder Reiss. Frank was born in the 1839 log cabin on our family farm on 9/27/1841 and Anna was born on 9/26/1844 in Popendorf Landgericht, Bordenstein Koenigreig Bayern, Germany. Her parents were George and Anna Sybilla Rau Feder so young Anna was named after her mother. However, we think her parents were married in 1845 so young Anna was probably adopted or may have been the daughter of a relative who could no longer care for her.

George, Anna, and 13-month old Anna sailed on a ship named Rajah from Bremen, Germany to the US along with his parents and siblings to arrive in New Orleans on 10/28/1845. George was 27 and his father who was also named George was 55. At the time of the 1850 census this double family of at least ten adults and children all lived together in Ridge Prairie which is about five miles north of Belleville. Today that area is part of Fairview Heights.

Fast forward 16 years to this letter from young George to his grown daughter Anna Syvilla who became Mrs. Frank Reiss on 4/9/1866:

Belleville, January 18, 1867

Beloved Franz and Sybilla,

I have received your letter on the 18th of this month with my own hand, when I was in Belleville again for the first time. I thank you for your worries you had for me. Thank God everything is better again, for ten days I had suffered great pain. But not of Bier, where many suffer, because it comes every day from 9 o'clock in the morning until 3 o'clock in the afternoon, who takes it again.

In your letter I have seen that you like Nani to hear the news from here. She intended to be at your house on Sunday the 20th of January, Jonn, Hennig, and Anna. But the weather is too cold and it is too cold for the trip. We have bought the old Schinos farm at "Rieschbrem" (Rich Prairie?) 140 acres for $15,250. 50 acres are rented out I get $6 per acre. 50 acres I get immediately for planting. The table is set for noon the 23rd of January, then I must pay $8,000, the rest over one year at 6% interest. We don't have the quarters yet, but I think we'll get it soon.

I cannot write you yet when we will move. I hope we will see each other soon so I can describe the matter in detail. Thank God we are all healthy what I also wish of you, with all my heart. I close my letter and hope that these lines will find you healthy. Many greetings to all, Father, Mother, Frank, Sybilla, Karl and wife.

From George Feder, Mother and another portion of
greetings from Jonn, Anno, Heiny, Kath, Mari, and Liesset

Here's a sketch showing the former George Feder farm crosshatched in red at a 45 degree angle to the world. It's in Section 15 of St. Clair/Belleville Township about four miles south of their previous home in Ridge Prairie. It's in the village of Swansea northeast of the intersection of state highways 159 and 161.

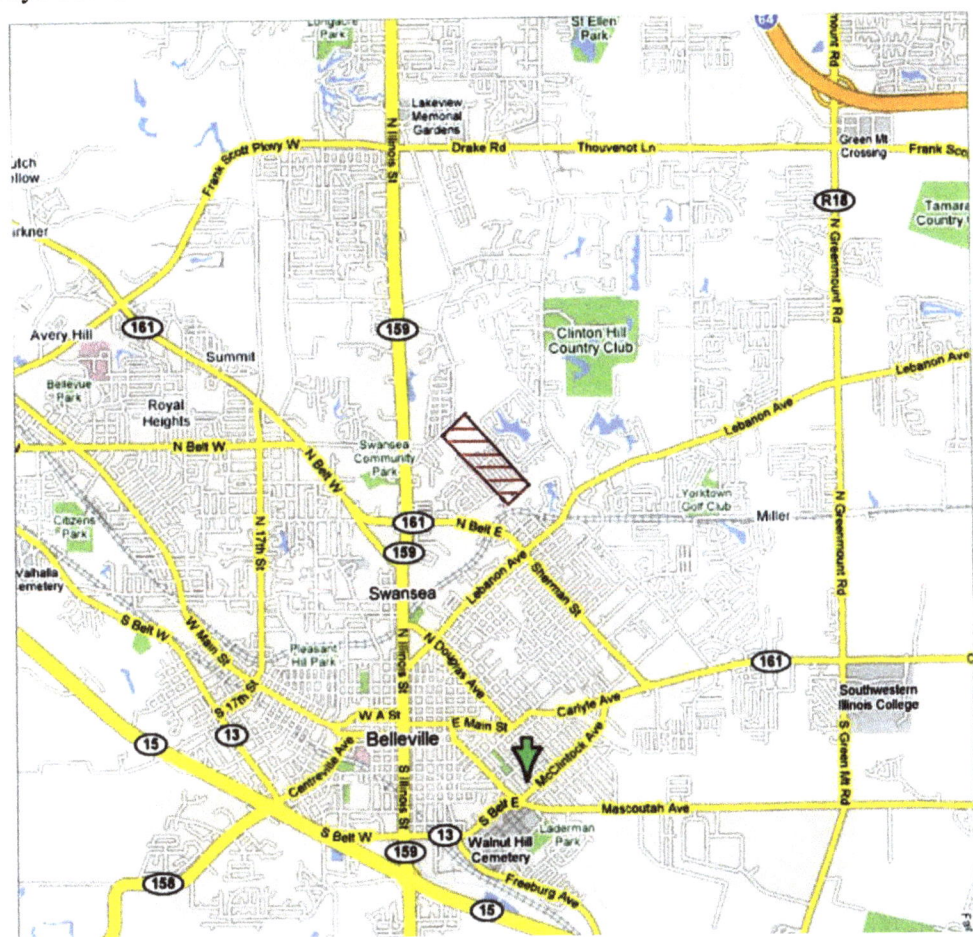

Will, Kayla, and Ava, we don't know how or when or where Frank and Ava first met, let alone carried on a courtship. Their two farms were 16 miles apart according to Mapquest. That would be a full day's ride in a horse and buggy each direction. Frank mustered out of service in the Union Army at the end of the Civil War on July 19, 1865 in Louisville, Kentucky. He still had to get back to the home farm from there. And then he and Anna got married less than 10 months later. Whatever that missing history is, everything worked out just fine because they had 11 children and were married for over 55 years.

Love, Granddad

Conrad Ebert Arrives on June 7, 1847

Dear Will, Kayla, and Ava,   September 2, 2013

<mark>This is exclusive breaking news!!! No one else in our extended family knows what I am about to tell you.</mark> After years of searching on www.ancestry.com and other genealogy websites, I finally determined when and where Conrad Ebert, your great great great great step-grandfather, arrived in the United States.

I typed "Conrad Ebert" into "ship passenger lists" on ancestry.com and found 22 men named Conrad Ebert who arrived in New York, Baltimore, New Orleans, or from Canada in the 19th century. There were another 6 men named Konrad Ebert and 49 additional men named C. Ebert who arrived in that same century. Which one, if any, of these 77 possibilities would be our relative? Below is the one I chose. Here is a partial listing of the 179 passengers and their ages on a clipper ship named Leodes which took 53 days to sail from Rotterdam, Holland to New Orleans, Louisiana to arrive on June 7, 1847.

P. Roller.   27.
J. Hayenstab.   31.
C. Ebert.   37.
F. Presently   24
Adam   „   1.
J. F. mast   24.

Here is even a semi-famous painting of that three-masted ship, Leodes, which was built in 1841 in Newburyport, Massachusetts. Weight was 445 tons, draft was 17 feet, and her captain was N. B. Robins.

Why am I convinced this is the correct Conrad Ebert? Fast forward 3.5 years to the Federal Census of 1850 which was taken on November 16. It appears on the next page. Notice that the census-taker spelled Conrad Ebert as "Abert" and that

he showed that misspelled name for all five of Conrad's stepchildren whose correct last name was Reiss. It shows Conrad's wife as Margaret who is your great great great great grandmother and widow of your great great great great grandfather, Adam Reiss, who had died of cholera 1.5 years earlier on May 23, 1849. Conrad and Margaret were married on April 2, 1850. They probably met at St. Michael's Catholic Church in Paderborn. I'm impressed that Conrad was willing to accept an instant family of five children under age 12 and to all live together in a

log cabin less than half the size of ours. He and Margaret eventually had four more children of their own.

Conrad Ebert	46 yrs	36	m		farmer
Margaret	"	32	f		
John H.	"	12	m		
Francis	"	9	m		
Charles	"	7	m		
Martin	"	5	m		
Catharine	"	3	f		
John Harsenstob		33	m		laborer

Notice that this census includes a hired hand working/living on the Reiss/Ebert farm. His name is John Harsenstob age 33. Now look at the name just above C. Ebert on the ship passenger list on the previous page. It's J. Harsenstab age 31. It's the same guy!!! Conrad and John emigrated from Germany together, traveled from New Orleans to St. Clair County, Illinois together, and even worked/lived together for over 3.5 years!!! Maybe John slept in our 1838 log granary.

I looked further on ancestry.com for later records of John Harsenstob. I found that name in East St. Louis and St. Louis but there were no major news items.

Will, Kayla, and Ava, I wrote to my fifth cousin, Marianne Walter, in Obernburg, Germany who is also a professional genealogist to see if she could find any records about Conrad Ebert who was born May 11, 1811 or his friend John Harsenstab who was born about 1817. We think Conrad was born in Obernau, Landgericht (county court) Aschaffenburg, Bavaria which is where Adam Reiss was born May 7, 1804 so perhaps they were childhood friends. Maybe that's why Conrad chose St. Clair County as his destination, never in his wildest dreams guessing that he would eventually marry the widow of his friend, Adam Reiss, and help raise his children!!! Here is Conrad Ebert's tombstone in St. Michael's Cemetery in Paderborn less than two miles from the Reiss Family Farm. He died on 7/23/1880 at age 69.

Love Granddad

PS: **Jerry Prouhet** wrote me from Foristell, Missouri saying that he was a descendant of Joseph Stein who has 49 letters in our book, It Takes A Matriarch. Joseph used the title of "aunt" when mentioning our matriarch, Margaret Basler Reiss Ebert. Joseph was a close friend of Margaret's son, Martin Reiss, but not a Reiss relative. Jerry is researching to see if Joseph is a descendant of Margaret's second husband Conrad Ebert. Here's our email exchange:

-----Original Message-----
From: Stephen Reiss <reiss_steve@yahoo.com>
To: Jerry Prouhet <jprouhet@tandninc.com>; Jerry Prouhet <jpwrrntn@aol.com>
Sent: Fri, Sep 13, 2013 6:47 am

Subject: Joseph Stein connection to the Reiss/Ebert family

Hi, Jerry. We communicated two years ago about my book, It Takes A Matriarch, which included 49 letters by your ancestor, Joseph Stein. Well, in April 2012 I started writing two email attachment stories to my very young grandchildren as a means of passing along important family history, major memories, funny stories, etc. I call these stories "Granddad's Mondays" because I have emailed two of them on each of the past 75 Mondays. Attached are two that deal with my great great grandmother Margaret, our "matriarch", and her second husband Conrad Ebert. Your Joseph Stein was in the habit of referring to my Margaret as "aunt." I think you mentioned the possibility of Joseph being a descendant of Conrad Ebert which would then make the "aunt" title a relative rather than simply a term of respect. I'm curious about your latest thinking and research. Thanks,

Steve Reiss
cell 309 472 5266

Jerry Prouhet

To: reiss_steve@yahoo.com

Hi Steve, it's great to hear from you!! I think Joseph Stein's mother, Catharine, was an Ebert. I found different spellings of Ebert, such as Evers and Evert. Have you come across those spellings? The only record I have found of her was the 1870 Census living with her daughter and son-in-law, Magdalena and Nicholas Simon. I cannot find a passenger list of when she came to the USA. I have found one for Magdalena and Joseph when they arrived in New Orleans on June 1, 1859.

Have you found any information on Conrad Ebert's siblings? The dates for Catharine are, born about 1805 in Germany and died April 20, 1872 in St Louis County. But these are not confirmed. I am trying to find an obituary for Catharine.

Through your years of research, do you know anyone in Germany that might be able to help me out?

Thank for your email,

Jerry

Cell 314-779-5598

The Dintelmanns Arrive in 1848, 1852, and 1853

Dear Will, Kayla, and Ava,   April 21, 2014

We are related to the second and third generations of Dintelmanns in the US so we have lots of double cousins. Here's the overall Dintelmann family tree starting with their first generation in the US (to which we are not related). Here it's in paragraph form for the first two generations and then later it's in outline form.

Johann Dintelmann was born on May 10, 1792 in Germany. He served nine years in the Germany military. He was in the Cavalry and fought in the Battle of Leipzig where Napoleon Bonaparte was defeated in October 1813. Johann's wife was Eva Mueller (8/8/1803 -- ??) whose parents were Conrad Mueller (1795 – 1847) and Anna Margarethe Volger (1805 – 1849) from Semd, Germany. Johann age 61 and Eva age 50 immigrated in 1853 to the Belleville, Illinois area. Johann died April 7, 1874 and Eva died on 8/1/1876. They are buried in Franklin Cemetery in Smithton.

Johann and Eva Dintelmann's children were John, George, Henry, Conrad, Philip, and Eva. The children had already immigrated to the Belleville area between 1848 and 1853. Initially George, Henry, and Philip were wagon makers as Dintelmann & Company located on South Illinois Street in Belleville between 5th and 6th Streets. John and Conrad Dintelmann were farmers and lived near Freeburg. Eva married Charles Reiss and lived on a farm near O'Fallon (more below).

John Dintelmann was born in 1825 or 26 in Darmstadt, Hesse, Germany and immigrated in 1848 to Belleville. Little is known about his wife, Susan, except that she was also born in Darmstadt. John and Susan were parents of five children. The family lived near Freeburg, farming on "Turkey Hill." Later John moved to Freeburg. He served one year as a Union soldier in the Civil War. John died in October 1907 at the home of his daughter, Mrs. Adam Culli in Mt. Vernon, Illinois. There is a John Dintelmann who appears in the 1880 census as age 54 (born 1826) born in Hesse D. Germany and working as a farm renter, wife Maria age 46 (born 1834) also in Hesse D. Germany, and three children all born in St. Clair County – Margaretha 13, Phillip 9, and Louisa 5. Another record shows he filed for a Civil War pension on 5/4/1886.

George J. Dintelmann was born in 1826 or 27 in Darmstadt and immigrated in 1852 to Belleville. His wife, Barbara Beyyons was born in 1830 in Darmstadt. George and Barbara were parents of eight children, five sons and three daughters. In 1862 George, his wife, and their son George moved to Nashville, Washington County, Illinois. George was a wagon maker for many years. Later, he was a farmer near Nashville, Illinois where he died August 6, 1897. Barbara died after 1897. There is a marriage record in St. Clair County between Johann G. Dintelmann and Barbara Bernius on September 14, 1851. Another record says her last name is Bernjus. Another record shows George J. Dintelmann born on 3/27/1860 in Belleville to father J. George Dintelmann born in Germany and Barbry Benyous born in Germany. George died on 3/1/1917 and is buried at Plum Hill in Washington County, IL. He was a farmer.

Henry Dintelmann was born September 10, 1833 in Darmstadt and immigrated in 1852 to Belleville. Henry's wife Elizabeth Keller, was born on April 9, 1836 in Darmstadt and immigrated with her family in May 1844. Henry married Elizabeth on February 10, 1861 and they were parents of ten children. Initially, Henry worked with his brothers George and Philip as wagon makers in Belleville. Later he was a farmer near Bellville city limits where he died on September 11, 1912. His wife Elizabeth died on August 24, 1900. They are buried in Walnut Hill Cemetery in Belleville.

Conrad Dintelmann was born in November 1836 in Darmstadt and immigrated in 1853 to Belleville. His wife Margaret Philip/Keller was born April 25, 1841 in Darmstadt and came to the US with her parents John Philip and Katherine Keller in 1844. Katherine was the sister of Elizabeth Keller, Henry's wife. Conrad and Margaret were married on April 17, 1864 and were the parents of one son, George. Conrad was a farmer and lived south of Freeburg just west of the Five Forks road intersection. Conrad died on December 6, 1911 and Margaret died on March 8, 1914. They are buried in Elmwood Cemetery. Their son George married Anna Margaret Reiss on 4/22/1908 and had two sons, George and Edwin. Anna was the younger sister of my grandfather George Reiss so she was my great aunt.

Philip Dintelmann was born in 1838 in Darmstadt and immigrated in 1853 to Belleville. Little is known about his wife Mary Bormann except that she was born in 1838 in Hanover, Germany. Philip and Mary were married on January 30, 1859 in St. Clair County and they were parents of seven children. Philip was a wagon maker for most of his life at the "Dintelmann and Brothers, Wagon Makers" in Belleville. After his brothers George and Henry, moved away, Philip and son Louis operated the wagon making business. Philip served with the 12th Missouri Infantry, Company A in the Union Army and fought in the Civil War "Battle of Pea Ridge" in northwestern Arkansas on March 6 to 8 of 1862. The battle took place at Pea Ridge Rocky Eminence and Elkhorn Tavern. That Union victory kept Missouri from joining the Confederacy. Philip died on March 11, 1906 in Belleville and is buried in Walnut Hill Cemetery.

Eva Dintelmann was born on June 25, 1844 in Darmstadt and immigrated in 1853 to Belleville. She married Charles Reiss on November 15, 1855 in Belleville. Charles was born on February 17, 1843 at the Reiss Family Farm in Prairie du Long Township of St. Clair County. His parents were Adam Reiss and Margaret Basler Reiss. His next older brother was my great grandfather Frank Reiss so Eva was my great great aunt. Charles and Eva were parents of seven children. They lived on several farms near O'Fallon. Eva Reiss died on November 29, 1910. Charles retired in 1910 and moved to O'Fallon. He died on May 13, 1931 at his home in O'Fallon. They are buried in Shiloh Cemetery.

Adam Reiss immigrated from Obernau, Germany to the US in 1833. He arrived in New Orleans and spent that first winter in Natchez, Mississippi before coming to St. Clair County, Illinois the following spring of 1834. I have tried to find his immigration record for well over ten years and I currently have a certified professional genealogist looking for it, all with no success so far. We have the same frustration trying to find Adam's first wife, Mary Schuessler. In the meantime we have found virtually everyone else as my past and future Granddad's Mondays will document.

This German aerial photo below shows Obernau where Adam Reiss came from, Darmstadt where the Dintelmanns came from, and Semd where our great great aunt Eva Dintelmann Reiss' maternal grandparents lived.

Here's the Dintelmann family tree in outline form. Count the Georges!

Johann Dintelmann (3/??/1792 – 4/7/1874) married Eva Mueller (8/8/1803 – 8/1/1876) on ??
They were born in Germany, immigrated in 1853 to Belleville, and are buried in Franklin
Cemetery in Smithton.

    John Dintelmann (1825/6 – 10/??/1907) married Susan ?? (?? – ??) on ?? He was born in
    Darmstadt, immigrated in 1848, and died in Mt. Vernon, Illinois.

        George Dintelmann
        Margaret Dintelmann
        Edward Dintelmann
        Anna Dintelmann
        Minna Dintelmann

    George J. Dintelmann (1826/7 – 8/6/1897) married Barbara Beyyons (?? -- ??) on ?? He
    was born in Darmstadt, immigrated to Belleville in 1852, and died near Nashville, IL.

        George Dintelmann
        Emil Dintelmann
        Karl Dintelmann
        Barbara Dintelmann
        Emma Dintelmann
        Louisa Dintelmann
        Amos Dintelmann
        Henry Dintelmann

Henry Dintelmann (9/10/1833 – 9/11/1912) married Elizabeth A. Keller (4/??/1836 -- <1910) on 2/10/1861. He was born in Darmstadt, immigrated in 1852 to Belleville, and is buried there in Walnut Hill Cemetery.

> Louis Dintelmann
> Henry Dintelmann
> Barbara Dintelmann
> Eva Dintelmann
> Caroline Dintelmann
> John Dintelmann
> Margaret Dintelmann
> George Dintelmann
> Elizabeth Dintelmann
> Conrad Dintelmann

Conrad Dintelmann (11/??/1836 – 12/6/1911) married Margaret Keller (4/25/1841 – 3/8/1914) on 4/17/1864. He was born in Darmstadt, immigrated in 1853 to Belleville, died near Freeburg, and is buried in Elmwood Cemetery. Note that Conrad and Henry (above) married the Keller sisters. We have another Keller in our family tree but I don't know if both Keller families are related. It was Adam Reiss' great great granddaughter Mary Ruth Ferkel (8/30/1913 – 9/22/1993) who married Clarence John Keller (5/22/1905 – 9/20/1967) on ?? She was born in Belleville. Several of those Kellers from Belleville came to our 175th Reiss Reunion in 2009.

George Dintelmann (2/1/1867 – 2/27/1945) married Margaret Reiss (9/20/1875 – 8/31/1940) on 4/22/1908 as his second wife.

> George Conrad Dintelmann (7/18/1913 – 4/13/1946) married Marjorie Ruth Pivoda (2/6/1915 – 6/2/2002) on 10/2/1937.
>
>> Dale Conrad Dintelmann (8/13/1940 --) married Jane Ellis Kendall (3/8/1942 --) and had two children. Later he married Eve Faith Ran (2/15/1965 --) on 7/2/2001.
>>
>>> Scott Dennis Dintelmann (12/19/1967 --)
>>>
>>> Dayla Janelle Dintelmann (9/30/1973 --) married Jasper Latimer Austin (6/19/1973 --) on 5/31/2008.
>>
>> George Dennis Dintelmann (6/3/1944 --) married Linda Kay Miller (7/31/1948 – 5/27/2008) on 6/22/1968 in Grayson County, Texas.
>>
>>> Jeff Miller Dintelmann (9/8/1973 --) married Jennifer McCutchen (9/??/1973 --) in 2006.

Drew Miller Dintelmann (12/8/1975 --) married Fawn Lind (6/9/1977 --) in 2006.

Edwin Louis Dintelmann (2/191916 – 10/28/1987) married Beulah Alvina Cox (2/11/1916 – 5/28/2006) on 6/8/1941.

Robin Ann Dintelmann (2/9/1944 --) married Richard William DeLeeuw (10/10/1940 --) on 11/26/1971. They live in Morgan Hill, California.

Lisa Ann DeLeeuw (7/21/1975 --) was born in Santa Clara County, California.

Terry DeLeeuw (10/9/1978 --) was born in Santa Clara County, California.

Judith Kay Dintelmann (4/3/1948 – 5/26/2012) married Douglas Peters (10/31/1942 --) on 5/21/1977. They live in Houston, Texas.

Philip Dintelmann (1838 – 3/11/1906) married Mary Bormann (1838 -- <1880) on 1/30/1859 in St. Clair County. He was born in Darmstadt, immigrated in 1853 to Belleville, and is buried in Walnut Hill Cemetery.

Louis Dintelmann
Mary Dintelmann
Philip Dintelmann
Louisa Dintelmann
Linda Dintelmann
Corinna Dintelmann
Henry Dintelmann
Lily Dintelmann
Hugo Dintelmann

Eva Dintelmann (6/25/1844 – 11/29/1910) married Charles Reiss (2/17/1843 - 5/13/1931) on 11/15/1866 in Belleville. She was born in Darmstadt, immigrated in 1853 to Belleville, died near O'Fallon, and is buried in Shiloh Cemetery.

William Henry Reiss (11/15/1867 – 3/14/1957)
Louisa Amelia "Lulu" Reiss (12/17/1869 – 8/29/1928)
George A. Reiss (9/??/1871 – 7/22/1957)
Charles Frederick "Tinker" Reiss Jr. (7/26/1873 – 10/28/1958)
Ferdinand Joseph Reiss (6/7/1875 – 11/18/1943)
Jeanette M. Reiss (9/16/1878 – 5/??/1967)
Meta K. Reiss (2/14/1880 – 11/??/1967)

Will, Kayla, and Ava, how many Georges, Conrads, and Steves did you find? Let's talk about the November 15, 1866 Dintelmann-Reiss wedding. An early thought was for Eva and Charles to be married on April 9, 1866 when Charles' brother Frank married Anna Syvilla Feder and his sister Kate married Charles Max Wittig in a double ceremony. That would have made it a triple wedding which is extremely rare, especially involving three siblings. In the end Eva and Charles decided to make it a special day for just the two of them. Their marriage lasted 44 years.

George and Margaret Reiss Dintelmann

Let's also talk about the April 22, 1908 Reiss-Dintelmann wedding which was 106 years ago tomorrow. The ceremony was conducted on the Reiss family farm as you can see in the group photo on the next page. Margaret and George made a handsome couple, thanks in part to his really cool moustache. Their marriage lasted 32 years.

Here is more about the group photo. In the front row from the left in the swing are bride's brother Henry Reiss and wife Emma, the groom's parents Conrad and Margaret Dintelmann, and the bride's parents Frank and Anna Reiss holding their granddaughter Syvilla Reiss, daughter of Louis and Hattie.

Standing from the left are Hattie Reiss who is married to the bride's tall brother Louis standing second from the right, then Lizzie Darmstatter whose husband George is fourth from the right, then the minister with the beard, then the bride's bachelor brother John Reiss who went on to found the Reiss Dairy, then Philip Petri whose wife Katy at the far right is the bride's sister, then the bride's bachelor brother George Reiss who owns the farm, then groom George and the bride Margaret Reiss Dintelmann.

Not visible in the picture because he was taking it was the bride's brother Will Reiss who went on to become a professional photographer. I don't know the Darmstatters connection.

The bride's dress was lace on China silk and was made by Margaret's cousin Barbara Reiss who lived on South Church Street in Belleville. At her neck is a gold locket which became a family keepsake. It was worn by Beulah Cox on 6/8/1941 when she married the Dintelmann's second son Edwin. Both that locket and Margaret's 1908 wedding dress were worn by their granddaughter Judith Dintelmann when she married Douglas Peters on 5/21/1977. Neat story.

Will, Kayla, and Ava, there are two more Reiss/Dintelmann marriages beyond the two in this story. They involve grandchildren and great grandchildren of the people named above and it gets a bit too complex. The only wedding keepsake in our family is the gold watch and chain that my grandmother Katie wore as a gift from her husband George when they were married on 4/16/1911. My sister has it now so maybe it can be borrowed for your weddings in a few decades. And I have my grandmother's wedding dress and grandfather's wedding ring if you're interested.

Here's a 1925 picture of six of the Reiss siblings surrounding their mother Anna Syvilla Reiss. There were eleven children born but only seven reached adulthood. The one missing here is Katy Reiss Petri. My grandfather George Reiss is on the front left with the farmer tan. The final picture below is the 4/22/1908 wedding of Margaret Reiss and George Dintelmann.

Love, Granddad

Back: William, Louie, Henry, John Reiss. Front: George, Anna Reiss, Margaret Reiss Dintelmann 1925

Wedding of Margaret Reiss and George Dintelmann 1908.
Standing L-R: Hattie Reiss, Lizzie Darmstatter, Minister; John Reiss, Phillip Petri, George Reiss, George Dintelmann, George Darmstatter, Margaret Reiss Dintelmann, Louis Reiss, Katy Reiss Petri.
Seated L-R: Henry and Emma Reiss, Mr. & Mrs. Conrad Dintelmann, Frank and Anna Reiss holding Svilla Reiss

The Dintelmann Family Farms

Dear Will, Kayla, and Ava,   April 21, 2014

My other Granddad's Mondays story of today mentions the Dintelmann family and how at least two of their generations married our Reiss relatives. This story is about various farms that Conrad Dintelmann bought over the years. Six of them appear in this aerial photo identified as "Dint" and so many acres. Total is 603 acres which is the most of all our farmer relatives in St. Clair County.

Here's a photo from about 1906 of the Dintelmann family and farm house just west of Five Forks south of Freeburg. Conrad and his wife Margaret are seated. Son George and his first wife Kate Altheim are standing. Don't know the guy on the back right.

Conrad Dintelmann bought his first two farms in partnership with his brother Henry. Remember their wives were the Keller sisters. Here's the indenture dated 6/29/1863 which was just a week before the Union victories at Gettysburg and Vicksburg in the Civil War. The total price for the Dint 80 farm in Section 18 and the Dint 20 farm in Section 14 was $3,600 or $36 per acre.

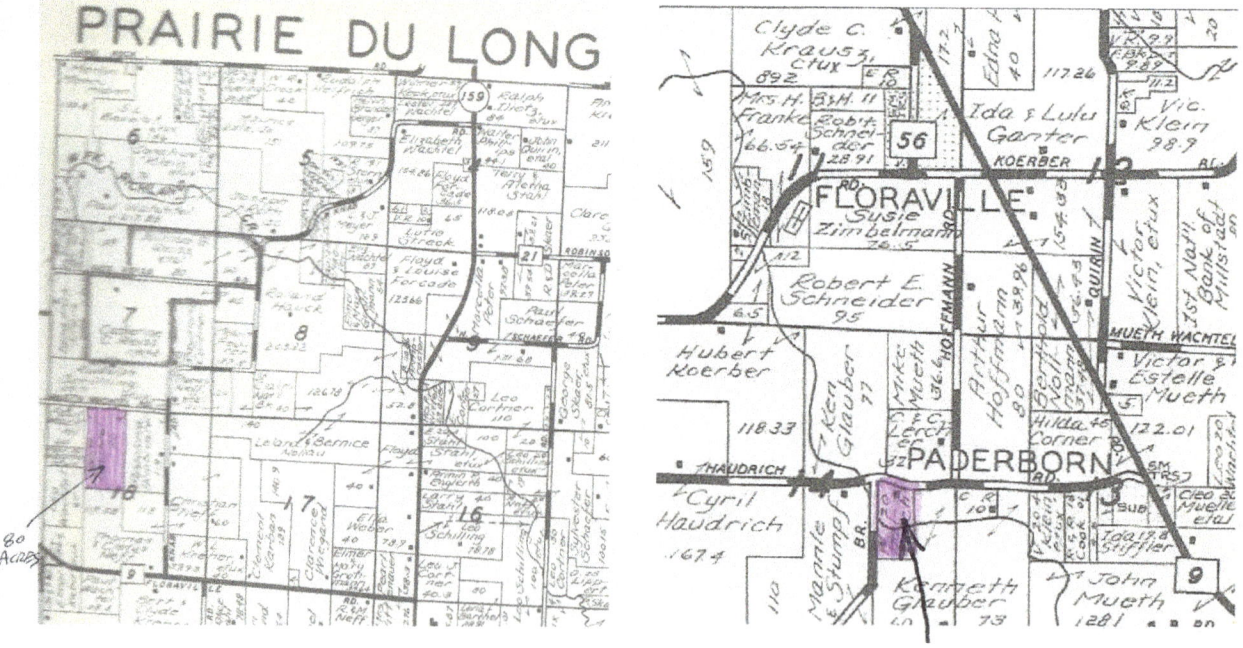

Below are plat maps of Dint 80 in Section 18 and Dint 20 in Section 14. Note that the 80 acres is just a quarter mile south of the Reiss Family Farm in Section 7. Maybe that's how young George Dintelmann got acquainted with Anna Margaret Reiss who he married on 4/22/1908. Later Conrad Dintelmann bought the Dint 160 and Dint 40 farms on 11/15/1883 for $7,900 or $39.50 per acre.

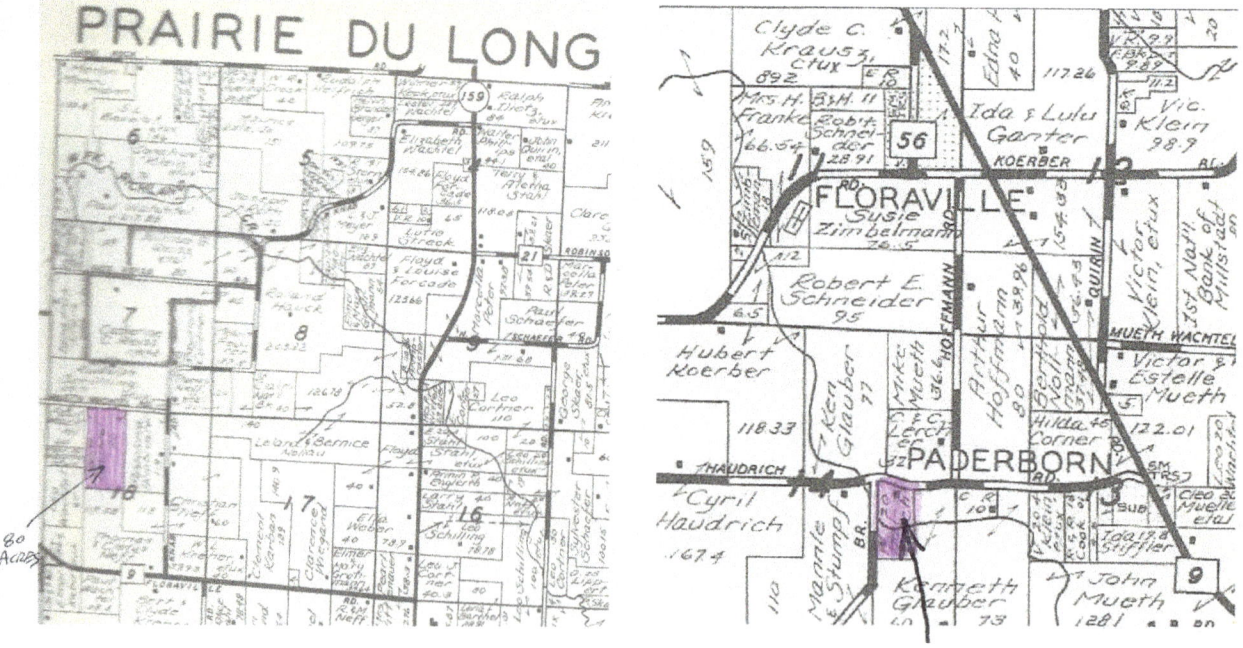

Now go back to the aerial photo and notice the "Dint 133" farm east of Smithton. Conrad Dintelmann died on 12/6/1911 so his son George is now the administrator for his dad's estate. Here is the indenture where George is leasing those 133 acres and farmhouse to Fred Hesse. Check out the restrictions at the bottom.

This Indenture, Made this ....1st.... day of ....August.... 19 12,
BETWEEN ..George Dintelmann, Admr. of Estate of Conrad Dintelmann of the
Town of New Athens, County of St. Clair and State of Illinois...................
party of the first part, and ..Fred Hesse of the Town of Prairie du Long in said....
County and State ....
party of the second part, WITNESSETH, That the said party of the first part, in consideration of the
covenant of the said party of the second part hereinafter set forth, do ..es.. by these presents lease to the
party of the second part the following described property, to-wit: A ..part of the north east...
..quarter of Section One (1), Tp. Two, South, Range Eight West, being the
farm formerly owned by A. Hamill containing one hundred thirty three
(133) acres more or less, situated in the Town of Prairie du Long, St.
Clair Co. Ill. ....
No timothy to be sown in orchard, nor hogs to be allowed in said orchard
No straw to be burned or removed which is raised on the premises.
No dances to be held in the house. ....

Will, Kayla, and Ava, this is a very interesting story, but kinda complex, don't you think? But I have left even more complexity for you three to figure out in the years to come like the Reiss – Dintelmann connection through the Kellers. Here's another one -- when Conrad's oldest brother John died in October 1907, his obituary mentioned his granddaughter, Mrs. Edward Reiss, but none of us know that connection. Here's a third one – that Hesse guy who was not allowed to dance in the Dintelmann farmhouse may be related to Anita Hesse who married my dad's oldest brother Bill. Here's a fourth one – the Dintelmann family branch that owns the Dintelmann Nursery south of Belleville has a great grandchild who married a Reiss. I'm going to sign off now. The 1935 plat map below shows the Dintelmann farms just left of Five Forks and at the bottom center in New Athens Township.

Love, Granddad

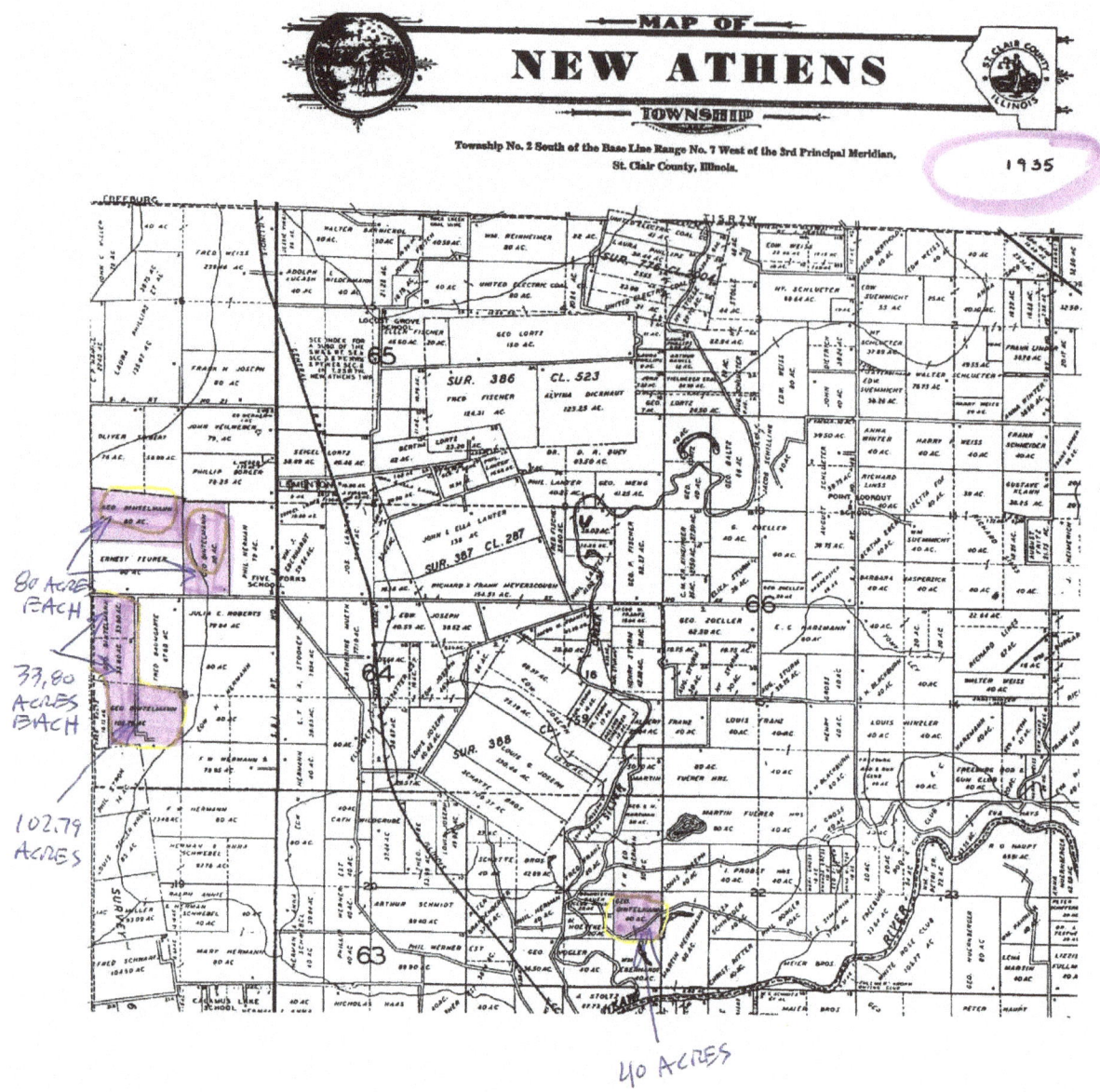

MAP OF
NEW ATHENS
TOWNSHIP

Township No. 2 South of the Base Line Range No. 7 West of the 3rd Principal Meridian,
St. Clair County, Illinois.

1935

80 ACRE BACH

33,80 ACRES BACH

102.79 ACRES

40 ACRES

As you'll see in my April 28, 2014 Granddad's Mondays story next week, our Adam Reiss bought his first 40-acre farm in Section 7 of New Athens Township on April 30, 1834. Adam sold it three years later in 1837 and it became lost to our family awareness and documented history. And then surprise, surprise, Conrad Dintelmann bought that same 40 acres 48 years later in 1883 as part of his "Dint 160" farm which you can see on both of the satellite pictures. The Dint 160 and the Dintelmann homestead are 200 yards west of the Five Forks intersection on the north side of the road.

That original Adam Reiss 40 acres is where I was standing on 4/1/2014 when I took this picture looking southeast toward the Dintelmann homestead. Sadly their original home shown in the page 1 photo burned several years ago. Just the outbuildings and a replacement double-wide trailer home are there now. You can see the same barn in both pictures.

Last Will and Signature of Adam Reiss

Dear Will, Kayla, and Ava,   May 19, 2014

Here is the last signature of your great great great great grandfather Adam Reiss –

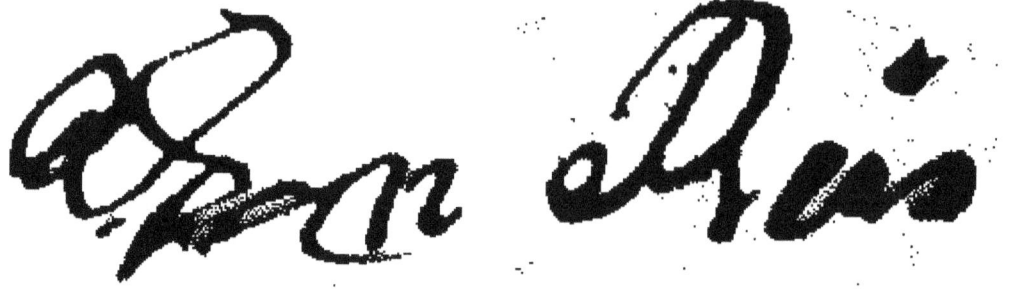

You can see it below at the end of his last will and testament that he signed on May 23, 1849, the day he passed away at age 45 years and 16 days which is 165 years ago this coming Friday. It was written in German and later translated into longhand English which I then typed.

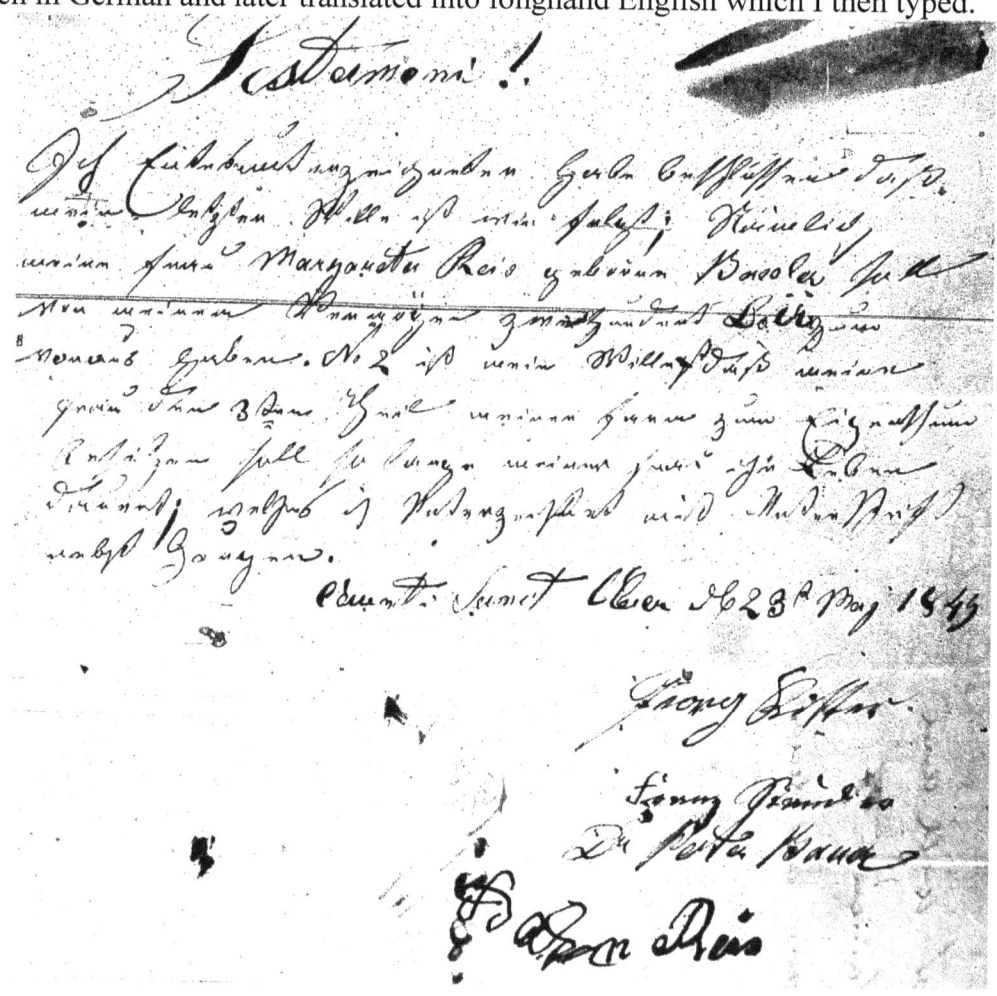

[Handwritten document reproduction:]

Translation

Last will & testament

I the undersigned have come to the conclusion, to make these presents my last will and testament to wit. My wife Margaret Reis alias Basler shall have and receive beforehand two hundred Dollars. 2° I devise to my wife one third part of my farm as her absolute property for and during her natural life; which I have signed with signature in presence of witnesses.

County St Clair this 23rd of May 1849.

Georg Ritter
Franz Stauder
Dr Peter Bauer
Adam Reis

Translation – Last Will & Testament

I the undersigned have come to the conclusion to make these presents my last will and testament to wit. My wife Margaret Reis alias Basler shall have and receive beforehand two hundred dollars. #2 I devise to my wife, one-third part of my farm as her absolute property for and during her natural life: which I have signed with signature in presence of witnesses.

County St. Clair this 23rd of May, 1849.
George Ritter
Franz Stauder
Dr. Peter Bauer
Adam Reiss

Will, Kayla, and Ava, above is the last of three signatures we have of our patriarch Adam Reiss who established the family in 1838 in Prairie du Long Township of St. Clair County, Illinois. A lot has transpired in the 165 years since his passing. He left behind his wife Margaret age 30 and 5 children under age 11. Worse yet, Margaret lost their sixth child who was stillborn sometime in 1849. They all lived in a one-room log cabin and would have been extremely challenged to eek out a living on the family farm. Can you imagine what they had to endure?

Love, Granddad

Adam Reiss Tombstone

Dear Will, Kayla, and Ava,   May 19, 2014

This story is about the tombstone of your great great great great grandfather Adam Reiss. It is located in St. Augustine Cemetery about a mile west of Hecker, Illinois or about five miles south of the Reiss Family Farm. Adam Reiss died 165 years ago this coming Friday on May 23, 1849.

Here are five pictures were taken in 1984 when 115 Reiss family members gathered at the Smithton Sportsman's Club to celebrate 150 years of Adam Reiss becoming an American farmer in 1834. The two on the left are my brother Ken taking a close up picture and the second one is another relative making a rubbing.

Below is more of the cemetery with the Adam Reiss stone at the right center. The second large white stone from the back left corner is a four-sided obelisk with each side naming one of Adam's four grandchildren who died young. They were children of his son Frank and his wife Anna Sybilla – Charles Martin Reiss (10/17/1867 – 11/18/1874), Adam Joseph Reiss (9/25/1869 – 11/5/1874), Catherine Reiss (11/11/1871 – 6/16/1872), and Elizabetha (Lizza) A. Reiss (7/1/1888 – 3/2/1889). Their ages were 7, 5, less than 1, and less than 1. The first two grandchildren died just 13 days apart in 1874. How tragic.

86

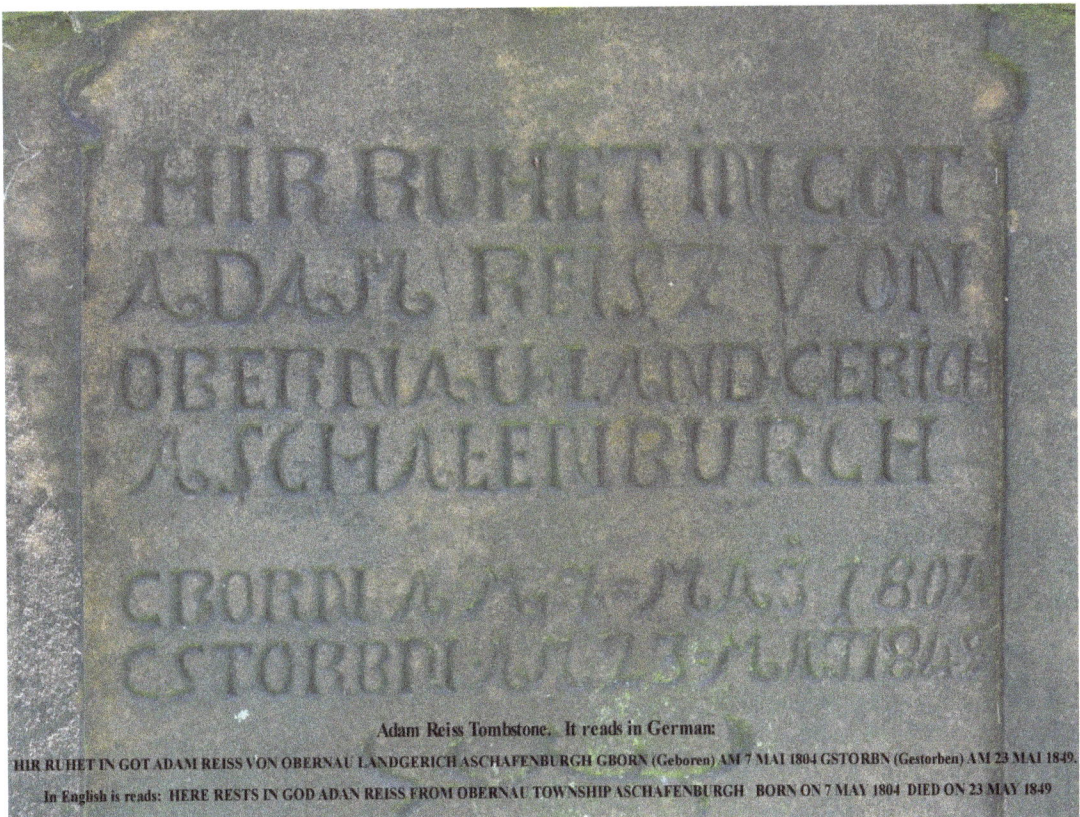

Grave site of Adam Reiss in St. Augustine Cemetery near Hecker Illinois

Adam Reiss Tombstone. It reads in German:

HIR RUHET IN GOT ADAM REISS VON OBERNAU LANDGERICH ASCHAFENBURGH GBORN (Geboren) AM 7 MAI 1804 GSTORBN (Gestorben) AM 23 MAI 1849.

In English is reads: HERE RESTS IN GOD ADAN REISS FROM OBERNAU TOWNSHIP ASCHAFENBURGH BORN ON 7 MAY 1804 DIED ON 23 MAY 1849

Will, Kayla, and Ava, we'll show you this cemetery in the coming years. There are other relatives buried here including Adam's second wife Margaret and her daughter Louisa by her second husband Conrad Ebert. Cemeteries can be emotional places to visit but they can also be great sources of family history. I think Adam's stone is a beautiful work of art. Notice that it's all written in German and that his last name is spelled Reisz.

Love, Granddad

1849 Probate of Adam Reiss Estate

Dear Will, Kayla, and Ava,   May 19, 2014

I wasn't real sure what "probate" meant so here is what I found on Google – **Probate** is a legal document. Receipt of probate is the first step in the legal process of administering the estate of a deceased person, resolving all claims, and distributing the deceased person's property under a will. A probate court (surrogate court) decides the legal validity of a testator's will and grants its approval by granting probate to the executor. In this case the probate court was a probate justice of the peace. The probated will becomes a legal document that may be enforced by the executor in the law-courts if necessary. A probate also officially appoints the executor (or personal representative), generally named in the will, as having legal power to dispose of the testator's assets in the manner specified in the testator's will.

At right is the original probate document for the will of our patriarch Adam Reiss who died on May 23, 1849. The original is fairly hard to read so I shrunk it for this story and typed the following copy:

State of Illinois, St. Clair County. Be it remembered that on this 9th day of June A.D.1849 personally appeared before me the undersigned Probate Justice of the Peace in and for the said County of St. Clair and State aforesaid, Francis Stauder and George Ritter. The subscribing witnesses to the instruments of writing hereto annexed as the last will and testament of Adam Reis deceased who after being duly sworn on their oaths deposeth and say that they were present and saw the said Adam Reis, the testator, sign the said will in their presence and he acknowledged the same to be his act and deed, and they then believed and still believe the said testator was of sound mind and memory at the time of signing and acknowledging said will and they attested said will in the presence and by the request of said testator and in the presence of each other who signed their names thereto as witnesses at the same time and they also witnessed the said will in the presence of the other subscribing who signed his name thereto as a witness at the same times.

Sworn to and subscribed before me this day and year above written. Johann Hughes P.J.P
Signed – Franz Stauder, George Ritter

State of Illinois, St. Clair County. I John D. Hughes, Probate Justice of the Peace in and for the said County of St. Clair and State aforesaid, do hereby certify that I do approve of the foregoing as the last will and testament of Adam Reis deceased and admit the same to the Record. Given under my hand and seal this 9th of June A.D.1849. Signed – John D. Hughes P.J.P.

We do solemnly swear that the instrument of writing hereto annexed is the true last will and testament of Adam Reis deceased so far as we know or believe and that said will will and truly execute the same by paying first the debts and then the legacies therein mentioned as far as his goods and chattels will thereunto extend and the law charges, and that we will make a true and perfect inventory of all such goods and chattels, rights, and credits as may come to our hands or knowledge belonging to the estate of the said deceased, and render a fair and just account of our administration when thereunto required by law to the best of our abilities, so help us God. Sworn to and subscribed this 9th day of June A.D.1849, John D. Hughes P.J.P.

Margaret Reiss, her mark X
Franz Stauder

After the Probate Justice of the Peace finalized the document above, Margaret and Franz continued the probate process by hiring an auctioneer to sell various farm items and animals to pay Adam's debts and to downsize the ongoing operation of the 120-acre family farm by 30-year old Margaret and her five children – John age 10 years 6 months, Frank 7 years 9 months, Charles 6 years 4 months, Martin 4 years, and Kate 2 years 3 months. Sometime in 1849 Margaret lost her sixth child Barbara who was stillborn. Here is one of two pages summarizing the results of that auction. It was hard to read so I shrunk it more and typed the entire summary on the next page.

Sold at Public Auction Vandue (*auction*) by Francis Stauder and Margaret Reiss, administrators of the Estate of Adam Reiss deceased on the 7th day of July 1849 the goods, chattels, and personal estate of the aforesaid Adam Reiss

Buyers Names	Description of Property	$	Cents
Francis Stauder	2 hoes		80
Peter Deschner	1 shovel & grubbing hoe		25
Edmond Brandt	hoe and grubbing hoe		25
Phillip Reitz	hoe and iron wedge		25
" "	1 oven with lid		25
Sebastian Richert	1 old grove		60
Phillip Reitz	2 iron wedges	1	00
Francis Reinhart	6 harrow teeth		70
Bartholomew Goldman	1 spinning wheel		80
Christian Scker	2 old scythes		20
Francis Reinhart	1 scythe with cradle		60
Lewis Demint	1 log chain	1	20
Phillip Reitz	1 cutting hoe for straw	1	05
Peter Deschner	1 barrel		40
Peter Metzger	1 pickling tub	1	15
Phillip Reitz	1 shotgun	2	00
Michael Schenborn	1 ox yoke	1	00
Jacob Rapp	1 " "		85
George Ritter	1 horse collar with harness	1	05
Phillip Etling	1 2-year old horse colt	46	00
Daniel Hermes	1 steer 3 years	8	00
Peter Deschner	1 bull	4	55
Jacob Barthold	1 cow with white face calf	11	10
Andrew Hurt	1 white & speckled cow with calf	13	75
Phillip Reitz	1 2-year old heifer	5	00
Michael Barthold	1 red cow with calf	8	10
John B. Thomas	1 2-year old steer	8	20
Phillip Reitz	1 white sided cow with calf	10	00
Daniel Barthold	1 2-year old heifer white face	5	00
Edmond Brandt	4 head of hogs, 1st choice	2	00
" "	4 " " , 2nd choice	2	00
Francis Stauder	8 " " , 3rd "	1	00
Francis Stauder	7 head of hogs, 4th choice		60
		$119	80

This is to certify that the foregoing is correct Bill of the Sale of the Personal Estate of Adam Reiss, deceased, this 7th day of July 1849.

Jacob Eyman, Clerk

Love, Granddad

Cholera in 1849

Dear Will, Kayla, Ava, and Blake,   May 18, 2015

Your great great great great grandfather Adam Reiss died of this dreadful disease on May 23, 1849 which was 165 years ago this Saturday. He was just 16 days past his 45th birthday and left behind a wife and five children under age 11, all living on a 120-acre farm in a log cabin with a dirt floor. How would they cope? Adam was buried in St. Augustine Catholic Cemetery in Hecker five miles south of the Reiss family farm.

Here is a paragraph from the published history of St. Michael's Catholic Church in Paderborn – "A cholera epidemic swept this area somewhere along the year 1849. It is claimed that fifty-two persons died and were buried in the old cemetery. Most of the graves were never marked, but the location was along the extreme west end of the old cemetery. This may be the reason that some family names recorded in the early church records are no longer here. The "Belleville" cholera epidemic claimed 236 lives from May 18 to July 31, 1849."

The disease came further north that summer to around Peoria where we live. Pekin lost 50 residents, Bishop Hill lost 60, Liverpool lost 13, and Germantown Hills lost 83 over the next 30 years.

Cholera is an infection of the small intestine caused by the bacterium *Vibrio cholerae*. The main symptoms are watery diarrhea and vomiting. This may result in dehydration and in severe cases grayish-bluish skin. Transmission occurs primarily by drinking water or eating food that has been contaminated by the waste products of an infected person, including one with no apparent symptoms.

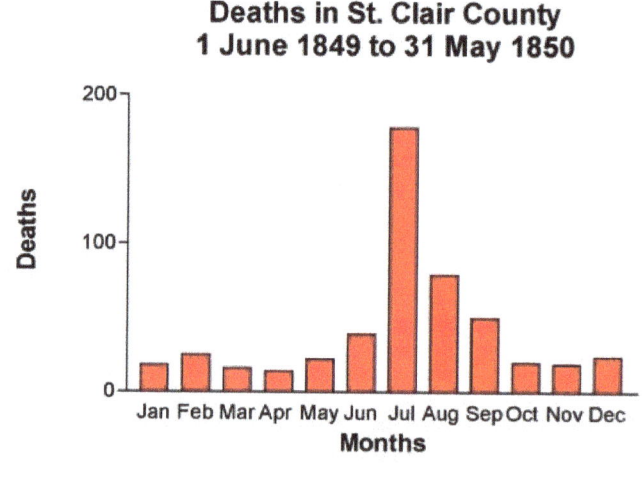

**Deaths in St. Clair County
1 June 1849 to 31 May 1850**

**Based on the 1850 Mortality Schedule
504 deaths reported.
257 (51%) in July and August.
346 (69%) in June to September.**

Data from: Rawlings, Issac D. et al. 1927.*The Rise and Fall of Disease in Illinois*. State Department of Health.

The severity of the diarrhea and vomiting can lead to rapid dehydration and electrolyte imbalance, and death in some cases. The primary treatment is oral rehydration therapy, typically with oral rehydration solution, to replace water and electrolytes. If this is not tolerated or does not provide improvement fast enough, intravenous fluids can also be used. Antibacterial drugs are beneficial in those with severe disease to shorten its duration and severity.

Worldwide, cholera affects 3 to 5 million people and causes 100,000 to 130,000 deaths a year as of 2010. Cholera was one of the earliest infections to be studied by epidemiological methods. And now the world is living through an outbreak of Ebola centered in western Africa.

Will, Kayla, Ava, and Blake, maybe there are several lessons for all of us to remember including:

- Wash you hands frequently
- Consume only safe foods and liquids
- Get all your vaccinations even if it hurts a little bit
- Support medical health workers and research around the world
- Get quick medical attention if you suspect a serious disease
- Count your blessings on where you live, advances in medical science, and conscientious parents

Love, Granddad

1850 -- 1859

1850 Population of St. Clair County is 20,180.

1850 States total 30, national population is 23.19 million. California is added in 1850, Minnesota in 1858, and Oregon in 1859.

1850 President is Zachary Taylor. Millard Fillmore is inaugurated in 1850, Franklin Pierce in 1853, and James Buchanan in 1857.

1851 The first YMCA opens in Boston, Massachusetts.

1852 The anti-slavery book, Uncle Tom's Cabin, is published, 300,000 copies sold.

1852 The Studebaker Brothers Wagon Company is established and would become the largest producer of wagons in the world. They started making electric automobiles in 1902 and gasoline models in 1904.

1852 Domingo Ghirardelli founded his chocolate company in San Francisco.

1853 The Gadsden Purchase finalized the borders of the continental US.

1853 Levi Strauss moved to San Francisco. He made his first pair of riveted blue jeans in 1871.

1854 The Republican Party is founded in Ripon, Wisconsin.

1854 The US Naval Academy at Annapolis graduates its first class.

1855 The first railroad train crosses the Mississippi River from Rock Island, Illinois to Davenport, Iowa.

1857 The Dred Scott Case regarding Negroes and slavery. Scott dies in 1858.

1857 First elevator is installed by Elisha Otis in New York City.

1858 Seven debates between Abraham Lincoln and Stephen Douglas.

1858 Rowland Hussey Macy opened his first successful department store in New York City as R. H. Macy & Co. on Sixth Avenue.

1859 First productive oil well is drilled by Edwin Drake in Titusville, Pennsylvania.

1859 John Brown attacks the US armory at Harper's Ferry, Virginia.

Matriarch #1 – Margaret Basler Reiss Ebert

Dear Will, Kayla, and Ava,   August 18, 2014

Your great great great great grandmother Margaret Basler was born on 10/22/1818 in this picturesque Swiss village of Niederzeihen (lower Zeihen). She was the second of ten children and the oldest daughter. Her father Johann Basler was the village mayor, burgermeister, or gemeindeammann about 1823. The second photo is their house near the village center.

Johann, his wife Katharina, and eight of their surviving children arrived in New Orleans on 11/28/1839 from Le Havre, France on a ship called Salem as family number is 292308. Their oldest son Nicholaus had previously arrived in New Orleans on 12/3/1836 and settled in Louisville, Kentucky.

The Basler family quickly moved north to settle in the German community of Paderborn, Illinois about two miles from the 40-acre farm which Johann Adam Reiss had purchased from Thomas Houghan on 9/1/1838. Adam built his log cabin that fall and moved in with his pregnant wife Mary. He also built an adjacent log granary. Both measured about 15 feet by 18 feet and had stone foundations. Their son John was born soon on 12/11/1838 but sadly Mary died during that childbirth.

Adam hosted Catholic church services on his farm in his log cabin, his log granary, or outdoors as the seasons allowed. He did that for about two years and may have started that practice with Mary. Anyway, those church services may have been where the Basler and Reiss families first met in late 1839. So here was Margaret age 20 and the oldest Basler child in the area. And here was Adam Reiss age 34, new landowner, handyman farmer, and widower with an infant son. Margaret and Adam were married on 9/10/1840. In less than a year she had gone from an upscale house with wooden floors in Switzerland, to a very small log cabin with a dirt floor in Illinois, to a wife and homemaker, and to a step-mom with an infant son. ==Awesome lady!!!==

The decade of the 1840s was challenging for Margaret with very high highs and very low lows. Here's a summary –

- Her mother Katharina died on 3/5/1841 and is probably buried in St. Michael's Cemetery in Paderborn. ==Margaret is now the family matriarch at age 22.==

- Her second son Frank Joseph Reiss was born on 9/27/1841.

- Her father Johann Basler bought a 40-acre farm northeast of Paderborn on 12/13/1841.

- Her next younger sister Sophia married nearby farmer Frantz Stauder on 3/28/1842. He was also a recent widower and was raising two small children under age 5.

- Her third son Charles Joseph Reiss was born on 2/17/1843.

- Her father Johann Basler sold his farm on 11/2/1843 and moved with his unmarried children to Louisville, Kentucky.

- Her fourth son Martin Charles Reiss was born 6/19/1845.

- Her first daughter Catharine Reiss was born 3/23/1847.

- Her second daughter Barbara Reiss was stillborn sometime in 1849.

- Her husband Adam Reiss died of cholera on 5/23/1849. Margaret is now a widow, age 30, five children ages 2 to 10, living in a small log cabin with dirt floor, on a 120-acre farm. ==Can you imagine!!!==

The next decade of the 1850s were kinder to Margaret but still had major highs and lows –

- Margaret married Conrad Ebert on 4/2/1850. He was born in Germany on 5/11/1811 so he is seven years older than Margaret. He arrived in New Orleans on 6/7/1847.

- Her third daughter Anna Maria Ebert was born on 9/14/1851. She did not reach adulthood because she is not mentioned in the 1860 census.

- Her two younger brothers moved to California in 1852. George Anselm Basler took a steamship from New York to Panama, crossed the isthmus, and took a second steamship to San Francisco. He later participated in gold rushes in Nevada and British Columbia. Martin Basler, his wife Anna Maria, and two month old son John took a covered wagon for 105 days along the California Trail from St. Joseph, Missouri to Sacramento.

- Her fourth daughter Louisa Ebert was born on 12/??/1853.

- Margaret and Conrad Ebert bought 40 acres on 1/5/1854 to square off their farm at 160 acres.

- Her father Johann Basler died in late 1854 in Louisville, Kentucky.

- Her fifth daughter Margaret Ebert was born on 10/29/1856.

- Her last child with a name we don't know was born about 1859 but did not survive because there is no mention in the 1860 census.

The next four decades of the 1860s through the 1890s included additional joys and sorrows –

- Brother Nicholaus Basler died on 4/11/1860 in Louisville. ==Margaret is now the oldest of seven surviving Basler siblings.==

- Son John Reiss married Maria Josephine Gass on 10/22/1861 and had ten children but lost four of them the week of 5/10/1888 to disease.

- Fighting in the Civil War with four different Illinois regiments were Margaret's brother George Basler with the 22nd, son John Reiss with the 43rd, son Frank Reiss with the 31st, and son-in-law Charles Max Wittig with the 82nd. All returned but two were wounded.

- Margaret and Conrad were subpoenaed on 4/18/1865 by the widow of Thomas Houghan over her dower rights to three 40-acre tracts sold by her husband to Adam Reiss in 1838, 1839, and 1842. The Eberts traveled to Springfield and were excused from the suit.

- Younger sister Sophia Basler Stauder died on 7/25/1865. Margaret is now the only Basler living in Illinois. Her parents are deceased. Two brothers are in California. Two sisters are in St. Louis. One brother is in a Civil War veterans' home in Dayton, Ohio. And one brother is in Sullivan, Indiana.

- Son Frank Reiss married Anna Antonia Syvilla Feder on 4/9/1866 and had eleven children but only seven reached adulthood.

- Daughter Kate Reiss married Charles Max Wittig on 4/9/1866 in a double ceremony with her brother Frank and Anna. They had five daughters with four reaching adulthood.

- Son Charles Reiss married Eva Dintelmann on 11/15/1866 and had seven children with all seven reaching adulthood.

- Margaret and Conrad bought 20 more acres on 5/13/1868 on the northeast corner of their farm.

- Her younger brother Ferdinand Basler died on 12/15/1873 in Sullivan, Indiana.

- Daughter Louisa Ebert married George W. Neff on 11/6/1873 and had one son before she died on 5/21/1875 when her clothes caught fire while making apple butter.

- Daughter Margaret Ebert married Conrad Charles Neff (George's younger brother) on 9/7/1877 and had five children who all reached adulthood.

- Margaret's husband Conrad Ebert's died on 7/23/1880 at age 69.

- Her younger brother Martin Basler died on 1/25/1881 in Sacramento, California.

- Son Martin Reiss married Margaret Williams in 1883 and had three children but only one reached adulthood. Margaret died in 1891 and Martin in 1898.

- Her younger brother George Anselm Basler died on 11/??/1888 in San Francisco.

- Her older brother Johann Jakob "George" Basler died on 9/7/1897 in Dayton, Ohio.

- The 1900 census shows Margaret with five of ten children still living. Stepson John was the first born, then five children with Adam Reiss, and four more with Conrad Ebert.

Will, Kayla, and Ava, our matriarch Margaret saved 780 letters written to her or her neighbor son Frank Reiss between 1852 and 1888. Writers were her siblings and spouses, her Reiss children, several grandchildren, and two friends. Only 22 of these letters were written by Margaret while she was visiting her daughter in Davenport or son in O'Fallon. Most were written in "old" German and were translated between 2004 and 2008. About 20% of the letters are in phonetic English and are just plain fun to read. All these letters with some linking italics to make them more self-explanatory were published by Author House in 2009 in a book titled It Takes A Matriarch. There are 412,000 words, a dozen photos, and 600 pages.

These letters show a consistent and very conscientious pattern of caring, leading, counseling, listening, sharing, and compassion. Margaret Basler Reiss Ebert was an outstanding matriarch, patriarch, and big sister. She was my great great grandmother and simply a great person. I hope to meet her in heaven some day!!! Here's her book and her obituary on the next page.

Love, Granddad

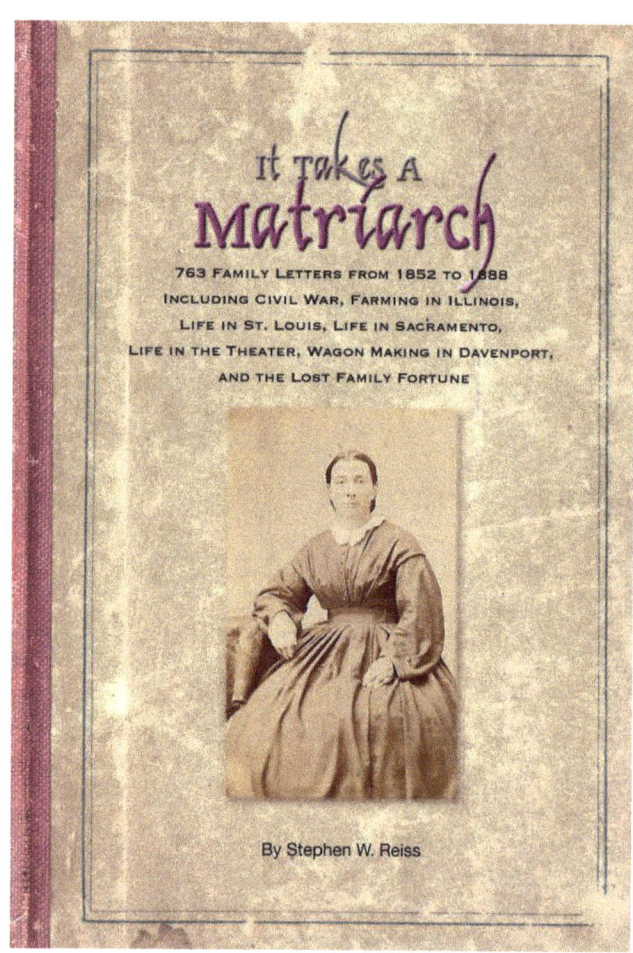

Huebinger Bros DAVENPORT, IA.

Here is Margaret's obituary as translated from a local German newspaper –

In the Prairie du Long Township died on Sunday morning Mrs. Margaretha Ebert at an age of 84 years and 9 months. Mrs. Ebert's maiden name was Margaretha Basler, she was the widow of Mr. Conrad Ebert. At the time of her death, Mrs. Ebert was living on the farm of her daughter, Mrs. Conrad Neff, 2 miles north of Hecker.

Mrs. Ebert was born in Switzerland and came to the United States in the year 1839. Her first husband Mr. Adam Reiss died in 1849. Her second husband Mr. Conrad Ebert died in 1880.

Mrs. Ebert is survived by her children: John Reiss in Belleville, Frank Reiss in Floraville, Charles on the Ridge Prairie, Martin in Missouri, Mrs. Max Wittig in Davenport, Ia. and Mrs. Conrad Neff as well as 31 grandchildren and 3 great grandchildren. Also her sisters Mrs. Charles Krone and Mrs. Samuel Perrow (*who died a week apart in July 1907*).

The funeral service has been on Wednesday morning at 8:00 o'clock in the Catholic Church in Hecker and the burial took place right after the service at St. Augustine Cemetery.

Martin and Anna Maria Basler

Dear Will, Kayla, Ava, and Blake,   April 27, 2015

Exactly 163 years ago this Friday your great great great great great uncle and aunt, Martin and Anna Maria Basler, left St. Joseph, Missouri by covered wagon to arrive 110 days later in Placerville, California. Their covered wagon followed a route called the California Trail. Typing those two cities into Mapquest shows a total distance of 1,661.84 miles and travel time of 24 hours and 6 minutes. So our relatives averaged less than 15.1 miles per day because their route would not have been as direct as that of modern interstate highways.

Martin was a blacksmith and harness maker. Harnesses are the leather straps and reins which connect horses/mules/oxen to the wagons/buggies/plows they are pulling. Martin was born on 11/11/1825 in Switzerland so he was age 26 when they embarked on this trip. Anna Maria was born on 7/31/1827 so her age was 24. She was born in Prussia which is now part of Germany. The most amazing part of this journey is that with them was their first child, an infant son John born 2/22/1852 who was just 10 weeks old. And all this is in the days before car seats, McDonalds, penicillin, email, Holiday Inns, cell phones, and GPS. Can you imagine, can you imagine, can you imagine making such a trip!!! It's absolutely awesome!!!

Here are two letters written by Anna Maria, one from Missouri before the journey started and one from California after it concluded. They were both written in German which I had translated into English. These are 2 of the 780 family letters in our book, It Takes A Matriarch. The first letter is addressed to Martin's sister Margaret who is the "matriarch" of our book. The second letter is addressed to Martin's younger brother George Anselm Basler who would join them in California in 1853. He arrived there in just 30 days by taking a steamship from New York to cross the Isthmus of Panama and then a second steamship to San Francisco.

Anna Maria did not keep a journal of their 110 days on the California Trail. I'm sure she had her hands full with their infant son John besides the other time demands of making such a trip. However there are hundreds of other women who did keep journals. Many are published in a series of books called Covered Wagon Women by Kenneth L. Holmes. I bought Volume 4 which is six 1852 journals just to get a good feel of daily life on the trail.

St. Joseph, Missouri
the 1st of May 1852

Dear brother-in-law and sister-in-law Margaretha!

We left St. Louis on the 14th of April and arrived here on the 21st of April in late in the night in St. Joseph and the next day arrived Johann L. Kohl with animals and wagons and despite the difficult trip, our animals are still in good shape, we also sold our pony for 60 dollars and bought a donkey to take its place, so now we have six donkeys and all are still well and are looking better than they did in St. Louis and we have done the best by leaving here, we also took 40 bushels of oats with us on the trip, to keep our donkeys in good condition until they can get grass, we also didn't regret yet that we started the trip, we could still make a good profit here if we would sell everything, because for the large donkeys, for which we paid 150 dollars in St. Louis, we could get 250 here and that's the same with the other utensils, wagon and provisions. But, dear friends, but what the things are worth for other people they are also worth for us, and for that reason, dear friends, take heart, because if we should do bad on the trip, then few would get to California.

Dear Friends, the weather here is also pretty fair, and we wanted to leave here on the 28th of April, but we were prevented from doing so because my sister's child, Mari, got the measles and got very sick of them, but now she is better and we will leave for sure tomorrow, the 3rd of May.

We also hope for our brother George Anselm Basler, who has promised to come after us, if he is able to get ready, because it was very hard on him to leave us. And if he would have had his money with him, then he would have gone with us right away, which we would have preferred. So, dear friends, as I said, we have a good carriage and are well provided with provisions and all the necessary things, as far as we know, and if we don't meet a special misfortune on the trip, then we don't have to worry.

I hope my letter meets you in good health as we are to date. I want to close my letter and with our best wellbeing and highest friendship, we are and remain your true friends.

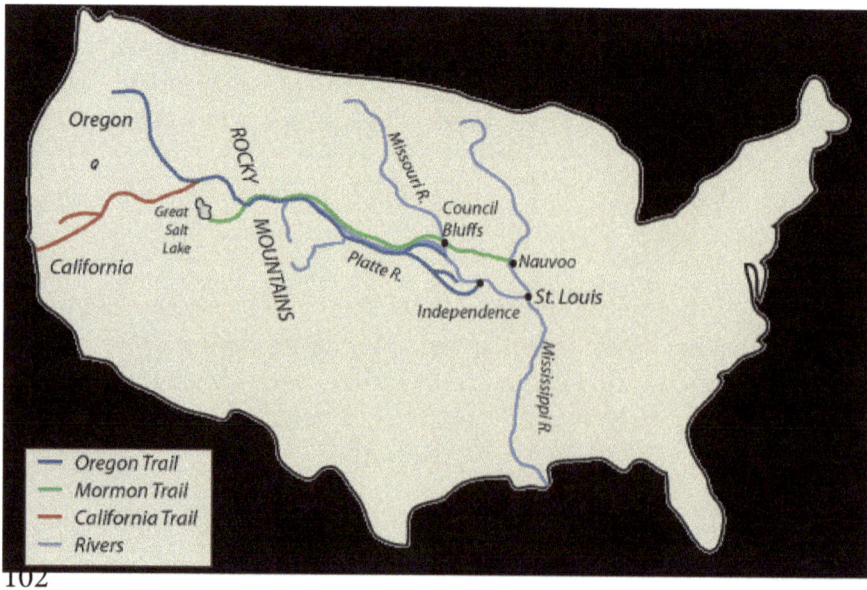

Your sister-in-law,

Anna Maria Basler

The California Trail accounted for 67.6% of all 296,000 covered wagon immigrants between 1840 ad 1860. The Oregon Trail was second with 17.9% and the Mormon Trail third with 14.5%. This map shows the three trails were almost identical until the east and west Utah borders. The year 1852 was by far the busiest with 23.6% of the 20 years of immigrants.

Sacramento, California
the 30th of January 1853

To G. A. Basler
Louisville, Ky.

Dear brother-in-law, sister-in-law and Father and Mother!

With the best intentions I take up the pen to tell you about our experiences, as best as I can. Dear Friends! We left St. Joseph the 4th of May and on the 5th it already started to rain and for 14 days we had to make small stations and could not go more than 5 to 10 miles per day until Fort Kane. This stretch is the prettiest area on the whole trip. From there to Fort Laramie we had a good road and grass, but for 14 days we had no wood and we had to collect the dung of the buffaloes, which is even better than wood when the weather is good. From Fort Laramie we had bad grass for a long while, and nothing but hills. At this long trip, one cannot see anything pretty or enjoyable, no pretty flower, no pretty tree, nothing but shrubs similar to wild Vermouth or juniper berries, also we often had dust a foot high then again sand, even higher, and we had to drive over stones 3 to 4 feet high, and also mountains that when one stands below them and looks at the mountains, one would think that one couldn't even get over them by foot, also there were areas where the water was bad, but one can differentiate from good water, also many hardships had to be overcome on the trip, but it can be endured if one is careful. One doesn't have to be afraid of the Indians, they only steal what they can. We were almost 4 months on this trip, until the 22nd of August when we arrived in Haengtaun (*now Placerville, California*). Here we sold donkey and wagon and therefore had 700 dollars, which is gone quickly here in California. From here we traveled to Sacramento where we quickly met an acquaintance, who had been here since 1850 and had a saddler shop, and because the two men knew each other well, they went into partnership and we bought half the shop for 800 dollars, of which we were able to pay only 500 dollars and still owed 300 dollars, and by now we have paid off everything and still have a little money, and we are also inclined to take over the shop by ourselves on the 1st of March, if we can do it, we also both work very hard and save as much as we can , so that in a couple of years we have enough to live well and happy.

Dear Friends, California is a wild area and no place where one can live happily, so one month after our arrival we had a terrible fire which almost laid the whole town into ashes. It was terrible. Many lost hundred thousands of dollars and are now poor people, even we had already cleared out everything but to our luck the wind turned when the fire was two houses away from us. Here was the 8th Street and pretty wide, one house was a hotel and the second our shop and behind it the residence which was already on fire but we could put it out so we were saved from the fire which was a great wonder.

That is the worst winter which has been seen here, we have rain almost every day and because of this lot of rain our town has already been flooded three times. We also had between 10 and 15 feet. And with a roof made out of linen cloth, we have it 3 feet off the ground so we don't get any water in it, but it wasn't high enough and we got 18 inches in the room. This happened on the 1st of January, a nice New Years present for the whole town and I and other women who fled to us jumped on the bed and we had to sit surrounded by the water. Much fun! Our men had to take large boxes and set the stove on it and cook, and use a little boat to go from door to door. This, dear friends, was true fun, and everything had to be carried by boat, and if one of the boats turned over then the unfortunate were laughed at. Also all the wells and ditches were filled with water, so everything became one and we had no choice but to use the water for cooking (very appetizing). Excuse me my friends, but that is the truth.

This destroyed the streets to such a degree that one could not drive on them with a wagon and they had to hitch the horses to boats to bring the necessary items from house to house but the horses or donkeys often got stuck in the mud and they often couldn't get them out anymore, they had to but a rope around their neck and use other horses to pull them out again.

Also the boots high up over the knees are much used here and even the women wear them proudly and unabashed, because without them one cannot leave the house, also there are houses which look more like a wood shack than a residence, because everything is made here to save money, and then to move on, because one doesn't have to think about pleasure here.

With all of this we are very satisfied, and we think we will make great business until Spring because one can still make money here when one has money and enough to start out and continue, but with a little one cannot do anything here. We have made great progress already and ask you, dear brother-in-law George to give father 50 or 100 dollars as much as he needs in our name and we will send it to you or bring it ourselves as soon as you tell us because father is now an old man and not able to work. The large coin, as large as a bus, I haven't found yet, otherwise I would have sent it. We also have written a letter to Margareth on the 1st of September and one to Lorenz Rich in St. Louis on the 1st of October and have no answer from either side.

Hope you will write soon again and let us know especially how it looks with brother Jakob's saga. We are all fresh and healthy and well content, as we hope of you. Hereby I will close and greet all of you.

Your sister-in-law and
daughter,

Anna Maria Basler
Martin Basler

Make the address Martin Basler Sacramento City, California. Excuse my bad handwriting and the crooked lines, which I made, because my mind is more at work and business, to make money than to write letters.

Will, Kayla, Ava, and Blake, there is a lot of family and national history in this Granddad's Mondays story. Some day we will travel to some of these cities and parts of these trails, but we'll go by air-conditioned car instead of covered wagon. And we'll average 500 miles a day instead of 15. Whaduyathink?

Love, Granddad

Here's an email exchange I had a year ago with Valarie Vine who was a volunteer at the Sacramento County Historical Society. One of my Basler relatives had donated her collection of old family photographs and related material to the Society. Valarie had found me in the Internet via our Matriarch book of letters and called, hoping I could identify people in those photos.

To valarievine@yahoo.com

Hi, Valarie. These Baslers were my great great great aunt and uncle. He was a younger brother of my great great grandmother Margaret Basler Reiss Ebert. She saved 780 letters written to her or her son Frank Reiss from 1852 to 1888. Most were written in old German. They have all been translated and now appear in my book, It Takes A Matriarch. There are 76 letters from these Baslers who traveled the California Trail by covered wagon in 1852 with a two month old baby son.

Do you have a connection with these Baslers? I can provide pictures of both of them if you would like to add that to your memorial. Thanks for doing all that you have done so far. Let me know. Thanks,

Stephen W. Reiss

Valarie Vine
To Me

Stephen, how wonderful that you have those historical letters and that you have put a book together! I was able to find some obits on several of the Basler family members tonight in the California Digital Newspaper Collection and added the information to their memorials.

Any photos you would like to add to their memorials would be great! It always adds so much to see the images of the pioneers. No, I am not related to the Baslers. I walk cemeteries in California and take photographs hoping it will be of help to family/genealogists. If you have bio material you would like me to add, I would be happy to do so.

Happy Genealogy Trails,

Valarie

George Anselm and Maria Basler

Dear Will, Kayla, Ava, and Blake,   April 13, 2015

This man is the youngest son of your great great great great great Basler grandparents who immigrated from Switzerland to arrive in New Orleans on 11/28/1839. Young George was born on 4/22/1831 and was 8.5 years old when he arrived in America, probably speaking only German.

George's second oldest brother was Johann Jakob Basler who was born on 7/24/1821 and arrived with the rest of the family in New Orleans. But for some reason JJB chose to also go by "George" about age 30 which makes the genealogy a bit difficult to follow. His Civil War service record is under George Basler as is his tombstone at the Dayton National Cemetery in Ohio. Anyway, the rest of this story is about the younger brother whose real name is George.

The oldest Basler son was Nicholaus Johann who was born on 12/13/1816 and who immigrated to America by himself to arrive in New Orleans on 12/3/1836. He settled in Louisville, Kentucky. When the rest of the family arrived three years later, NJB's younger siblings moved in with him in Louisville while his parents and older siblings settled in St. Clair County, Illinois. Five years later NJB got married in 1844 and his younger sibs then boarded with the Sackstetter family in Louisville. The **1850 census** shows GAB age 18, sister Kate age 16, and 3 boarders all enumerated with the Sackstetter family of parents and 7 kids. Sounds like a houseful. GAB, the Sackstetter son John, and boarder Anthony Kern all worked as sign and house painters.

Here's a letter George wrote in German on 5/4/1852 to his sister Margaret and her husband Conrad Ebert thanking them for his recent Easter Sunday visit on 4/11/1852 to the Reiss family farm in St. Clair County, Illinois.

Louisville, Ky
The 4th of May, 1852

To Mister Konrad Ebert
Belleville, Illinois (Received the 15th of May)

Beloved brother-in-law and siblings,

We are all still healthy here and hope the same of you. I left brother Martin on Tuesday after Easter in St. Louis. Martin left St. Louis on Wednesday the 14th of April. I had a quick and very pleasant trip. I arrived here on Thursday, the 15th of April. I am very sorry that I couldn't stay with you longer. I think that I and the sister will stay with you for a couple of weeks next winter. Louisa and Katarina want to see you again very much. I haven't heard anything from brother Jakob since I was at your house. He is still at the old place in Lexington. Brother Martin said that we can't expect a letter from him before the month of December because he usually doesn't write until he is at his final location. Brother Ferdinand also wants to go to California next spring if Martin likes it.

Beloved siblings and in-laws, I don't have any news to write. I am going to send you three newspapers with this letter. When you write back, let me know if you received the papers or not. But I hope that you don't wait too long to write because all of us are waiting with longing for news. With this letter I will close my present day "Infangelium." Best Wishes to your father and siblings.

Yours truly,
Brother Georg A. Basler

I don't know what that last word "Infangelium" means, so I Googled it. And guess what, this 1852 letter of George's was the only hit that popped up and it came from our book It Takes A Matriarch. So I still don't know what it means!!!

In early January 1853 George traveled to San Francisco. He took steamships from Louisville to New York, departed there on 1/20/1853 on an ocean steamer to Panama, crossed over the isthmus, and then took another ocean steamer to San Francisco arriving on 2/19/1853. In 1852 George's older brother Martin had driven a covered wagon from St. Joseph, Missouri to Sacramento, California which is a Granddad's Mondays story by itself. I mention it here because George and Martin connected for the next ten years in Sacramento. George found work as a sign and house painter. Here's his fascinating letter in phonetic English from early 1861.

#428 – English

January the 10th, 1861
Sacramento City

Dear Sister Kate Basler,

It affords me great pleasure to inform you that I have just returned from San Francisco this morning. Wen I got on board, I found a young man on board how (*who*) I knew wel in Louisville. His name is Mr. Kraft. He is a tinner by trade and a were (*very*) nice young man. He is going to Louisville by this steamer wish leafs San Francisco tomorrow. Kate I would of send a letter by Mr. Kraft but I had no tim to weight. I gave him one of my cards and told him to cal on you. He promist to do so. He learned his trade on Jerfson Street between Preston & Jackson with Mr. Krauth a tinner.

I rec'd your letter on last Friday of December the 3rd, 1860 and I also rec'd one of Wm. H. Basler & one of Sister Margretha Ebert. One of Mr. Ziteler has not yet come to hand.

Kate, Mr. Kraft wil com back here after a stay of three or fore weeks in your city. If you and Frank Rice are coming out here, I wish you to com with him for I don't know of a more gentelmanly man for you to come with.

Dear Sister Kate. I can in sure you you will find your self mush better off here. In fact I think I would like to have you all here with us Kate. I wil tell you more this time than wat I have told you be fore. Brother Martin and Sister said to me last Sunday that thay are going to remain here for their futer home. Martin & my self have bought six hundred & forty akers of land with a house on it 12 mils be low Sacramento City and then Martin has bought three hundred and twenty ackers 15 mils above Sacramento City with house & fenc on part of it and he now lifs on it and is inproffing it and doeing well. I have a horse and go to see them every Sunday and com back on Monday. Also I ride very fast. Som time I ride up to his plase in two hours. I spent my Christmas & New Year with them eating turkey & co. Sister Mary would lik for our Brother in Law Mr. Ebert with all of his family to come out to Cal. For he would do wel here with all of his boys in a fewe years. Thay would be rich on a farm I think. Besides it is a helthy country and inproffing every day. I am hapy to say that my business is inproffing very mush and I expect to stick to it for som years yet for I am well knowen in this city by this time. It wil be my foster home all tho not married yet nor any hops to mary. I wish you could see the letter Sister Margret wrote to me about me not being married yet. She makes some excelent remarks. She talks to me like a Dutch Uncal. She closet her letter as fowlos.

Dear Brother George, I wish you for the New Year a good young wife or a butifull young gairl and for you to make a wife of her. I have no dat but she is right but she per haps dos not know the value of ladys in Cal. Or the skersety of them. She said probely I would like to mary until as Fleckenstin said for fore weeks and if she did not suite me to send her off again. I think that would please me best. Jack would not eate supper be cause.

It pleased me very mush to here that Brother Ferd had bin to Ill. To see our sisters Sophe & Margret. I would afford greate plasure to you all. Kate if you have no money (*to*) com with, let me know. If you wish to com I will send it to you or borrow it and I will pay it back with entrest with the gratest of plasure. You have never given me any answer if you wish to com or not. I hope you wil give me an answer to som sadisfacton and let me know about Frank Rice. My love to all. I remain,

Your loving & affecenant,
George A. Basler, Sac City, Cal.

The **1860 Census** shows George Basler born in Switzerland, age 25, living in Sacramento, working as a painter, and sharing a residence with another painter Duncan Gillis age 28 from Scotland. The **1870 Census** has a Charles Bassler age 40 born in Switzerland and working as a painter plus wife Mariah age 50 born in Ireland living in San Francisco. The **1880 Census** shows George age 49 working as a house painter, wife Maria age 50 born in Ireland and living on Market Street in San Francisco with no children but with a boarder working as a sign painter. The **1889-1891 San Francisco Directory** shows Maria, widow of George A. Basler, living at 607 Hyde Street. The summary below shows years and home addresses for George from those respective San Francisco City Directories. Those 1 thru 8 locations appear on the following map of San Francisco. North is at the top. George died in November 1888. The 1890 address is that of his widow Maria. We don't know where either is buried.

1	1864	309 Tehama Street
2	1868 - 72	3 Harriet Street
3	1875 - 80	29 Pearl Street
4	1881	1006 Market Street
5	1882	923 Market Street
6	1882	28 Geary Street
7	1883	19 Seventh Street
8	1890	607 Hyde Street

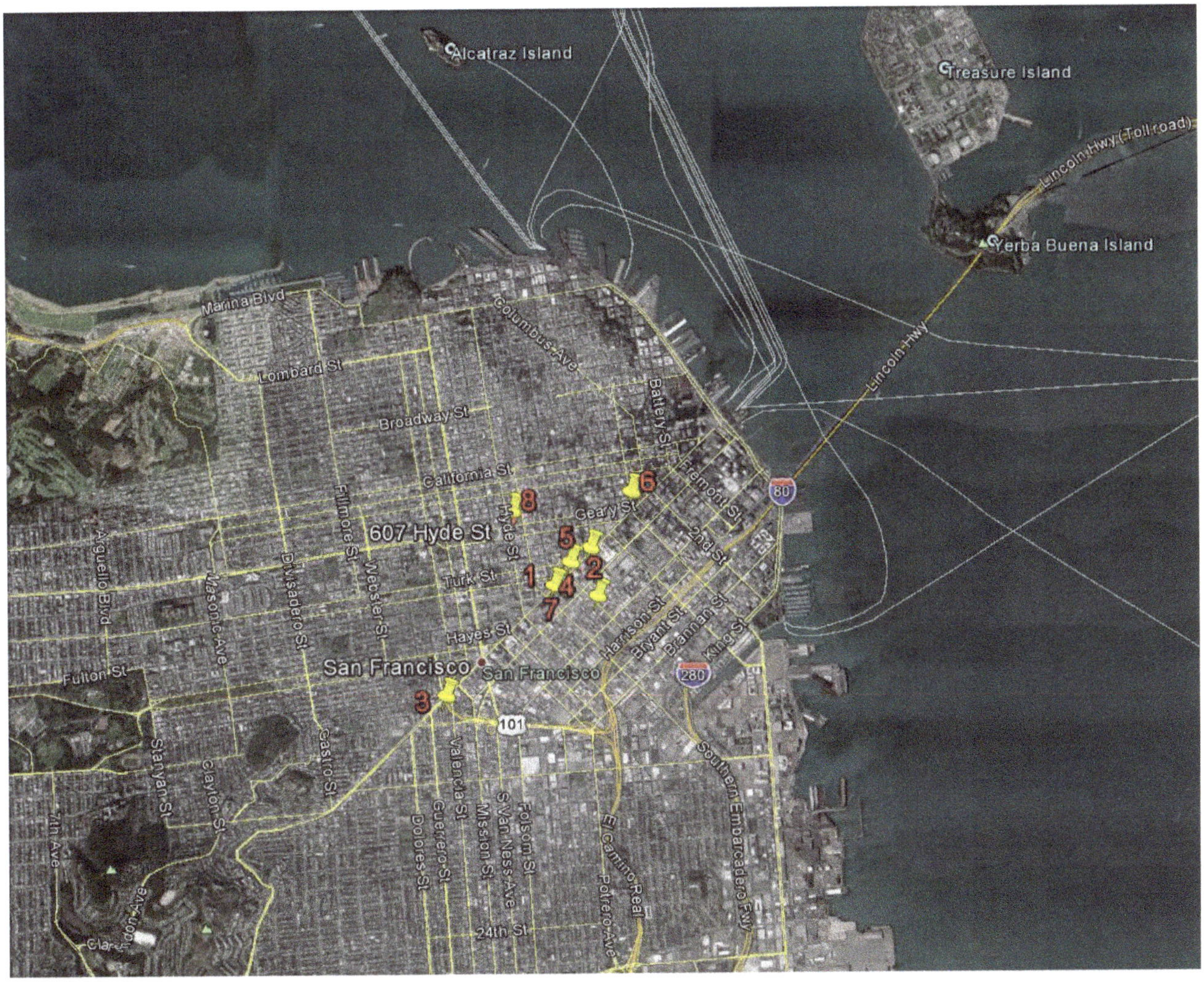

By 1870 there were 37 states and 38.5 million people in the United States. San Francisco was the 10th largest city in the country with 150,000 people. This second map with East at the top is from 1876. Market Street is the main drag angling northeast toward Treasure Island. You can see that the Basler homes were all in the middle of city life.

At 5:12 a.m. the morning of April 18, 1906 San Francisco was hit by a devastating earthquake and resulting fire that lasted for three days. About 80% of the city was destroyed and over 3,000 people died. The shaded area in the upper right shows the fire boundary. It's obvious that every one of the addresses where the Baslers lived for over 25 years was destroyed. George had passed away in 1888 and I assume Maria did not live to experience this catastrophe.

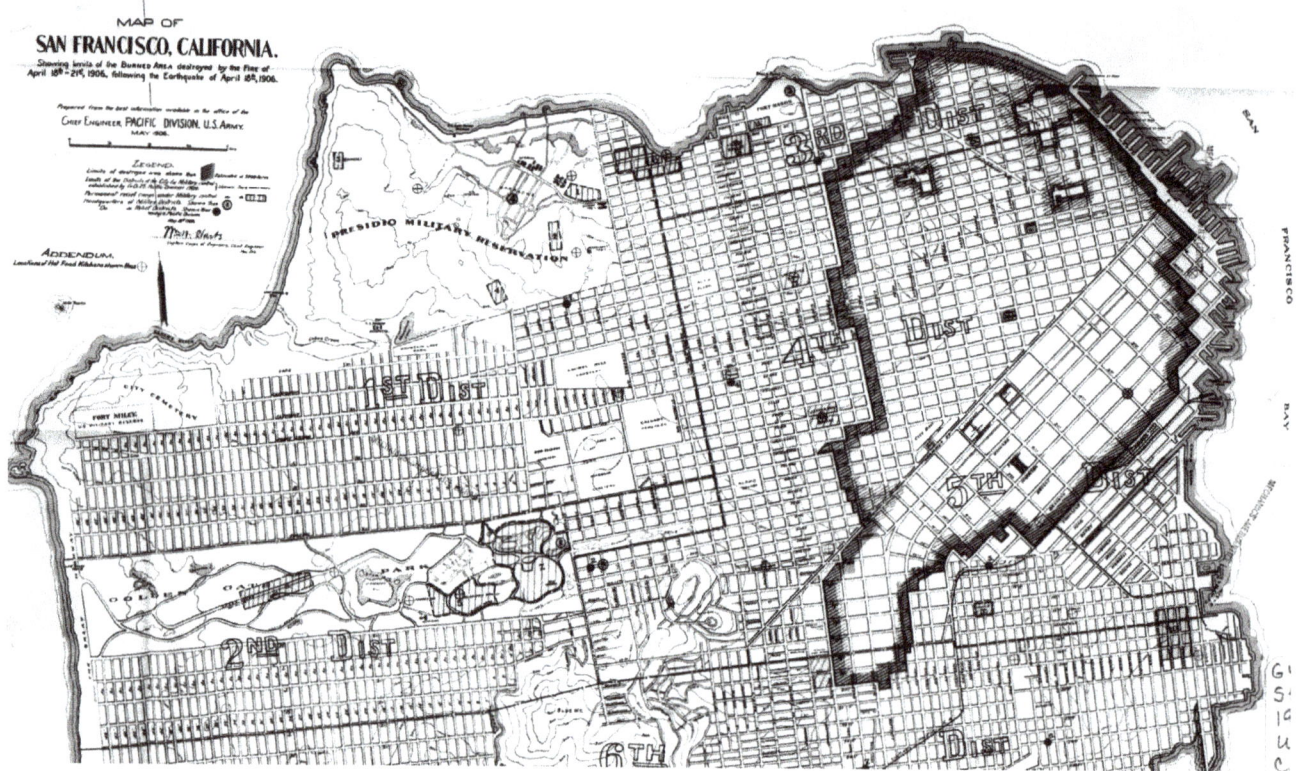

Gold rushes – We have only nine letters from George. All were written between 1852 and 1861 except one in 1882 to his sister Margaret mentioning the passing of their brother Martin in Sacramento. There may have been more letters but those nine are all that Margaret saved which now appear in our book, It Takes A Matriarch. Here is part of a letter from Martin's wife, Maria Basler, to Margaret on 8/4/1858 about brother George's first gold rush – British Columbia, Canada in what is now modern day Vancouver.

"Brother George has left California two months ago, he went to Fraser River, it is about a 60-day trip from here over land, but very difficult due to the large mountains and also very dangerous because of the many Indians. No company with less than 300 men may attempt to undertake this. George left by water first, the trip took 8 days with a steamboat, until Victoria, this is the main place, a town which already has about 20 houses and huts. Until there it costs 150 dollars. From there on they must go with small boats over the Fraser, the river is so strong that the steamboats can't get up there and the trip takes 3 weeks and is also very dangerous. This is still a real wilderness and is occupied by the worst Indians which exist anywhere, and it is still

110

unknown if this place belongs to the United States or to England. But the English have the court jurisdiction until now. This place was advertised as the richest gold area in the world, so rich that some are supposed to have made $2000 in 3 hours. This made a larger spectacle here than I am able to write to you, all the people wanted to go. If one owed someone money, then he would be sued right away, almost 200 stores in Sacramento went out of business, who didn't have the money didn't get any either, one could not sell anything for half the price. They sold things in Sacramento for 5 or 6 dollars which originally cost 100. They sold hay for 5$ a ton.

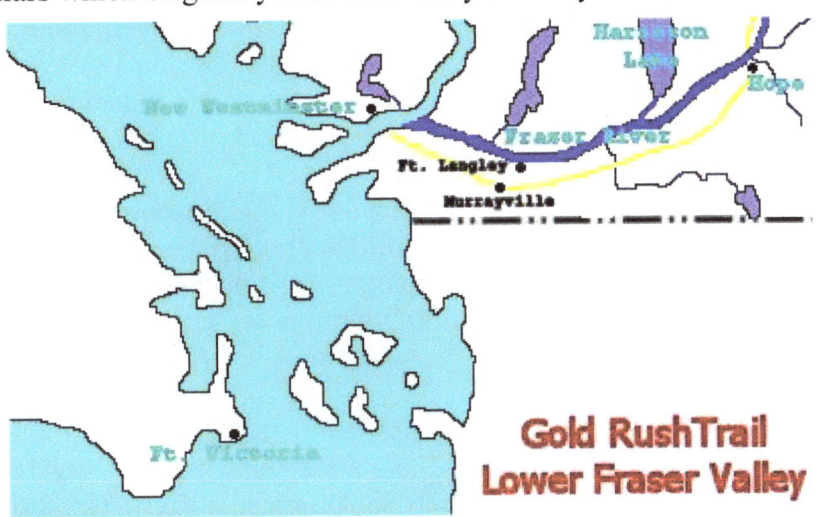

Gold RushTrail
Lower Fraser Valley

Wheat was 75 cents per 100 pounds, and other items where similar. Now it is starting to get a little better again, it seems that the whole thing was a humbug and the more than 20,000 men who sold off their things here to get the money for the trip in April, most of them don't have enough money to return, they are suffering of hunger there and are in pretty bad shape, I don't think that George is faring any better. He would have had enough money to come back from Victoria, but he wrote in his last letter on the 6th of July that he wanted to see the place where the gold was supposed to have been, because if he is supposed to pay to see the elephant, then he wants to see him too."

Here's a partial letter from Martin Basler dated ==3/4/1869 about brother George's second gold rush== – "Brother Georg was here the 18th and 19th of February, he is traveling again to the new gold mines. They are about 700 miles from here, but pretty much high in the mountains. You can imagine that it is no pleasant trip at this time of year, when the pound of freight costs 12 cents to send it here. I think that most of the people, who are here so early, will keep the costs down. But the new mines are supposed to be very rich. Many people are going there from here, and one believes generally that laborers will be rare here this summer. Georg has left his family in San Francisco. He has two in the family, his wife, a cat, and his horse. I am sending you brother Georg's picture. He had it taken in Sacramento in the same clothes he is wearing to cross the mountains."

Here's another partial letter from Martin dated ==9/20/1869== – "Brother Georg came back sick from ==White Pine==. I didn't see him, he went straight to San Francisco."

We don't know if George went on these two gold rushes to look for gold, to paint signs and buildings, or just to see what else made sense for him. Neither is mentioned in his letters to his family. Here's what I found on White Pine.

"Rush to White Pine" or "Rush of '69" was perhaps the most sensational mining stampede in the history of the west. Within a few months more than 25,000 adventurers - 5,000 more than flocked to Comstock 10 years earlier - swarmed over Treasure Hill. The first discovery in the district, however, was not on Treasure Hill but on the west side of Mount Hamilton. In the spring of 1865, prospectors from Austin explored east-ward until their attention was drawn to the prominent White Pine Mountain (Mount Hamilton). By the summer of 1869, 10 stamp mills were in operation and by the fall there were 15 with six more under construction. At one time there were 23 mills running simultaneously. During 1869 the yield of 34 mines was $1,822,868 according to tax records; nearly 200 mines were producing profitable ore, and more than 13,000 claims had been filed. Today, Ely is the seat of White Pine County, Nevada.

Will, Kayla, Ava, and Blake, what do you think about our adventurous uncle George Anselm Basler? A long trip to California. Two gold rushes when he was single and footloose. He apparently did pretty well as a painter. His brother's letter of 7/17/1874 says George has 20 to 35 employees. Too bad he didn't write more letters that survived for his descendants to read and appreciate.

That Fort Victoria that George visited in 1858 is now Victoria, British Columbia, Canada. That's where my mom, Mary Leone Stephenson Reiss, was born on 3/15/1921 just 63 years after George was there. Her dad was an American citizen. Her mom was born in Canada but became an American citizen automatically by marrying an American citizen. I think Mom had dual citizenship until about 1955 when she formally renounced her Canadian connection. Anyway, I contacted the Canadian Consulate in Chicago to see if I could have dual citizenship. There first answer was "no" but I'm still investigating. That will be another Granddad's Mondays story someday.

Love, Granddad

Nicholaus Johann Basler

Dear Will, Kayla, Ava, and Blake,   July 6, 2015

Nicholaus Johann Basler was the older brother of my great great grandmother Margaret Basler Reiss Ebert. You also know her as our family matriarch who saved 780 letters from 1852 to 1888 from her siblings, children, and grandchildren. Sadly, none of those letters are from Nicholaus so most of what we know about him is from public documents via Ancestry.com.

Nicholaus immigrated to the US by himself at age 20. I'm impressed!!! He sailed from the port of Le Havre, France on a ship named Ernest to arrive in New Orleans on December 3, 1836. His record is transcribed as N. Joh. Barber with National Archives Series Number of M259-14. He settled in Louisville, Kentucky.

His parents, Johann and Katharina, and eight siblings appear in the New Orleans immigration records under the family name of Badler arriving on November 28, 1839 from La Havre on a ship called Salem. Both parents are listed as "Catha" and as female. Family Number is 292308 and National Archives Series Number is M259-19. The older sons moved to Louisville to live with brother Nicholaus but the parents and the rest of the family moved to St. Clair County, Illinois. Two of the older sisters married there – Margaret in 1840 and Sophia in 1842. Their mother died there in 1841 after which Johann sold his farm and moved with his younger children to Louisville, Kentucky to be near Nicholaus and his young family.

Nicholaus Johann (or N. John or N. J.) Basler (12/13/1816 – 4/11/1860) married Anna Catherine Betz (or Bates) (5/22/1821 – 8/5/1887) in 1844. The **1850 Census** shows husband N. J. age 33 born in Switzerland living in Louisville, wife A. C. age 28 born in Germany, William H. age 6 born in Kentucky, Elizabeth A. age 2, and twelve boarders in a building valued at $5,000. Also in Louisville are John's brother George Anselm Basler age 18 and his sister Catharina Basler age 16 who are boarding with the Sackstetter family of John age 30 a painter, Johanna age 32, seven children, and six boarders. The **1856 Louisville City Directory** shows Nicholas J. working as a notary public and living on Market Street between 5th and 6th Streets. The **1858-59 and 1860 Louisville City Directories** show Nicholas. J. working as a notary public living on Brook Street between Main and Market Streets. The **1860 Census** shows Cath Basler age 39, no husband, no boarders, personal property valued at $100, and six children – William H. age 16 working as a clerk, Cath L. age 12, Caroline age 10, John age 7, Peter age 5, and Mary age 3. If Cath was pregnant during this census, there is a George T. Basler in the 1910 Census age 50 who was born in Kentucky. Also living in Louisville are her late husband's sister Kate Basler age 27 boarding with the Yettler family.

The **1870 Census** shows Anna C. age 49 keeping house, Kate age 21 working as a tailoress, John age 17 working in a chair factory, Alex R. age 15 apprenticed to a saddlery, and Mary age 12 at school all living in Louisville. The **1880 Census** shows Annie age 59 born in Prussia, Kate age 31, John age 28 working as a caner in a chair factory, August age 25, and Mary age 22 working as a dress maker all living in Louisville. The **1884 Louisville City Directory** shows Anne C. as the widow of Nicholas J. living at 711 E. Green Street. The **1886 Jefferson County Directory** shows four Baslers living at 711 E. Green Street in Louisville – Anna C., John L. working as a caner, Mary E. working as a clerk, and Peter A. working as a clerk. The **1887 Louisville Directory** shows Anna C. as the widow of N. J. Basler, John working as a caner, Mary as a dressmaker, and P. Alexander as a clerk. **Our letter #378 dated 6/16/1887** mentions the recent death of Mrs. J. John Basler at age 66 leaving four children to mourn. Here is her gravestone in Section A of St. Michael's Cemetery in Louisville. The **1890 Louisville Directory** shows Alexander working as a policeman, Mary A. working as folder, and Katherine L. all boarding at 711 E. Green Street. It shows Mary boarding at 306 3rd Street. The **1900 Census** shows no record.

William H. Basler (1843 – 9/??/1881) married Julia ?? (1852 -- ??) on ?? The **1870 Census** shows William age 26 working as a store clerk, Julia age 18 born in Virginia, and Katie age 10/12 living in Louisville. The **1880 Census** shows William age 36 working as a shipping clerk, Julia age 27, Katie age 10, Willie age 8, Carrie age 6, Nellie age 4, and Walter age 1 living in Louisville. All were born in Kentucky except Julia who was born in West Virginia. The **1900 Census** shows no record. The **1910 Census** and **1920 Census** show no record. The database for **Cave Hill Cemetery** in Louisville shows William H. Basler interred on 9/29/1881 in Section A, Range 70, Grave 18 at right.

Katie Basler (8/??/1869 – ??)
Willie Basler (1872 – ??)
Carrie Basler (1874 – ??)
Nellie Basler (1876 – ??)

Walter H. Basler (1879 – 7/29/1921) married Josephine ?? (1857 – 8/16/1911) in 1899. The **1910 Census** shows Walter age 32 married 11 years working as a clerk on a steam railroad living on South Eighth Street in Louisville, wife Josephine age 53 born in Indiana in her second marriage at 11 years as mother of 3 children with 2 still living but not living with them. Living with them is uncle Alex R. Basler age 55 born in Kentucky with a Swiss father and German mother, and a boarder. The **1920 Census** shows no record. The **Kentucky Death Index** shows a Walter H. Basler death at age 42 on 7/29/1921 and a Josephine Basler at age 53 on 8/16/1911 both in Jefferson County. There is a **9/12/1918 Draft Registration Card** for Walter Wade Basler born 9/27/1878, married to Lena, living at 814 E.

Walnut Street in Louisville, working as a clerk at the Big 4 Railroad, with height of 5' 7.5", build "slender", eyes "light blue", and hair "dark".

Catherine L. Basler (7/11/1846 – 9/8/1926) The **1900 Census** shows no record. The **1910 Census** shows unmarried Katie Basler age 62 working as a hotel chambermaid living on Beckenridge Street in Louisville with her sister Mary E. and brother-in-law Louis Steuerle and their two children. The **1920 Census** shows no record. The **Kentucky Death Index 1852 – 1953** shows Catherine Basler died on 9/8/1926 in Jefferson County of chronic dysentery. Informant was Louis Steuerle of 1020 E. Breckenridge in Louisville.

Caroline Basler (1850 - <8/1887) The **1870 Census** and **1880 Census** show no record.

John L. Basler (1851 – 12/10/1907) The **1886 Jefferson County Directory** shows him working as a caner and living at 711 Green Street in Louisville. The **1887 Louisville Directory** shows him working as a caner. The **1900 Census** shows a John Bozler age 44 born 2/??/1856 in Kentucky as a boarder on West Broadway in Louisville working in a chair factory. The **1910 Census** shows no record.

Peter Alexander Basler (1/31/1855 – 5/22/1914) The **Kentucky Birth Records 1852 – 1910** shows Peter Alexr born 1/31/1855 to N. J. Basler and A. C. Betz. The **1886 Jefferson County Directory** shows him working as a clerk and living at 711 Green Street in Louisville. The **1887 Louisville Directory** shows him working as a clerk. The **1900 Census** shows no record. The **1910 Census** shows Alex R. age 55 living on S. Eighth Street in Louisville with his nephew Walter Basler. The **Kentucky Death Index 1852 – 1953** shows Alexander Basler born 1/31/1855 and dying of tuberculosis on 5/22/1914 with father Nicholaus Basler and mother Katie Bates.

Mary A. Basler (8/1/1857 – 7/17/1920) married Louis Steuerle (10/??/1859 – 8/30/1933) in 1892. The **Kentucky Birth Records 1852 – 1910** show Mary born 8/1/1857 to N. J. Basler and Cath Bates. The **1886 Jefferson County Directory** shows her working as a clerk and living at 711 Green Street in Louisville. The **1887 Louisville Directory** shows her working as a dressmaker. The **1890 Louisville Directory** shows Louis working as a binder at Bradley & Gilbert Company at 2717 Bank Street. The **1900 Census** shows Lewis age 40 working as bookbinder, Mary age 41 married 8 years and with 2 of 2 children still living, Leola age 5, and Louis age 3 living on Breckenridge Street in Louisville. The **1910 Census** shows Mary age 50 in her first marriage of 17 years with 2 of 2 children still living, Louis Steuerle age 49 in his second marriage born in Kentucky working as a foreman in a binding company, daughter Leola age 15, and son Louis age 13. Living with them is her sister Katie Basler age 62 born in Kentucky with a Swiss father and German mother who works as a hotel chambermaid. They live on Breckenridge Street in Louisville. The **1920 Census** shows Mary age 61, Louis age 58 working as a foreman at a printing company, Leona M. age 25 working as a music teacher, and Louis J. age 23 working as a linotyper at a printing company. They own a house on Breckenridge Street in Louisville. The **1930 Census** show no record but the **Kentucky Death Index** does show both Mary and Louis.

Leola Steuerle (6/??/1894 -- ??)

Louis J. Steuerle (6/7/1896 – 8/6/1987) married ?? (?? -- ??) on ?? The **Social Security Death Index** and **Florida Death Index** show his final residence as Sarasota, Florida. The **1920 Census** and **1930 Census** show no record.

Will, Kayla, Ava, and Blake, we're used to seeing letters and photographs from this generation. This story is kinda plain without all that. It looks like most of Nicholaus' children never married and those that did apparently lost several children to disease. Furthermore, we know that my great great great grandfather Johann Basler died in Louisville in late 1854 but we can't find his grave. Maybe on one of our snowbirding trips to Florida, Grand DD and I will stop in Louisville and walk St. Michael's and Cave Hill Cemeteries.

Love, Granddad

PS: I tried to find 711 Green Street in Louisville on Google Earth and Mapquest. No such place now, not even a street by that name. Bummer.

1860 – 1869

1860 Population of St. Clair County is 37,694.

1860 States total 33, national population is 31.44 million. Kansas is added in 1861, West Virginia in 1863, Nevada in 1864, and Nebraska in 1867.

1860 President is James Buchanan. Abraham Lincoln is inaugurated in 1861, Andrew Johnson in 1865, and U. S. Grant in 1869.

1860 The Pony Express carried mail from St. Joseph, Missouri to Sacramento, California for 1.5 years.

1860 Eberhard Anheuser and William D'Oench bought a nearly bankrupt St. Louis brewery. Adolphus Busch married Anheuser's daughter in 1861 and bought D'Oench's share in 1869. The Budweiser name appeared in 1876.

1861 The Confederate Army attacks the Union's Fort Sumter to begin the Civil War.

1862 The battle of the ironclads. The USS Monitor defeats the Confederate Virginia at Hampton Roads, Virginia.

1862 The Homestead Act is approved granting 160 acres to settlers in many states who meet requirements.

1863 Lincoln's Emancipation Proclamation goes into effect.

1863 Union victories over Confederate troops at Gettysburg and Vicksburg on July 4.

1863 Lincoln's Gettysburg Address on November 19.

1865 General Robert E. Lee surrenders at Appomattox Court House on April 9. President Lincoln is assassinated on April 14. The 13th Amendment abolishing slavery takes effect on December 18.

1865 Marshall Field and partners entered the dry goods business in Chicago. He became sole owner in 1881. He donated $1.0 million in 1894 to what became the Field Museum of Natural History.

1866 The Grand Army of the Republic is formed in Decatur, Illinois.

1867 The US buys Alaska from Russia for $7.2 million.

1867 The Grange organizes to protect the interests of the American farmer.

1869 The Union Pacific and Central Pacific Railroads connect at Promontory Point, Utah.

Civil War – George Basler with the 22nd Illinois Infantry Regiment

Dear Will, Kayla, and Ava, and Blake,   February 2, 2015

Your great great great great great uncle Johan Jakob "George" Basler was a brilliant and very articulate individual in both German and English. He was also quite outspoken which often got him into trouble with family members. That nature contributed to his marriage failing after less than ten years. All three of his young children died before George enlisted in the Civil War at age 40. He was educated as a school teacher but also worked several years as a confectioner. From age 52 until he died at age 76, George lived at the National Soldiers Home for disabled volunteer veterans in Dayton, Ohio where this picture was taken. He was buried in Dayton National Cemetery (Section K, Row 23, Site 24) the day he died on 9/7/1897. His is a sad but complex story. I have visited his grave twice and am probably the only relative to do so.

We have 99 letters which George wrote between 9/6/1862 and 6/20/1894 which total 131 pages and 61,000 words. He is the #2 author, after the Wittig family, in our book It Takes A Matriarch.

His first 6 letters are individual two-week journals covering 90 days of the Civil War leading up to the Battle of Stones River near Murfreesboro, Tennessee where he was wounded on 12/30/1862. Parts of his letters appear below.

After his Civil War service, George moved back to St. Clair County, Illinois where he was a school teacher for about five years. One of his students was his niece, Kate Reiss, who later married our other Civil War hero, Max Wittig.

From about 1867 until he moved into the Dayton Home, George worked as a confectioner in my hometown of Sullivan, Indiana. His brother Ferdinand had moved there in 1849 so that was a good fit. Those two had previously been in the candy business together in Galena, Illinois in 1848.

Here are some of George's war letters. He writes beautifully.

Union Portrait Co.,   32 & 34 S. Main St., DAYTON, O.

Nov. 7, 1862 Today's cold makes for grim faces, it permeates the whole day through tents and clothes. Last year around this hour was the Battle of Belmont. The memory of it will always remain in my thoughts. An invisible hand had guided me wonderfully though the enemy and his bullets. Fresh troops continue to arrive here. The hills of the tent city and the number of troops increase visibly.

Nov. 11, 1862 A large part of the Western men, who arrived daily and whose number increased like a swarm of bees, has already found a channel out. With the town in their back for many an hour, brigades and divisions, led by their commanders, marched on various roads and directions towards a faraway target. Some of them followed the pikes towards Murfreesboro and Chattanooga. The shooed-away Butternuts collect again in fragments behind their backs. The authorities are patient and merciful. They only catch the small fry, the culprits, they let them go. The Rebels want to come to their senses only slowly and without disgrace. The usual camp business takes over in these morning hours, nothing seems to point to the fact that something special is to happen before the end of the day: Artillery and cavalry moved out to drill. Sentinels move back and forth. Orderlies ride back and forth with their couriers. Here and there one from the high command rides by and reciprocates the greetings condescendingly and often obligingly. The clear sky and the friendly sun illuminate and gild the buildings and houses of the Arabs in the poor section. On the shaved hills, the wind plays with the fallen leaves of the trees like young cats with mice. Individual soldiers clean their clothes, others cook and some clean their guns and accoutrements, when suddenly the order flew in for Revue and Inspection for noon, 12 o'clock. The troops under the command of Negley and G. Palmer were to be inspected today by Major General Rosecrans. So that no one is missing, we were replaced by other troops from our Guard duty. At the determined hour we marched through the main streets of the town and from there out to a large, flat, mowed grassy area. Set up by brigade and division lines, our batteries in the center, the steely gleaming gun weaponry at our front, in straight line, the many blue and gold decorated status and large regiment and country banners planted and we many thousand, loaded like Arabian camels, with knapsack, haversack and canteen, waited for the arrival of the field-tested, great Commander. Canon fire announced his presence at our line. The noble figure, the great commander exposed his head and greeted wonderfully. He rode on the head of the staff through our line. He glanced left and right with his eyes, he measured the troops up from head to the soles of their shoes. Nothing escaped his eyes. He promised to rectify the inadequacies. After the inspection, the number of 15,000 troops defiled in various maneuvers on the Revue field: The short grass, which allowed the soldiers to be seen from head to toe in their march and the location of the terrain itself significantly increased the military beauty of the day. A number of ladies and gentlemen honored and adorned the fest by their presence. Happily smiling faces met our glances. The return greeted us with jubilation. The 22nd and Belmont accepted many a Hurrah. It was 7 o'clock before we were able to unbuckle our "Maulesel" (*muzzle donkey or hinny, the offspring of a stallion horse and female donkey*) from out backs and take in our supper.

December 2, 1862 The duty for Grand guard and Brigade engages our whole camp this morning. When a number of Cavalry arrived on the Lebanon Pike with 12 prisoners, Butternuts, we heard about the troops and what they are doing out there in the country. Three weeks ago they formed a sort of Cavalry to scout and roam through the countryside from volunteers from our regiment, about 50 or 60 men strong. This type of Cavalry has done much already in this short time. Among ourselves, we call them jokingly "The sore ass or Jackass Cavalry." Last Sunday, the 30th of last month, this Cavalry, with the aid of a part of the Infantry took 100 prisoners at Baird's Mill, 7 miles from Murfreesboro. A few hours later, this same Cavalry took another 12, 2 of the prisoners had crawled all the way up a chimney. As black as they were, they had to come down, if they didn't want to have bullets blown up their butt. Some of ours posed as rebels to the ladies in the houses, and this way, they found out something about the strength of the enemy and the thoughts of the dowagers and matrons. A wagon came in, loaded with pies, cornbread and other fresh food, in addition to clothes and boots and similar items. Fr. Schilling from our company brought the same with the rebel playing actors into the camp of Colonel Smith of the 16th Illinois Volunteers. The same gave a receipt for it and his compliments to the Guerrilla Morgan. This receipt was brought back by the driver who didn't know about it and as a result, the Guerrilla Morgan fled immediately. From Arkansas we hear news that General Curtis beat the rebels there in 2 battles. Many of the rebel troops in Virginia are fleeing and come over here into our lines. The main reason is lack of clothes. If the rebel army would know how bad they are off and how bad their clothes depots are, then most of them would run away, which in turn would prevent further bloodshed. Here with us we are also missing many things, especially socks. But one still helps as long as one can, and he who loves Freedom and the country does not care to complain.

Wednesday, Dec. 3, 1862 This noon we signed the payroll for two months. Why we didn't get our whole four month pay, I don't know, somewhere there must be a hidden hole in the sack. We are in debt because all prices are too high, and what remains is not worth to carry in the sack. Someone told me that the paymasters loan out the money for their own interest. O American humbug, it is your curse. A fatherly Government not only makes laws and regulations, it also ensures that the same are followed obediently. The 42nd Illinois volunteer was foraging today on the Harding Pike, about 12 miles from our camp location. The Pike carries the name of the estate, which belongs to Mr. Harding. The estate is 7 miles square, it contains the prettiest land you can see around Nashville. Mr. Harding used to be the Commanding Rebel General at Fort Donelson. After his capitulation, he was in Uncle Sam's care for 8 months in Alton. Then he took the oath and was released. Uncle Sam forages on his estate and will probably pay him for what he needs. This evening, Quartermaster Sam Hood and a Brigade quartermaster were taken prisoners by the Guerillas, as they sat at the table and wrote their receipts which they had received for the forage. They were careless and didn't protect the train in the rear, as is the regulation. Voila toutes.

Dec. 5, 1862 We foraged today on the Harding's farm on Harding Pike. The Harding name is in bold relief over the entrance to their mansion. We loaded by 900 wagons with hay. We were there to cover the trains of the 22nd Ill. Volunteers and the 19th Illinois, in addition to 2 canons and some cavalry. It snowed from early morning to noon uninterruptedly. It was very cold. In a short time, the snow was far and wide and every tree and bush was covered as with powdered sugar and full of cotton. Every tree in the forest and all branches had a white cap. We ourselves were covered in snow and crystallized as on New Years Day the large figures at the sugar bakers. There were pointed lips and ears, blue faces and cold feet. When we went home, the streets were dirty and slushy. We marched quickly home and the candles were already burning when we arrived. To the devil with all the foraging and war duty in and around Nashville. The movement of fresh troops did not make our service much easier.

120

Dec. 9, 1862 In the morning I received your December letter. No date is given. The Floraville post office says Dec. 4, 62. I am happy with the letter and will answer later. Every minute at the present strengthens my hours. We are packing our knapsacks, where to is unknown. I am sending two dollars for Christmas gifts for the two little ones. Greetings to you and everyone. I am in a hurry. Dec. 9, 2 o'clock in the afternoon.

Fast forward to 6/20/2004 when Grand DD and I were in Nashville, Tennessee. It was a Sunday afternoon so we visited a drugstore to look at local postcards for ideas on what sites we might visit. We chose the Belle Meade Plantation simply because it included the oldest and best preserved antebellum home in the area. We parked near the former slave quarters log cabin gatehouse and walked 100 yards to the mansion where I saw the Harding name over the entrance!!! I got goose bumps on top of goose bumps when I realized this is where my great great great uncle George Basler had foraged (aka stolen) 900 wagonloads of hay. I

apologized on his behalf to the young lady tour guide in period costume at the entrance. She said we should come back in two weeks for a Civil War reenactment followed by a Blue-Grey Ball. She also explained that Uncle George and friends had not been interested in their thoroughbred race horses 142 years earlier because they are too skittish for war horses. This visit was a real serendipity?

Fast forward again to 9/5/2014 when Grand DD and I were in Lexington, Virginia. Here are notes from my journal – After visiting Stonewall Jackson's home, Washington and Lee University and VMI, we walked next to Wolf and Company Antiques where I took a picture of a

painting by Isaac F. Eaton called "Foraging Party." It was painted in 1882 but the action it depicts happened in October 1863 at Baltimore, Virginia. It reminded me a lot of my great great great uncle George Basler doing the same thing during the Civil War prior to the Battle of Stones River in January 1863.

On the back of the painting is an extensive inscription which includes the mother's plea, "Leave enough for the baby and the cow." The painting is for sale at $3,500 in "as found" condition. There is damage above the second story window and to the right of that. Visit wolf@wolfandcompany.net.

Illinois Adjutant General's Report (Through the Battle of Stones River)

The Twenty-second Infantry Illinois Volunteers Regiment, 1st Division, 14th Corps was organized at Belleville, Illinois May 11, 1861 and was mustered into the United States service for three years at Caseyville, Illinois June 25, 1861 by Captain T. G. Pitcher, U.S.A.

On July 11, 1861 the Regiment moved to Bird's Point, Missouri. On November 7, seven companies engaged in the battle of Belmont – three being left to guard transports. Loss – 144 killed, wounded, and missing. *George Basler's letter dated 8/28/1887 says he was wounded on the right side of his face in this battle, probably by a bullet fragment.*

July 14, 1861 made a reconnaissance under General Grant into Kentucky in the rear of Columbus. The Twenty-second was on detached duty a great deal of the time, and not infrequently had single-handed engagements with the enemy.

On August 19, 1861 Colonel Dougherty with Companies A, B, C, D, and E attacked Colonel Hunter at Charleston, Missouri in the night and drove him from his camp to the town in a hand-to-hand fight, capturing many prisoners and horses. In this engagement the Twenty-second lost 1 killed and 11 wounded, including Colonel Dougherty whose shoulder was broken with the butt of a gun and Captain Johnson who received a gunshot through the right leg. After this engagement, the Regiment returned to Bird's Point.

Early in the spring of 1862 the Regiment left camp with one day's cooked rations to engage General Jeff Thompson who was known to be in the neighborhood in force. Coming up with him at Sikeston, a running fight ensued when he was driven to his fortifications at New Madrid. In this engagement the Twenty-second captured two guns and a few prisoners and returned to camp the third day without the loss of a man. *Sikeston is the future home of the Reiss Dairy.*

April 8, 1862 expedition to Tiptonville under General Paine to intercept retreating enemy from Island No. 10. Captured 4,000 prisoners, 2 generals, and a large quantity of stores, ammunition, arms, and guns.

May 3, 5, and 9, 1862 skirmished before Farmington and battle of Farmington.

The Regiment was engaged in the siege of Corinth and in pursuit of the enemy two weeks into June. The last day of the siege Captain Johnson was again wounded, receiving a gunshot through the head.

The Twenty-second was engaged guarding Memphis & Charleston Railroad until August 26, 1862 when it fell back to Nashville by forced marches, arriving September 11 where it remained the balance of the year. *This is when George's daily journal entries were written.*

After the return of the Regiment to Nashville, it was besieged in the city for months without receiving communication of any kind from the outside world and it was forced to send out foraging parties daily to obtain supplies.

December 31, 1862 and January 1 and 2, 1863 the Regiment was engaged in the Battle of Stones River near Murfreesboro, TN where it lost 199 out of 342 men going into action. Lieutenant Colonel Swanwick was wounded and taken prisoner and remained at Atlanta and Richmond (Libby) until May 1863. It is a singular fact that at the Battle of Stones River, every horse belonging to the Regiment including the Battery was wounded.

Here's part of the quartermaster's clothing issue for soldiers of the 22nd Illinois Infantry Regiment. I found it on eBay. It's for Company G in January 1864 but I'm sure it was the same for Uncle George's Company K in 1862. Soldiers had to rely on sutlers and camp followers for additional needs, laundry, etc. Pretty basic.

STATEMENT *exhibiting the allowance of Clothing to each sold. during his enlistment, and his proportion for each year respectivel. as established by the Secretary of War.*

CLOTHING.	FOR FIVE YEARS.					Total in the five years.
	1st.	2d.	3d.	4th.	5th.	
Hat, trimmed	1	1	1	1	1	5
Forage Cap	1	1	1	1	1	5
Uniform Coat or Jacket	1	1	1	1	1	5
Blue flannel Sack Coat	2	2	2	2	2	10
Trousers	3	2	3	2	3	13
Flannel Shirts	3	3	3	3	3	15
Flannel Drawers	3	2	2	2	2	11
Bootees, pairs	4	4	4	4	4	20
Stockings, pairs	4	4	4	4	4	20
Leather Stock	1	....	1	....	....	2
Great Coat	1	....	....	....	....	1
Stable Frock	1	....	1	....	....	2
Fatigue Overall	1	1	1	1	1	5
Blanket	1	....	1	....	....	2

January, 1864

Notes from George Basler's Civil War Pension File

1. He volunteered on June 11, 1861 to serve 3 years. He was born in Switzerland. He was age 36, height of 5' 5.5", fair complexion, brown hair, and brown eyes. His profession was teaching. *Since George was born on 7/24/1821, he must have fibbed about his age.*

2. His Casualty Sheet shows him wounded and taken prisoner on December 30, 1862 to January 3, 1863 which probably means an exchange of prisoners after four days. He was wounded in battle at Stones River, Tennessee near Murfreesboro.

3. His Certificate of Disability for Discharge reads, "Gun shot ball entering at joint of 4th toe passing diagonally through the foot emerging at tarso-metatarsal joint of the great toe and resulting in partial loss of use of foot. Disability one-third." He was discharged June 8, 1863 in Louisville, Kentucky and returned to Floraville, Illinois.

4. His pension was $4/month commencing June 8, 1863 on certificate #37842. In May 1870 at age 48 he applied for a pension of $8/month sighting extended disabilities. Request was denied. He was a resident then of Sullivan, Indiana and listed his trades as confectioner and school teacher.

5. On December 31, 1879 at age 58 and a resident at the National Military Home in Montgomery County, Ohio, he applied for a pension increase which was denied. Again on February 18, 1880 while still living at the National Military Home he applied for a pension increase which was denied. Another request on May 23, 1887 was denied. But another request on June 5, 1891 for the original gunshot wound plus an injury to the right hand for senility was approved to $12/month.

Will, Kayla, Ava, and Blake, can you imagine what our uncle endured – a failed marriage, loss of all three children, 1.5 years in a military tent, twice wounded in battle, never owning a house, 24 years in a veterans home, minimal pension, no estate, no grandchildren, a basic funeral, etc. But Uncle George does leave a legacy with his letters. It's obvious that he experienced significant European and American history. He was a free spirit, maybe too free.

Love, Granddad

Civil War – Charles Max Wittig with the 82nd Illinois Infantry Regiment

Dear Will, Kayla, Ava, and Blake,   February 2, 2015

Perhaps you remember this relative from my Granddad's Mondays story of 11/17/2014 which was largely Max's autobiography before and after the Civil War. It mentioned his immigration from Germany, his marriage to your great great great great aunt Kate Reiss, and their life together with five daughters in Davenport, Iowa. But that story did not include Max's military service because it's worthy of a story all by itself. Here it is in his own words.

Grand DD and I stayed for a week in north central Virginia last September specifically to round out this story by researching the Battle of Chancellorsville and other nearby Civil War sites. We had previously visited Wilson's Creek National Battlefield in Missouri which Max mentions below. This story today is about Max's double military service with the 1st Missouri Infantry Regiment and with the 82nd Illinois Infantry Regiment.

Charles M. Wittig Autobiography

I, John Charles Max Wittig, was born 16 day January year 1838 in Duchy of Coburg-Gotha, Thueringen, Germany. Was the 9th child to my parents, prominent citizen Johan George Wittig (occupation proprietor brewing – bakery in business) who was married to my mother about year 1820 Anna Barbara Brotzman, daughter of Burt Brotzman, rope manufacturer. Receiving education in public school until Easter Sunday 1851 confirmed.

Following tradition learning trade was sent to city Meingen to relatives, Mr. and Mrs. Grau, old lady a kin of Brotzman who died in December 1852. By will the property was left to daughter of Michael Grau, valued 5,000 thaler (*silver German coin*).

In spring 1853 Father concluded to emigrate with whole family to America starting month May to sail, leaving Coburg by mail coach to Gotha, taking railroad to Hamburg on the Elbe, on arrival meeting brother Adolph, clerk employed at iron works at Rendsburg, who helped arrangements in voyage ready to enter bark Magdalena Oldenburg, ship 2 masts, 80 passengers in all, a boat ready May 15th, 1853. Sail set crossing the Atlantic Ocean, 56 days made journey on 5th day July 1853 landed in quarantine Staten Island. A house was rented on 3rd Street, Avenue C, three rooms, Father, brother Herman, Emil and myself occupying 1 room, bedding on floor; the girls Augusta, Hildegard, Carolina, Clara, Anna in the other part of lodging. The girls soon finding employment sewing all by a furrier, later on millinery, clothing store.

Myself attending public school for six months, fatigue around passing time gathering coal and wood at ship yard on East River for home use. First job to strike was during recess of school, attending cigar store Ave. C near Houston Street, later on learning art of carving wood by John Albach (Broome and Mott St.) had joined Turnzogling (gymnastic school) Franz Zigel Turnwatt.

During month October 1855 Father, Anna and myself moved to St. Louis, Missouri with desire of my brothers Herman and Emil together to help support Father and youngest sister Anna.

October 21st, 1856 Father died. Disease was dysentery. Age 57 years. Buried Lutheran graveyard on Gravoy, Arsenal Street, brother Emil furnishing marble stone. Max made picket fence in memory his resting grave at St. Louis, Missouri. (*The St. Louis City Death Records 1850 – 1908 show a John George Wittig, born in Germany, died 10/27/1856, and buried in Holy Ghost Cemetery at 7153 Gravois.*)

With the death of Father (Mother died Aug. 1847 Coburg) orphan boy was left to paddle his own canoe for earning support. Brother Herman left St. Louis for Kansas, never to see him again. One meager report it was said he was killed in fight at Mountain Meadow in Mormon War, Utah 1860. Brother Emil, his health failing, ailment caused by hemp dust he was exposed to in working factory, had returned to New York City, sick.

I was placed in trade to learn to build wagons by William Dresher on 8th and Franklin, binding myself three years faithful service. With springtime St. Luis became disturbed rebellion state of Missouri, on secession question. April 21, 1861 the St. Louis Turner 10th and Market St. suspending the organization in order to enlist, forming 3 full companies responding to the call made by President Abraham Lincoln for defense to save the Union of America suppress the conflict by enforcing law of U. S. Constitution protecting government property defending flag U.S. America.

==April 23rd, 1861 was enrolled Private Comp. B, First Regiment Missouri Volunteers to serve 90 days.== The First Regiment Missouri Infantry was commanded by Capt. Nathaniel Lyon. The government treasury unable to supply clothing, uniform and substance, we paid out of our own pockets during term military service. Pay received for said service Sept. 18th was no coin money received. The first series of greenback (claim gold) repudiated money of value! Was about all compensation from government.

August 10 – Gen. Nath. Lyon, U.S. Army Southwest unable to get reinforcement, refused by order of Gen. John Fremont in command at St. Louis, concluded to attack the Rebel force of 30,000 men at Wilson's Creek 10 miles S. W. Springfield with our force, in all 5,000 men to fight, gaining our honest retreat and safe return to St. Louis. Casualty during action lasting from daybreak till noon, about ten o'clock occurred the death of Nat. Lyon. Also at eleven-thirty, death and killing of color guard 7 men, members of Co. C, by 1st shot fired at close of battle, by the Rebels with a captured piece of canon of Sigel Battery with ammunition done job. Wounded: Adolph Fisher, Matthes Muller, Max Wittig, J. T. Minzmeier.

August 21, camping at Rolla, received $10.

August 27, camping at St. Louis, College Hill, North St. Louis. It was a pitiful sight for us heroes reception, with sunburned faces, dirty rags of clothes, marching from Union Depot on 14th St. to Market, down to Broadway Court House, up to Bremen N. St. Louis, later pitching tents on College Hill Ground, N. Park called Camp Schofield where the Regiment Organization during month being organized into artillery of First Missouri Light Artillery; forming three batteries fit for duty, sent to the front, left St. Luis during September on the 17th day while resting in line, draw ration, close to fireplace (three sticks cordwood with two camp kettles on) had slipping, had my feet scalded and by order of Florence Cornyn, surgeon, forwarded to my boardinghouse at Schnider Hotel for treatment. No hospital. Paid expense boarding. Having faithfully served during the campaign military service to U. S. government without receiving any compensation; spending my own money for necessary during sickness for clothes, board, medical aid while incapacitated and unfit for duty besides suffering ailments from wound by a ball arrested in turnbuckle of my cap during action August 10 battle at Wilson's Creek. Exposure unlimited for common men endure resulted besides injuries, diseases typhoid, malaria without any aid of Company official, was left deserted. Crisis followed consequence.

While sick suffering injuries, unable to appear date Sept. 30, 1861 for mustering, my name not been taken up in other Company, not having received my discharge, no pay or settlement, while at home having paid expenses own pocket till stranded, was ordered out on the street unable to pay board, the poor orphan boy without friends asking charity was forced to depart from St. Louis under military martial law authority. Landed crossing Mississippi River, moved into Illinois, St. Clair County, arriving month Nov. by relative farmer George Geyer, Scotch Hill (*could be Dutch Hill*). Stayed at his home until March, leaving for St. Louis. To Fritz Beinert for short time. Steamboats had commenced open traveling. While convalescent and recommended by physician order to recover by change of climate, took passage up the river to Muscatine. Stayed during month at the home of Mr. Gottfried Aumiller, entered in order to follow up to St. Paul or New Ulm, Minn. No show for employment to earn support, on return stopped at La Crosse, Wis. Intended going to New York to my sister. Only succeeded to Chicago. There the 13th day August 1862 re-enlisted U. S. Army as private in Comp. B of 82nd Illinois Regiment of Infantry.

In order not to be deemed a deserter, had re-enlisted August 16, leaving Chicago with Capt. August Bruning to Camp Butler, Springfield, waiting order to Washington, D.C. Pitched camp on Arlington Heights opposite capitol, Wash., D.C. Dec. 8th marched to Alexandria, Va. Dec. 10th camping at Dumfries, drawing of rations 5 days, Fairfax Court House, Va. Dec. 12 – 15 at Stafford Court House, Va. during battle at Fredericksburg. Later tenting on Aquia Creek until order Jan. 1863 Gen. Burnside. Flanking march onto Kelley Ford, mud with blizzard made the memorable sticking in mud campaign. Winter quarters Stafford on Potomac Creek until April 30 while the whole people observing prayer, our column moved to Germania Ford, Culpepper, Chancellorsville. On picket 16 hours right in Wilderness April 30. Wilderness Church in camp.

May 2 evening about 6 o'clock attack by Rebel Gen. Stonewall Jackson. Co. B army flanking 11th Corps Army Potomac during action resisting advances 3 divisions. Received gunshot wound to left ankle, laying 16 days disabled without attendant or food. In this battle my tentmate William Berger, Cook County, Illinois, instantly killed. May 14 transported. . . . . . .

Memoranda of a Pioneer Citizen
Chas. M. Wittig
2322 Farnam Street
Davenport, Iowa

1838   Born January 16, 1838 in Duchy of Coburg-Gotha, Thueringen, Saxony, Germany

1853   Year 1853 the family emigrated. Landed at New York date opening Worlds Fair.

1856 Father died St. Louis, Missouri, month November

1861 Responded to President's Call to Arms Order to suppress rebellion. ==Enrolled private in Company B, Regiment Missouri Infantry Volunteers.==

    May 10 Captured Camp Jackson, St. Louis
    June 12 Captured state capital, Jefferson City
    June 17 Skirmish Booneville, Missouri
    August 10 Battle Wilson's Creek, Springfield, Missouri
    August 29 Returned St. Louis great pain, sick, wounded, unfit for duty
    September 20 Sent home, no hospital
    September 30 Not present for mustering, was not transferred any company. Not being discharged until act Congress of Febr. 13, 1891.

1862 ==Aug 1862 had re-enlisted Private Company B, 82nd Regiment Illinois Infantry Volunteers==

1863 Wounded during action Battle of Chancellorsville, Virginia May 2nd, 1863. Total disabled gunshot wound left ankle.

1864 Was discharged hospital New York

1865 Came home Davenport, Iowa

1866 Married Miss Kate Reiss, Belleville

1885 Built house on 321 E. 4th Street, worked in the wagon trade.

Civil War Record by Chas. M. Wittig of Davenport, Iowa

Born in Germany, Jan. 16, 1838. Landed in NY in 1853. Went to City of St. Louis and was wagon maker. Member Turn Verein (*gymnastics organization*).

In response to Pres. Lincoln's first call for 75,000 men, he ==enlisted April 23, 1861 in Company B, First Regiment Missouri Volunteers,== under Col. Frank P. Blair. Was with Gen. Nath. Lyon in Missouri. Was transferred June 10, 1861 to Company C, First Missouri Artillery (same rgmt.). Was in constant service in Gen. Lyon's campaign restoring State of Missouri to the Union.

By reason of injuries, wounds, and disease was at home sick and was unable to report on re-organization of regiment Sept. 30, 1861. After that was honorably discharged from that service by Act of Congress Feby. 13, 1891.

==Enlisted again in August 1862 as a private in Company B, Eighty-second Illinois Infantry.== Was wounded May 2, 1863 at the Battle of Chancellorsville, Va. from the effects of which he has always been disabled. Was inmate of different hospitals till Sept. 1864 when he was discharged as "Unfit for any duty in the military service of the United States."

Had pension granted June 9, 1865, Certificate No. 43703. Pension increased January 3rd, 1898 allowing $17 per month, being the limit allowed for the gunshot wound in the left ankle.

Mr. Wittig claims that for disabilities and sickness resulting from his first service in Missouri, the most severe service he had, he has no consideration. According to General Order No. 15 of the Secretary of War, dated May 4th, 1861, making allowance for said service of those that responded to the President's call for 75,000 men, dated May 3rd, 1861.

In Mr. Wittig's present condition, owing to his age and disability resulting from wounds and service in the United States Army, he is incapacitated to perform any manual labor. This disability is certainly equivalent to the loss of a hand or foot. He has made application for pension on account of such disability and for his Missouri service and the same was rejected in the year 1894. Any further information to make this application successful will be cheerfully furnished.   Signed: Charles M. Wittig, 327 East 4th Street, Davenport, Iowa

82nd Illinois Infantry
Regiment History
Adjutant General's Report (excerpt)

Under General Oliver Otis Howard's command of the 11th Corps, the 82nd moved from Stafford Court House on April 27 and marched towards Chancellorville. By the morning of April 30, they had formed a line of battle along the Fredricksburg Pike. On the morning of May 1, small rifle pits were dug and barricades made. At noon May 2, the Regiment was placed in position, facing south, in the second line of battle with the 157th New York. About five o'clock p.m., the enemy attacked from the west which routed and drove several units to the rear. The second line, comprising the 82nd Illinois and the New York Regiment, held the enemy in check until a new line was formed to their rear, when it fell back about fifteen yards, leaving seventy killed and wounded on the ground it had occupied. The losses of the 82nd, before it re-joined the Brigade, were 156 killed or wounded including 7 commissioned officers.

The 82nd participated in the engagement on May 4, and then returned to camp Stafford Court House, where it had a much needed rest until June 12, when it moved on the Gettysburg campaign.

Civil War Record of Charles Max Wittig

- Private Charles Wittig enlisted on August 13, 1862 in Chicago. He was born in Germany. His age is 24, height is 5' 2.5", fair complexion, blue eyes, light hair, and profession of wagon maker. Actual muster-in date is September 26, 1862 at Camp Butler, Illinois.

- Memorandum from Prisoner of War Records shows him captured at Chancellorsville, Virginia on May 3, 1863 and paroled for medical attention on May 15 with a gunshot wound to the left ankle. He was admitted to the camp hospital and then sent to

Washington, D.C. (*Max's wound was treated by a Confederate doctor before he was exchanged 12 days later for Confederate prisoners held by the Union.*)

- Letter from Charles Max Wittig dated June 24, 1864 to Assistant Surgeon Samuel A. Stornow at the Filbert Street Hospital in Philadelphia stating, "I have the honor to request a transfer to New York City or to my State which is Illinois. I have been in this hospital for ten months having received a severe wound at the Battle of Chancellorsville. I have some relatives in New York, also in Illinois, and as it has been some time since I have seen any of them, I would respectfully request a transfer to either place. Signed Chas. M. Wittig."

- A Certificate of Disability for Discharge shows Max Wittig at the U.S.A. General Hospital in Central Park, New York on September 18, 1864 with a "false inchylosis of the left ankle joint the result of a gunshot wound received at the Battle of Chancellorsville May 2, 1863. He is unfit for the Veteran Reserve Corps. Degree of disability – one-third."

- Company Muster Roll for September and October 1864 states, "Discharged for disability caused by wounds, in Central Park Hospital, New York City, September 21, 1864 by and of Major General Dix."

- There is a memo dated March 2, 1891 from the War Department Record and Pension Division stating under Previous Action: "While a deserter from Company C, 1st Missouri Volunteers where he served under the name of Max Wittig, he enlisted in this organization (Illinois 82nd) in violation of the 22nd Article of War. Date - November 2, 1883. Under Present Action: "The preceding notation of November 2, 1883 is cancelled."

- Charles M. Wittig was granted US Citizenship on November 7, 1864 by the County Court of St. Clair County, Illinois.

I took this picture below last September. It shows where Max was camped with his 82nd Illinois Regiment. The Wilderness Church is just out of the picture to the right. The Fredericksburg Pike is just behind me to the south which is the direction from which General O. O. Howard, who commanded the Union's 11th Corps, expected Generals Robert E. Lee and Stonewall Jackson to attack.

Despite orders from his superior General Hooker, General Howard had failed to protect his west flank from possible attack. It was all a heavy woods called The Wilderness. As you can see in the next three battle maps, that failure by O. O. Howard to protect his west flank, resulted in a Confederate victory even though the North outnumbered the South by more than two to one. Chancellorsville has been called as Robert E. Lee's greatest victory. It caused General O. O. Howard to be nicknamed "Oh Oh" Howard.

The May 1 map below shows 120,000 Union troops in blue and 60,000 Confederate troops in red. The city of Fredericksburg is to the right. The one-house "village" of Chancellorsville is an inch below the name "Hooker" at left center. The May 2 map shows Stonewall Jackson making a daring 12-mile left flank maneuver with 28,000 men to surprise General Howard from the west.

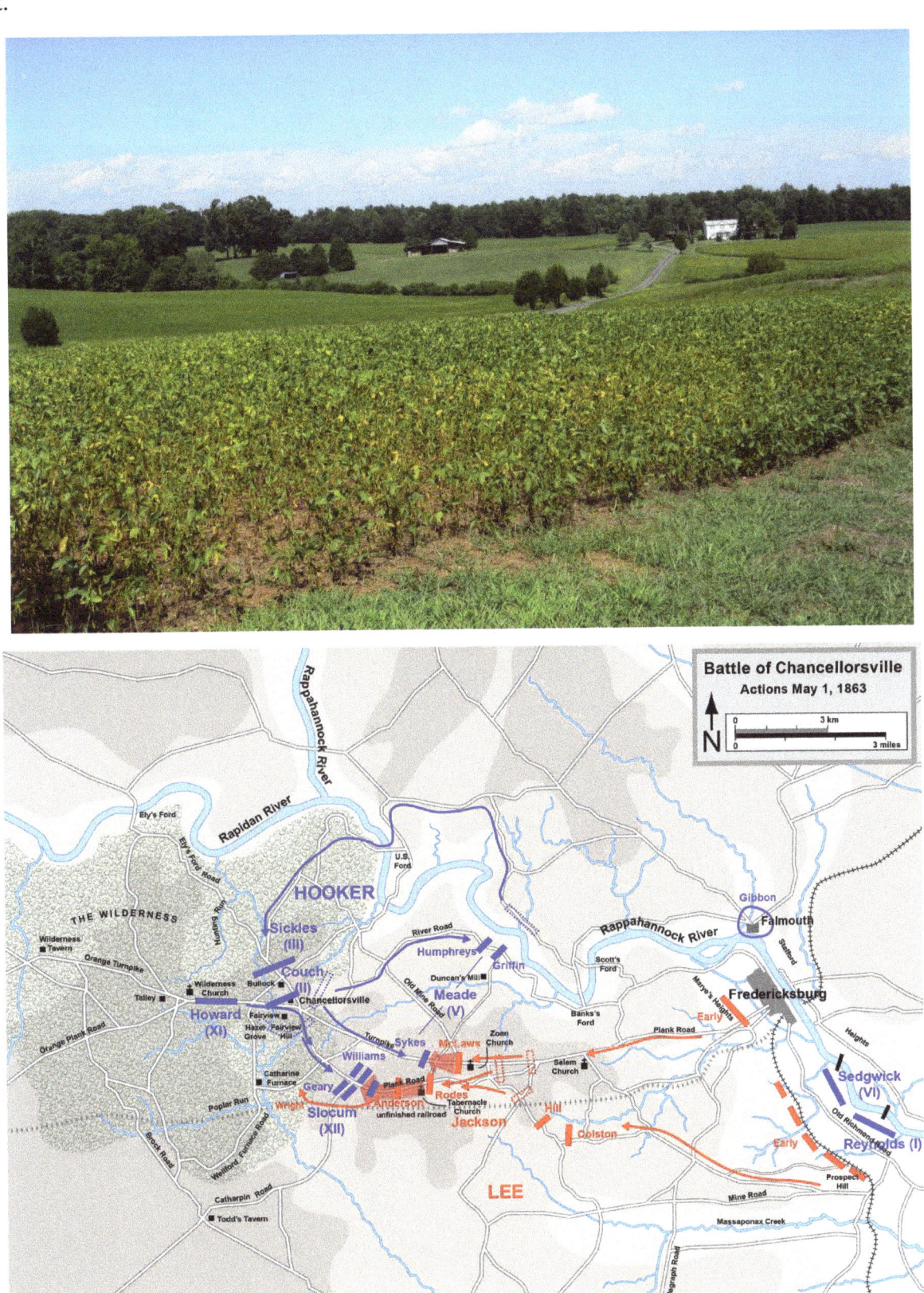

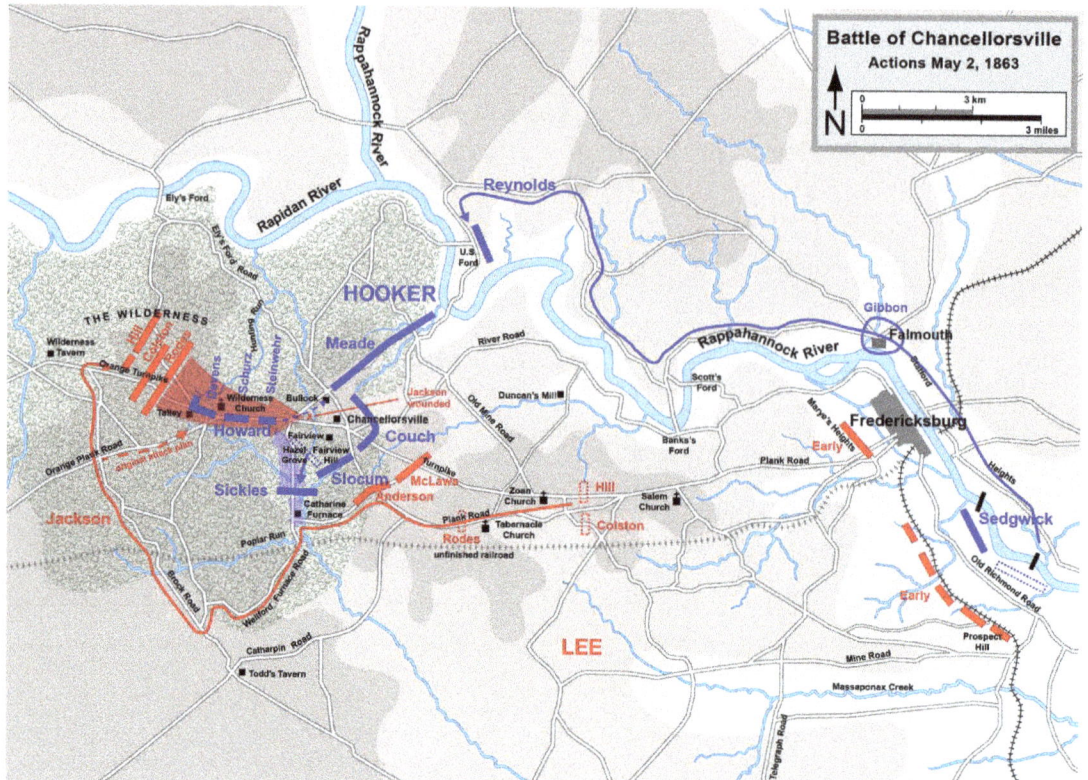

Below is an enlarged view of Jackson's attack from the west. You can see the Wilderness Church just below the point of the arrow. A bit further left you can see the original positions of the 157th New York and 82nd Illinois. The Union soldiers had stacked their rifles and were preparing to eat supper as dusk was approaching. All of a sudden there was a rush of wildlife running through camp from the west which was immediately followed by Rebel yells and panic amongst Union ranks. The Rebels had caught the Union totally by surprise. Max Wittig defended his new position as best he could despite being wounded in the left ankle.

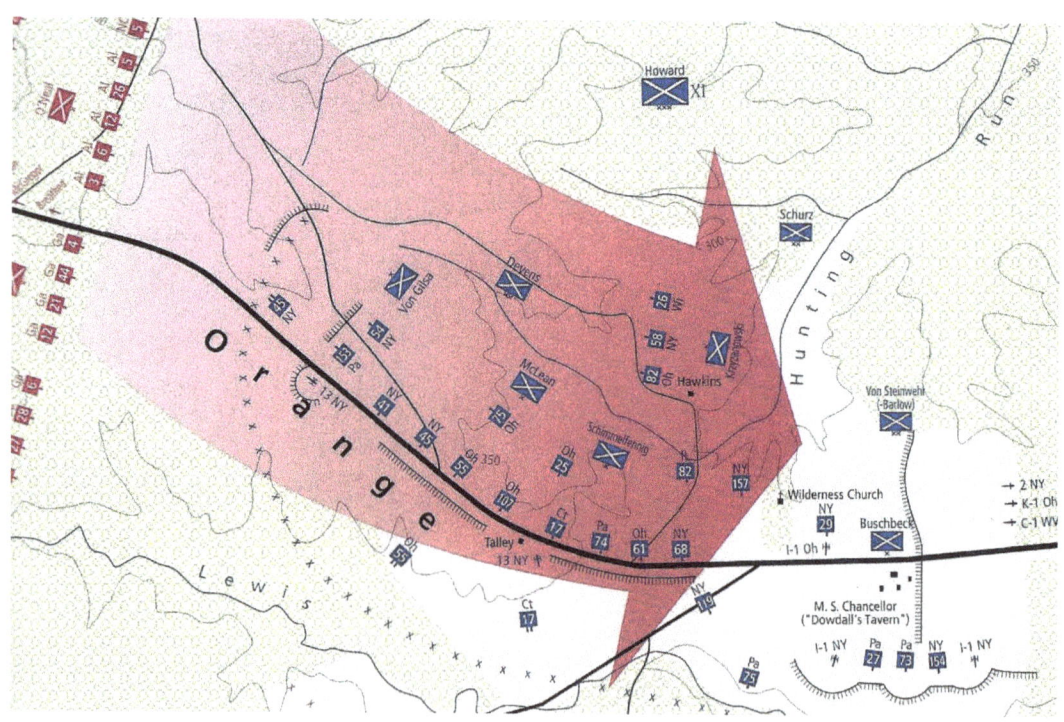

If it's any consolation, Stonewall Jackson was accidentally wounded by his own troops about 10:30 that evening as he was reconnoitering on horseback. His arm was amputated to save his life but he died anyway a week later of pneumonia. General O. O. Howard also made mistakes at Gettysburg a month later but he improved his reputation with later battles in the Civil War. He went on to found Howard University in Washington, DC and Lincoln Memorial University in northeastern Tennessee. He was eventually awarded the Congressional Medal of Honor.

I just finished reading an excellent book, <u>Yankee Dutchmen under Fire, Civil War Letters from the 82nd Illinois Infantry</u> by Joseph R. Reinhart. He mentions the formation of the 82nd at Camp Butler near Springfield, how the unit was predominately German immigrants, how they were frustrated being treated as second-class citizens, and how they were eventually very proud of their service during that war. Here is one of Reinhart's summary statements: "The 82nd Illinois and other German regiments succeeded in raising awareness of German participation and sacrifice in the Civil War well beyond the level that would have been achieved if their members had been scattered in Anglo-American-dominated units."

Will, Kayla, Ava, and Blake, I'll contact Joseph Reinhart shortly and make sure he is aware of Max Wittig's 22 Civil War letters about the 82nd Regiment as well as the 278 Wittig family letters which appear in our book, <u>It Takes A Matriarch</u>. We should all be very proud of our Uncle Max. He served in Missouri and Illinois infantry regiments and was twice wounded. We are blessed with his service and with his writings.

Love, Granddad

Charles Max Wittig at Lincoln's First Thanksgiving (1863)

Dear Will and Kayla,   November 26, 2012

Thanks for coming home this week to celebrate Thanksgiving on Thursday which was the fourth Thursday of November. We all ate too much thanks to the excellent cooks in our family. What was your favorite dish? Did you know that Thanksgiving was celebrated on the last Thursday of November until President Franklin Roosevelt changed it to the fourth Thursday in 1939? But when November has only four Thursdays, the fourth and the last Thursdays are the same date.

President Abraham Lincoln formalized Thanksgiving around the last Thursday in November in his 1863 proclamation below. Here is brief mention of it in a letter from your great great great great uncle, Charles Max Wittig, in his letter dated November 27, 1863 (149 years ago tomorrow). He was writing to his future brother-in-law, Frank Reiss, who is your great great great grandfather whose picture in my den. Max was in a military hospital in Philadelphia, recovering from a gunshot wound to his ankle at the Battle of Chancellorsville, Virginia on 5/2/1863 during the Civil War. His wound was extremely slow to heal properly so Max was in hospitals in Philadelphia and New York for 16.5 months. Here is Max's letter dated 11/27/1863 from the Philadelphia hospital, originally written in German, and then translated to English. It's in our book called It Takes A Matriarch.

Dear friend Franz!

I want to address these few lines to you to give you an opportunity to send me soon again a few words. Even though it is very enjoyable for me to correspond with your sister Catharina (*Max's future wife*) who took over since you don't have time to write, but I am at the end without wanting to fall out of her favor, according to her last report she wrote probably while I was in New York. From the 26th of October until the 15th of November I was in New York on leave "on general expenses." This means the trip to and from was free. It was for the New Yorkers so they could vote at home but I was not able to stay there. I won't be able to get to Illinois either for New Years, but we want to hope that we can get together by Easter or Whitsuntide, maybe at your wedding. You just have to think about the old proverb which fits for us soldiers: "Der Mensch denkt, Gott lenkt" or "Eile mit Weile". ("*Man thinks, God directs" or "More haste, less speed*"). So you can imagine yourself how things are here.

As a friend you have to make excuses for my negligence to your sister Catharina. I would have written her a long time ago if I would not have always thought that we would leave here, and for that reason I wanted to wait until I was certain where we would be going to. I was sorry but one can't make a permanent union with fate, one must take heart.

That my foot is on the way of getting better. You can believe when I tell you that I was in the gym here for the Thanksgiving Day Party* without crutches just with a cane, but dancing wasn't that great yet, more the eating and drinking. The New York excursion cured my foot the best, he liked to ride on the train and on the bus. As soon as the bullet can be cut out, the foot will be as good as before, since the bone was not hurt even though I have suffered some pain like an old horse. My greetings to all acquaintances and friends, your parents and siblings and I wish that you may spend the holidays healthy and happy. Greetings from your friend,

Max

*Lincoln's 1863 Thanksgiving Proclamation

Lincoln's Thanksgiving Proclamation that follows is taken from the collection of Lincoln's papers in the Library of America series, Vol II, pp. 520-521.

The year that is drawing towards its close, has been filled with the blessings of fruitful fields and healthful skies. To these bounties, which are so constantly enjoyed that we are prone to forget the source from which they come, others have been added, which are of so extraordinary a nature, that they cannot fail to penetrate and soften even the heart which is habitually insensible to the ever watchful providence of Almighty God. In the midst of a civil war of unequalled magnitude and severity, which has sometimes seemed to foreign States to invite and to provoke their aggression, peace has been preserved with all nations, order has been maintained, the laws have been respected and obeyed, and harmony has prevailed everywhere except in the theatre of military conflict; while that theatre has been greatly contracted by the advancing armies and navies of the Union. Needful diversions of wealth and of strength from the fields of peaceful industry to the national defense, have not arrested the plough, the shuttle, or the ship; the axe had enlarged the borders of our settlements, and the mines, as well of iron and coal as of the precious metals, have yielded even more abundantly than heretofore. Population has steadily increased, notwithstanding the waste that has been made in the camp, the siege and the battle-field; and the country, rejoicing in the consciousness of augmented strength and vigor, is permitted to expect continuance of years with large increase of freedom.

No human counsel hath devised nor hath any mortal hand worked out these great things. They are the gracious gifts of the Most High God, who, while dealing with us in anger for our sins, hath nevertheless remembered mercy. It has seemed to me fit and proper that they should be solemnly, reverently and gratefully acknowledged as with one heart and voice by the whole American People. I do therefore invite my fellow citizens in every part of the United States, and also those who are at sea and those who are sojourning in foreign lands, to set apart and observe the last Thursday of November next, as a day of Thanksgiving and Praise to our beneficent Father who dwelleth in the Heavens. And I recommend to them that while offering up the ascriptions justly due to Him for such singular deliverances and blessings, they do also, with humble penitence for our national perverseness and disobedience, commend to his tender care all those who have become widows, orphans, mourners or sufferers in the lamentable civil strife in which we are unavoidably engaged, and fervently implore the interposition of the Almighty Hand to heal the wounds of the nation and to restore it as soon as may be consistent with the Divine purposes to the full enjoyment of peace, harmony, tranquility and Union.

Abraham Lincoln

I don't know about you, Will and Kayla, but I'm hungry all over again after reading this long letter and proclamation. Help yourselves to some more turkey, sweet potatoes, and a few Thanksgiving cookies for a snack.

Love, Granddad

Civil War – John Reiss with the 43rd Illinois Infantry Regiment

Dear Will, Kayla, Ava, and Blake,   February 16, 2015

John Reiss was born on 12/11/1838 to Adam Reiss and his first wife Mary who did not survive that delivery. Almost two years later on 9/10/1840 Adam married Margaret Basler as his second wife. They had five more children who were half-siblings to John. The oldest of those was Frank who was also a Civil War veteran with the 31st Illinois Infantry Regiment.

John married Maria Josephine Gass on 10/22/1861 in Paderborn. They relocated to Belleville where John worked as a cobbler making shoes for John Birnstreib. The Reiss' daughter Louisa arrived on 7/31/1862 followed by another daughter Mary on 12/23/1863 as a Christmas present. But then John was drafted into the Union Army as a replacement soldier on 9/20/1864.

The 43rd Illinois Infantry Regiment Volunteers was organized at Camp Butler near Springfield, Illinois in September 1861 for a three-year enlistment. It was mustered into service on 10/12/1861.

Fast forward to 9/10/1863 when the 43rd Illinois was part of the Union Army which captured Little Rock, Arkansas. Little Rock was the capital of Arkansas but still a small town of less than 4,000 people. Folks there knew their days were numbered after Vicksburg, Mississippi had fallen to General Grant on 7/4/1863. The Union Army used Little Rock as a base for the next year to harass and engage Confederate units in southern Arkansas through the end of the war.

The 43rd Illinois remained in Little Rock until their original three-year enlistment expired. Not quite three-fourths of those veterans however re-enlisted in continuing service before their commander Colonel Engelmann retired on 12/16/1864. He had succeeded in prevailing on the Illinois authorities to assign a sufficient number of drafted men to the 43rd Illinois so that Lieutenant Colonel Dengler could be promoted as Engelmann's replacement.

One of those replacement soldiers was John Reiss who was drafted as a substitute soldier and mustered into service on 9/20/1864 in Company H in Little Rock. His company was later consolidated into Company E. John was mustered out on July 6, 1865 so he served about 9.5 months in an army of occupation. Military records show him with blue eyes, light hair, fair complexion, and height 5' 8", and rank of private. His pension certificate number is 651504. His widow's pension certificate number is 877316.

The 43rd Illinois remained in Little Rock until 11/30/1865 when it mustered out and returned to Camp Butler for final pay and discharge 12/14/1865.

John returned to Belleville, his wife and two daughters, and his job as a cobbler. Eight more children arrived in the next 18 years – Emma on 4/30/1867, George in 1869 who died on 5/13/1888 at age 19, Katherine on 9/30/1871, John on 11/28/1873, Barbara on 1/31/1875, Charles in 1877 who died on 5/17/1888 at age 11, Josephine on 6/12/1881 who died on 5/13/1888 at age 7, and Anna in 1883 who died on 5/10/1888 at age 5.

The **1870 Census** shows John age 30 working as a boot and shoe maker living in Belleville. The **1880 Census** shows John age 42 working as a coal miner. The **1890 Belleville City Directory** shows John working as a shoemaker for L. A. Vogel at 126 East Main Street and living at 120 South Church Street. The **1900 Census** shows John Reiss age 61 working as a shoemaker. The **1910 Census** shows John age 71 working as a shoemaker and married 49 years. John died on 6/18/1919. The **1920 Census** shows John's widow Maria Josephine age 75 living with daughters Barbara Reiss and Louise (and George) <u>Meehling</u> on South Church Street in Belleville. She died shortly thereafter on 12/2/1920. Both are buried in a family plot in Walnut Hill Cemetery in Belleville.

Will, Kayla, Ava, and Blake, this is the headstone in the John Reiss family plot in Walnut Hill Cemetery in Belleville. My second cousins Wendy Reiss George and Roya Reiss Singleton (with camera) and I visited a dozen or more family stones during our 2009 family reunion at the Sportsmen's Club which celebrated 175 years in Illinois. We couldn't find two stones which should have been there so I later contacted the cemetery office. They determined the stones had been covered over by creeping grass and did an appropriate trim.

It looks like Uncle John Reiss had a fairly safe job during his service in the Civil War. Perhaps he never fired his rifle in anger. But look at what happened to his family of ten children. Four of them died of cholera in one week in May 1888, two on the same day. My heart aches for what John, his wife, and their six other children endured.

Love, Granddad

Civil War – Frank Reiss with the 31st Illinois Infantry Regiment

Dear Will, Kayla, Ava, and Blake,   February 16, 2015

This is the only picture I have of your great great great grandfather Frank Reiss without a beard. Pretty handsome guy, don't ya think? He was born on 9/27/1841 so this picture was definitely taken before he was drafted into the 31st Illinois Infantry Regiment on 12/2/1864 at age 23.

Here is a letter which Frank's youngest brother Martin Reiss written in phonetic English to his middle brother Charles Reiss on 1/5/1865 regarding Frank being drafted. Martin believed, as many others did, that a disproportionate number of German immigrants were being drafted into the Civil War. Martin calls them Duchman but the correct spelling would be "Deutsch man."

Mattoon, Ills.
Thursday Night Jan. 5th, 1865

Dear Brother (*Charles*),

Yours came to hand today this morning. I have been looking for it for some time. I have been in Indiana sins you got my last letter. I left here last Monday a week. I got back Tuesday night last. The first place I went to when I got back was to the Post Office as I thought I had about 6 letters there. But there was only one & that was from St. Louis from a fellow in the shop where Joseph Stein used to work. But that did not sattisfie me as I wanted one from you or Frank to hear the news from Frank. But when it came from you, I did not like it at all. Poor brother Frank. I would have rather lost a finger from my right hand than to see him go to this damd war. God bless & protect him for this year.

Chas, you say you wished the Yankees was in Hell. I think you are now seeing the evils of the Republican Party which I have told you last fall & begin to think that I was right. I have seen enough of this war sins the last two years part. I say every German man is a damd fool if he joyns this war unless he is drafted into it & bount to go. I do not care where you go it is always the handy word, dam Duchman. They want alone the Duchman to have the upper hand in this damd war or any other place. Look at Sigel he was a good general but because he was a Duchman he had to be knocked out of his office & that is always the case. & after the war is over, the Duchman's will get there asses kicked so bad that they can't help themselves & the Irish the same way.

It's only the blue belly Yankees that will have the name, but the Duchman has to fight it out. The Germans are getting there back part kicked now but they are to blind to see it. I have made up my mind to do as it sais in a Sutten song – it sais so let the conscribt come when it will. I will be gry & happy. I still – I am very sorry for Frank but it is no use to gry after spiling milk – I would die right here before I shoulder a musket for Old Abe or the Negros.

I am a Democrat & will live to die as one. & you will see that this country will be ruined as long as the Republican Party has the upper hand. Let a good loyal Democrat get in as President & we will see peace & happy days but not before the Republican Party was the ruination of America.

I could not enjoy myself any in dinner as I could not get Frank out of my mind. I always keep thinking of you at home & special of Frank & Mother. I reckon it gose very hard with her to see Frank go.

Well it is 10 o'clock & I have to write to Kate yet before I go to bed. Let me here from you soon as soon as possible. Give my love to Mother & all.

Your true loving Brother,

Martin

Here is the Illinois Adjutant General's Report published in 1902 for the 31st Illinois after Frank Reiss joined them in Savannah, Georgia. Frank participated in all these activities in the next paragraph and the two-day Grand Review celebration parade through downtown Washington, DC on 5/23-4/1865. In October 2011 Grand DD and I visited Beaufort, SC and then followed the route the 31st Illinois took through South and North Carolina before we returned home to Peoria.

On the 4th of January 1865 the Thirty-first bade farewell to Savannah and shipped on the steamer Harvest Moon, and after the novel experience and sights of a sea voyage, disembarked at Beaufort, South Carolina where it remained, enjoying the luxury of fresh oysters at low prices, until the 13th. To this succeeded some skirmishing at Fort Pocotaligo – "Poke-'em-till-they-go" as the men called it which was evacuated by the enemy. On the 30th of January the march began through the Carolinas by way of Salkahatchie, Orangeburg – which was captured after some fighting by the Regiment's skirmishers, Columbia – scourged by destroying flames – Winsborough, Cheraw, Fayetteville – captured by foragers – and Bentonville – scenes of the last great struggle of Johnston's army, and the Regiment came out of the swamps, out of the pine forests, "out of the wilderness", the men ragged, dirty, many of them barefooted, to Goldsborough, North Carolina, where it arrived the 24th of March 1865, and where letters from home and news from the world were received. These and the prospects of the nearing of the end were cheering and refreshing to the men who for 54 days had been without communication with home or the world, and were weary with long marching and fighting.

On the 14th of April 1865 the Regiment was with the army at Raleigh, North Carolina. Signs of the ruin of the Confederacy and the dispersion of its armed forces were apparent on every hand. Soon came the surrender of Johnson's army – the only force which could oppose the onward march of the Union troops to Richmond, and the Regiment formed a part of the host to which that army surrendered.

140

On the 9th of May the Regiment was at Richmond, on the 19th at Alexandria, and on the 24th of May, with faded and tattered uniforms but with martial step and bearing, in the column of company, eyes front, it marched through the principal avenues of the capital, in the ==Grand Review== of the returning armies in presence of the great leaders, civil and military, of the republic – the most magnificent and imposing spectacle ever witnessed by the city of Washington. The end had been attained!

Soon afterwards the Regiment was moved to Louisville, Kentucky arriving at the place on the 11th of June where it was assigned to provost guard duty. On the 19th of July 1865, it was mustered out of the service by Lieutenant Aug. P. Noyes, A. C. M. 3rd Division, 17th Corps. It was then moved to Springfield, Illinois where it arrived on the 23rd of July 1865, and there on the 31st of the same month, the men received their final discharge and separated for their homes – those who were left of them.

At the time of the discharge there were present 25 officers and 677 enlisted men. When first organized the Regiment numbered 1,130 men. It had recruited 700. The casualties including men discharged before final muster-out, amounted to 1,128. In the course of its existence the Regiment had been commanded by four Colonels, and had had five Lieutenant Colonels and six Majors. Of the 25 officers discharged at the final muster-out, all save the chaplain had risen from the ranks.

In the campaigns of Sherman this Regiment had marched 2,076 miles. This part of its history is included in that of the Brigade to which it belonged – the 1st Brigade, 3rd Division, 17 Corps, Army of Tennessee. The Regiment marched 2,000 miles under Grant, and on expeditions other than those of Sherman. It served in the hostile States of Missouri, Kentucky, Tennessee, Mississippi, Louisiana, Georgia, Alabama, North Carolina, South Carolina, and Virginia. Before January 1, 1863 the history of the Regiment is comprised in that of the 1st Brigade, 3rd Division, Reserve Army of Tennessee.

Always efficiently commanded and evincing soldierly qualities in its first battle, the Regiment became in the days of its "veteran" existence, one of the best drilled in the service. It was, while encamped at Black River, Mississippi, after the Vicksburg Campaigns, that the Regiment under the skillful management of Lieutenant Colonel Pearson, attained that high degree of discipline and proficiency in drill for which it became known, and towards which it had been directed, under Logan and White, in the earlier days of the war. The latter fell at Donelson and deserved the title "The bravest of the brave".

Colonel Pearson had seen service under General Prentiss before the organization of this Regiment and early showed an aptitude for tactics and drill which made him a favorite with the field and staff, while his soldierly qualities displayed at Henry and Donelson endeared him to the rank and file. Hence he rapidly rose from the ranks being promoted to Commissary Sergeant March 1, 1862; to Adjutant May 16, 1862; to Major February 4, 1863 by unanimous vote of the officers; to Lieutenant Colonel July 1, 1863; and to Colonel September 26, 1864. On the 13th of March 1865, he was brevetted Brigadier General of Volunteers for gallantry during the war.

Many of the officers and soldiers of the Regiment deserve special mention and lasting remembrance, but the space allotted forbids a more extended account. To some of the men were awarded medals for gallantry, among them Sergeant George W. White of Company C who, severely wounded in the battle of Atlanta July 22, 1864, resolutely and persistently refused to be carried to the rear.

The fighting qualities of this Regiment were displayed in 14 battles and 25 skirmished of various degrees of importance. It witnessed the surrender of Buckner and the garrison at Donelson, the capitulation of Pemberton and his army at Vicksburg, the humiliation of Johnson and his force at Bentonville, and their final surrender near Raleigh. And a brilliant gem in its crown of glory is the fact of its organization as a "veteran" Regiment at a time when the Union cause stood so much in need of trained and tried soldiers to complete the overthrow of armed rebellion and to establish upon the ruins of anarchy and slavery, "a government of the people, by the people, for the people."

Here are notes from Frank's pension file and a few items that I added. Frank Reiss was drafted on 12/2/1864 as a private in Company G of this unit and was mustered out of service on 7/19/1865 in Louisville, Kentucky. His first day of service was 12/9/1864 at Camp Butler near Springfield after which he probably joined his Company in Savannah, Georgia in January 1865. His regiment was part of the 1st Brigade, 3rd Division, of the 17th Army Corps.

His Civil War pension file under #757904 also mentions various details including:

1. He was 5' 7" tall, fair complexion, black hair, hazel eyes. His weight at age 50 was 144 pounds and at age 61 was 130 pounds. His profession was farming.

2. He married Anna Antonia Sevilla Feder on 4/9/1866 by Catholic priest F. Lohmann in Millstadt, Illinois. She was born 9/26/1844 in Bavaria, Germany.

3. Their children were Charles Martin born 10/17/1867 and died 11/18/1874 at age 7, Adam Joseph born 9/25/1869 and died 11/5/1874 at age 5, Catharine born 11/11/1871 and died 6/16/1872 at age 7 months, George William born 4/23/1873, Anna Margaretha born 9/20/1875, John Jacob born 11/4/1877, Henry William born 3/30/1880, Louis Philip born 9/7/1883, Louise Katie or Katie Louise born 9/22/1885, Lizzie A. born 7/4/1888 and died 3/2/1889 at age 7 months, and William Martin born 9/17/1890. That's eleven children with seven reaching adulthood.

4. His pension was $6/month from 9/21/1891, then $8 from 9/21/1906, then $12 from 9/21/1907, then $15 from 10/19/1911, then $19 from 6/11/1912, then $22.50 from 9/27/1916, and eventually $50 when he died 11/21/1921 at the age of 80 years, 1 month, and 24 days.

5. He was born and raised in a log cabin which his father Adam Reiss had built in 1838. He continued living in that cabin after his wedding on 4/9/1866 and through the birth of the first ten of their eleven children. In 1889, Frank and Anna built a modern house next door where their last child was born in 1890. That home still exists on the

old Reiss homestead. Cause of death was pericarditis and chronic nephritis with complications of chrones intestinal catarah. Burial was in Franklin Cemetery in Smithton, IL on November 24, 1921.

6. His wife Anna received widow's pension of $30/month from December 21, 1921 and $40/month from June 4, 1928. Her account number is 915002.

We have only five letters from Frank Reiss while he is away serving with the 31st Illinois. Below is the first one where he mentions returning his civilian clothes from Camp Butler near Springfield. I do not recognize Frank's two friends' names as being his neighbors near Floraville. The next letter is 5/28/1865 when Frank is still camped near Washington, DC following the Grand Review on 5/23–24/1865. The last three letters are from Louisville, KY when he is preparing to be mustered out on 7/19/1865. We have no letters from him marching through the Carolinas and Virginia.

                                                            12/1864 at Camp Butler in Springfield

Dear Brother,

I and P. R. and Max are sending back our clothes to you, the ones we don't want to drag along, by A. Ex. You or Jack R. can have them, they are addressed to you and sent by me. Leave Max's at your house or at J.'s, at whoever gets the box, until he comes home. Mine are in a bag, Max's also, they are marked with our name. P.'s are not together with my clothes. Also there is a paper in there, with the gold futures, give them to Kate, she shall keep them for me. I want to close now, and send my greetings to you and all.

                                                            Your faithful brother F. J. Reiss.

Will, Kayla, Ava, and Blake, General Robert E. Lee surrendered his Confederate Army exactly four months after your great great great grandfather Frank Reiss entered military service on 12/9/1864. The yellow highlighted paragraph above on page 2 is what Frank would have experienced in those four months. Much of the overall history of the 31st Illinois that follows that paragraph happened before Frank joined that unit. Fortunately Frank survived the Civil War such that he married and fathered eleven children. But it's very sad that he and Anna lost four of their children, the two oldest in just 13 days in November 1874. How tragic. Give your parents an extra hug. Here's his Civil War tombstone in Smithton.

Love, Granddad

Civil War – Andrew Bicknell with the 72nd Illinois Infantry Regiment

Dear Will, Kayla, Ava, and Blake,   February 23, 2015

You've seen four stories this month about four of our Reiss and Basler relatives who fought in the Civil War with four different Illinois infantry regiments. This story today is about a fifth relative who fought with yet another Illinois unit. Only difference is that he is a relative on my mom's side rather than my dad's side.

Andrew Bicknell was born 9/6/1834 in Warwick, Kent County, Rhode Island. Here's more –

1. The **1830 Census** shows the Bicknell family of parents, 2 sons, 1 daughter, and two grandparents living in North Kingston, Rhode Island. Only the father's first name of Jesse is mentioned. The **1840 Census** shows the Bicknell family of parents, 6 sons, and 2 daughters living in Warwick, Rhode Island. Only the father's first name of Jesse is mentioned. The **1850 Census** shows Andrew age 16 living in Warwick, Rhode Island with his parents and 11 children. He is the middle child of 6 boys and 5 girls. Andrew, 4 siblings, and his father all worked in a nearby textile mill. The **1860 Census** shows Andrew married to Mary Owen age 21 and living in Mobile, Alabama with a daughter born in 2/1858. Both parents and several of Mary's siblings worked in a nearby textile mill. They all lived in company housing. It's not known how/when/why he relocated from Rhode Island to Alabama and then to Illinois.

2. Civil War records at the National Archives show Andrew J. Bicknell enlisting in the 72nd Illinois Infantry Regiment on 12/29/1863 at Danville, Illinois for a period of three years. He was living in Champaign, Illinois at the time. He joined Company U but later joined Company D. He was age 29, 5' 6.5" tall, blue eyes, dark hair, fair complexion, profession of laborer, and was paid a bounty of $60. He appears as a private in Springfield, Illinois for training at Camp Butler on 1/13/1864.

3. Owen relatives researched their extended family genealogy in the 1950's. It shows Andrew Bicknell's lineage beginning with his parents as Jesse Bicknell born 2/16/1802 in North Kingston, RI married to Susannah Tourjee born 8/24/1803 in the same place. Before him was Jesse Bicknell born 8/21/1770 in Attleboro, MA married to Elizabeth Austin born 3/1/1776 in North Kingston. Before him was Japhet Bicknell born 11/19/1750 in Attleboro married to Molly Carpenter born 12/21/1754 in Cumberland, RI. Before him was Japhet Bicknell born in 1711 in Middleboro, MA married to Martha Metcalf Turpin born 1718 in Attleboro. Before him was Thomas Bicknell born 1670 in Weymouth, MA married to Ann Turner born 8/18/1679 in Doxbury, MA. Before him was John Bicknell born 1623 in Barrington, England married to Mary Porter born in 1635 in Weymouth. Before him was Zachary Bicknell born in 1589 in England married to Agnes Anna Lovell born in 1598 in England. And before him was Zachariah Bicknell born in 1556 in Barrington married to Joanna ?? born in 1560 in Barrington. So that's eight generations from 1556 covering 278 years leading up to our Civil War relative, Andrew J. Bicknell. After him in our line is Andrew Stephenson born in 1856. After him is Andrew Stephenson born in 1892. After him is Mary Reiss born in 1921. After

her is Stephen Reiss born in 1944. After him are Adam Reiss born in 1976 and Grant Reiss born in 1979. After them are the four of you born in 2010 through 2015. So that's seven more generations from 1834 covering 181 years leading up to the four of you. Grand total is sixteen generations and 459 years. Pretty neat history, don't ya think?

4. Andrew Bicknell married Mary Owen, a sister of James Tine Owen who was the grandfather of my grandfather Andrew Stephenson. That makes James Tine Owen my great great grandfather and it makes Andrew Bicknell my great great great uncle. Add two more "greats" to describe your connection to all three of those ancestors. Maybe my grandfather Andrew Tine Stephenson and his father Andrew Henson Stephenson were even named after their uncle Andrew Bicknell. Your dad/uncle Grant Andrew Reiss was named for my grandfather Andrew and for Grand DD's grandfather Andrew Wynd. Thus Grant is probably named after Andrew Bicknell.

The Owen family, of which Mary Owen is a part, dates from Revolutionary War times in America. Mary is the fourth generation in the US. I have ten generations of Owen names in my family tree. On 2/14/2007, Grand DD and I hosted lunch in Tulsa, Oklahoma for Sandi Owen Livingston who is my fifth cousin. Her husband owns several orthopedic clinics and has lots of money such that Sandi is very comfortable flying off to other cities to visit cemeteries for data on her extensive family tree. She has 130,000 names in her database and is related to 11 different US presidents. There used to be bi-annual Owen reunions where hundreds would gather near Dallas, Texas. So being an Owen is a big deal. You're aware of Owen as a first or middle name in several of your young cousins. It's a very proud family.

So anyway, per Item 2 above, Andrew joined the 72nd Illinois as a replacement soldier. Their original compliment of about 1,000 men had been recruited in Chicago per this poster or handbill with bounty incentives. That original $302 bounty would be worth $5,700 today.

The 72nd Illinois Infantry Regiment Volunteers was organized at Chicago as the first Regiment of the Chicago Board of Trade. Its first hand bills were put out for one Company, calling itself the "Hancock Guards," on July 23, 1862, and, exactly one month later the entire Regiment was complete and mustered into the service for three years. The very day of their muster they headed for Cairo, Illinois where they arrived on the 24th. Their strength at that time was 37 officers and 930 men.

Fast forward to 10/18/1863 when the 72nd Illinois went on provost guard duty at Vicksburg, Mississippi where they remained until

10/30/1864. Vicksburg was already in Union hands following General Grant's siege victory there on 7/4/1863 which is also the same day the Union won at Gettysburg. Andrew Bicknell would have arrived in Vicksburg in late February 1864. During this year of comparative inaction as an army of occupation, the 72nd Illinois went on only two expeditions. The first of these was to Benton, Mississippi on 5/7/1864 and the second was to Grand Gulf, Mississippi, on 7/18/1864.

Sadly Andrew Bicknell died of consumption (pneumonia) on 9/5/1864 a day before his 30th birthday in the Vicksburg regimental hospital. He is buried in plot L-843 at the Vicksburg National Cemetery.

On 8/6/1865, the 72nd Illinois was mustered out of the service at Vicksburg and then marched directly home to Chicago. During their term of service they received some 450 recruits and when ordered home they transferred 270 of those to the 33rd Illinois Veteran Volunteers at Meridian, MS. They brought home 22 officers and 310 men. Here are various statistics:

Number of officers belonging to Regiment at date of muster-in	27
Number of enlisted men belonging to Regiment at date of muster-in	930
Number of officers returning with Regiment	22
Number of enlisted men returning with Regiment	310
Number of officers killed in service	7
Number of men killed in service	78
Number of officers died of disease	3
Number of men died of disease	130
Number of officers wounded	10
Number of men wounded	120
Number of officers taken prisoner	3
Number of men taken prisoner	76
Number of battles fought	7
Number of skirmishes	11
Numbers of miles traveled since entering service	9,280
Number of days under enemy's fire	145

Grand DD and I visited **Vicksburg National Military Park** and nearby **Vicksburg National Cemetery** on 4/14/2003 which was the 138th anniversary of the assassination of President Lincoln. We visited the Illinois Memorial which is the largest of 1325 monuments and markers in the park. We also visited the cemetery which is the second largest national cemetery after Arlington in Virginia. It contains 18,244 interments of which 12,954 are unknown. I was not aware of my extensive Owen genealogy at that time, so we didn't know to visit the grave of Andrew Bicknell.

Here is the Illinois Monument at the Vicksburg National Military Park. There are 47 steps in the long stairway, one for each day of the Siege of Vicksburg. Modeled after the Pantheon in Rome, the monument has sixty unique bronze tablets lining its interior walls, naming all 36,325 Illinois soldiers who participated in the Vicksburg Campaign. The monument stands 62 feet in height and originally cost $194,423.92, paid by the State of Illinois. We'll have to revisit Vicksburg to find Andrew Bicknell's name in this monument and on his tombstone.

Will, Kayla, Ava, and Blake, now you know about all five of your relatives who fought with five different Illinois infantry regiments in long bloody war to preserve the Union. You should be very proud. But someday I'll write several stories about your 35 other relatives on the Owen and Stephenson side who fought for the Confederacy. Most were from Alabama and Texas. About half of them did not return home.

Love, Granddad

Camp Butler

Dear Will, Kayla, Ava, and Blake,   December 7, 2015

Four of your Civil War relatives went through basic military training at this camp six miles northeast of Springfield, Illinois. They were Charles Max Wittig who enlisted on 8/13/1862, Andrew Bicknell who enlisted on 12/29/1863, John Reiss who was drafted on 9/20/1864, and Frank Reiss who was drafted on 12/2/1864. The two Reiss men were sons of Adam Reiss by different moms and Max was their future brother-in-law. Andrew Bicknell was a relative on my mom's side. Here's a sign at the entrance to Camp Butler which is now a National Cemetery.

CAMP BUTLER

CAMP BUTLER WAS ESTABLISHED IN 1861 AS A CIVIL WAR TRAINING CAMP AND MOBILIZATION CENTER FOR ILLINOIS RECRUITS. SELECTED BY STATE OFFICIALS AND BRIGADIER GENERAL WILLIAM T. SHERMAN AND NAMED FOR ILLINOIS STATE TREASURER WILLIAM BUTLER (1859-1863), CAMP BUTLER WAS THE SECOND LARGEST RECRUITMENT FACILITY IN ILLINOIS AFTER CAMP DOUGLAS IN CHICAGO. BY THE END OF THE WAR IN 1865 NEARLY 200,000 UNION SOLDIERS PASSED THROUGH THIS CAMP.

THE CAMP LATER SERVED AS A PRISONER OF WAR (POW) FACILITY FOR THOUSANDS OF CONFEDERATE SOLDIERS CAPTURED IN BATTLES ALONG THE CUMBERLAND, TENNESSEE, MISSISSIPPI, AND ARKANSAS RIVERS, SUCH AS FORT DONELSON AND FORT HINDMAN (ARKANSAS POST). LIVING CONDITIONS WITHIN THIS CAMP, FOR BOTH RECRUITS AND PRISONERS, WERE PRIMITIVE AT BEST.

DISEASE WAS WIDESPREAD WITHIN CAMP BUTLER. PNEUMONIA, SMALL POX, DYSENTERY, AND OTHER ILLNESSES CLAIMED THE LIVES OF 639 UNION AND 866 CONFEDERATE SOLDIERS, MANY OF WHOM WERE BURIED WITHIN THE CONFINES OF THE CAMP. INCLUDED AMONG THE CONFEDERATES WERE SOLDIERS FROM TEXAS, ARKANSAS, TENNESSEE, MISSISSIPPI, LOUISIANA, AND ALABAMA. TODAY THE CONFEDERATE GRAVES ARE DISTINGUISHABLE BY THEIR POINTED HEADSTONES.

ALTHOUGH THE CAMP WAS DEACTIVATED IN 1866, THE CEMETERY REMAINS AN ACTIVE MILITARY BURIAL SITE. IN 2011 THE NATIONAL CEMETERY OCCUPIED OVER 53 ACRES AND IS THE FINAL RESTING PLACE FOR MORE THAN 20,000 U.S. VETERANS AND ELIGIBLE FAMILY MEMBERS. ALSO INTERRED HERE ARE POW SOLDIERS FROM WORLD WAR II, WHOSE REMAINS WERE RELOCATED FROM VARIOUS CAMPS AND FORTS THROUGHOUT THE MIDWEST.

SPONSORED BY THE ILLINOIS SESQUICENTENNIAL CIVIL WAR ROUND TABLE COMMISSION AND THE ILLINOIS STATE HISTORICAL SOCIETY.

Here are parts of two letters from Max Wittig which mention his time at Camp Butler.

German   Chicago, the 19th of August 1862

Dear Friend (*Frank Reiss*)!

I wrote you before I left Deutschhuegel and wanted to go to New York. But in St. Louis I changed by plan and traveled through Iowa where I stayed for 3 weeks in Muscatine, from there to Minnesota into the wilderness among the Indians, New Ulm, Fort Riggly, St. Peter, St. Paul, then back to Wisconsin, where I worked for 12 weeks in LaCrosse. I got $10 a week there and now I am in Chicago, enlisted in the Hecker Regiment, Cpt. Bruening as Teamster, to fight again for the fatherland. I hope to find you also in the camp in Springfield as a soldier. Greet your parents and siblings again from me. The last day I stayed at Mr. William Drescher, where Heinrich was and where our colleague Emil Metzger worked. Had a friendly reception but I had called in St. Louis. I didn't want to fight for $100 as they do here.

You are unmarried or promised already? Again, greetings to your sister Kath as well as your sister-in-law. In the hope that these lines find you healthy, I will wait until after the war before I get married so that I don't have to worry about a family during the long absence, who in the end might leave me anyway.

Greetings to all who ask about me. I am in the new Hecker Regiment Cp. Bruening, Camp Butler, Springfield, Ills. where you can still write to for the next three weeks if you want to.

Your old friend and colleague of the science of wheelwrights,

Chas. Max Wittig

Rally boys for the bounty 175 dollar no humbug. Cash down afterward nothing.

German   Fairfax Court House, Virginia
                                                the 1st of December 1862

Friend Franz Reiss!

Because the weather is bad today and we don't have to exercise, the morning is destined for you and to learn something about me and where we are roaming around even though you probably heard something from our colleagues Balser and Mollis. I sent my greetings every time but you didn't let anyone at all hear from you, and actually I shouldn't even write first before I have received a letter from you.

It's old hat now that we have been for almost 3 months in Camp Butler and the boys still had plenty of bounty money to spend in beer and liquor. But now it blows from another side because the money is little and also the hope to get some soon.

Now I want to write you about our trip from Camp Butler to here to determine yourself if the boys still have something to lament about! On the 3rd of November we abandoned our camp to go to Chicago when a drunken teamster ran over some and demolished things because he refused to do what he was ordered to. The end of the song was that one of the officers shot him and blew a bullet through his head of which a lot of stuff was written in the newspapers. . . . . . .

We have no letters from Andrew Bicknell, but Civil War records at the National Archives show him enlisting in the 72nd Illinois Infantry Regiment on 12/29/1863 at Danville, Illinois for a period of three years. He was living in Champaign, Illinois at the time. He joined Company U but later joined Company D. He was age 29, 5' 6.5" tall, blue eyes, dark hair, fair complexion, profession of laborer, and was paid a bounty of $60. He appears as a private in Springfield, Illinois for training at Camp Butler on 1/13/1864.

We have no letters from John Reiss, but here's a short one from Frank Reiss at Camp Butler –

#158 – German   12/1864 at <mark>Camp Butler in Springfield</mark>

Dear Brother.

I and P. R. and Max are sending back our clothes to you, the ones we don't want to drag along, by A. Ex. You or Jack R. can have them, they are addressed to you and sent by me. Leave Max's at your house or at J.'s, at whoever gets the box, until he comes home. Mine are in a bag, Max's also, they are marked with our name. P.'s are not together with my clothes. Also there is a paper in there, with the gold futures, give them to Kate, she shall keep them for me. I want to close now, and send my greetings to you and all.

                                        Your faithful brother F. J. Reiss.

Will, Kayla, Ava, and Blake, some day we will all take a tour of the **Camp Butler National Cemetery**. The initial camp is a significant part of our family history and of Illinois history. Of the 167 regiments of Illinois infantry, cavalry, and artillery who saw action in the Civil War, 114 were created, reorganized, discharged, or saw service here. Today, nothing remains of the original site. Most of the land on which the stockade and west camp stood has been returned to cropland or is occupied by a few private residences. Parts of the south camp and its adjacent drill fields are now part of Roselawn Cemetery. I took several photos on the next page. Those gravestones with the angled top are Confederate soldiers who died here of disease when part of Camp Butler was also a prisoner of war camp.

Love, Granddad

From *The Bivouac of the Dead*
By Theodore O'Hara

The muffled drum's sad roll has beat
The soldier's last tattoo;
No more on life's parade shall meet
That brave and fallen few.
On Fame's eternal camping-ground
Their silent tents are spread,
And Glory guards, with solemn round,
The bivouac of the dead.

Grand Review at the End of the Civil War

Dear Will and Kayla,   May 21, 2012

Your great great great grandfather, Frank Reiss, took part in the world's largest military parade 147 years ago this Thursday on May 24, 1865. It celebrated the Union victory to end the Civil War after four long years of fighting in which thousands of soldiers died of wounds, infection, and disease. Here is a photograph showing soldiers marching down Pennsylvania Avenue in Washington, DC from the Capitol in the background to the White House nearby.

The **Grand Review of the Armies** was a military procession and celebration in Washington, D.C., on May 23 and May 24, 1865, following the close of the American Civil War. Elements of the Union Army paraded through the streets of the capital to receive accolades from the crowds and reviewing politicians, officials, and prominent citizens, including the President of the United States, Andrew Johnson.

On May 10, Johnson had declared that the rebellion and armed resistance was virtually at an end, and had made plans with government authorities for a formal review to honor the troops. One of his side goals was to change the mood of the capital, which was still in mourning following the assassination of Abraham Lincoln the month before at Ford's Theater. Three of the leading Federal armies were close enough to participate in the procession. The Army of the Tennessee arrived via train. The Army of Georgia (including grandpa Frank Reiss), also under the command of William T. Sherman, had just completed its Carolinas Campaign and had accepted the surrender of the largest remaining Confederate army, that of Joseph E. Johnston. It arrived from North Carolina in mid-May and camped around the capital city in various locations, across the Potomac River from the Army of the Potomac, fresh off its victories over Robert E. Lee in Virginia. It had arrived in Washington on May 12. Officers in the three armies who had not seen each other for some time (in some cases since before the war) communed and renewed acquaintances, while at times, the common infantrymen engaged in verbal sparring (and sometimes fisticuffs) in the town's taverns and bars over which army was superior. Sherman, concerned that his Westerners would not present as polished an image as the eastern army, drilled his forces and insisted that uniforms be cleaned, buttons and brass shined, and that bayonets glistened.

At 9:00 a.m. on a bright sunny May 23, a signal gun fired a single shot and Maj. Gen. George Gordon Meade, the victor of Gettysburg, led the estimated 80,000 men of Army of the Potomac down the streets of Washington from Capitol Hill down Pennsylvania Avenue past crowds that numbered into the thousands. The infantry marched with 12 men across the road, followed by the divisional and corps artillery, then an array of cavalry regiments that stretched for another seven miles. The mood was one of gaiety and celebration, and the crowds and soldiers frequently engaged in singing patriotic songs as the procession of victorious soldiers snaked its way towards the reviewing stand in front of the White House, where President Johnson, general-in-chief Ulysses S. Grant, senior military leaders, the Cabinet, and leading government officials awaited. At the head of his troops, Meade dismounted when he arrived at the reviewing stand and joined the dignitaries to salute his men, who passed for over six hours.

On the following day at 10:00 a.m., Sherman led the 65,000 men of the Army of the Tennessee and the Army of Georgia, with an uncharacteristic semblance of military precision, past the admiring celebrities, most of which had never seen him before. For six hours under bright sunshine, the men who had marched through Georgia and those who had destroyed John Bell Hood's army in Tennessee now paraded in front of joyous throngs lining the sidewalks. People peered from windows and rooftops for their first glimpse of this western army. Unlike Meade's army, which had more military precision, Sherman's Georgia force was trailed by a vast crowd of people who had accompanied the army up from Savannah – freed blacks, laborers, adventurers, scavengers, etc. At the very end was a vast herd of cattle and other livestock that had been taken from Carolina farms. Within a week after the celebrations, the two armies were disbanded and many of the volunteer regiments and batteries were sent home to be mustered out of the army.

Will and Kayla, our family has many relatives who fought in the Civil War. You already saw my Granddad's Monday of April 9 which mentions five relatives who fought with five different Illinois regiments. Well, there are another 35 men on my mother's side who fought with various Confederate units. I'll tell you about them in later editions. Keep all these soldiers plus others from other wars in mind for the upcoming Memorial Day at the end of this month.

Love, Granddad

Martin Charles Reiss (later Rice)

Dear Will, Kayla, Ava, and Blake,   August 31, 2015

Martin is the youngest brother of my great grandfather Frank Reiss whose picture hangs in my den. Note the brothers wore the same beard which must have been the fashion in the 1860s. Their middle brother Charles also had the same beard.

Martin is one of our most interesting and colorful relatives. You really need to read his 59 letters which appear in our book, It Takes A Matriarch, to get a feel for Martin's interests, mobility, and views on life. His profession was making harnesses which are the leather straps which connect a horse to its rider or driver and whatever they were pulling. He occasionally made saddles. Those skills were in high demand back then since there were no cars or motorcycles. Everything went by horsepower. As a harness maker, Martin was able to easily get a job as he moved about in his bachelor days. He lived in boarding houses.

Here's a list of 18 cities in 18 years where Martin lived/worked and the date of the first letter he wrote from each. There may have been other cities but without letters. These 52 bachelor letters are really interesting.

Born	6/19/1845	Letters
Sullivan, Indiana	?/1862	1
Terre Haute, Indiana	2/8/1863	2
St. Louis, Missouri	3/13/1863	1
Terre Haute, Indiana	3/19/1863	4
St. Louis, Missouri	3/20/1864	2
Mattoon, Illinois	12/4/1864	6
St. Louis, Missouri	1/28/1866	1
Leavenworth, Kansas	3/4/1866	5
St. Joseph, Missouri	5/24/1866	1
Maryville, Missouri	6/3/1866	2
Savannah, Missouri	8/26/1866	7
St. Joseph, Missouri	11/3/1867	2
Atchison, Kansas	6/12/1868	0
St. Joseph, Missouri	8/12/1868	7

Halleck, Missouri	1/13/1872	1
St. Joseph, Missouri	11/15/1872	2
Toledo, Iowa	11/1875	0
Dawn, Missouri	11/7/1880	8

Martin spent the spring of 1866 in Leavenworth, Kansas and seriously considered employment driving and maintaining commercial wagon trains crossing the plains to the west. He changed his name from Reiss to Rice in early 1867. He sold his inherited share of the Reiss home farm to his brother Frank in 1873.

Martin finally settled in Dawn, Missouri and married Margaret Williams on 1/1/1883. He was born on 6/19/1845 and was age 37. She was born on 3/23/1862 in Wales and had immigrated with her parents and siblings about 1865. She was almost age 21.

Martin and Maggie had three children, Jennie on 9/17/1883, Milton on 7/1/1888, and a stillborn child in 1891. They really enjoyed being parents but sadly, little Jennie died of gastroenteritis at 7:00 a.m. on 9/2/1885 just two weeks short of her second birthday. She is the subject of three letters which follow. They are the last letters we have from Martin and Margaret Rice.

548 – German

Dawn, Mo.
Nov. 17, 1885

Dear Mother,

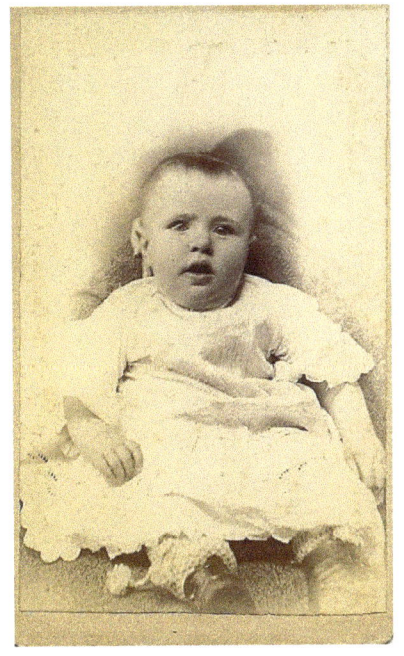

I wanted to write to you already long ago, but didn't find time. Your letter is dated 18th September, I still think of my dear Jennie. We buried her on Sunday. I am so sad to have lost her, she was so good to me, always wanted to sleep next to her father. My wife is crying all the time but she is away now and we won't see her again in this world. She was such a happy child, all people said so.

Half an hour before she died she said "bye, bye Daddy". I thought my heart would break, she spoke so clearly, but what can you do. You cannot have all you want to have. Times are bad here like it is everywhere else and no money. Since Jennie is dead, my wife has always been ill ever since Jennie was born and it would be cheaper to hire a girl to do the work.

There is no more I can report, I wrote to Kate long ago. She wrote such a nice letter which I answered.

Well, I want to close now, hoping that these line will reach you in good health. All our love to you. Write soon to you loving son.

Martin C. Rice

#107 – English

Dawn, Missouri
December 1885

Dear Mother,

Your letter came a Christmas gift for us. Mart's eyes filled with tears when reading it. It is not because I did not intend to write but thought many times. But did not carry it out. Am sorry I have neglected it now three years. Will try and do better in the future. I feel acquainted with you through Mart and know I would like you. Would like if you would live with us. I want to see you so much and sister Kate, brother's Frank and Charley. And do hope we shall see each other before long. It would be a great pleasure for me to have a long talk with you. We are boarding with a real nice family. We have a pleasant warm room. I have a south window full of flowers. Hear is a bouquet of them for you.

Have all the reading I can be able to read. Mart does everything in his power to make it pleasant and comfortable for me and you could not be happier family than we three were. As we idolized our little girl. She was just what we wanted in everything. She was perfection in all she would do in looks and ways.

The leaves of this little bouquet is taken of the same plant that we had made for little Jennie when she was buried. There was a white rose bud in the center and then white verbena and the green leaves all around. Well I hope you are feeling better by this time. Wish you a Happy New Year.

Maggie Rice

(This letter was written by Martin's wife shortly after their daughter Jennie died in 1885. The little bouquet she mentions was still enclosed in the envelope.)

108 – German

Dawn,
December 30, 1885

Dear Mother,

We received your dear letter of 23rd on Christmas 25th. My wife has just written to you as well. She was very happy to hear from you and often tells me to write to you. She resembles you and often says she would like to see you. She often says to me, you have a good mother. She also has good parents and they also like me very much and so do I for they are good people. Since Jennie is dead we ???, because she is not healthy and too weak to work. Everything is expensive, times are very bad, everything goes slowly and poorly. We have got no money. Pigs and animals are very cheap, also grain and I think it is getting better in spring because times are rough for more than one year now.

That's all for today, I hope these lines will reach you in good health. I wish you a very happy New Year.

Your loving son,

Martin C. Rice

Maggie died at age 29 on 8/5/1891 so maybe it was during her third pregnancy when neither survived. Martin died a few years later in 1898 at age 53. We don't know that exact date. No records were available at the Welsh Cemetery in Dawn, Missouri or at the Livingston County Clerk's office in Chillicothe or at the Missouri State office in Jefferson City. Martin and Maggie's middle child Milton was orphaned at age ten and was raised by his maternal Williams grandparents. He had a full life and died on 3/6/1959. His obituary appears below.

Grand DD and I visited the Rice graves in the Welsh Cemetery just outside Dawn, Missouri in 2008. Here is little Jennie's tombstone. It is the largest of five Rice and several Williams stones. There is no tombstone for Martin. Perhaps the money issues he mentions in his last letter prevented the purchase of a stone.

Will, Kayla, Ava, and Blake, it was 130 years ago this Wednesday that little Jennie passed away. A lot has happened in our extended family since then. We are so blessed. Give your parents a super hug.

Love, Granddad

Milton Joshua Rice

Chillicothe Constitution-Tribune Newspaper - 7 March 1959

Funeral services for M. J. (Milton) Rice, well known Chillicothe insurance man, will be held at 2:30 o'clock Monday afternoon at the chapel of the Keeny Funeral Home. Mr. Rice's sudden death occurred at 9:40 Friday morning at his home, 929 Elm Street. He was 70 years old.

A native of Livingston County, he was born July 1, 1888, at Dawn, Missouri, the son of Mart and Margaret Williams Rice, on Nov. 20, 1918. He married Lora Anne Culver of Excelsior Springs, Missouri. They resided in Tulsa, Oklahoma until 1921 at which time they moved to Chillicothe and purchased the Hoffman Insurance Agency which became known as the M. J. Rice Agency. Mr. and Mrs. Rice conducted the business until January, 1953 when they retired.

For many years Mr. Rice was active in city and church affairs and was a member of the Presbyterian Church for 42 years. He served on the city council and the welfare board and was a charter member of the Chillicothe Kiwanis Club. He leaves his wife, of the home; one son, Hadley F. Rice, Townsend, Montana; one daughter, Mrs. Robert (Nancy) Stepp, Lincoln, Nebraska, and three grandchildren, Robert Earl, Milton Lawrence and John William Stepp of Lincoln.

Our Matriarch's Children – One Missing

Dear Will and Kayla,   September 2, 2013

Our oldest family matriarch is your great great great great grandmother, Margaret Basler Reiss Ebert. She is the one who saved the 780 letters written between 1852 and 1888 that now appear in our book, It Takes A Matriarch. She was a very special person. I only recently realized that two of her ten children did not appear in my version of our extended family tree. But thanks to help from my third cousin, Peggy Ray who is also a serious family genealogist, we now know about one of those two missing children.

We know Margaret had ten children because the 1900 Census mentions ten children of which five were still living when the census was taken. Let's assume that Margaret counted her stepson, John Reiss, as her first child since she raised him from age 21 months following her 9/10/1840 marriage to John's father, Adam Reiss. Below are nine of her children that we know about. You can see that five were still living in 1900. Can you imagine outliving five of your children? How sad.

- John R. Reiss (12/11/1838 – 6/18/1919) born to Adam Reiss and his first wife Mary Schuessler Reiss.

- Frank Joseph Reiss (9/27/1841 – 11/21/1921). He is your great great great grandfather.

- Charles Joseph Reiss (2/17/1843 - 5/13/1931)

- Martin Charles Reiss (6/19/1845 – 1898)

- Catherine Reiss (3/23/1847 – 4/2/1916)

- Barbara Reiss who was stillborn sometime in 1849 and was the last child of Adam Reiss because he died that year as well

- Anna Maria Ebert born 9/14/1851 to Margaret and her second husband Conrad Ebert who married on 4/2/1850. She was baptized on 9/20/1851 at St. Michael's Catholic Church in Paderborn per the third entry on the scan below. I only recently learned about her thanks to cousin Peggy. Anna Maria does not appear in the 1860 Census so she apparently died before age nine.

- Louisa Ebert (12/??/1853 – 5/21/1875). She was baptized at St. Michael's on 1/4/1854. Her great great granddaughter is Peggy Ray who found Anna Maria's baptism record.

- Margaret Ebert (10/29/1856 – 4/19/1926)

This list is only nine children. The 1860 Census mentions seven living children – Frank, Martin, Catherine, Louisa, and Margaret. Sons John and Charles are living nearby as farm laborers and enumerated there. My guess is that Margaret (10/22/1818 – 6/23/1902) had another child in late 1858 when she would have been age 40 and that that child also died before the 1860 Census.

Will and Kayla, this is where our story about our matriarch's children must end for now. Maybe by the time you get to my age, there will be billions of additional documents found, scanned, and available on the internet. Please let me know what you find. Thanks,

Love, Granddad

The Luetzelschwab Family Arrives on August 3, 1865

Dear Will and Kayla,   October 28, 2013

Besides summarizing the arrival of one branch of our extended family, this story is also a lesson on how a family name can be misspelled by national census takers. The correct spelling appears above. Count the highlighted misspellings as you read on.

Johann Baptiste Luetzelschwab (11/27/1824 – 4/26/1916) was born in Magden, Switzerland. He married Maria Anna Stuber (11/12/1828 – 2/26/1878) in 1849 and had four children, but young son Albert died at age 1.5 in 1854. In early 1865 as the American Civil War was ending, they left Magden in the Swiss state or canton of Aargau, sailed to New York on a ship named "Energie," and arrived on 8/3/1865. Their language was German because their canton bordered Germany.

This new American family consisted of Johann age 39, Maria Anna 35, Rosalia 14, Johann Arnold 7, and Jacob 6. They settled first in Missouri and later moved to Granite City, Madison County, Illinois. The **1870 Census** shows John Litzilshaw age 46 working as a farmer, Mary 42, Rosie 26, Arnold 14, and Jacob 12. Living nearby is the Herman Hoelscher family which includes daughter Charlotte age 7 who becomes Jacob's wife 11 years later (see next paragraph). Maria Anna died in 1878 and is buried in St. John's Cemetery in Granite City. The **1880 Census** shows John Litxelschaup age 58 working as a farmer in Nameoki, Madison County, daughter Rosa Dogita 30, granddaughter Anna Dogita 9, and Jacob Litxelschaup 22.

The next generation includes John Jacob Luetzelschwab, Sr. (7/14/1858 – 10/28/1940) who was born in Magden, Switzerland. He married Charlotta Hoelscher (11/15/1862 – 4/23/1925) on 5/26/1881. About 1883 they moved with baby daughter Mary to a farm about 3.5 miles south of Millstadt in Section 33, Township 1, Range 9 West. His father John joined them in 1892 and lived with them until his death in 1916. Her grave is in Evergreen Cemetery in Millstadt. The **1900 Census** shows Jacob Litzetschwaab age 41 working as a farmer, Charlotte 37 married 19 years with 9 of 9 children still living, John 17 working as a farmer, Minnie 14, Herman 12, Katy 12, Charlotte 7, Lena 5, Jacob 4, Frank 2, and his widowed father John age 75. The **1910 Census** shows Jacob age 51 working as a farmer, Charlotte 47 with 11 of 11 children still living, John 26 working as a carpenter, Herman 22 working as a carpenter, Charlotte 17, Lena 15, Jacob 14, Frank 12, Carolina 7, Edna 4, and his widowed father John age 85. Daughter Catherine Charlotte Lueteelschwab age 20 was enumerated with the George Reiss household working there as a servant. The **1920 Census** shows Jacob Suetzelschuab age 61 working as a farmer, Charlotte 57, Herman 32 working as a farmer, Jacob Jr. 24 working as a carpenter, Frank 22 working as a farmer, Caroline 19, and Edna 14 all living on a farm on Columbia Road. The **1930 Census** shows widowed Jacob Ludzetschcoab age 71 working as a farmer, Herman 41 working as a farmer, and Frank 29 working as a farmer living on their home farm.

Below is a Luetzelschwab family photo taken in 1919 of all eleven children and their parents. Front row from the left are John, Herman, Jacob, Charlotte, Jacob Jr., and Frank. Back row from the left are Mary (Weihl), Minnie (Sponemann), Catherine (Reiss), Charlotte (Sander), Lena

(Becker), Caroline (Gummersheimer), and Edna (Lang). The yellow highlights indicate a connection with the Reiss family farm as you'll see below.

All eleven children of John Jacob and Charlotte Luetzelschwab reached adulthood which is amazing given the times. Here is a brief summary in birth order of each of them.

Mary (baptized Anna Maria Charlotte) Luetzelschwab (6/14/1882 –1/21/1971) married Jacob Weihl (3/7/1878 – 6/4/1937) on 5/8/1900 at home.

John Charles Luetzelschwab (12/10/1883 – 11/22/1976) was born in Millstadt and married Katherine Keim (9/23/1891 – 2/6/1952) who was also born in Millstadt on 10/8/1911. The **1920 Census** shows John Luetzelschwa age 36 working as a carpenter contractor, Katie 28, Edgar 7, and Roland 6 owning a house on Laurey Street in Millstadt. The **1930 Census** shows John Lustzetichwab age 46 working as a concrete contractor, Katie 38, Edger 17, Roland age 16, Peral 4 1/12, and Adam Lutzelichwab 36 as a boarder working as a concrete laborer on White Street in Millstadt. John built the 1940 home of my grandparents, George and Katie Luetzelschwab Reiss, on our family farm.

Minnie (baptized Wilhelmina) Luetzelschwab (11/24/1885 – 2/17/1947) married John Sponemann (1873 – 6/4/1940) on 10/7/1909 in St. Louis.

Herman F. Luetzelschwab (12/6/1887 – 3/14/1961) never married.

Catherine (Katie) Charlotte Luetzelschwab (3/25/1890 – 10/17/1986) married George William Reiss (4/22/1873 – 8/16/1964) on 4/16/1911 at home. Witnesses were Herman

162

F. and Lottie H. Luetzelschwab. They are buried in Franklin Cemetery in Smithton. The **1910 Census** shows George 37 as head, his parents Frank 68 married 44 years and Anna 65 with 7 of 11 children still living, and servant Katie Lueteelschwab 20 who he married in 1911. A 1919 auto-owners directory shows him driving a Ford. George's **9/12/1918 World War I Draft Registration Card** shows him as a self-employed farmer with height "tall", build "medium", eyes "hazel", and hair "dark brown". The **1920 Census** shows George age 46, Katherine 29, William 7, Franklin 4, Irwin 2, father Frank 78, and mother Anna Syvilla 75 living on the home farm. The **1930 Census** shows George age 56 owning his own farm, Katy 40 married 19 years, William 17, Franklin 14, and Irwin 12 living in Prairie du Long Township. George and Katie hosted the **1934 Reiss Centennial**.

Charlotte "Lottie" H. Luetzelschwab (10/18/1892 – 10/11/1984) married Edward Sander (10/4/1888 – 2/11/1958) on 8/23/1914.

Magdalena (Lena) Luetzelschwab (12/17/1894 – 3/8/1989) married Joseph A. Speichinger (5/22/1891 – 4/27/1927) on 2/??/1915.

Jacob Luetzelschwab Jr. (11/9/1895 – 3/1/1965) married Cora Muskopf (10/17/1896 – 12/21/1977) on 2/12/1925 in Millstadt.

Frank Luetzelschwab (1/3/1898 – 7/1/1976) never married.

Caroline Luetzelschwab (12/7/1900 – 6/1/1983) married Elmer Gummersheimer (10/25/1897 – 3/15/1980) on 3/14/1920.

Edna Luetzelschwab (10/16/1905 – 11/25/1990) married Henry G. Lang (1/2/1900 – 1/12/1978) on 8/14/1927. They are the parents of Lavern Lang who farmed our family farm from 1954 to 1995.

Will and Kayla, you can see that three of these eleven Luetzelschwab siblings have a connection with the Reiss Family Farm.

- Katie Luetzelschwab married George Reiss, raised three sons, and lived on the Reiss farm for 70 years. They are your great great grandparents.

- John Luetzelschwab built the new Reiss farm home in 1940.

- Lena Luetzelschwab's son, Lavern Lang, farmed the Reiss farm for 45 years.

That's quite a connection, don't you think. The Luetzelschwabs will hold their sesquicentennial family reunion on 6/6/2015 on the Lang family farm just south of Millstadt, Illinois.

Love, Granddad

The Luetzelschwab Family Farm

Dear Will, Kayla, and Ava,   June 2, 2014

My other Granddad's Mondays story of today was about the Lang Family Farm which came into our extended family by marriage on 11/20/1895. This story below is about the neighboring Luetzelschwab Family Farm which started on 9/12/1882 when your great great great grandfather Jacob Luetzelschwab and his father John Baptiste Luetzelschwab bought the first 80 acres. You can see both in this plat book scan with the Lang farm in brown and the expanded 160-acre Luetzelschwab farm in purple. The village of Millstadt is about three miles north.

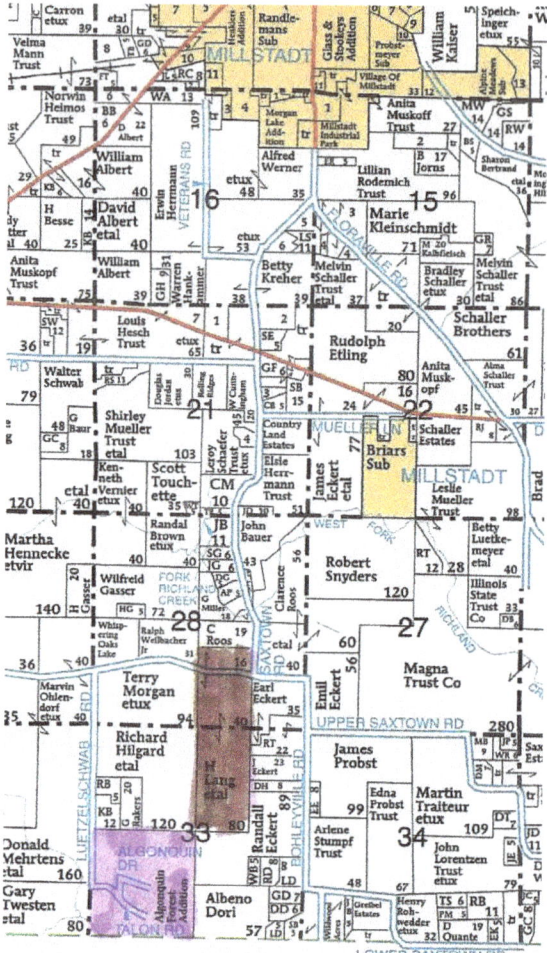

Jacob was born in Magden, Switzerland on 7/14/1858. He arrived in New York harbor with his parents and siblings on 8/3/1865 at age 7. They settled first in Missouri and later moved to Granite City, Illinois where his mother died on 2/26/1878.

Jacob married his neighbor Charlotte Hoelscher on 5/26/1881. Their first child, a daughter Mary arrived on 6/14/1882. Three months later, the young family and Jacob's widowed father bought 80 acres as the south half of the southwest quarter of Section 33 in Millstadt Township. They built a house and moved in during the summer of 1883.

Jacob and Charlotte had a total of eleven children with all of them reaching adulthood which was really a blessing given the times. There were seven daughters and four sons. My grandmother Catherine Charlotte Luetzelschwab Reiss was child #5 born on 3/25/1890. Edna Luetzelschwab Lang was child #11 born on 10/16/1905. All the children except the first and last were born on the 80-acre Luetzelschwab Farm. Two sons, Herman (12/6/1887 – 3/14/1961) and Frank (1/3/1898 – 7/1/1976), were lifelong bachelors and spent their entire lives on the family farm.

This chart and the table below show how the farm doubled from 80 to 160 acres over 63 years and how the bachelor brothers bought out their siblings after their father Jacob died on 10/28/1940. Charlotte had died on 4/23/1925. Eventually ownership resided only with Frank Luetzelschwab who died 7/1/1976. His estate was liquidated with three outside couples named Peebles, Guenther, and Ritter buying the 160-acre farm on 9/15/1977. Now there are a dozen or more homes there.

Book : Page	Description Price	Grantor	Grantee	Date transacted / date recorded
168: 339-341	S ½ SW section 33 80 acres $3000.00	John Frederick Broetje and Maria Dorothea his wife	John Lutzelschwab and Jacob Lutzelschwab	12 September 1882 / 2 December 1882
262: 258	S ½ SW section 33 and personal property thereon[1] $500.00 QUIT CLAIM	John Lutzelschwab	Jacob Lutzelschwab	20 July 1898 / 20 July 1898
890: 343	E ½ NW SW section 33 $1.00	Christina Mehrtens and Herman Mehrtens, her husband	to Jacob Luetzelschwab Sr	28 May 1938 / 31 May 1938
943: 609-610	S ½ SW; NE SW; E ½ NW SW section 33 $2700.00	Mary **Weihl**, widow not remarried, Lottie **Sanders** and Edward Sanders her husband' Caroline **Gummersheimer** and Elmer Gummersheimer her husband, all of Monroe County, Ill; John C **Luetzelschwab** and Katie Luetzelschwalb his wife, Jacob **Luetzelschwab**, Jr and Cora Luetzelschwalb his wife, Minnie **Sponeman**, a widow not remarried, Edna **Lang** and Henry Lang, her husband, all of the town of Millstadt, St Clair Co., Ill; Lena **Becker** and Edward Becker her husband, of Belleville, St Clair Co., Ill; and Katie **Reiss** and George Reiss her husband of Smithton, St Clair Co., Ill	to Herman Luetzelschwab and Frank Luetzelschwab, of town of Millstadt	24 January 1942 / 20 February 1942
1046: 514	W ½ NW SW section 33 $1.00	Christina Mehrtens and Herman Mehrtens her husband	to Herman and Frank Luetzelschab	3 Apr 1945 / 16 Apr 1945
2014: 503	road across NW SW section 33 $1.00	Frank Luetzelschwab, bachelor	Millstadt Township	3 September 1965 / 24 May 1966
2427: 1922	SW ¼ section 33 $195,000.00	Frank Luetzelschwab **by executor**	Terry L **Peebles** and Linda L Peebles his wife in joint tenancy to an undivided ¼ interest; and Harry E **Guenther** and Judith Guenther his wife in joint tenancy to an undivided ¼ interest; and Robert F **Ritter** and Karen G Ritter his wife in joint tenancy to an undivided ½ interest	15 September 1977 / recorded date too faint Note: the grantees secure a mortgage on this parcel; see Deed Record 2427: 1924 15 Sept 1977

Notice the footnote in the second line of boxes where John sold his personal property to his son Jacob. That included a black mule age 20 years, three cows being yellow, red/brown, and black aged 3, 6 & 13 years respectively, several hogs, and 4 pigs. John lived with Jacob and Charlotte from 1892 until his death on 4/26/1916 so that continuity made all of his animals very happy.

Here's part of the original deed from 9/12/1882 where John Luetzelschwab and his son Jacob bought their first 80 acres.

This Deed, made and entered into this Twelfth day of September A.D. Eighteen hundred and Eighty two, by and between John Frederick Droetje and Maria Dorothea his wife, of the County of St Clair and State of Illinois, of the first part and John Lutzelschwab & Jacob Lutzelschwab of the County of ___ and State of Illinois, of the second part, Witnesseth that the said parties of the first part, for and in consideration of the sum of Three Thousand ($3000) Dollars, the receipt of which is hereby acknowledged, have granted, bargained and sold and by these presents do grant, bargain and sell, convey and confirm unto the said part of the second part, ___ heirs and assigns forever, all that certain lot, tract or parcel of land lying and being in the County of St Clair and State of Illinois and described as follows: The South half of the South West quarter of Section Thirty three (33) Township one (1) South Range Nine (9) West of the 3rd prin

Here are two pictures of the Luetzelschwab homestead from different angles. The original dog trot log cabin portion of the home was moved in the late-1970s to Foley Park between Millstadt and Smithton.

Here's a picture of Jacob and Charlotte taken about 1905. Or maybe it was taken in 1900 when daughter Mary married Jacob Weihl, or in 1909 when daughter Minnie married John Sponemann, or in 1911 when daughter Catherine married George Reiss, or in 1911 when son John married Katherine Keim. Charlotte died on 9/23/1925 at age 62 and missed the marriage of her last child Edna to Henry Lang.

Jacob and Charlotte had 11 children and 27 grandchildren which meant they had 47 birthday and anniversary cards to send each year, almost one per week. All the Luetzelschwab genealogy is wonderfully documented in two books that were published by family members for recent reunions. The first is The Luetzelschwabs, Our Swiss Heritage by Gladys Wittenauer Thiele and Ardell Roider in August 1994. The second is The Luetzelschwab Family, History and Descendents by John Luetzelschwab in May 2009. There will be another Luetzelschwab family reunion on 6/6/2015 at the adjacent Lang Family Farm to celebrate the sesquicentennial of the Luetzelschwab arrival in 1865.

Here is the entrance to Freivogel Cemetery southwest of Millstadt and the grave of John Luetzelschwab who started it all by emigrating from Switzerland to the US on 8/3/1865.

Next is an aerial photo showing the Luetzelschwab farm as it is today, a rural subdivision with a dozen or more homes surrounding a big lake. Looks pretty nice. There may not have been much tillable land originally. The original homestead was on the right as you turn onto Algonquin Road.

Below are my overview details from the Luetzelschwab family tree. Note how the census-takers really butchered the Luetzelschwab family name.

John Baptiste Luetzelschwab (11/27/1824 – 4/26/1916) was born in Magden, Switzerland and married Maria Anna Stuber (11/12/1828 – 2/26/1878) in 1849 and had four children. They left Magden, Aargau, Switzerland and arrived in the port of New York on the ship "Energie" on 8/3/1865. The family consisted of Johann age 39, Anna Maria age 35, Rosalia age 14, Johann Arnold age 7, and Jacob age 6. They settled first in Missouri and later moved to Granite City, Illinois where Maria Anna is buried in St. John's Cemetery. She was born in Canton Berne, Switzerland. He is buried in Freivogel Cemetery in Millstadt. The **1870 Census** shows John Litzilshaw age 46 working as a farmer, Mary age 42, Rosie age 26, Arnold age 14, Jacob age 12, and laborer Chas. Stanger age 35 living on a farm near Collinsville in Madison County at Township 3, Range 9. Living nearby is the Herman Hoelscher family which includes daughter Charlotte age 7 who will becomes Jacob's wife 11 years later. The **1880 Census** shows John Litxelschaup age 58 working as a farmer, daughter Rosa Dogita age 30, granddaughter Anna Dogita age 9, and Jacob Litxelschaup age 22 working as a farmer living in Nameoki, Madison County, Illinois. The **1900 Census** shows widowed John B. Litzelschwaab age 75 living with his son Jacob and family near Millstadt. The **1910 Census** shows widowed John B. Luetzelschwab age 85 living with his son Jacob and family near Millstadt.

Will, Kayla, and Ava, now you know more about your Luetzelschwab heritage and how it makes each one of you 8% Swiss. You should be very proud.

Love, Granddad

Immigrant Trunk (1865) and Wardrobe (1920)

Dear Will and Kayla,   September 3, 2012

These are two "family" pieces of furniture in the front bedroom of our lake house in Sullivan, Indiana – an immigrant trunk and an oak wardrobe. Both are associated with the Reiss Family Farm south of Belleville, Illinois.

The trunk carried clothes and personal belongings of your great great great great grandparents John Baptiste and Maria Anna Luetzelschwab who emigrated from Magden, Switzerland to Millstadt, Illinois in August 1865. They were your grandfather's grandmother's grandparents. His dates are (11/27/1824 – 4/26/1916) and hers are (11/12/1828 – 2/26/1878) so they lived to ages 91 and 49.

Immigrant trunks contained essential things that allowed its owners to survive and to prosper in the New World. Contents included weapons with extra ball and shot for hunting or defense, nails and hand tools, vegetable and fruit and flower seeds, shoes, extra buckles, a bolt of cloth, a smidgen of available spices, medicinal potions, needles and thread, a priceless thimble, and a Bible.

There are eleven immigrant trunks on eBay right now. Starting prices range from $395 to $2,200 with an average price of $1,016. Most do not have the painted designs that ours does. Our trunk was passed down from the original immigrants to their son Jacob, to his daughter Katie, to her son Irwin, and then to me. Not sure how we can determine the next owner, so keep your fingers crossed.

Will and Kayla, the oak wardrobe in that lake house bedroom was used by your great great grandparents George and Katie Reiss. It was in their upstairs sleeping area and contained blankets, sheets, and general storage. I remember seeing it on every visit but I have no ideas about where it came from. Grandma Katie was known to buy furniture items at farm auctions and may have paid less than $5 for something like this in the 1930s or 1940s. There are 54 "antique oak wardrobe" listings on eBay right now with prices ranging from $350 to $3,500. Most are fancier than ours however and have a large single door with a mirror.

Love, Granddad

A Double Wedding on April 9, 1866

Dear Will, Kayla, and Ava,   October 27, 2014

A double wedding was celebrated at St. James Catholic Church in Millstadt, Illinois on April 9, 1866. Your great great great grandfather Frank Reiss married Anna Sybilla Feder and his sister, your great great great great great aunt Kate Reiss, married Charles Max Wittig. The priest was Father Francis Lohmann who served there only from January 1866 to August 1866.

For some reason St. James archives show only Frank and Anna being married on that date. Their names are written in Latin as Franziscum Josephum Reiss and Anna Ottilium Feder.

Both men had been friends for five years or longer because we have an old letter from Max to Frank dated 8/19/1862. Both men had served in the Civil War – Frank with the 31st Illinois Infantry Regiment and Max with the 82nd Illinois Infantry Regiment. Our oldest letter is from Max to his "friend" Kate Reiss on Christmas Day 1861. We have 19 letters from Max while he is recovering in hospitals in Philadelphia and New York from a gunshot wound he received 5/2/1863 at the Battle of Chancellorsville, Virginia. We have 3 more letters from Max while he is living in Davenport, Iowa setting up his blacksmith and wagon making business. Those 22 letters are from before the double wedding and are part of the 780 letters which appear in our book It Takes A Matriarch. The matriarch in this case is Frank's and Kate's mom Margaret Basler Reiss. Very neat lady.

Here's what St. James looks like today. This lawn view is a bit more attractive than the street view. The church dates from 1851.

Here's Kate before the wedding. Maybe the photo was taken at the rehearsal dinner or a bridal shower because the background doesn't quite look like her family home which was a log cabin with a dirt floor built in 1838 by her father Adam Reiss.

Kate was born on 3/23/1847 so she is a month short of age 20. Max was born on 1/16/1838 so he recently turned 28.

Frank was born on 9/27/1841 so he is 24 and Anna was born on 9/26/1844 so she is 21. Note that their birthdays are only one day apart.

Kate Reiss before marriage to Max Wittig

171

Here are the two couples on their shared wedding day. You would think the backgrounds would be identical but they're not. Note that the style back then was for the groom to sit and the bride to stand with her right hand on her new husband's shoulder. My grandparents, George and Katie Reiss, had the same photo poses when they married 45 years later. Your parents (aka aunt/uncle) Hany and Grant had the same poses when they married 143 years later. You four grandkids can think about those poses when you get married about 170 years later!!!

May I introduce Mr. and Mrs. Reiss on the left and Mr. and Mrs. Wittig on the right.

Frank and Anna Reiss had 11 children with the first 10 being born in the Adam Reiss log cabin which measured only 15 by 18 feet. Sadly 4 of those children died and did not reach adulthood. The Reisses built a modern house in 1889 and had one more child there. The log cabin was demolished in 1957 but the 1889 house is still there and rented to others.

Kate and Max Wittig had five daughters in Davenport, Iowa. The first one died at age 23 months which was very sad as mentioned in our Matriarch book of letters. Altogether we have 300 letters from the Wittigs between 1861 and 1886 – 176 letters from Kate, 102 from Max, and 22 from their daughters.

Frank and Anna Reiss celebrated their golden wedding anniversary in April 1916 at their family farm. Compare the before and after photos above and below and note that their hairstyles, goatee, and clothes sizes are still the same. But the "after" picture has them both sitting.

Sadly Kate Reiss Wittig died on 4/2/1916 just two weeks shy of their golden wedding anniversary. The Reiss marriage lasted another 5.5 years before Frank passed away on 11/21/1921. I really like Anna's smile.

Will, Kayla, and Ava, there are over 100 years of history between these two couples who started married life together. Some of it is sad with the loss of children. Most of it is harsh by modern standards because there was no electricity, indoor plumbing, penicillin, automobiles, etc. Both men were self-employed and supported by their able spouses. There is a lot we can learn from all four of our ancestors. If you're ever unhappy with your surroundings and situation, look over those old letters and count most of your differences today as blessings.

Love, Granddad

The Charles Reiss Family Farms

Dear Will, Kayla, and Ava,   May 12, 2014

Maybe you know that my great grandfather Frank Reiss and his younger sister Kate were part of a double wedding on 4/9/1866 where Frank married Anna Sybilla Feder and Kate married Charles Max Wittig. It was almost a triple wedding which would have included their middle brother Charles Reiss who married Eva Dintelmann seven months later on 11/15/1866.

Soon after their wedding, Charles and Eva moved to a farm they rented near O'Fallon about 19 miles north northeast of the Reiss farm where Charles was born on 2/17/1843 and spent his first 23 years. The rest of this story summarizes Charles and Eva's farm history whether it was land they rented or owned. Eva died on 11/29/1910 and Charles died twenty years later on 5/13/1931. They had seven children, were married for 45 years, and are buried in Shiloh Valley Cemetery in nearby Shiloh.

The **1891/92 Farmers and Land Owners Directory** shows Charles renting land in Section 29 of O'Fallon Township. The **1900 Census** shows Charles age 57 working as a farmer and Eva age 55 married 34 years with 7 of 7 children still living. The **1910 Census** shows Charles Sr. age 69 and Eva age 66 married 42 years with 7 of 7 children still living and occupying a house in Caseyville Township with son Charles age 36. The **1920 Census** shows widowed Charles age 76 and daughter Louise age 50 living in O'Fallon. The **1930 Census** shows widowed Charles age 87 and daughter Jeanette age 50 living at 305 East Washington Street in O'Fallon.

Here is downtown O'Fallon. You can see Section 29 in the middle. We don't know how many acres Charles rented in what is now called Penn's Addition.

Obituary – Charles Joseph Reiss, respected O'Fallon citizen and pioneer St. Clair County resident, died yesterday morning at 3 o'clock at his residence, 305 East Washington Street, at the ripe old age of 88 years, 2 months, and 26 days.

Charles J. Reiss was born in Prairie du Long Township, St. Clair County, February 17, 1843, a son of the late Adam and Margaret Reiss, nee Basler. He was united in marriage at Belleville, November 15, 1866 to Miss Eva Dintelmann, who died in this city November 29, 1910. Seven children were born to the union. Those surviving are four sons, William R. Reiss of Lebanon; George A. of East St. Louis; Charles F. and Ferdinand J. of this city; two daughters, Jeanette M. Reiss at home and Meta K., wife of Slade R. Young of Atlanta, Ga. He also leaves eight grandchildren and three great-grandchildren. He was the last surviving member of a family of seven, all his brothers and sisters having preceded him in death.

Mr. Reiss was a practical farmer and for many years engaged in this vocation. After his marriage he located to a farm in Ridge Prairie (*now Fairview Heights*) where he remained one year. The couple then moved to a place near Willard's east of O'Fallon. Later he rented the old Bond estate now largely owned by his son Ferd north of this city. In those days the land extended far into the then village of O'Fallon, the present City Hall site being cultivated in wheat and corn by Mr. Reiss. He was a man of keen intellect and delighted in telling of the early history of O'Fallon when it was a mere village. Twenty-one years ago he retired from active farming (*thus he farmed from 1867 to 1910 or 43 years*).

Our book, It Takes A Matriarch, includes 23 letters written by Charles Reiss and 4 by his children between 1865 and 1888 to his mother or his brother Frank. Here's part of my favorite letter written in Charles' own phonetic English. He cautions his brother Frank about loaning a team of mules to any neighbor.

#268 – English   Jan. the 7th 1869
                                                     O'Fallon

Brother Frank,

I am giting consarn for not hearing anney news of Brother Martin or of anney one of yours. Martin I gas is not com & you I expected to com Chrismas or New Years but you dit not so, how ever the weder (*weather*) dus not alweys alou satch as travling wit familay.

Frank I will let you know to bee careful next time in loning your team. That fallow of corse went out the Collinsville Road. At least he was at his broter in laws & I think or have heard so that tha had a fallin out togater & so he come up to me yet after we hat spoken & he told me storey that tha hat been at the graveyard at her Faters so long. We knot (*knowed*) in the first quarter of an hour that the men drove them. The poor mules was awful hukray (*hungry*) and tursday (*thirsty*), but don't you tell him about it at least not of me. I gave him corn along & told him partickler to feed tham in Balleville. But it is doutful if he has dun it. I du dispice the fallow now. Some how I think he had to much back at home.

Will, Kayla, and Ava, can you just imagine sitting at your great great great great uncle Charles' knee and listening to his old time stories, especially with his ==heavy German accent==. My guess is that your great great great grandfather Frank Reiss had that same accent as did their parents, Adam and Margaret Basler Reiss. Hopefully we can meet all these people in heaven some day and then sit back and talk about old times. Wouldn't that be absolutely wonderful!!!

Here's another letter which Charles wrote to his mother 15 years later. It was written in German and is translated below in English. It mentions the Bond farm he is renting just northeast of O'Fallon. The paragraph and plat map after this next letter mention an 80-acre farm which Charles purchased in 1891 which is the only farm he formally owned. It was in Caseyville Township, the next one west of O'Fallon Township.

#24 – German   O'Fallon, Ills.

Dec. the 28ᵗʰ 1884

Dear Mother!

The dear Christmas is gone and the sun is already setting for the last time in this old year but it will rise again and announce the New Year and wish you a dear and peaceful new year, this is my dearest wish. I have thought about you the whole time, how you could do your work when the weather was so cold, it was a hard piece of winter. A German has told me that the farm which was called Bond's Farm for 25 years will be sold and that Mr. Joseph Penn in Belleville is the buyer, you will have seen it in the Belleville paper, for the sum of $20,000. I was present myself and the only witness. I have the promise from Mr. Penn to be able to stay on it. He hasn't been here since then, the weather was too bad and it also isn't urgent. I have time till next summer for plowing for wheat. Brother Frank has chosen a fortunate time for his visit here, when the weather arrived, we were just finished with shocking and had brought in corn feed and hay, so that we could look the weather in the eyes. The teacher in our school got smallpox two weeks ago, so we had to close the school until the 5ᵗʰ of January. Till now it looks like it hasn't spread, the boys are fishing and hunting, they shot about 60 rabbits and 17 partridges this fall and winter.

I have not received any letters lately, I have already written to Kate Wittig and want to write a few more soon to Conrad Dintelmann. Did they already visit you since they left here? Maybe with the sled?

I haven't heard anything from Aunt Lou since 3 weeks, I don't know what she is doing. George Perrow wanted to be home by the 15ᵗʰ and then they want to see what they will do. I had made the suggestion to buy something in O'Fallon and to auction something. That should have been done in time, several weeks before Christmas, so that it would be completed before the holidays. I am glad, with this bad weather and the terrible harvest prices, that she didn't do it. I don't know what else to write you, other than that the weather is terrible. I will visit you before spring.

With an always faithful heart I remain your son,

Chas. Reiss

Seven years later on 8/20/1891 Charles paid $8,350 for 80 acres of farmland in Caseyville Township. You can see it on the plat map on the next page as the east half of the northeast quarter of Section 27. It's exactly four miles west of Bond's Farm in O'Fallon Township where Charles had farmed before. He sold just the mineral rights of 79 of these acres on 5/17/1917 to Prairie Coal for $14,220 which is 70% more than his original deal and he still has the surface. Sweet! On 8/1/1919 Charles sold one acre of surface and minerals to Kinloch Long Distance Telephone Co of Missouri for what might be a relay tower.

Charles was also involved in founding the First National Bank O'Fallon. Here's a partial history from 1965 which includes two of his sons. In 1903 a number of citizens felt that one of the chief needs of the city of O'Fallon was a financial institution. There had been a private bank, owned and managed by outside persons, in the late 1890s which had failed rather disastrously. While its deposits were not large the bank's closing had seriously affected the community and its citizens. The primary purpose of the organization of the First National Bank was to give the people of O'Fallon and vicinity a safe and sound banking institution and to provide for its patrons every convenience and favor that conservative banking would permit.

That their efforts have been appreciated is evidenced by the steady growth of its resources and deposits through the years as shown by comparative operating statements. Original stockholders included Charles Reiss, Sr., William Reiss, and George Reiss. It is interesting to note that the majority of the shares issued to the above are still held by the original owners or their heirs.

William and George were born in 1867 and 1871, respectively, as sons of Charles and Eva. Today this O'Fallon bank is one of 16 branches of the First National Bank of St. Louis with combined assets of $1.4 billion. Don't know if any of Charles' descendents today in 2014 are still part owners of the greater institution.

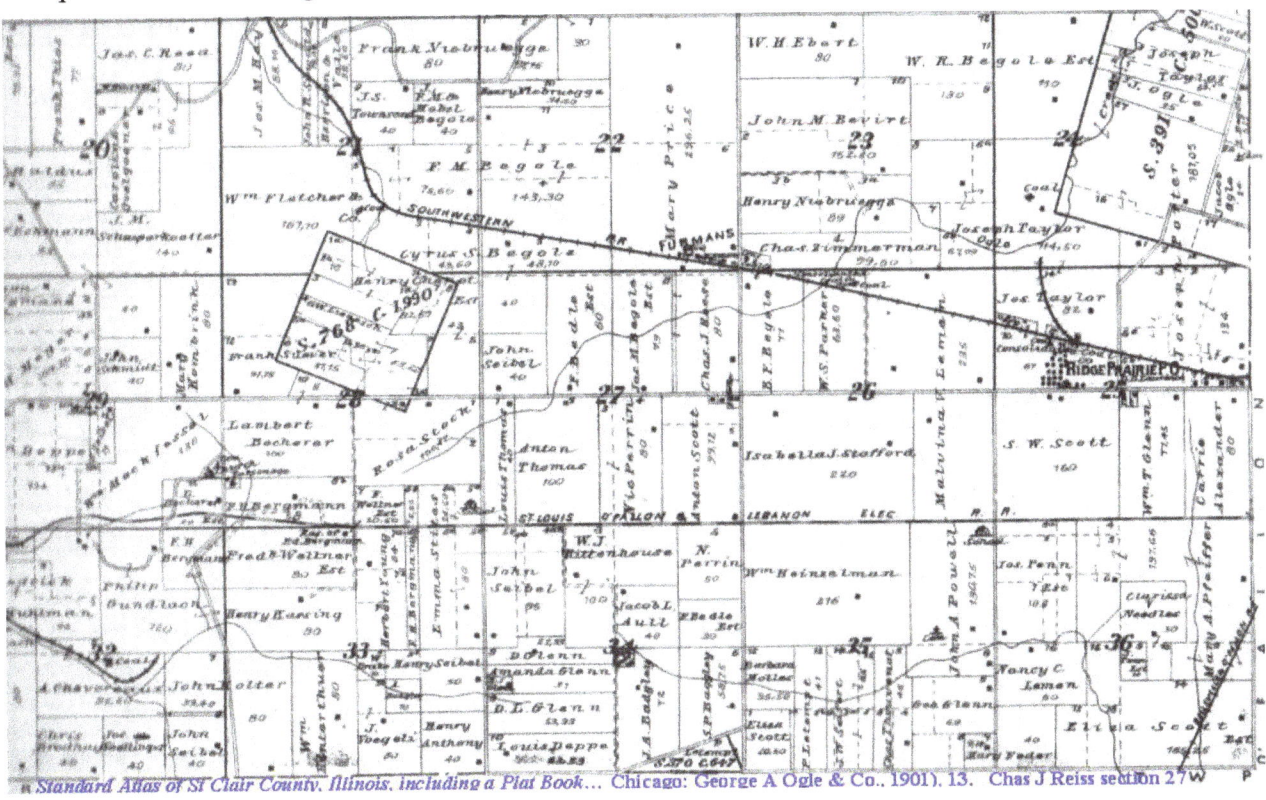

Standard Atlas of St Clair County, Illinois, including a Plat Book... Chicago: George A Ogle & Co., 1901). 13. Chas J Reiss section 27 W

Will, Kayla, and Ava, your great great great great uncle Charles Reiss was quite an entrepreneur, don't you think? He was also a very highly regarded and appreciated citizen of the O'Fallon area. I think he was pretty good at writing letters and speaking his mind. I'm glad we're all related.

Love, Granddad

The Ebert House

Dear Will, Kayla, and Ava,   October 6, 2014

Here are the various 20- and 40-acre fields of the Reiss family farm and the years they were purchased. My great great grandfather Adam Reiss bought the first three in 1838, 1839, and 1842. His widow Margaret and second husband Conrad Ebert bought the next two in 1854 and 1868 shown in pink. My grandparents George and Katie Reiss bought the next five in 1917. The rest of this story is about just the 40 acres bought by the Eberts in 1854.

Conrad Ebert married Margaret Reiss and her family of five children on 4/2/1850. Her children were John born 12/11/1838, Frank born 9/27/1841, Charles born 2/17/1843, Martin born 6/19/1845, and Kate born 3/23/1847. The Eberts had four more children, Anna Maria born 9/14/1851, Louisa born 12/??/1853, Margaret born 10/29/1856, and another whose name and birth date we don't know. The first and last of the Ebert children did not survive infancy.

All nine Reisses and Eberts lived in the log cabin which Adam Reiss built in 1838. It measured only 18 by 15 feet and had a dirt floor. Kinda crowded don't you think with an average of 30 square feet per person!!! That cabin and adjacent farm buildings appear as the "homestead" in the 1838 box.

I'm sure the Eberts wanted at least one of their children to marry, take over the family farm, and have lots of kids so they could enjoy their senior years spoiling their grandchildren. That meant they would need a second house perhaps as soon as 1859 when their eldest son John turned 20. So they made the 1854 land purchase because it was for sale, because it squared off the family farm with the homestead right in the middle, and because it could address their future need for two houses each with its own space.

Here's the house the Eberts built on their 1854 land but we don't know the year of its construction. Their oldest son John married on 10/22/1861 and moved to Belleville. Their next son Frank returned from the Civil War on 7/19/1865, married on 4/9/1866, and expressed major interest in buying the family farm. Frank's first child, Charles Martin, was named for his two brothers and arrived on 10/17/1867. So my guess is that Frank Reiss helped his mother and step-father build the Ebert house in the last half of 1865 after he returned from the Civil War.

This is the only picture we have of the Ebert house. A note on the back reads, "Home of Margaret Basler R. Ebert, Ebert Place. First "landscape" taken by Wm. M. Reiss." Will Reiss was Margaret's youngest Reiss grandson who was born on 9/17/1890. He was a professional portrait photographer all his life but this was his first landscape. If he was age 20 when he took it, then the photo dates from about 1910. The home looks like it is occupied.

Conrad Ebert died on 7/23/1880. At that time he and Margaret had only one surviving daughter, Margaret, who had married Conrad Neff on 9/7/1877 so maybe both families were living together in this Ebert home. With her husband gone, Margaret probably did not want to live alone on a farm. The 1900 Census shows Margaret Reiss Ebert living with her son Frank in the modern home he built in 1889 adjacent to the 1838 log cabin on the Reiss homestead. Margaret

Reiss Ebert died on 6/23/1902 at the home of her daughter Margaret but we don't know if it was this home or another.

Here's the 1901 plat map showing the Ebert home in the southeast corner of the 40 acres they bought in 1854. The Reiss homestead is just left of the "7" for that section. It shows Frank Reiss as the owner of 118.42 acres which his father Adam originally purchased. Frank would eventually buy out the Ebert descendents to take over those additional 60 acres. The Ebert house was abandoned and existed only as foundation stones when I first saw it about 1952.

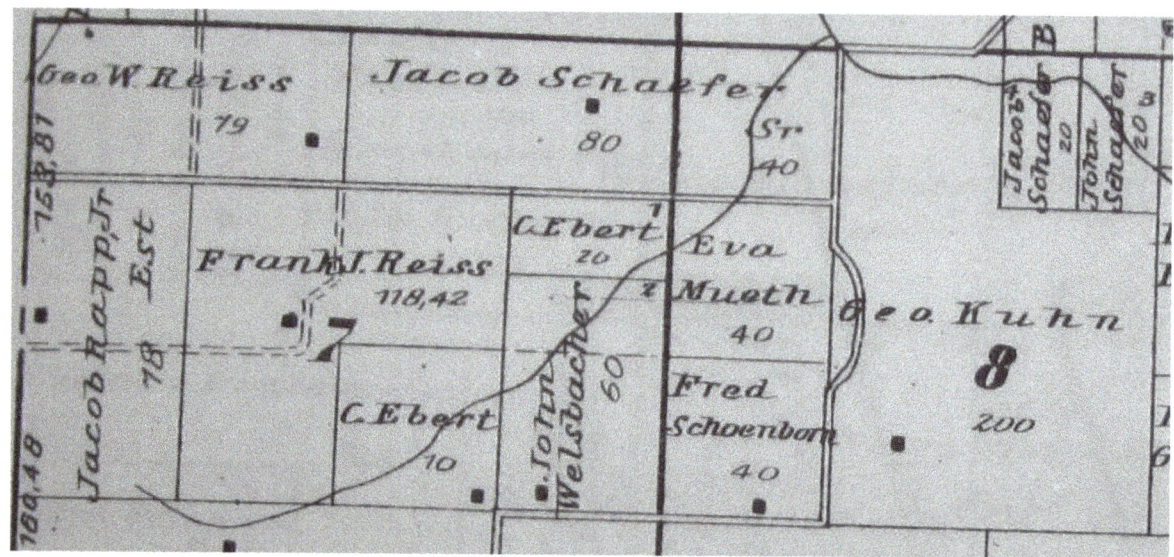

Bulldozer work was done on that southeast corner of the farm in 1958 to clear more land for farming. Here's some kid who looks like me crossing the nearby stream on a fallen log in 1958 on his way to inspect that dozer work. I don't remember if they used Caterpillar machines or some knock-offs. Today there is probably little chance of me finding any Ebert house artifacts with my metal detector but I'll still make that effort in next June when we're in the area for the Luetzelschwab Reunion celebrating 150 years of their arrival in the USA.

Will, Kayla, and Ava, what do you think we're doing in this field in 1958 where the Ebert house once stood? The answer is "looking for four-leaf clovers." That's my grandma Katie on the left who was the best four-leafer ever. Maybe you remember the very first Granddad's Mondays story I wrote way back on 4/2/2012. It was titled "Four Leaf Clovers" and contained the following paragraph:

"I learned about four-leaf clovers from my grandma Katie Reiss on the family farm south of Belleville, Illinois. She would find a few such clovers per week all summer long. She saved them between the pages of several books in her home. The books kept the clovers flat and let them dry out slowly. There were several hundred that she saved that way. I still have a few of them from her books that are now over 75 years old."

Look in the distance to the right of center and you can barely see the red barn of the Reiss homestead. That direction is northwest which will help with your bearings.

Love, Granddad

1870 – 1879

1870 Population of St. Clair County is 51,068.

1870 States total 37, national population is 38.56 million. Colorado is added in 1876.

1870 President is U. S Grant. Rutherford Hayes is inaugurated in 1877.

1870 Standard Oil Company is incorporated by John D. Rockefeller.

1870 The last former state of the Confederacy, Georgia, is readmitted into the Union, and the Confederated States of America is officially dissolved.

1870 The 15th Amendment is ratified giving the right to vote to black Americans.

1871 The Great Chicago fire.

1872 Yellowstone, as the world's first national park, is established.

1872 Susan B. Anthony, women's suffragette, illegally casts a ballot at Rochester, New York.

1873 San Francisco cable cars begin operating.

1873 Jesse James and the James-Younger Gang engage in the first successful train robbery in the American West in Adair, Iowa.

1875 The first Kentucky Derby is run at Churchill Downs in Louisville, Kentucky.

1876 Battle of Little Big Horn where Lt. Colonel George Custer and his 7th U.S. Cavalry are killed.

1878 Thomas Edison patents the cylinder phonograph.

1878 Frank W. Woolworth opens the first five and dime store in Utica, New York. business.

Matriarch #2 – Anna Antonia Sybilla Feder Reiss

Dear Will, Kayla, and Ava,   August 18, 2014

This lady is your great great great grandmother. She was born in Popendorf Landgericht, Bordenstein Koenigreig Bayern, Germany on 9/26/1844 so next month she would be age 170. Her parents were George Feder who was born in 1817 and Anna Sybilla Rau Feder who was born in 1825. They were married in 1845. We think they adopted infant Sybilla who may have been a niece so they could all make a new home in the United States. **Immigrations Records** show a George Feder age 27 as Family Number 46250 arriving in New Orleans on 10/28/1845 from Bremen, Germany on a ship called Rajah. Included in his extended family were Johann age 23, John age 13, and Catherine age 9. Another George Feder was on that same ship at age 55 and Family Number 46135. This double family settled on a farm about two miles north of Belleville, Illinois in 1846.

The **1850 Census** under <u>Fader</u> shows a double family living together in Ridge Prairie in St. Clair County as George age 61, Anna age 60, George age 32, <u>Sevilia</u> age 27, John age 27, John age 18, Catharine age 15, <u>Sevilia</u> age 6, John age 2, and Anna age 1. Underlined names are misspellings.

A dozen or more years later, young Sybilla somehow met Frank Joseph Reiss who was born on 9/27/1841 so he was one day short of three years older than her. Their farms were 14 miles apart so they weren't neighbors, school friends, or church friends. Frank was away serving in the Civil War with the 31st Illinois Infantry Regiment from 12/2/1864 to 7/17/1865 as part of the Army of General William Tecumseh Sherman. Maybe they exchanged letters or maybe they met after he returned. We just don't know.

Anyway, here is their wedding picture when Sybilla and Frank were married on 4/9/1866 in a double ceremony when his sister Kate Reiss married Charles Max Wittig who had also served in the Civil War with the 82nd Illinois Infantry. Sybilla and Frank moved into this log cabin on the Reiss family farm where he had been born. Here's how it looked in 1957.

Frank's older and younger brothers had already moved out on their own and his sister was newly married to Max. Frank's mother Margaret and step-father Conrad

Ebert had already built their new home on the southeast corner of the Reiss family farm. This log cabin had been built by Frank's father Adam Reiss in 1838 and measured 15 by 18 feet. It had a dirt floor. You can see a brick chimney for heat from a stove rather than a fireplace.

Sybilla and Frank lived 23 years in this small log cabin where 10 of their 11 children were born and where 4 of them died. Those four share this tombstone in St. Augustine Cemetery in Hecker where each child has a side. Their last child was born in a new house next door which they built in 1889. Sybilla and Frank raised seven children to adulthood who all did very well in life. Here are the details on all 11 children –

- Charles Martin was born on 10/17/1867 but died seven years later on 11/18/1874.

- Adam Joseph was born on 9/25/1869 but died two years later on 11/5/1871.

- Catherine was born on 11/11/1871 but died seven months later on 6/16/1872.

- George William was born on 4/22/1873. He bought 160 acres of land in Lamb County, Texas on 10/18/1907, married Catherine Luetzelschwab on 4/16/1911, they raised three sons, took over the family farm, and doubled its size. They were my grandparents.

Tombstone of Adam, Charles, Catherine and Lizzie Reiss, four very young children of Frank and Anna Reiss. There is one name on each side.

- Anna Margaret was born on 9/20/1875. She married George Dintelmann in 1908.

- John Jacob was born on 11/4/1877. He married Mary Etta Sellards in 1907. They founded the Reiss Dairy in Sikeston, Missouri.

- Henry William was born on 3/30/1880. He married Emma Caroline Eberlein in 1906 and Bertha Richards in ?? He was a pharmacist in St. Louis.

- Louis Phillip was born on 9/7/1882. He married Harriet "Hattie" F. Wright on 1/7/1904. He worked as a refrigeration engineer in Texas.

- Louisa Kathryn was born on 9/22/1884. She married Philip Heinrich Petry on 6/2/1909.

- Elizabetha (Lizza) was born on 7/1/1888 but died nine months later on 3/2/1889.

- William Martin was born on 9/17/1890. He married Mabel Golden in 1913 and Rose Freant on ?? He was a professional portrait photographer.

Here's a photo of the 1838 log cabin at left and the new 1889 house at right. Notice the log cabin chimney is at the side instead of on top like the newer photo above. Notice also that the front and side porches on the new house are not yet enclosed like they are today.

Here are Sybilla and Frank celebrating their golden wedding anniversary. April 9, 1916 was a Sunday so that's probably the exact date of this photo. Their hair and beard styles did not change in 50 years, only the color!!! I like her smile.

Notice in the birth summary above that George is the oldest surviving child and the next to the last one to get married. He was obviously a very busy and successful farmer, a strong handsome guy with a good tan, but he was also kinda shy. He didn't get out much. So in 1910 Sybilla had a plan to find a wife for her son. Besides, Sybilla was age 65 in that spring and all her other children had left home. She needed help around the homestead. Shortly before the Census on 4/25/1910 she hired attractive 20-year old Catherine Luetzelschwab as a live-in domestic to help with chores like laundry, cooking, cleaning, quilting, chickens, etc. Katie appeared in that census but they

butchered her last name as Luietcelschwab. Well, 37-year old George was no dummy so it didn't take him long at all to realize that ==Katie was a keeper==. She maintained a good house, was outgoing and social, spoke German like he did, was very comfortable living on a farm, and would make an outstanding wife and mother. They were married a year later on 4/16/1911 which is one week and 45 years after Sybilla had married Frank Reiss. Sybilla and Frank were married for 55 years and Katie and George were married for 53 years. ==Sybilla gets an A+ as wife, mother, and matchmaker!!!==

New Subject – The deathbed will of Adam Reiss on 5/23/1849 gave 1/3 of his 120-acre farm and homestead to his wife Margaret Basler Reiss. That meant his sons John, Frank, Charles, Martin, and daughter Kate inherited the remaining undivided 2/3 share. Those children came of age 15 and more years later and married. Frank and Sybilla eventually negotiated to buy out his mother and his siblings to consolidate the farm ownership under their names. In the meantime, Margaret married Conrad Ebert on 4/2/1850 and had two more daughters who reached adulthood and married the Neff brothers. Margaret and Conrad also bought adjacent 40- and 20-acre farms. Conrad Ebert died on 7/23/1880 without a will. Frank and Sybilla negotiated to also buy out his mother again and his step-siblings. All these buy-outs happened over a 37-year period. Here are more details –

12-18-1869	Warranty Deed from Chas. Reiss and wife to Franz Joseph Reiss for $1,000 as heirs of Adam Reiss deceased for the northeast quarter of the southwest quarter, the southeast quarter of the northwest quarter, and the southwest quarter of the northeast quarter of Section 7, township 2 south, range 8 west. This is Charles' share of the 120 acres he inherited from his father.
11-4-1872	Indenture between Martin C. Reiss of the County of Buchanan, State of Missouri and Franz Joseph Reiss for $670 for Martin's share of the 120 acres he inherited.
7-31-1880	Letters of Administration whereas Conrad Ebert died intestate 7-23-1880 therefore Margaretha Ebert became administratrix.
5-12-1884	Quit Claim deed made 4-13-1875 and filed 9-9-1875 from Catharina and Charles M. Wittig to Frank J. Reiss for $950 for her share of the 120 acres she inherited.
7-15-1887	Letter to Margaretha Ebert from attorneys Dill & Schaefer saying her son called on them with her power of attorney to sell 20 acres instructing her to sign a petition to the County Court.
12-9-1887	Administrator's deed from Margaretha Ebert administratrix of the estate of Conrad Ebert to Charles J. Reiss, made 11-25-1887. Defendants named were Margaret Neff, Conrad Neff, George Neff, and George Neff, Jr. for $555 for the 60 acres she and Conrad Ebert had purchased.
1-12-1888	Quit Claim deed from Charles J. Reiss and wife Eva who had bought the Ebert 60 acres at an estate auction signing it back to Margaretha Ebert.

9-15-1900	Warranty deed from Adam Rapp and Jacob Rapp to Frank J. Reiss for $40 for a strip of land 16.5 feet wide which became the west entrance lane.
8-11-1906	Warranty deed from George Neff Jr., Margaret Neff and her husband Conrad Neff Sr. (heirs of the late Margaret Ebert deceased) for $500 to George W. Reiss for the 20 acres the Eberts had purchased.
8-11-1906	Warranty deed from George Neff Jr., Margaretha Neff and her husband Conrad Neff Sr. (heirs of the late Margaret Ebert deceased) for $800 to Frank J. Reiss and Anna S. Reiss for the 40 acres the Eberts had purchased.

Our story continues with Sybilla and Frank living on the family farm with Katie and George from 1910 onward. They were big helps when their three grandsons were born – William on 5/6/1912, Franklin on Halloween night of 10/31/1915, and Irwin on 9/18/1917. As live-in grandparents they were both blessed and a blessing. Frank died on 11/21/1921 and Sybilla on 5/14/1930. They are buried in Franklin Cemetery in Smithton. They have a tombstone together and Frank also has this Civil War stone.

Here's a family photo probably taken at Frank's funeral. Back row left to right is William, Louis, Henry, and John. Front row is George with the tan, Sybilla with the same smile, and Margaret. Kate is missing.

Will, Kayla, and Ava, you can easily see why I consider your great great great grandmother Sybilla a matriarch. She was an outstanding mother and wife nurturing a young family under very challenging living conditions. She was a farm business partner, a teacher for her children, and an astute matchmaker. I'm sure you are all equally impressed and very proud.

Love, Granddad

188

The Ebert Sisters Marry the Neff Brothers

Dear Will, Kayla, and Ava,   December 1, 2014

You know that your great great great great grandfather Adam Reiss died of cholera at age 45 on 5/23/1849 leaving his widow Margaret with five children under age 11, a 15 by 18 foot log cabin with a dirt floor, and a 120-acre farm. What a challenge! But Margaret found a second partner in Conrad Ebert and married him on 4/2/1850. Conrad and Margaret Ebert then had three children (perhaps four) but only two reached adulthood. They were Louisa born 12/5/1853 and Margaret born 10/29/1856. Those girls are your half-aunts because everyone had the same mother but they had a different father.

At age 20, Louisa married George Neff on 11/6/1873 at St. Augustine Catholic Church in Hecker. He was born on 11/16/1849 so he was age 24. They quickly had a son George Neff Jr. on 2/1/1874 before she died on 5/21/1875. George remarried and had more children but none of them are our relatives. We have no photographs.

At age 21, Margaret married Conrad Neff on 9/7/1877 in St. Michael's Catholic Church in Paderborn. Conrad was born 12/26/1853 so he was age 22. They had their first son Conrad Charles Neff, Jr. on 8/22/1877, two weeks before their wedding. That delivery was even faster than Jimmy Johns!!!

After Conrad Jr., Conrad senior and Margaret had four more children – Mary on 1/17/1879, Adam on 1/11/1882, Ignatius on 6/18/1887, and August on 2/16/1895. Here's a family photo with all but Conrad Jr. who is missing so it must have been taken about 1899. Looks like the boys all went to the same barber.

John Fietsam,   Traveling Photographer.

Here's the home of Conrad and Margaret Neff. The lady at the right front looks like her mother who your great great great great grandmother Margaret Basler Reiss Ebert who was living with her daughter and family in her final days. Her obituary says she died at her daughter's house which would be this place on 6/23/1902. Mrs. Ebert is survived by her children: John Reiss in Belleville, Frank Reiss in Floraville, Charles Reiss on the Ridge Prairie, Mrs. Max Wittig in Davenport, Ia. and Mrs. Conrad Neff as well as 31 grandchildren and 3 great grandchildren. Also her sisters Mrs. Charles Krone and Mrs. Perrow in St. Louis.

Here is Conrad Neff Jr. who was missing from the first picture. He was born in 1877 so this picture must date from about 1910. His registration for the military draft on 9/12/1918 at age 42 shows him working as a fireman at the New Athens Bearing Company with brown eyes, black hair, height – tall, and build – stout. My guess is that he was operating a heat treatment furnace to harden bearing parts before finish grinding.

Will, Kayla, and Ava, now you know more about a step-branch of our extended family. Interesting information, don't ya think?

Love, Granddad

190

Here is the tombstone of Conrad and Margaret Neff from St. Augustine Cemetery just west of Hecker, Illinois. The graves of her mother Margaret and her sister Louisa are nearby.

Neff Family Farms

Dear Will, Kayla, and Ava,   December 1, 2014

Our connection with the Neff family in St. Clair County, IL is that two of their sons married two daughters of Conrad and Margaret Basler Reiss Ebert. Margaret is your great great great great grandmother and Conrad is her second husband after her first husband Adam Reiss died in 1849. Here are tidbits about the Neff farms which are half a mile south of our Reiss farm. Both were in Prairie du Long Township. We are in Sections 7 and 8 while they are in sections 29 and 30.

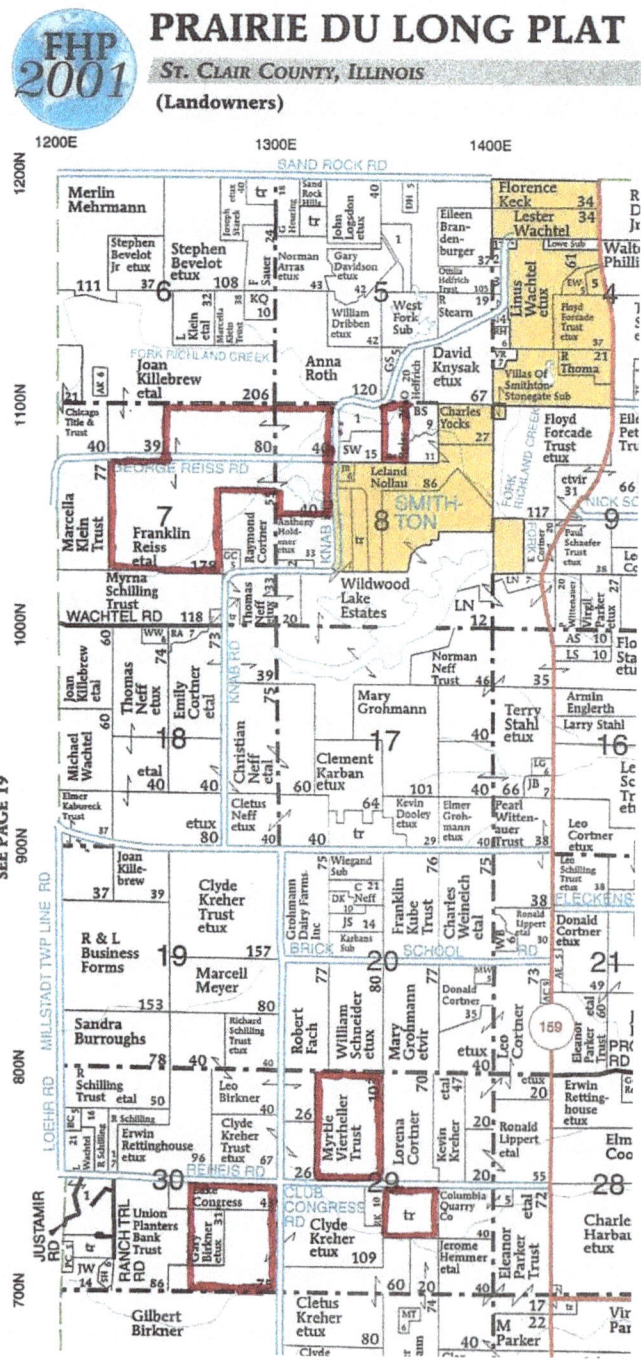

George Neff married Louisa Ebert on 11/6/1873 and Conrad Neff married Margaret Ebert on 9/7/1877. The Neff brothers are sons of Ignatius and Anna Eva Neff who both emigrated from Germany in 1837 and were married in St. Louis on 7/18/1840. Here is his picture:

Below is the 1874 plat book showing Ignatius Neff owning two farms in Section 29. Northwest of that number "29" is 107 acres and southeast is 40 acres. He bought them between 1850 and 1860. Their home is that small black square in the south center of the larger farm.

Warner and Beers, compilers, *An Illustrated and Historical Atlas of St. Clair County, Illinois*, (Chicago: Warner and Beers, 1874), 43 Township 2 South Range 8 West

Ignatius Neff died on 1/5/1891 and Eva on 1/24/1913. Below is the 1901 plat book showing two of the Neff children owning these two farms. Mary has 87 acres and George has 60 acres including the homestead. Mary eventually married Nic Cortner.

Notice also in 1901 that Conrad Neff owned 160 acres with a house as the southeast quarter of Section 30. That farm was owned by Lorenz Berkel in 1874 who had married the Neff brother's oldest sister Appolonia Neff on 2/4/1862. So Conrad bought out his brother-in-law some time after 1874.

The 11/5/1903 "Waterloo Republican" newspaper reported: George Neff, a well-known farmer near Hecker, shot himself with a 32 caliber rifle Saturday. Family troubles had been at work some time, which broke out desperately in September, causing his wife and children to leave the home. He was aged 55 years. His farm of 40 and 20 acres was in Section 29 of Prairie du Long Township. Sad story.

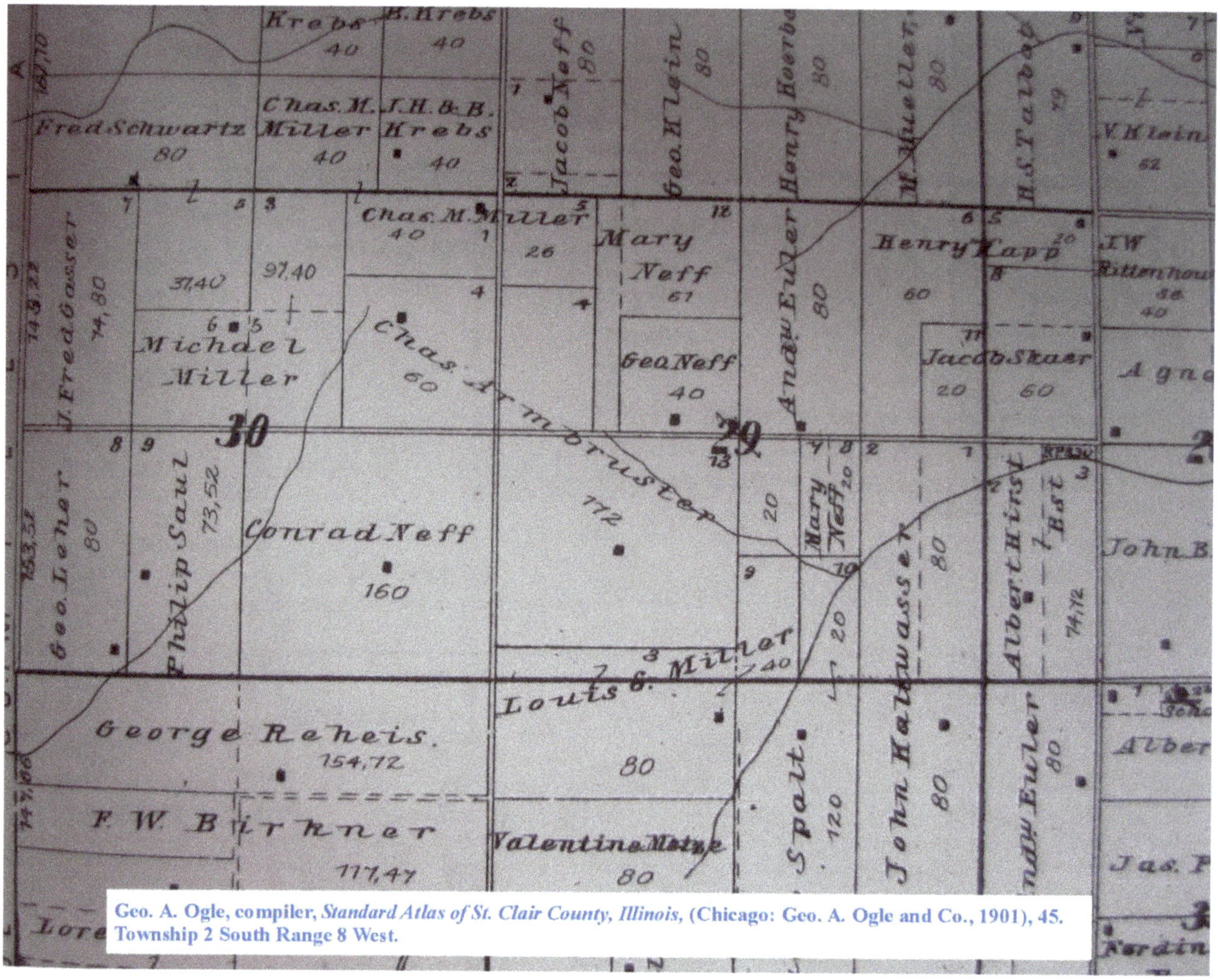

Geo. A. Ogle, compiler, *Standard Atlas of St. Clair County, Illinois,* (Chicago: Geo. A. Ogle and Co., 1901), 45. Township 2 South Range 8 West.

Will, Kayla, and Ava, here is the tombstone of Ignatius and Anna Eva Neff in St. Michael's Cemetery in Paderborn. Remember that it was your great great great great great grandfather Johann Basler who donated two acres for St. Michael's Church and cemetery in 1843. So that's yet another connection between the Neff, Reiss, and Basler families.

Love, Granddad

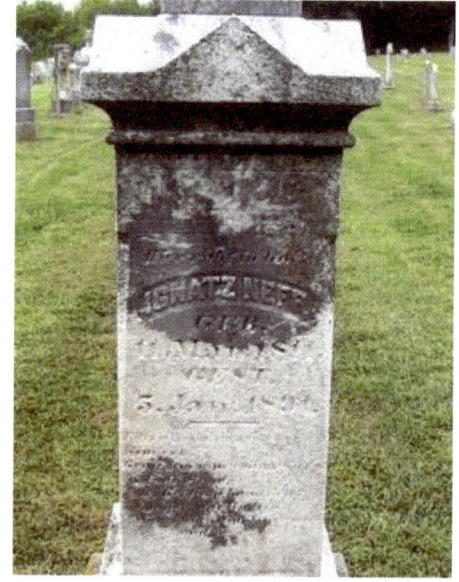

Bringing in the Sheaves

Dear Will and Kayla,   April 29, 2013

This is your great great great grandfather's cradle scythe which he used in the 1860s and 1870s to harvest wheat on the Reiss Family Farm in St. Clair County, Illinois. It's on display overhead in our log cabin so I put it on that cabin porch to take the picture below. The manufacturer's name was no longer visible. There is another picture below from Google.

A

cradle (also called cradle scythe, or grain cradle) is an agricultural tool, a form of the scythe, used to reap grain. It is a scythe with an arrangement of fingers attached to the snath, snathe or snaith (handle), such that the cut grain falls upon the fingers and can be cleanly laid down in a row for collection.

As agriculture (and particularly the cultivation of grain) developed, the end of a season was the harvest. Grain could be pulled or, more typically, cut and the sickle was the usual tool, leaving sheaves of grain to be gathered. The scythe improved the process, because the long handle allows the reaper to work standing up.

Reaping with a scythe before the invention of the cradle

readily resulted in the grain forming a muddled carpet on the field, making gathering and transport very time-consuming. In 1794, a Scottish farmer invented "a most marvelous and wonderful machine for cutting grain." This was the cradle, which revolutionized the harvesting of grains.

The cradle was commonly used throughout the 1800s and into the beginning of the 20th century, in part because many of the smaller farms were not designed for mechanical reaping and in part because there were still a great number of smaller farms where the mechanical reaper was not economical.

The cycle of wheat production involved a number of operations: preparing the ground, planting the seed, helping the crop grow, cutting the ripe plants, binding the wheat stalks into sheaves, stacking the sheaves into shocks in the field, bringing in the sheaves to the barn, separating out the grain (threshing), and finally grinding the grain into flour.

Cutting the wheat and tying it into sheaves -- have been described as involving some of the most laborious and tedious work a farmer did, one job the farm family could not do without hiring or exchanging labor. Inventions seeking to make this work more efficient and less backbreaking date from at least Roman times, but up until the mid-nineteenth century nothing worked well enough to provide widespread and permanent relief. For almost ten millennia technology virtually stood still. From the earliest days of agriculture about 10,000 years ago until the late 1700s farmers harvested wheat by stooping down, gathering, and cutting a handful of wheat at a time with a short handled sickle.

The cutting blade improved from using pieces of chipped stone to metal but not much changed otherwise. The cut grain was raked into sheaves (bundles) that were tied together using several stalks of wheat twisted together. Ten or twelve sheaves were then leaned against each other, heads up, in arrangements called shocks. By shocking the wheat, the farmer created a field storage system that promoted further drying while protecting against the effects of wind and rain, which sometimes caused the wheat to "lodge" (to go down). Later the shocks were taken apart and the sheaves collected for threshing. Using this method a farmer could only harvest up to an acre each day and the work required constant stooping.

The scythe, essentially a long handled, longer bladed sickle used for mowing hay, was not suitable for harvesting grain because the grain head often shattered as the stalk of grain

196

fell, resulting in losses. However, in the late 18th century a cradle of four or five long fingers was attached to the scythe to catch falling stalks and allow the worker to lay them on the ground in neat piles that could then be raked into sheaves.

Using this cradle-scythe, or cradle, the farmer could stand up to cut the grain, although there was still stoop work to do to rake and bind up the sheaves. Now a single farmer could cut two or three acres each day. But additional workers were needed to rake, tie sheaves, and shock the wheat.

Both sickle and scythe were used well into the 19th century. The big breakthrough in mechanization came in the 1830s with the work of Cyrus McCormick and Obed Hussey who independently invented horse-drawn machines that cut wheat stalks close to the ground using a cutting bar powered by one of the machine's wheels.

Once cut by the knives on the bar, stalks fell onto a wooden deck and then were automatically swept off to the ground, forming a continuous swath. These machines became generally available about 1850. A farmer could now ride a reaper and cut his grain. But, he still needed laborers to rake and tie it in sheaves and build shocks. The reaper only did part of the process automatically but the number of workers needed was dramatically reduced. For cutting the grain the farmer had progressed from stooping, to standing, to riding but all that really tedious and painful raking and tying by children, grandchildren, wives, and hired hands was still there.

Will and Kayla, think about how this process of gathering wheat to make flour has now been replaced with walking to Krogers to buy a loaf of bread. Now we're more concerned about whether the bread is whole wheat, cracked wheat, enriched, and many other options. Here's a song about the wheat harvest that is popular in our church.

Love, Granddad

"Bringing In the Sheaves" is a popular American Gospel song used almost exclusively by Protestant Christians (though the content is not specifically Protestant in nature). The lyrics were written in 1874 by Knowles Shaw, who was inspired by Psalm 126:6, "He that goeth forth and weepeth, bearing precious seed, shall doubtless come again with rejoicing, bringing his sheaves with him." Shaw also wrote music for these words, but they are now usually set to a tune by George Minor, written in 1880.

Sowing in the morning, sowing seeds of kindness,
Sowing in the noontide and the dewy eve;
Waiting for the harvest, and the time of reaping,
We shall come rejoicing, bringing in the sheaves.

Refrain: Bringing in the sheaves, bringing in the sheaves,
We shall come rejoicing, bringing in the sheaves,
Bringing in the sheaves, bringing in the sheaves,

We shall come rejoicing, bringing in the sheaves.

Sowing in the sunshine, sowing in the shadows,
Fearing neither clouds nor winter's chilling breeze;
By and by the harvest, and the labor ended,
We shall come rejoicing, bringing in the sheaves.

Refrain

Going forth with weeping, sowing for the Master,
Though the loss sustained our spirit often grieves;
When our weeping's over, He will bid us welcome,
We shall come rejoicing, bringing in the sheaves.

Refrain

Max and Kate Reiss Wittig

Dear Will, Kayla, Ava, and Blake,   November 17, 2014

My Granddad's Mondays story of 10/27/2014 mentions a double wedding where Kate Reiss married Charles Max Wittig and where Kate's brother Frank Reiss married Anna Sybilla Feder in a double ceremony on 4/9/1866. Let's learn from ==Max's autobiography== about what transpired in his life prior to the Civil War and prior to him marrying into the Reiss family. It's pretty interesting – his words:

"I, John Charles Max Wittig, was born 16 day January year 1838 in Duchy of Coburg-Gotha, Thueringen, Germany. Was the 9th child to my parents, prominent citizen Johan George Wittig (occupation proprietor brewing – bakery in business) who was married to my mother about year 1820 Anna Barbara Brotzman, daughter of Burt Brotzman, rope manufacturer."

"Receiving education in public school until Easter Sunday 1851 confirmed." (*That's age 13 or about grade 7.*)

"Following tradition learning trade was sent to city Meingen to relatives, Mr. and Mrs. Grau, old lady a kin of Brotzman who died in December 1852. By will the property was left to daughter of Michael Grau, valued 5,000 thaler" (*German silver coin*).

Kate Reiss before marriage to Max Wittig

"In spring 1853 Father concluded to emigrate with whole family to America starting month May to sail, leaving Coburg by mail coach to Gotha, taking railroad to Hamburg on the Elbe, on arrival meeting brother Adolph, clerk employed at iron works at Rendsburg, who helped arrangements in voyage ready to enter bark Magdalena Oldenburg, ship 2 masts, 80 passengers in all, a boat ready May 15th, 1853. Sail set crossing the Atlantic Ocean, ==56 days made journey== on 5th day July 1853 landed in quarantine Staten Island. A house was rented on 3rd Street, Avenue C, three rooms, Father, brother Herman, Emil and myself occupying 1 room, bedding on floor; the girls Augusta, Hildegard, Carolina, Clara, Anna in the other part of lodging."

"The girls soon finding employment sewing all by a furrier, later on millinery, clothing store."

"Myself attending public school for six months, fatigue around passing time gathering coal and wood at ship yard on East River for home use. First job to strike was during recess of school, attending cigar store Ave. C near Houston Street, later on learning art of carving wood by John Albach (Broome and Mott St.) had joined Turnzogling (*gymnastic school*) Franz Zigel Turnwatt."

"During month October 1855 Father, Anna and myself moved to St. Louis, Missouri with desire of my brothers Herman and Emil together to help support Father and youngest sister Anna."

"October 21st, 1856 Father died. Disease was dysentery. Age 57 years. Buried Lutheran graveyard on Gravoy, Arsenal Street, brother Emil furnishing marble stone. Max made picket fence in memory his resting grave at St. Louis, Missouri." (*The St. Louis City Death Records 1850 – 1908 show a John George Wittig, born in Germany, died 10/27/1856, and buried in Holy Ghost Cemetery at 7153 Gravois.*)

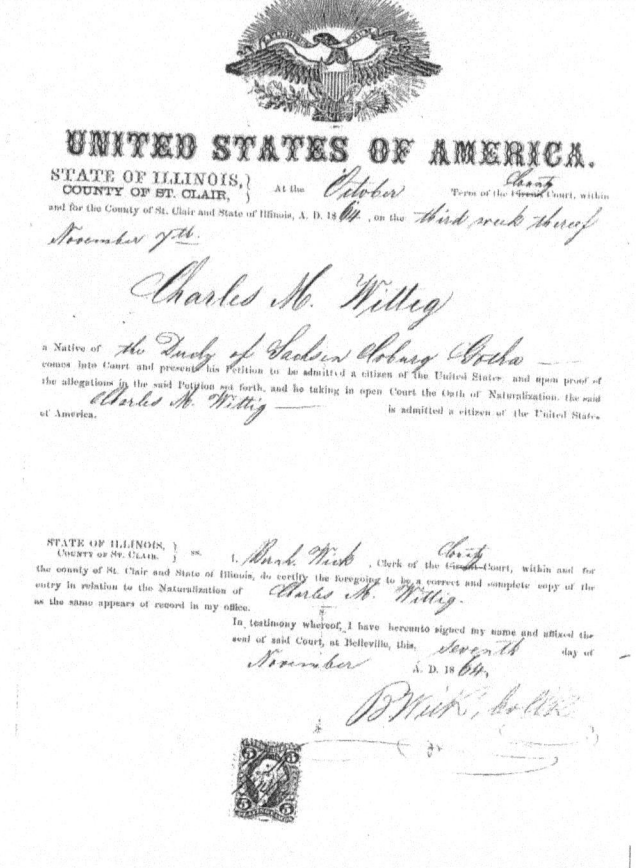

"With the death of Father (Mother died Aug. 1847 Coburg) orphan boy was left to paddle his own canoe for earning support. Brother Herman left St. Louis for Kansas, never to see him again. One meager report it was said he was killed in fight at Mountain Meadow in Mormon War, Utah 1860. Brother Emil, his health failing, ailment caused by hemp dust he was exposed to in working factory, had returned to New York City, sick."

"I was placed in trade to learn to build wagons by William Dresher on 8th and Franklin, binding myself three years faithful service. Granted US Citizenship on November 7, 1864 by the County Court of St. Clair County, Illinois."

Max's next older sister Clara Meta Wittig (3/??/1836 – >1900) married Julius vom Hofe (8/??/1834 – >1900) in 1863. He and

his father owned a fishing tackle factory. They made high end salt water reels which you now see on eBay for big bucks.

We have 22 letters from Max to Kate Reiss or her brother Frank before Max and Kate were married on 4/9/1866 in Millstadt. It was actually a double ceremony which included Frank Reiss marrying Anna Sybilla Feder. Over the next 20 years to 8/15/1886 we have another 80 letters from Max, 176 letters from Kate, and 22 letters from their daughters. All 300 Wittig family letters appear in our book, It Takes A Matriarch which contains 780 letters altogether. Thus the Wittig family represents 38.5% of all letters. Your homework some day is to read that book. It's fascinating to learn what our relatives witnessed, endured, and accomplished. You will be proud.

Kate and Max Wittig had five daughters in Davenport, Iowa. The first one died at age 23 months which was very sad as mentioned in our Matriarch book of letters. Her name was Carolina Matilda Wittig. Her nickname was Tildchen where "Tild" comes from the second syllable of Matilda and "chen" means little one or young one. It's the same way that Gretchen comes from the second syllable of Margaret as "Gret" followed by "chen." Here is Kate holding young Tildchen who was born 3/5/1867 and died 1/31/1869.

The **1870 Census** shows Charles Wittig age 32 working as a blacksmith and wagon maker, Catherine age 23, and Meta 1 living in Davenport, Iowa. The **1880 Census** shows Charles Wittig age 42 working as a wagon maker, Kate age 32, Meta age 11, Amelia age 8, Emma age 5, and Frida age 1 all living in Davenport. The **1900 Census** shows Chas age 62 married 34 years and working as a wagon maker, Catherine age 53 with 4 of 5 children still living, Meta age 32, Emma age 25, and Frida age 21 living in Davenport. The **1910 Census** shows no record.

Here are the four surviving Wittig daughters who all married but only two had children. Somewhere in all these marriages over two or three earlier generations is a connection to Roger Williams, the founder of the State of Rhode Island. Here is the Wittig family about 1890.

- Meta Clara Wittig (4/17/1868 – 10/28/1942) married William Burger (1855 -- <1930) in 1903. No children.

- Emilie Margaret Wittig (3/9/1872 – 1962) married Henry C. Gilbert (1870 – 1934) on ?? No children.

- Emma Wilhelmina Wittig (7/25/1874 – 1958) married Merle Edwin Keener (1880 – 1925) on ?? Had one daughter who married and had one son. Grand DD and I met both in California in 2007.

- Frida Catherine Wittig (9/28/1878 – 1961) married Ernest Fred Colville (3/1/1876 – 1963) in 1903. Three daughters who married, two had children – five sons and a daughter. Grand DD met two of these grandsons in 2007 and 2009.

Frida Wittig was salutatorian of her high school graduating class of 62 students in Davenport, Iowa. Here is the speech she gave at that ceremony on 6/21/1896. It was printed in the "Davenport Daily Leader" as below:

"Again the swiftly circling year has passed, and here we meet for the last time as a class with you, our friends. Your presence betokens kindly interest in our welfare. We greet you and it is my pleasant privilege to welcome you to our commencement exercise."

"With these words the speaker turned her attention to the "fads".

"There is no new thing under the sun," said she, proclaimed King Solomon. "There must be," replies the 19th Century, and true to its convictions, it scales the loftiest mountain, and plants its banner where human foot has never trod: it traverses pathless regions which the eye of man has never seen: it invents kinetoscopes and motorcycles and discovers X-rays. Men are constantly struggling to be individual."

"Doubtless the fad is an outgrowth of civilization, for whoever heard of its existence among barbarians? Possibly the Fiji Islanders have their fashions in war paint and facial decorations, but if their ladies have a weakness for bangles one month and gay feathers the next, such accounts have never reached us."

"What is this vain thing that men call a fad? Every handsomely furnished home must have its little store of bric-a-brac, and the bride of four months, just returned from a honeymoon, is laden with spoils of the old world. It is the idea that makes the craze. There are many different fads. We have the philosophic fad; the social fad; the literary fad; the musical fad, and the Trilby* fad."

"Fads die young: the few that became fashions illustrate the survival of the fittest. But when the fad becomes preeminent and dominates society, literature, education, religion, and even the home, man has perverted his opportunities, and we are tempted to exclaim, with Shakespeare, 'What fools these mortals be.' "

*Trilby is the heroine of an 1894 novel by George du Maurier in France about a young lady hypnotized by Svengali into becoming a great singer, famous in European theaters. The book was very popular in the U.S. and was serialized in "Harper's Monthly". The name Svengali continues to this day for those practicing unethical hypnosis.

Here's another article from the Davenport Daily Leader of 1/22/1899 which involves Max Wittig's business:

An Attempted Safe Blowing
Stapleton Saloon Entered on Saturday Morning

"Early yesterday morning some time after 2 o'clock some party or parties entered the saloon of P. Stapleton on the southeast corner of Fourth and Perry Streets and attempted to crack the safe. In this way they were unsuccessful because of the lack of time as they were probably scared away by Mr. Stapleton coming back into the saloon at about 4:45 o'clock."

"The safe was in the front bar room under the cigar counter and was dragged into the back room where the operations were commenced. A hammer and a cold chisel stolen from the wagon shop of Mr. Wittig further east on Fourth Street were the tools used and the knob of the time lock was broken off with the hammer. Some nitroglycerine was poured into the hole thus made, but the would be burglars got no farther. If they had, they would have been well repaid for their trouble as there was over $300 in cash in the safe. When the attempted burglary was discovered, the police were notified but there was no clew to work on."

"Expert Ferbig of Rock Island was called to open the safe but seemed unsuccessful. When the safe was rolled on the sidewalk to be loaded on the wagon, the door swung open. The burglars had done a better job than they knew and could have easily opened the door. As it was, nothing was unsecured as all the cash was in the safe and not even a cigar was missing."

Will, Kayla, Ava, and Blake, Max enjoyed good success as proprietor of his wagon making business. He even made a wagon for his brother-in-law Frank Reiss which is mentioned in one of his letters. He experienced occasional pain and discomfort from the Civil War wound to his left ankle but nevertheless was quite proud of his service to his adopted country. Max died on 1/30/1918 and Kate on 4/2/1916 which was just two weeks short of what would have been their golden wedding anniversary. Grand DD and I visited their grave in Davenport and took this picture. They were good people.

Love, Granddad

Hedge Rows

Dear Will, Kayla, Ava, and Blake,   March 9, 2015

Here's a playhouse that some trespasser built in a Springfield backyard last summer. Maybe you recognize it from your previous visits and workouts. The trees in the background are Osage orange trees which were planted over 100 years ago to make a hedge row or "living fence" to keep cattle and horses confined to a pasture. There would have been a barn, farmhouse, and cropland nearby. This hedge row is now protected and serves as a border between two adjoining neighborhoods.

The fruits of Osage orange trees are called hedge apples. They are yellow, somewhat lumpy, sometimes sticky with white juice, and the size of a softball. Will, maybe you remember "bowling" hedge apples down the inclined road just beyond your house. The neighbor who donated the bowling balls probably appreciated your help but the one downhill probably didn't.

Below is page 316 from our book It Takes A Matriarch. It's the last letter written by Frank Reiss and consists of two similar paragraphs, one of which might become a sale bill for the family farm. In 1887 the farm included three 40-acre fields originally bought by Adam Reiss and willed in 1849 to his wife Margaret and five children. The farm also included 40- and 20-acre fields originally bought by Conrad and Margaret Reiss Ebert and willed in 1880 to Margaret and their two daughters. Frank eventually negotiated with all these owners such that he ended up as the sole proprietor on everything except the Ebert 20 acres. That parcel did indeed go up for public auction and was purchased by Frank's brother Charles Reiss who promptly sold it back to Frank. A land sale or auction is a tool which some families use in settling an estate. Anyway, having mentioned all this history, I wanted you to see that ==hedge rows are an asset==. Even the hedge row in your backyard, Will and Ava, is protected and cannot be removed.

No. 1   Farm for sale

A farm of 140 acres, three miles southwest of Georgetown (Smithton) in Prairie du Long, 100 acres in cultivation, 20 acres pasture, a pretty creek runs through it, with sufficient and healthy water for the animals, also growing on the same is the prettiest young wood for miles in the whole area, the other 20 acres are regular heavy woodland, also there is a spacious house on the same, with 4 rooms, garret, cellar and porch, barn 20x20, fruit house 16x18, surrounded with fence, also smoke house, chicken house, oven, cisterns, and a well which never gets dry, with healthy water, young orchard with the latest types of fruit, apples, peaches, plums, blackberries, strawberries, 100 fruiting grapevines of various types, all the best, a number of ornamental and shade trees, etc.

For details contact the owner at the place. Frank J. Reiss

No. 2   For sale

A farm of 140 acres, 3 miles southwest of Georgetown (Smithton) in St. Clair Co. Illinois, one of the best wheat growing areas in Southern Illinois, ==the same farm is also suitable for animal husbandry, because the owner has planted several miles of hedge for fencing==. The farm consists of 100 acres of cultivated land, 20 acres of pasture and the same is also planted with young rich wood, also a creek with sufficient water is running through it, the other 20 acres are regular heavily wooded, etc. When a plan is ready, you must check with mother or someone else to have it rewritten for better orthography. Contact F. J. Reiss at the place or in writing to the same Floraville, St. Clair Co., Ill.

Why don't we see many hedge rows still in use on cattle and horse farms? The main reason was the invention of barbed wire which made living hedge rows obsolete and their annual trimming unnecessary. Here is that history.

Barbed wire is a type of steel fencing wire constructed with sharp edges or points arranged at intervals along the strand(s). It is used to construct inexpensive fences. A person or animal trying to pass through or over barbed wire will suffer discomfort and possibly injury. Barbed wire fencing requires only fence posts, wire, and fixing devices such as staples. It is simple to construct and quick to erect, even by an unskilled person.

The first patent in the United States for barbed wire was issued in 1867 to Lucien B. Smith of Kent, Ohio, who is regarded as the inventor. Joseph F. Glidden of DeKalb, Illinois, received a patent for the modern invention in 1874 after he made his own modifications to previous designs.

Barbed wire was the first wire technology capable of restraining cattle. Wire fences were less expensive and easier to erect than their alternatives. When wire fences became widely available in the United States in the late 19th century, they made it affordable to fence much larger areas than before. They made intensive animal husbandry practical on a much larger scale.

As you know, the predecessor to barbed wire was Osage orange, a thorny bush which was time-consuming to transplant and grow. The Osage orange later became a supplier of the wood used in making barb wire fence posts because it is very hard and almost impervious to decay. Grand DD and I have Osage orange posts with barbed wire along our south line which measures 3/8th of a mile. We also have an isolated Osage orange tree in our lower west end which produces hedge apples and another tree in our front yard which is still too young for fruit. Here's an abandoned hedge row and a hedge apple.

Will, Kayla, Ava, and Blake, why don't the four of you plant a new hedge row at the Springfield house. It could go in front yard near the sidewalk so Deegan would have more space to run. You could plant seedlings like this picture or do what nature does and plant the entire hedge apple. Each one has a zillion seeds. Check out the next page from the Forest Park Nature Center bulletin. That's where your dad/uncle Adam enjoyed an internship. He knows all about Osage orange trees and could help you plant that new hedge row in his front yard. Whadoyathink?

Love, Granddad

Species Spotlight
by Mike Ingram

Which tree species in Illinois grows the longest? How about the straightest? Or which one branches off at perfectly right angles? All of these characteristics are typical of a common Illinois tree, but not a tree from Illinois. Osage orange, *Maclura pomifera*, is the answer to my trick question. It grows the "longest" by its former affinity by livestock owners for being used as living fences for animals, frequently extended for a mile or more and branching off on property lines to completely enclose pastureage. Another common name, therefore, is hedge.

Osage orange can grow to a prodigious size, often in excess of 30 inches in diameter, but that was historically not the case—at least in Illinois. To be used as a living fence that preceded barbed wire, the tree had to be kept small and relatively short. That trait alone would not have kept wandering cows at bay if not for the hedge tree's most formidable characteristic—stout thorns all along its branches. Here was barbed wire long before there was a patent for it! The thorns are relatively short, up to an inch long, but very stout and able to repel cattle very effectively for many years until barbed wire became the fashion. I suspect it wasn't so much the effectiveness of the shrubby tree that was an issue for containing cows over wire, but the maintenance of the long lines of trees that tilted the balance toward the wire eventually. At the time, to keep hedge trees from becoming too large to be effective as a fence, cattlemen maintained the fences by burning off the tops of the trees. This caused the trees to re-sprout aggressively and keep their shrubby, dense character. I recall one old black and white picture of a group of men spraying burning kerosene for miles along the hedge fences to keep them down! Before the trees could grow large enough to need repeat burning, the very stiff and dense wood could, although dead, still offer plenty enough armor to encourage cows to stay put. This re-sprouting characteristic explains why most hedge trees locally are composed of several stems as opposed to a single bole like an oak. These large trunk masses can exceed five feet or more in diameter, although no one trunk may be a single foot thick. This also explains why none of the trees are very old as compared to an oak of 200 years or more of similar size. As more and more cattle owners transitioned towards barbed wire, the trees often remained and grew, as many hedgerows still contain traces of posts and wire fences through them attest. The wood is very tough and dense as well, and

Hedge tree & hedge apples

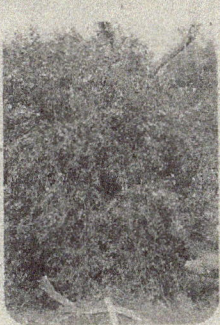

Osage Orange Tree Barrier

Hedge apple

I've commonly found old fence posts of hedge wood still with traces of wire sticking out of them—the wire has long since rusted away, but the wood remains. It does make excellent firewood, but burns very hot so use caution should you acquire some. It's best to mix it with other types of wood, as I have heard rumors of osage orange wood melting cast iron andirons in fireplaces as well as cracking bricks. I recall one cold and snowy day where I built a small warming fire of hedge wood and before very long at all, much of the snow had melted around the campfire to a distance of several feet! Imagine on a zero degree day, not being able to get close to your campfire!

Osage orange trees can be a management concern in Illinois woodlands, but seldom to a large degree. It's either one extreme or the other—a monoculture of hedge or scattered large specimens. Occasionally, in prairies, small examples exist, but for the most part they are not a huge issue. In Peoria and surrounding rural areas, you still can find them in their hedgerows within several neighborhoods in town, where they are seen growing as straight as they ever did. In this way, they have as much a history as any oak, hickory or sugar maple in our woodlands of today.

8

The Lost Family Fortune

Dear Will, Kayla, Ava, and Blake,   January 26, 2015

By now you know that my great great grandmother Margaret Basler became the second wife of Adam Reiss when they married on 9/10/1840. Adam had one son John with his first wife Mary Schuessler who died in that childbirth. Adam had five more children with Margaret so the majority of our descendents today have Basler DNA. Well, the brother of Margaret's mother Katharina Basler was Anton Basler. He was born in the 1797 in Zeihen, Switzerland. You'll also remember that both of Margaret's parents had Basler as a family surname because they were first cousins and had to get permission from the Catholic Church to marry. Anyway, Anton had a lot of money, he lived in Vienna, Austria, he had no children, and he planned to leave his estate to Katharina's children. Anton would be your great great great great great great great uncle. That's seven "greats."

Margaret had seven brothers and sisters in America in the 1870s and they agreed it would be nice to find out what happened to Uncle Anton's money in Vienna which was their anticipated inheritance. Here are parts of twelve letters by Margaret's siblings and spouses discussing their options and plans. Most were written by Margaret's brother Martin Basler and his wife Anna Maria in Sacramento, California. All these letters are in our book, It Takes A Matriarch, but they are scattered in author and date order rather than by subject like "show me the money."

                                            Sacramento County
                                            September 16, 1871

Dear brother-in-law and sister, Conrad and Margreth Ebert,

I have thought so often about Uncle Anton Basler, who died in Italy, and who had left such a great fortune. Father wrote us about it a year before he died, that the uncle had written to him that he is old and would like to leave his assets to his sister Kathrina's children, and as he said that himself, I cannot understand that he is supposed to have given the estate to his housekeeper, since he surely knew that he had friends who were in need, how often did we talk about that.

                                            Martin Basler

                                            Sacramento County
                                            December 11, 1871

Dear sister-in-law Margreth!

We have received your last letter four weeks ago, after a long wait, even though we are so careless about writing, we still would like to hear from you. Uncle Georg was here for a visit in September. I have talked to him about Uncle Anton's estate, he said he would do what is right and also would be willing to check into everything and we promised him to write as soon as we have received your letter which we did right away. He went to the Swiss consul and he wrote a letter for him to the American consul in Vienna, it cost $5 and we should receive an answer in three months. If we get a good answer, then Mr. Basler will go to Germany and take care of everything and if he goes, then he will visit you first. He intends to go as soon as we get a positive answer. So I will get my wish, finally, because I can't believe that a man, as educated as Uncle Anton was, and as of high class, that he would write to Father as he did, that he now was an old man and that he wanted to give his large assets to his beloved sister's children. That's what Father wrote us.

Also sister Kate had written us that the Uncle had died and that his large assets had been given to one of his servants, but she did not write from whom she had received the letter; and since we read in her letter and saw that it was a brother of Uncle Anton, who had written to the girls, so it is even more clear that he wants to keep everything for himself, and just told us that he had given it to his servant. A man with a good mind doesn't do something like that, if he has poor relatives, whom he really loved as he loved Mother. I also think that if he wanted to do that, then he would not have written to Father only to make his mouth water. I can't say how often I have thought about this or talked about it, but I am still satisfied, because since we have lost already so much, this can also be part of it, and if something is there for us, then we shall have it, and I don't doubt that the Uncle had made out a last will or testament, I only am afraid that we are too late.

Many greetings,

A. M. Basler

Sacramento County
the 4th of March 1872

Dear Sister Margreth,

I wrote you in my last letter that I would write you as soon as I have an answer from the Swiss consul. Yesterday I have received a letter from him. He writes that the Consul in Vienna has checked all records and all books where he could have looked, and he wasn't able to find the least about money or other property, not even as much as the name Anton Basler. He said himself that it was impossible that the Uncle has lived in Vienna, otherwise there would have to be a trace of him and I never knew anything else but that the Uncle Anton Basler lived in Naples, in Italy, but since you are older than I am, I thought you would know better, and I therefore asked them to write to Vienna. Now I wish, if you are not certain where the Uncle lived and died and when he died, in what year, then write me right away without waiting for a long time, because the Consul said that the laws in Austria are such that when one does not contact them within 10 years, then one looses all rights to an inheritance. So, write soon. We have started it and now we should see it to the end, because as Father, may God rest his soul, had written shortly before his death, the Uncle had written him that he is old and that he would not live too much longer and that he would pass on his assets to us children. And because the Uncle in Liebensville (*Louisville*) had written to Mr. Sagstaedter (*Sacksteter*) that Uncle Anton had given his assets to his servant, so I think because our Father and the Uncle in Liebensville have the same name, so it is easily possible that the pot hangs there and that Uncle John Basler himself has the assets in his possession and the Haseln (?) will have helped him to it.

Your brother,

Martin Basler

1872????

In regards to our Uncle Anton's history, I don't know what to think about it. It seems that Ferdinand and Jakob in Indiana could find out something about Dr. Flacher in Louisville, where the uncle had lived and in what college he was, what the name of his lady caretaker was, and what his assets were and what it consist of. As much as I could learn from the letters, it is certain that Uncle made a testament and if he would not have bequeathed us his assets, then he would not have sent John a testament. Write to Jakob and Ferdinand about this, and when you find out something, Brother George said he would then gladly go there if he would get the trip and the expenses paid for. Next summer is the World's Fair in Vienna, then it only costs half the price to travel there.

I would be willing to do my part, if Georg or Ferdinand would go, I don't have much confidence in Jakob. I think if the Uncle would have been willing to give him his assets, then it would at least be our obligation to see, what happened to it. Write to Ferdinand yourself, it's not too late. I want to send you an example, where you can see it yourself in print. We are all sending our greetings,

Your brother,

Martin Basler

Sacramento County
June the 7th, 1872

Dear Sister Margreth Ebert,

I have received your letter from Davenport, also Brother Jakob's letter, we have received them on the same day. You think it might not be so much in assets, and even if it would be only 1/10th, then we are still responsible to check on it and to see how the matter is. If the uncle would have wanted to give his assets to someone else, then he would not have taken the trouble to send his testament. I can't understand how indifferent all of you are, especially Lou, Kate and Ferdinand. We think if brother John has received the testament, then one must be able to find it among his papers, and if you could find it, then it would be proof enough, and also Mr. Fletscher from Louisville, as Lou said, this gentleman had known them both, the uncle and his female caretaker, you should be able to find out more from him. The servant or caretaker was probably younger than he was, and maybe she is still alive, we could probably find out a lot from her, and

Mr. Fletscher might be able to tell you where they lived, maybe even the street and her name and maybe much more, where we could find out more about the inheritance and he also might know how the laws are in Vienna, because the answer we had received from the consul is too suspect, and we can't believe that nothing can be found out about the uncle because we all know that not even a beggar dies in Europe without being recorded. The assets are there, and we think that he or those who have the assets in their hand are trying to write us off and the more we know the more we believe that there is some swindler behind this. We are all convinced that it was the intention of our Uncle to leave his assets to his sister's children and if we are being cheated out of this, then it still is our responsibility to check on it to satisfy our questions, and that we have done what is expected of us.

M. L. & A. M. Basler

December 16th, 1872
Sullivan, Indiana

Dear Brother Martin Basler,
Sacramento City, Cal.

I should have written you long ago in relation to the Vienna Legacy, but I have not been, nor am I now able to come to any final conclusion on the subject. I had at one time concluded to go and make a thorough investigation of the matter in person. I have been in St. Louis, Louisville, and have written to Margaret about it and have made all the investigation that can be made without going there and am not able to find a will nor any one who ever saw a will from Uncle Anthony to our mothers' children and finally I learn from Jacob and indirectly from Margaret that at one time Uncle Anthony at Vienna had an heir, a daughter, an illegitimate child, which if true, will cut quite a figure in the case, if she lived at the time of his death, without a will, would be the heir of the whole estate if she survived him, then the estate would fall to her mother and other relatives. . . . if he left no heir and no will, or died without a will and without an heir, the estate would go to the Austrian Government and the Government will hold it until legal heirs by due course of law prove themselves entitled to the estate, the whole subject is wrapped up on mystery and likely covered up beyond recover, I am satisfied it will require an amount of labor and as great outlay of money to recover the estate. I am willing to assist in doing anything thought best to investigate the affair fully but I have no inclination to go to Vienna and overhaul the history of Uncle Anthony and the records of the courts and the government. I think it requires a good attorney, one who is well acquainted with the laws of nations and particularly with the laws of Austria. If you or Brother George think you can attend to it, and either of you wish to, or will go, I will pay my share of the expenses. I think Margaret and Loo will also pay their shares, but as to the others I cannot say. Kate has a fine and good man but he has nothing to spare and he may not be able to assist. Jake has nothing and yet he wants something done in the matter, of course he thinks he is the proper man to send, he is very childish and not capable of doing anything without a boss or guardian, he has been living with me for about a year.

Another idea has just struck my mind, next year the World's Exhibition is to be held at Vienna, each state sends one delegate. I am now a member of our state Board of Agriculture. The State

Board of Agriculture recommends the delegate to the governor of the state and the governor appoints the delegate. The governor of this state (Thomas A. Hendricks) is a good and warm friend of mine. I think our state board will give me the recommendation and the governor will give me or some special friend of mine the appointment. Under these circumstances I may go, at least I will have our delegate to look after the matter. I will write you again about this or meet and spend a week at Indianapolis the 7th day of January next at which time the appointment will be made, after which I can give you more of a satisfactory answer. I can only assure you now that if I go in search of it, I will find the last dollar of it, providing there is any dollars in it for us.

Ferdinand Basler

partial letter

And the more we talk about it, the more we are convinced that it can't be true, it is almost unbelievable. I feel strongly convinced that there is a big fraud behind it, we talked to a public notary recently, he is a friend of us, and he also thinks as we do, there must be something behind it. We want to have it checked out by the Italian consul of San Francisco and the American consul in Naples, and we don't think that this should be too difficult. We want to check this out as soon as possible, you probably know who could provide the best information, when he died and anything what you know in regards to him. Please write us as soon as possible, because we want to wait until we have an answer from you. I think it is very careless of the whole family that this hasn't been checked out a long time ago.

Many greetings to all,

A. Maria Basler

Sacramento County
the 23rd of February 1873

Dear sister-in-law Margreth Ebert,

We have received a letter from Ferdinand in January regarding of Uncle Anton's assets, Ferd says he thinks he could get an opportunity to go to Vienna as a representative to the World's Fair and that would be the best opportunity for us and Ferdinand could find out everything. But we haven't heard if he was chosen or not, and we are waiting for an answer. If Ferd should not be going, then we think we should just let it go, the costs would be too high to send someone and we believe that others know more than we do, but I still can't believe anything other than that the uncle has bequeathed us the money.

Many greetings,

A. Mari Basler

Sacramento County
June 12, 1873

Dear sister-in-law Margreth Ebert,

This spring we have received several letters from Brother Ferd. He said he is probably going to Vienna and would probably be traveling when we are receiving his letter, the next letter he said that he is going on 1 May and then Jakob wrote that he is going on 1 June and now we have received a letter that he is not going until he hears from us. Jakob writes that if we don't send $300 by express or telegraph then Ferd is not going and the inheritance will be lost. We haven't answered the letters yet, I mean the ones from Jakob. I wish you would check what he says about this, now you know our circumstances are pretty good and what do you think about this. We have promised $100 for September 1, and if that is not enough than so be it.

Many greetings to all,

A. M. Basler

Evansville & Crawford Railroad.
Sullivan Station, Indiana
July 7th 1873

Mr. Frank Reiss, dear Nephew!

My brother Fr. Basler is sailing this week for Europe in the interest of Indiana. It may take 2 months of his time. If he is doing something or is able to do something for my interests, fate and the Gods may decide. One accommodated him too unresponsive from my side, and since he now wants to stay in Vienna, he must be happy if he can find board and lodging for 10$ in gold or God's peas. His business affects the matters regarding certain establishments in various countries, the Exhibition is the least, or just a figurehead and the trip depends on the thickness of his wallet.

Greetings to you,

Your Uncle George A. Basler

Vienna
Thursday Aug. 14, 1873

Dear Sister Lou,

Yours of the 28th came to hand yesterday. I was truly glad to hear from you but more sorrow to learn of your bad health. I wrote to Mr. Taylor on Tuesday and to my family on Wednesday. I have no doubt you will see all of my letters and thus keep posted as to my doings and movements therefore I will not repeat much of what I have already written.

I have already spent considerable time labor and money in search of the affairs of Anton Basler. I found where he had lived and died and visited those places also found a few old settlers who knew him, but no intimately, his associates were generally professors, merchants, and bankers.

In about 1850 he was still professor of language. In 1856 he was enumerated as born in Unterzeihen, Canton Aargau, Switzerland in the years 1797 and lived at No. 189. The place is now called Neuther No. 1. It is in the center of the city. I visited the house. It had changed ownership about ten times since he lived there. There he was simply recollected as a professor of languages and trades.

I then went to the office of register of deaths, examined the books for 1857 & 1858 but some how overlooked his name. But next day found him registered as having died March 29, 1857 at another house. He had a housekeeper whose name was Agnes Binder from Langenlois, Austria. I cannot find her now whereabouts.

The register says he was 58 years of age when he died. I find the records of the death of an infant child illegitimate of A. Basler. I don't remember the date year or name. It was a female name. At the time he died he was engaged in the manufacture of artificial flowers on an extensive scale. During his sickness he made two wills in which he willed a sum of money to his said housekeeper.

The Records of Deeds shows he owned city property but after a half a day's examination, I was politely informed that it was contrary and against the law of the Kaiser Konig to suffer an inspection of the books without a special written permit from the king himself and the desk was at once locked. I was not able to find what became of the stock of flowers and the real estate. The will does not cover it nor does it cover his pother personal property, nothing but a certain sum of money. I would get at the bottom of this affair, money will do it. I mean and am assured that nothing but money and underhanded bribery will ever do any good. I will get more information when on the cars and ready to leave the Government of Austria. There is an unrevealed mystery and I believe forgery in the matter. I am now satisfied that nothing but personal attention and lengthy perseverance will ever bring success, which I have no desire to undertake for I would take another journey across the ocean and live as I now have to live for all the money my brothers, sisters, and myself are worth. I had made you all a very liberal offer. You should have furnished the money early in the season. I am of the opinion that it would have paid well. If any of you desire to take the contract and want such fun as I am and have had since I left home, but more specially in the searching business. I will contribute my part, but I want no more of it myself. I am indeed sorry for all of you and look upon it as a great loss to us all. The will on its face is a lie. It says "that in as much as I have no children and no blood relations, I will and bequeath to my housekeeper Agnes Binder ---- gilders". As no real estate nor other personal property is mentioned and yet on the records in half a days examination, I found five or six deeds on record where he has bought and leased property, but find no sales or disposal of any, also the other property must have been disposed of.

I am glad to learn that my family is doing well and feel contented, but think that a large portion of the contested part is manufactured to ease my mind. Also it is not natural for any of them to show, or rather make their discontinuations and troubles public. On the contrary silence predominates.

I rest easy for I am tired every night singular as it may appear. I never once dreamed of any one in Sullivan since I left NY and yet think of you all before going to bed. It is now nearly one o'clock and I must sleep some tonight. I would like to say much more. Show my letter to all of them. Give my love to all and save this as a memorandum for future reference.

Your brother,

Ferdinand Basler

Here is part of the memorandum that Ferdinand Basler sent from Vienna to his siblings in the US in August 1873.

Anton Basler was Professor of Languages in Vienna for several years. In the enumeration of 1856 he is registered as born in Neiderzeihen, Canton Aargau, Switz. A.D. 1797. In 1856 he was engaged in the manufacture of artificial flowers and street speculation generally. Generally associated with professors, merchants, and bankers. He died March 28, 1857 at the age of 58 years (this don't G). He had a housekeeper, Agnes Binder of Langenlois, Austria. (*Langenlois 45 miles northwest of Vienna. Its population in 1865 was 7,000.*) He made two wills in each of which he willed a certain sum of money to his housekeeper. In 1856 he lived in No. 189 now called Neuther No. 1. It is about the center of the city. The records show he owned real estate. Found nothing as to what disposition was made of it. Jacob Hauser No. 55 Neubourg or Department of Chief of Police.

Saw Max Mantelbaum a special associate and a d-d rascal. Saw wife of Anton Galotzy (office holder) lives in Florina Gasse No. 19. She knew Anton Basler well. He lived in the same house as did her mother. Saw wife of Jacob Hauser flower manufacturer No. 25 Breite Gasse. His wife learned the trade at Anton Basler's establishment. She said that he at one time was married. Wife died. Left no children. His housekeeper had nothing to do with the business. She was a Sooder. Described Anton B. his sickness (Gleider Kronkheit) said he had plenty money, gold watch, fine jewelry, furniture too. Saw him at one time have a small sack of diamonds. Speculated generally, business was worth 50 to 100,000 guilders. Carried on very extensive . . . .

Here is a short notice in the Sullivan, Indiana newspaper about Ferdinand Basler's travel after leaving Vienna to visit his home town of Zeihen, Switzerland . . . . . I left Zurich Sunday evening and came by rail to Brugg, thence by stage to Hermessen, and next morning had my landlord Birri haul me to this place, Hotel Roessli, formerly owned by my father.

Grand DD and I spent most of September 2008 in Europe. On 9/26/2008 we drove to Zeihen, Switzerland to explore, meet relatives, and stay two nights at the Hotel Roessli which was owned by great great great grandfather Simon Basler around 1820. Below is what it looks like today.

We had an upstairs room on the front. We hosted dinner for my fifth cousin Kaspar Basler, his wife Roseli, and the town clerk Frantz Wuelser. It was fun and we learned a lot about our ancestral village. The Baslers hosted brunch the next morning at their farm on the edge of town.

My brother Ken and I are trekking for ten days in the Swiss Alps this coming August. That package will include parasailing off a 1,000 foot cliff. Assuming we survive, we plan to also visit Zeihen, stay again in this Hotel Roessli, and host dinner with our cousins.

Will, Kayla, Ava, and Blake, it's obvious that Ferdinand Basler followed many leads in Vienna trying to learn what had happened to Uncle Anton's estate. But at the end of the day, he had struck out, departed Vienna for Switzerland, and eventually returned to Sullivan, Indiana. But he returned home sick with cholera or typhoid fever which he probably caught on the ship. He never left his home and died a few weeks later on 12/15/1873 at age 46. Maybe if he hadn't finagled a free trip to Austria from the State of Indiana, he would have never left Sullivan and might have lived another 30 years or more. The other "maybe" is that maybe Uncle Anton's money is still there somehow.

Maybe we should pay our own way to Vienna and start another search. Whaduyasay?

Love, Granddad

Ferdinand Basler and Sullivan, Indiana

Dear Will, Kayla, Ava, and Blake,   September 1, 2014

Today is Labor Day and our three families are celebrating it together at our Lake House in Sullivan which is the County Seat of Sullivan County, Indiana. Therefore let me tell you about our extended family that has lived here since 1848 or 166 years. Here's a map from 1876 that I bought on eBay which will help with addresses and general orientation.

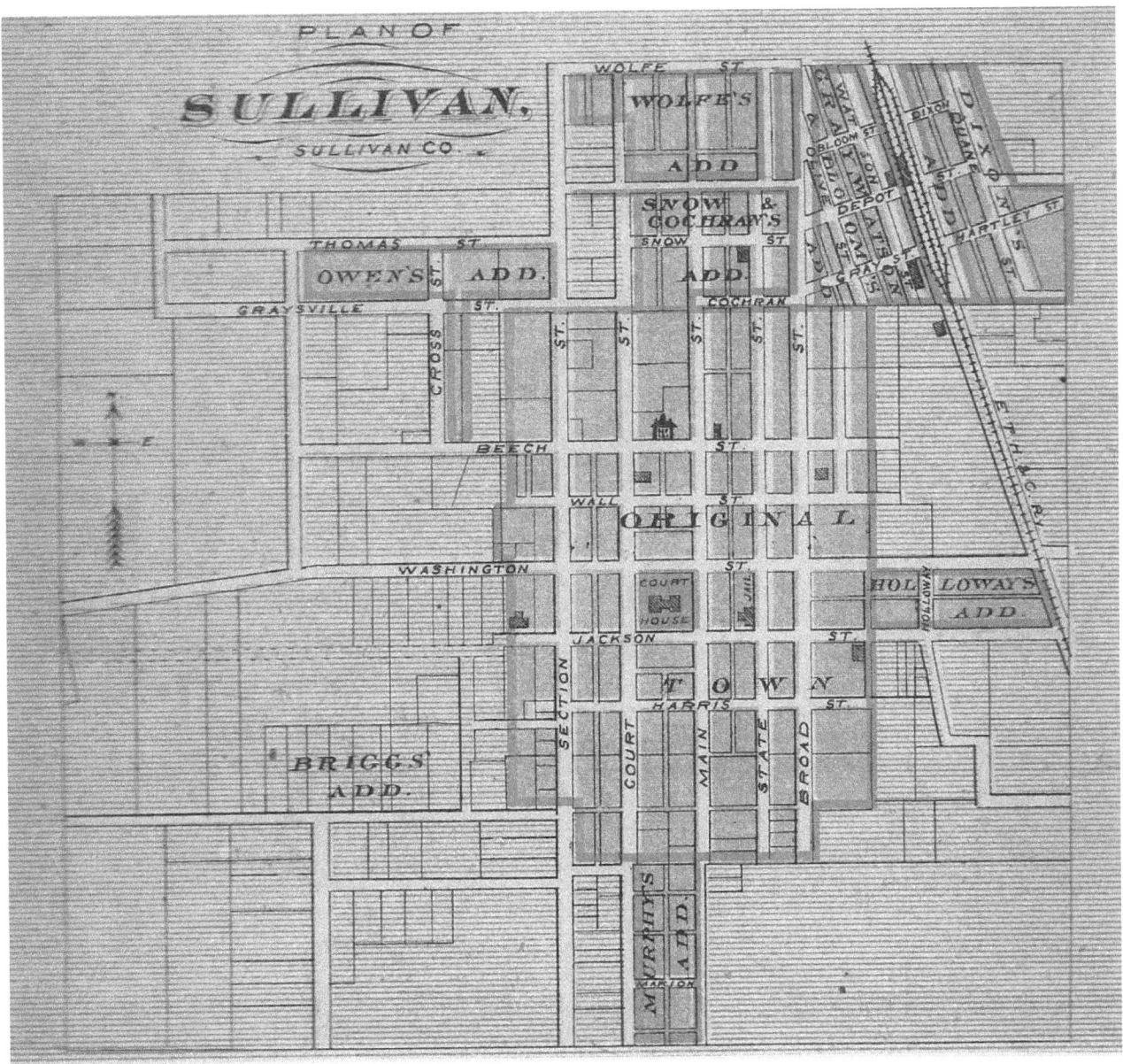

Our first relative to arrive here was Ferdinand Basler in 1848. He was born in Neiderzeihen, Switzerland on 6/13/1827, arrived in New Orleans with his parents and siblings on 11/28/1839, and settled with his family in Paderborn, Illinois. His oldest sister Margaret Basler married my great great grandfather Adam Reiss on 9/10/1840 and settled on his nearby farm to raise a family. His next older sister Sophia Basler married Frantz Stauder on 3/28/1842 and settled on his nearby farm to raise a family. Their mother had died in Paderborn on 3/5/1841.

Ferdinand's father Johann Basler bought 40 acres of land just northeast of Paderborn on 12/13/1841. He sold his farm on 11/2/1843 and moved his family (less the two daughters) to Louisville, Kentucky. Ferdinand and his six-year older brother Johann Jakob Basler (born 7/24/1821) next appear in Galena, a bustling city of 14,000 people in northwest Illinois where lead mining dominated the local economy.

"The Galena Directory and Miner's Annual Register for 1847-8" shows J. J. and F. Basler

operating a confectionary at 118 Main Street which was renumbered to 213 South Main in 1900. Their store was the right side entrance of this downtown building. The "1848-9 Register" shows Jacob Basler working as a confectioner at J. Armour's at the renumbered address of 201 South Main. The "Jo Daviess County, Illinois Marriages Book A for December 4, 1849 to December 5, 1855" shows John Basler marrying Cornelia Weck on 12/5/1849. So sometime in 1848 Ferdinand Basler moved to Sullivan, Indiana.

Ferdinand Basler married Esther Ann Catlin on 6/??/1849 in Sullivan. She was born on 6/??/1831 and was age 18 to his 22 when they married. The **1850 Census** shows Ferdinand age 23 working as a merchant, Esther age 19, Delpha age 1/12, his sister Louisa Basler age 15, and a boarder Peter Higdon age 24 working as a clerk. So Louisa is the second Basler in Sullivan.

The 1860 Census in Sullivan shows Ferdinand age 33 born in Switzerland working as county auditor, Esther Ann age 28 born in Indiana, George W. age 7, Ferdinand age 5, Josephine age 2, and servant Elizabeth O'Haver age 16. Their daughter Delpha had died in 1851. The **1868 Sullivan, Indiana Business Directory"** shows Ferdinand as a real estate agent on Court Street and his brother Jacob Basler operating a Confectionery on Washington Street. So Jacob is the third Basler in Sullivan.

Another relative moved to Sullivan in 1862. It was Martin Reiss was the fourth son of Adam and Margaret Basler Reiss. He stayed briefly with his uncle Ferdinand Basler. Martin was born 6/19/1845 so he is age 17. He was looking for a job as a harness maker apprentice in Sullivan or Terre Haute. Here are two letters he wrote in German which I had translated, first to his mother Margaret and second to his brother Frank.

218

Sullivan
14th of ??, 1862

Dear Mother,

It's with pleasure that I take my pen to write you the truth. Please don't think that I have forgotten you. I wrote a letter to you already eight days ago – whether you received it – I don't know. Dear mother, you don't think I have forgotten you, do you? I have already written seven letters without any answer. That's not nice – I am going to the post office twice a day waiting for some news – in vain. There should be one of the seven, take pity of me and write back. It has been raining for almost three days now and I don't think it is going to stop today. You can nearly go by boat into town.

Whether it is good here I don't know, yet – but I think it is – as I am becoming fat. Joseph (*Stein*) says you would not recognize me if you saw me now.

Amen. Write often,
Your true son Martin Reiss

Terre Haute
February 22nd, 1863

Dear Brother Frank,

It's a pleasure to write to you to let you know that I still love you and always loved you. You are offended that I haven't written yet which I can understand. Let me explain why I haven't written by now. I always thought you had a lot of writing to do and you don't like writing. I received your letter on Monday at 7:00 p.m. after supper. Please forgive me that I haven't written but I am no longer in Sullivan. I am in Terre Haute now. I am here for two weeks and I like it quite well. The wage is as I wrote to Charles.

Joseph (*Stein*) came with me from Sullivan but as he didn't like it here and he didn't find a good job. He left last Friday, where he is now, I still don't know. He left here at 2:00 o'clock and at 7:00 o'clock I received your letter so I couldn't give him your greetings. He promised to write as soon as he has got a permanent residence. I am very excited to hear from him soon. When we said goodbye, we cried. Now every one of us is alone.

Dear brother you think that I am annoyed with you, knowing the reason, then you know more than I do. It is true that I was cross with you a few times and the other way around as well. So please write.

Our uncle (*Ferdinand Basler*) is going to visit you soon. He wrote this week that he would be coming here on Friday, but he didn't come. He will probably be coming here this week then be travelling on to St. Louis and after that, he will be visiting you. That's all for today, hope you are well. Write as soon as possible. Amen.

Your true brother,
Martin Reiss

The 1870 Census in Sullivan shows Ferdinand age 43 working as a lawyer with a net worth of $13,000, Esther age 39, George W. age 18, Ferdinand age 16, Josephine age 13, Flora age 11, Kate M. age 9, and Maggie age 5. ==Ferdinand's brother Jacob still lived in Sullivan==, working as a candy maker, and boarding with the Henry Morris family.

Ferdinand Basler died on 12/15/1873 at age 46 from cholera which he had been exposed to during a trip Vienna, Austria when he represented the State of Indiana at the Weltausstellung World Exposition which had 26,000 exhibiters. He returned sick and never left his home at 415 Court Street.

Attending Ferdinand's funeral was his nephew Charles Reiss who wrote this letter in phonetic English and German to his brother Frank about the experience. Also attending were Ferdinand's older brother Johann Jakob who went by "George", his younger sister Louisa Perrow, and his older sister Margaret Reiss Ebert who is the mother of Charles and Frank.

GENERAL TELEGRAMS.

OBITUARY.

THE HON. FERDINAND BASLER.

[By Telegraph to the Sentinel.]

SULLIVAN, Ind., Dec. 16.—The Hon. Ferdinand Basler, member of the Board of Agriculture from this district, died Monday evening at fifty-five minutes past eleven. He will be buried Friday morning at ten o'clock. Deceased has recently returned from Vienna, where he officiated as general delegate from this State.

12/21/1873 Sunday

O'Fallon Station (*Illinois*)

Brother Frank,

I arivt home at 8 o'clock last knite and fount my famley all wright and wel. (*Last*) Thursday we left O'Fallon at 8:40 an arrivt Vensents (*Vincennes*) 1:15. Left 7:40 for Sullivan arrivt thear at 8:30 the am. There the bus driver hollered "free bus to the hotel, any other plase 25 cts." Don't want you. I stucks my hat in the ticket office, I seen a lot of young men in thear but dit not know anney of them. Then I hollers "is anney of the Baslers in?" ("What, I replied") How are you Charley hollers a Basler. Stout young man & it was Ferd (*junior*) also George & little George setten. The boys finished up and we all went to Baslers together. Than was nobody but Uncle F. J. Basler but nobody I of noblase (?) and Aunt Esther crying in Mothers arms. . . . . . Then went in the parlor near to see Uncle. He was thear laying in his last house the fantest (*fanciest*) coffen ever I seen. It was felt not silk white. The outside was the finest avable (*available*) magani (*mahogany*) with 6 silver pulls . . . . (*next page and a half are in translated German*) 38 screws held on the cover, and also so many silver plates under the screws. The cover with two glass panes and then two covers above the glass.

After half an hour arrived Aunt Lou and Max, joy and sorrow at once. George and Ferd are two haughty men. They wear ¾ stove pipe (*hats*). .... The uncle hasn't changed any at all, he could have laid there another 8 days. At 10 o'clock on Friday arrived the Masons, and the Brothers of the Knights Templar, which is the highest order of the Masons, and in this order our Uncle had reached the 6th degree. Their uniform resembled an otter tail, together with a white feather and a saber, a foot long.

From the house it went in the Free Presbyterian Church where his personal history and the ceremony of the order were recited, with song and piano music, from there to the gravesite, where he was lowered into the grave at 11 o'clock, west of O'Sullivan, on a nice hill which drops down to the east. I have left mother there, I don't know when she is coming. Georg Basler will bring her to Vensents.

Your brother Chas J. Reiss

Ferdinand had been on the board of directors of the new Center Ridge Cemetery just west of Sullivan when he died. That resulted in the Basler family plot being a prime location at the top of the center ridge. There are a dozen or more Basler graves there now.

The 1880 Census in Sullivan shows Esther age 50, her mother Delphi Catlin age 81, Ferdinand E. age 25 working as a railroad agent, Josephine age 20, Florence E. Age 18, Kate L. age 17, Maggie E. age 11, and Harry C. age 8.

The 1900 Census in Sullivan shows Esther age 68 as head of the household living on Court Street with daughter Florence age 38 who has been married 17 years and is the mother of 3 children all still living, son-in-law James Russell age 42 born in Indiana and working as proprietor of a transfer company and their two daughters, Marie age 8 and Ruth age 3.

Esther Basler died on 8/28/1903 and is buried next to her husband. Her daughter Florence Russell and her husband are buried nearby. In the fall of 2009 I was walking the Basler family plot and noticed new plastic flowers on the Russell grave. I returned and placed a typed and laminated "To whom it may concern" letter under a brick on top of that Russell stone. The letter explained my connection and asked the flower person to contact me which she eventually did. It turned out to be my fourth cousin Jill Anderson who was a Russell great grandchild. Today she owns a local jewelry store in Sullivan and lives one block north of the house where I grew up.

The Irv Reiss family moved to Sullivan in late 1948. We may have been within weeks of when Ferdinand Basler moved there 100 years earlier!!! Dad had taken a new job with Meadowlark Farms which was based in Sullivan as the farming subsidiary of Ayrshire Collieries which engaged in surface and underground coal mining. I was age 5, brother Ken was 3.5, and sister Mary Kay was 2. Our house was at 437 West Thompson Street which is two blocks further west from that kink at the end of Jackson Street. We three kids lived here through high school and college and my sister is still in Sullivan. Our parents lived here until Dad died on 4/11/2007 and Mom on 5/16/2010. Both were age 89 and are buried in Center Ridge Cemetery about 200 yards south of the Basler family plot.

Will, Kayla, Ava, and Blake, that's a complicated history summarizing how four of our relatives from St. Clair County, Illinois ended up in the small town of Sullivan, Indiana 100 years before we did. Even though it is the county seat, the Sullivan population has been level at 5,000 for at least the last 65 years. There just aren't a lot of jobs there so most young adults move to bigger cities like Peoria for careers with companies like Caterpillar. There are more pictures on the next pages.

Love, Granddad

Below is our house at 437 West Thompson Street where I grew up. This photo was taken at Christmas 1969 because I was still driving that 1967 Corvette convertible. The sun porch on the right side was not yet added. And it was still six weeks before I met Diane Peterson on Friday the 13th of February 1970. You know her better as Grand DD.

Above is the home of Ferdinand and Esther Basler at 415 N. Court Street. It is now owned by Mr. and Mrs. Nick Sider. Two of the Basler daughters owned the next two houses north.

Here is the home of Ferdinand Basler Jr. and his wife Allie French who were married on 10/4/1881. Her parents sold the house to them for $1.00. It's at the corner of Jackson and Section Streets and is now owned by attorney Ed Powell who handled our farm purchases from Peabody. He lives upstairs and has done an outstanding job preserving/restoring his home/office. Maybe you can make out his name on the sign at left.

Louisa Basler Perrow

Dear Will, Kayla, Ava, and Blake,   March 2, 2015

This lady is my great great great aunt as the youngest sister of my great great grandmother Margaret Basler Reiss Ebert. She usually went by Lou. We have 28 of her letters in our book, It Takes A Matriarch. The first six letters are from when she lived in my hometown of Sullivan, Indiana. They date from 1873 to 1880 before she moved to St. Louis for the rest of her life. All but one letter was in German. Here is Lou's first letter was to her oldest sister Margaret on 12/13/1873 which was two days before their brother Ferdinand Basler died of cholera.

"I have received your dear letter yesterday evening and I always have to cry when I receive or read your letters. I slept at home yesterday and this morning I went to Ferdinand and told him that I have received a letter from you. Oh, if you could have just seen him, he looked at me like an innocent child and asked me 'O, my dear sister read me the letter from my dear sister. Oh, how would I like to see my dear sister.' Then he waited about 5 minutes and said: 'Dear sister, I want you to go with me to Margrets.' I said: 'Certainly I will go with you, as soon as you can travel, we go to Margrets.' Then he bubbled over for joy and he started to cry like a little child 'Oh my dear, dear sister Margret, oh I want to see her', he cried really loudly and I tried to comfort him like a little child." (*Their brother Ferdinand died two days later on 12/15/1873 at age 46.5 from cholera contracted either at the World's Fair in Vienna, Austria which he visited three months earlier or onboard ship on the way home.*)

Lou was born 3/5/1836 in Switzerland as the youngest of nine children. Grand DD and I visited her parents' homes in Zeihen and in Herznach and even stayed two nights in the Hotel Rossli which was owned by their uncle. One of Lou's siblings died in Switzerland but then the rest of the family, parents and eight children emigrated to the US, arriving in New Orleans on 11/28/1839. Lou was just four months older than you are today, Kayla, when she landed in New Orleans to start life on a new continent. Your mom can tell you what that's like.

The **1850 Census** shows Louisa Basler age 15, born in Switzerland, and enumerated with her brother Ferdinand Basler age 23 in Sullivan, Indiana. Lou married Samuel R. Perrow on 12/1/1856. He was born in Louisville, Kentucky so maybe that's where the wedding was. He may have worked harvesting trees. She is definitely a dressmaker and had her own shop in St. Louis for many years. Here are entries from city directories in New Orleans and St. Louis:

1859	George L. Perrow born			Kentucky
1863	Samuel Perrow born			New Orleans, LA
1867	S. R. Perrow	Dry goods	Levee & Mary streets,	Carrolton, LA
1868	Lou, Sam	Dressmaker, Sawyer	Levee & Jackson	New Orleans, LA
1869	Lou, Sam	Dressmaker, Sawyer	Levee & Jackson	New Orleans, LA
1870	S. R. Perrow	Sawyer	Mary & 4th Streets	Carrolton, LA
1881	Aloise, George	Selling notions	2518 Carondelet Ave.	St. Louis, MO

1882	Lou, Samuel	Selling notions	2518 Carondelet Ave.	St. Louis, MO
1883	Lou, Samuel		2518 Carondelet Ave.	St. Louis, MO
1884	Louisa, Samuel	Selling notions	1518 Franklin Ave.	St. Louis, MO
1887	Lou, Samuel	Selling notions	2219 Chouteau Ave.	St. Louis, MO
1890	Lou, Sam, George	Dressmaker	2102 Walnut	St. Louis, MO
1891	George		5576 Vernon	St. Louis, MO
1892	George		2804 Morgan	St. Louis, MO
1892	Lou, Samuel		209 S. Madison	Peoria, IL
1893	George	Teacher	2102 Walnut	St. Louis, MO
1895	George	Teacher	2102 Walnut	St. Louis, MO
1899	George, Teacher - Bryant & Stratton College		2946 Clark Ave.	St. Louis, MO
1900	Census showing Louise, George, his family		2946 Clark Ave.	St. Louis, MO
1907	Lou Perrow dies on July 20 and is buried at Calvary Cemetery			St. Louis, MO

That address in Peoria is now underneath the Twin Towers across from City Hall. **Decatur Street** in New Orleans was named after Stephen Decatur. It is near the Mississippi River in the French Quarter and was formerly known as "**Levee Street**" or "Rue de la Levée". The street starts at Canal Street (across Canal Street, the equivalent street is Magazine Street) running across the French Quarter roughly paralleling the Mississippi River, and comes to its terminus at St. Ferdinand Street in the Faubourg Marigny neighborhood.

The most famous sights on Decatur Street are Jackson Square and nearby Café du Monde. For about a century, upper Decatur Street (the portion closer to Canal Street) had many businesses catering to sailors visiting the port of New Orleans. In the late 20th century, it was redeveloped and became more upscale with commercial business such as the House of Blues. In the late 20th century, lower Decatur Street became a center of local punk and goth subculture. The Street contains various bars and music venues and is not far from the Frenchmen Street venues, across Esplanade Avenue in Faubourg Marigny. The Palm Court Cafe is a famous traditional jazz venue.

Will, Kayla, Ava, and Blake, you'll have to read Aunt Lou's letters which are in our book. One of my favorites is where she mentions her ideal home as a senior citizen would be a small cottage with a garden and a cow. I think she was a pretty cool lady and probably really enjoyed living in New Orleans. We don't know what happened to her husband. My guess is he is buried in Louisiana.

Love, Granddad

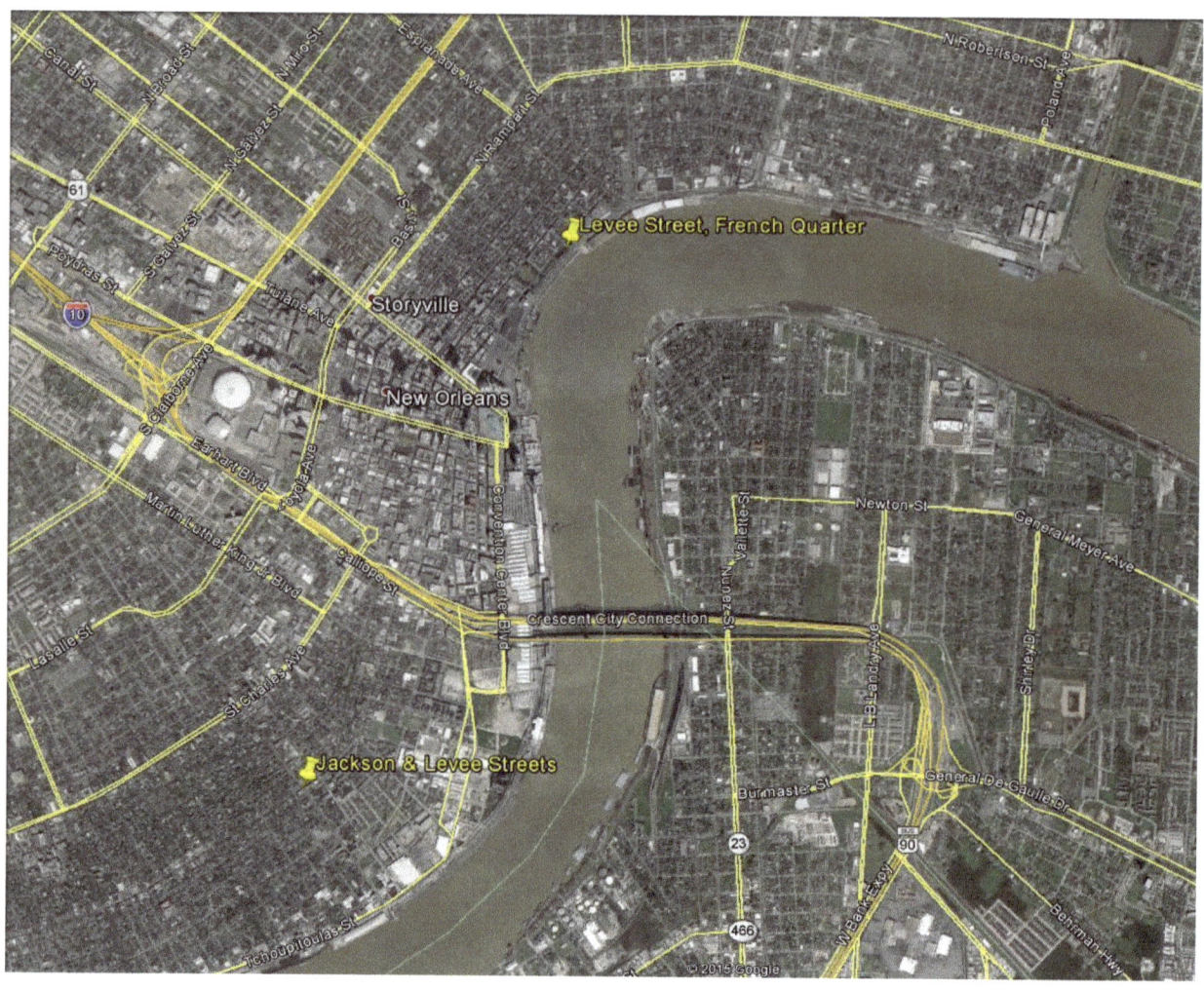

Charles and Kate Basler Krone

Dear Will, Kayla, Ava, and Blake,   March 16, 2015

I'm writing stories about my great great grandmother Margaret Basler Reiss Ebert and each of her siblings. You have seen some stories already and more are in the works. This one is about her second youngest sister Kate and her husband Charles Krone who was an actor in St. Louis, Missouri and in Louisville, Kentucky.

A year ago I received a phone call from Yvonne Juhl in St. Louis who was preparing an article on Charles Krone for the St. Louis Genealogical Society. She had found our book, It Takes A Matriarch, which contains the 780 family letters that Margaret had saved from 1852 to 1888. There were 97 letters from the Krones and Charles' autobiography. Yvonne had several questions and also wanted permission to quote from our book and use our pictures which, of course, I granted.

When Yvonne's mother died in 1989, one of the things in her mom's treasure trunk was a book written by a prominent German playwright in 1869. Inside the front cover of that book was Charles Krone's name and address of 1822 S. 7th Street in St. Louis. Why was that book in her mom's trunk, who was Charles Krone, and what was his connection to her mom? Yvonne spent nearly two years answering those questions and preparing her article for the SLGS. It turns out that the Krone's third child, Jeanette who was born on 11/21/1868, was the piano teacher for Yvonne's mother. Jeanette never married, lived with her parents, and gave lessons in their home. I have Yvonne's permission to use excerpts below but otherwise you need to see her full 20-page article via the SLGS quarterly, Volume 47.

Charles A. Krone was born Carl August Springmeier on February 24, 1836 in the Province of Hanover, Germany, son of Frederick Wilhelm Springmeyer and Josephine Delzmann. Charles, his parents, and his sister Marie came to America, arriving at Baltimore in the spring of 1839. They then traveled to Cincinnati and six months later ended up in St. Louis. Frederick died in late 1845 and his widow married Charles Krohne on 12/15/1850. They later Anglicized it to Krone.

About the time Krone's mother remarried, he discovered the theater. In an interview late in his life, the actor was asked when he became interested in acting. He replied:

The first time I saw a real play, . . . I was 15 years old and had learned the printer's trade. My firm had the contract to print tickets and programs for Bates Theatre, that was built on Pine Street, between Third and Fourth streets, and part of the printing bill was commonly paid passes. When it came my turn to receive one of the tickets, it happened that Elize Logan, the leading woman, was playing the title role in Shell's great tragic drama, Evadne, with Charles Fleming in the strong, but revolting character of "Ludovico." I was in the gallery, but I couldn't have told, to save my life, whether I was on sea or land. I was absolutely lost to everything but the stage. . . . My first appearance was in the cellar under my mother's kitchen. It was a big cellar, and I started by whitewashing it and building a stage at one end. Then I got together a lot of furniture and accessories, and some ambitious boys who wanted to act. We had a curtain and footlights, and an orchestra consisting of a flute, a violin and two guitars. . . . We played every Sunday night to a crowded cellar.

In 1858 Krone signed a contract to act during the summer season at de Bar's theater in St. Louis for $10 per week. In September 1859 he received a letter with a job offer from the Louisville Theater in Louisville, Kentucky, and thus he left St. Louis. Louisville is where he met young Kate Basler. He wanted to get married but first had to improve his finances by working a second year in Louisville.

The Civil War broke out in April 1861. As there were many soldiers coming and going out of the city and looking for entertainment in their leisure time, the theater business in Louisville was booming. He stayed in Louisville until July 1862. Theater business in St. Louis was not as good in the previous year, but he was able to get another job at Ben de Bar's theater for $12 per week. Kate Basler moved to St. Louis with Charles Krone. They were married on October 12, 1862 at St. Marcus Evangelical Church in St. Louis where church records show their names as Catharina Basler and Carl Springmeyer.

Their first child, Charles Ferdinand, was born on December 15, 1863 in St. Louis and baptized at St. Marcus Church on June 26, 1864 under the name of Carl Ferdinand Springmeyer. His aunt Esther and uncle Ferdinand Basler from Sullivan, Indiana were sponsors. Their second child, Josephine Marie Leocardia Caroline, was born on November 12, 1865 in St. Louis and baptized with the surname of Springmeyer on July 29, 1866 at the same church. Sadly this daughter died on August 27, 1866, about a month after her baptism. Their third child at right, a daughter Jeanette, was born on November 21, 1868 in Louisville, Kentucky, where Kate and Charles were living at the time.

Their son Charles was educated in St. Louis and became a successful lawyer. He was elected to the Missouri State Senate in Jefferson City. His personal life was less successful however because he was thrice married and had issues with alcohol, temper, and abuse. He had no children of his own. And since Jeanette never married, the Basler-Krone name ends with this generation. Charles Krone remarked about his children: *I have now entered upon my eighty-eighth year, and thanks to the noble generosity of my son Charles and the indefatigable industry and heroic pluck of my most excellent daughter Jeanette Krone, who, since my faithful wife's death seventeen years ago, not only has succeeded in keeping our home intact but has been busy as a teacher of vocal and instrumental music and a singer of acknowledged merit.*

From their marriage in October 1862 to the summer of 1869, the Krone family moved back and forth between St. Louis and Louisville, depending on what salaries were offered for actors. They moved back to St. Louis in 1869 and stayed there the rest of their lives. Acting was not a reliable way to make a living. There were times when Kate, working as a seamstress, made more money in a week than Charles did.

In January of 1864 at de Bar's St. Louis Theater in St. Louis, Charles appeared with John Wilkes Booth in Shakespeare's Richard III, Booth as Richard III, and Krone as King Henry. There may have been other times when the two men worked together. Here Charles comments on Booth:

John Wilkes Booth possessed a slender and graceful figure like his brother Edwin, though apparently somewhat taller and more closely knit and wiry, revealing a larger amount of animal spirits and love of action. Hair and complexion were dark, and his face though meditative in expression was illumined by a pair of dark and brilliant eyes, which rather bespoke a genial temper and lover of good fellowship and pleasure. As he differed in personal appearance from Edwin, so did he differ in his acting, which was more forcible, and manifested itself in stronger colors and bursts of passion. His speech was musical like his brother's, but stronger and more rapid, though clear and distinct. In the fullness of youth, life and passion, with the glorious record and talents inherited from his father at his command, he gave promise of achieving the highest. Most men of that day considered him superior to his brother and predicted great things in his favor. He was very much liked by his colleagues, as his manner of directing and sociability was frank, manly and cheerful, and no one could have ever divined that this kind and courteous young man would soon become the principal actor in one of the saddest tragedies in the world's history.

Our Matriarch book of letters includes Charles Krone's autobiography. Here's an excerpt. The date is not certain but my guess is that it was early 1865.

One gloomy Sunday afternoon, while strolling towards the theatre for a walk, I saw a man in a long whitish overcoat leaning against some mill-stones in front of a store in the Masonic Temple opposite the theatre. As the face was familiar to me, I stood and observed him awhile. Presently, the man looked up and seeing me cried out: "Hello, Mr. Krone, is that you?" and came over to shake hands with me. It was John Wilkes Booth, who had played an engagement in St. Louis, and was laying over in Louisville to take the night train for Baltimore. He told me of his hardships in coming from Omaha to fill his date in St. Louis, and that he had made the greater part of the journey in sleds, all of which I had read about in the papers. He looked worn out, dejected and as melancholy as the dull, gray sky above us. After some talk about St. Louis, he asked me if I did not know some quiet and respectable beer saloon, where we could sit down and enjoy a social chat. I took him to Dannerman's on Third Street, a resort frequented by actors, musicians, and professional people generally. After ordering beer, he sat gloomily and silent for a time, and upon my asking him the cause, he smilingly answered that no doubt it was the rough experience he had passed through lately. He then advised me to procure an engagement with McVicker Chicago, and called for pen, ink, and paper and wrote me a flattering recommendation, which he handed to me with wishes for my success. I remained with him until evening, when he suddenly got up, shook hands with me, and left. I never saw him again. The letter I never made use of, and later it was lost.

Kate Krone died on February 14, 1907 and Charles A. Krone died on January 9, 1926. The newspaper article about his death mentions his library of dramatic works including the book found by Yvonne Juhl in her mother's treasure trunk. Also in that trunk was Yvonne's mother's diary. There were eight entries between September 1930 and December 1934 that mentioned her mother taking piano lessons from Jeanette Krone. The connection between Yvonne's mother and the Krone family was now explained and confirmed.

Yvonne says in her article "I also wanted to find a new home for the book. At the time I decided to do this research on the Krone family, this country was in the middle of a five-year observance of the sesquicentennial of the Civil War. Thus, I thought about giving the book to Civil War re-enactor or an actor who had portrayed John Wilkes Booth. I had some leads on that possibility. I did not anticipate that I would find any relatives of Krone, however distant they might be. But that changed when I bought the book It Takes a Matriarch by Stephen Reiss and found out that his great-great-grandmother, Margaret Basler, was a sister to Kate Basler Krone. He readily agreed to accept the book; by the time you read this, he will have it and used it when he tells stories to his grandchildren about that part of their family tree, Charles and Kate Basler Krone."

"Among the people I want to thank is Stephen Reiss whose book gave me new insight into the Krone family and who allowed me to use photographs of Charles, Kate, and Jeanette Krone in this article."

Will, Kayla, Ava, and Blake, isn't that a wonderful story. We are so blessed by volunteers like Yvonne Juhl who solve a mystery like a found book and turn it into a fascinating story for the general public. Below is the title page of the book Yvonne gave me. The outside cover is just cloth with no words. I emailed this scan to Elke Hall in South Carolina who had translated all the German letters in our book. Her two replies are below.

Love, Granddad

Steve, I think this is the greatest present that you were able to provide answers to so many different people mentioned in the letters and that some of them were able to provide answers to you.

Heinrich Laube was a German playwright. His play is called "Die Karlsschueler," "The Karl Students."

He tells a story about what happened in the castle in Stuttgart on the 16th and 17th September 1782. The main character is Herzog Karl von Wuerttemberg.

Actually been there many times, you know that I am from Stuttgart. I worked at city hall and often ate my lunch on the castle steps. The Karlsgymnasium is right around the corner from there, still in existence. . . . . Elke

Here's another comment by Elke after reading Yvonne's article:

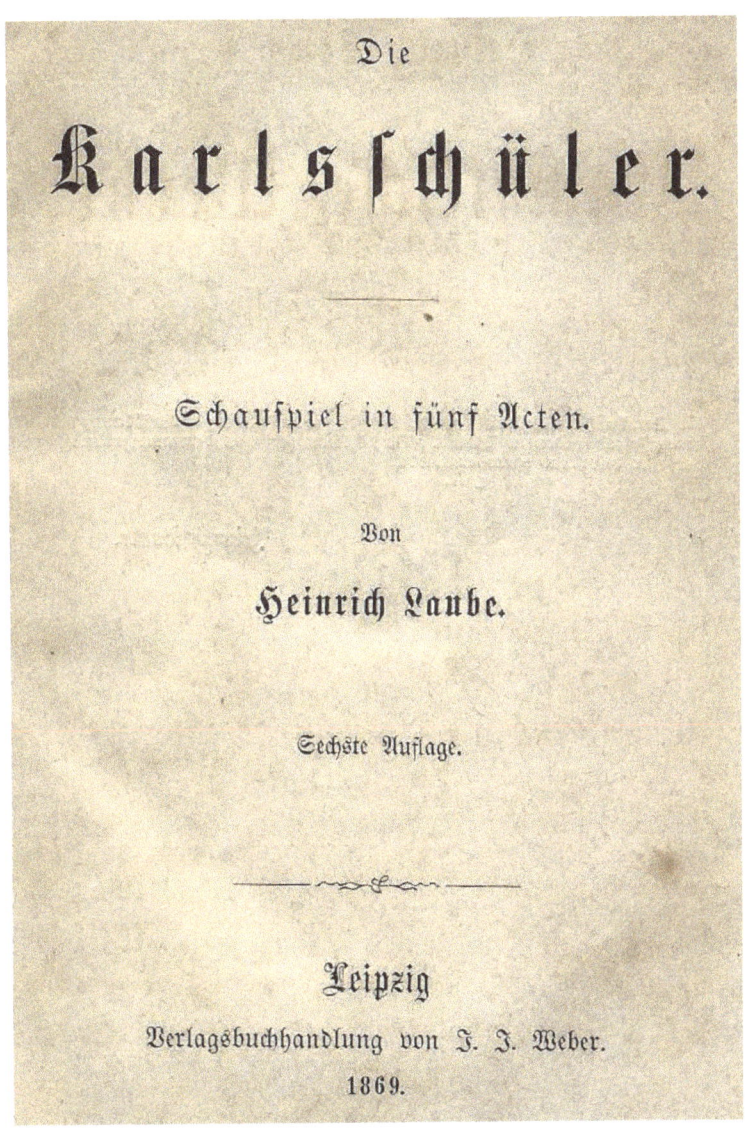

Die

Karlsschüler.

Schauspiel in fünf Acten.

Von

Heinrich Laube.

Sechste Auflage.

Leipzig
Verlagsbuchhandlung von J. J. Weber.
1869.

Steve, I am blown away! Am I in a movie? It's incredible. My God, that makes Genealogy soooo worthwhile. What else can we find in history? So much better than just a date, born and died! You need to write another book about all of this. Thank you so much for sharing it with me. Elke

1880 – 1889

1880 Population of St. Clair County is 61,850 which is third largest behind Cook and LaSalle Counties.

1880 Farm animals in St. Clair County totaled 7794 horses, 9559 cattle, 5183 mules, 5605 sheep, and 22,805 hogs.

1880 States total 38, national population is 50.19 million. North and South Dakota, Montana, and Washington are added in 1889.

1880 President is Rutherford Hayes. James Garfield is inaugurated in 1881, Chester Arthur in 1881, Grover Cleveland in 1885, and Benjamin Harrison in 1889.

1880 The French begin construction on the Panama Canal.

1883 Five standard time zones are established by the United States and Canadian railroad companies to end the confusion over thousands of local time zones.

1883 Bernard Henry Kroger opened his first grocery store in Cincinnati.

1884 The Washington Monument is completed at 555 feet after 37 years of work.

1886 The Statue of Liberty is dedicated in New York harbor.

1886 Dr. John Pemberton, a Georgia pharmacist, invented Coca-Cola.

1886 Richard Warren Sears and Alvah Curtis Roebuck founded a catalog mail order business. Retail locations were added in 1925.

1887 Pearl Harbor naval base is leased by the United States Navy.

1889 Oklahoma lands are opened to white settlement with the first of five land runs. More than 50,000 people waited at the starting line to race for 160-acre parcels.

The Estate of Conrad Ebert

Dear Will, Kayla, and Ava,   October 20, 2014

By now you know that your great great great great grandparents were Adam and Margaret Basler Reiss. Adam founded and operated the family farm in St. Clair County, IL from his first land purchase on 9/1/1838 until his death almost eleven years later on 5/23/1849 at age forty-five. He left behind a 120-acre farm and five children under age eleven. His will stipulated that Margaret would inherit one-third of his farm and his five children the balance. A year later his widow Margaret married Conrad Ebert on 4/2/1850 so he is became your GGGG step-grandfather.

The Eberts managed the family farm for the next thirty years. They continued with the farm buildings and equipment that Adam Reiss had purchased and used. The Eberts expanded Margaret's farm by 40 acres on 1/5/1854 and by another 20 acres on 5/13/1868 for a new total of 180 acres. Here's our current farm map which includes yet another 180 acres which Margaret's grandson George Reiss purchased on 4/12/1917.

The Eberts had four children in addition to the five they were raising from Margaret's marriage to Adam Reiss. Sadly only two of the Ebert children reached adulthood, Louisa born on 12/??/1853 and Margaret born on 10/29/1856. Louisa married George Neff on 11/6/1873 and very quickly had one son George Neff Jr. on 2/2/1874 before she died on 5/21/1875 when her dress caught fire while she was cooking apple butter. She was probably "salvaging" old shriveled apples stored from the previous fall harvest. Margaret married Conrad Neff (George's brother) on 9/7/1877, three weeks after their son Conrad Neff Jr. was born on 8/22/1877. Their second child that decade was Mary Neff born on 1/17/1879.

Conrad Ebert died on 7/23/1880 at age 69 leaving a wife, seven children, three grandchildren, and a 180-acre farm, 120 acres of which was transitioning to Margaret's son Frank Reiss. Maybe Conrad was just worn out from farming and raising nine kids. His funeral and grave were at St. Michael's Church and Cemetery in Paderborn. That's also where his four children were baptized and where both of his daughters were married. That was very appropriate because the two acres for that church were donated by Margaret Reiss' father Johann Basler on 1/24/1843.

Here is the petition naming Conrad's widow Margaret as executor of his estate. Note that his Personal Estate is described as 60 acres of land, stock (animals), farming implements, and household furniture all valued at $500. It mentions his survivors as wife Margaret, daughter Margaret Neff, and grandson George Neff Jr. His older daughter Louisa had already died in that cooking fire so her son George got his mom's share.

PETITION FOR LETTERS OF ADMINISTRATION.

PETITION OF *Margaretha Ebert*

In the matter of the estate of *Conrad Ebert* deceased, for Letters of Administration.

To the Honorable *Frederick W. Pieper*

Judge of the County Court of St. Clair County, in the State of Illinois.

The Petition of the undersigned *Margaretha Ebert* respectfully represents, that *Conrad Ebert* late of the County of St. Clair aforesaid, departed this life at *Richland Precinct* in said County, on or about the *23d* day of *July* A. D. 1880 leaving no last will and testament so far as your petitioner *knows or believes.*

And this Petition further shows, that the said *Conrad Ebert* died *seized* and *possessed* of Real and Personal Estate consisting chiefly of *about 60 acres of Land, Stock, Farming implements, household & Kitchen furniture &c.*

all of said personal estate being estimated to be worth about *Five Hundred* Dollars. That said deceased left surviving him, *Margaretha* his widow and *Margaretha Neff his child and Georg. Neff his grand child*

as heirs. That your petitioner (being *the widow* of said deceased,) and believing that the said estate should be immediately administered as well for the proper management of said *Estate* as for the prompt collection of the assets, by virtue of *her* right under the Statute, *she* therefore pray *s* that your Honor will grant letters of Administration to *her* in the premises, upon *her* taking the oath prescribed by the Statute and entering into Bond in such sum, and with securities, as may be approved by your Honor.

STATE OF ILLINOIS, } ss.
County of St. Clair.

Margaretha Ebert

being duly sworn, deposes and says, that the facts averred in the above petition are true, according to the best of *her* knowledge, information and belief.

Sworn to and Subscribed before me,
LOUIS C. STARKEL, Clerk of the County
Court of St. Clair County, this *31st*
day of *July* A. D. 1880

Margaretha Ebert

Notice the signature at the bottom by your GGGG grandmother Margaret Ebert.

Just as an FYI, Conrad's son-in-law who had married Louisa, did remarry and have more children but they are not Ebert or Reiss relatives. Conrad's daughter Margaret had more children with husband Conrad Neff but they were born after Conrad Ebert's passing. Those additional children are Neff and step-Reiss relatives.

The next two pages are an appraisal list of Conrad Ebert's goods, chattels, and personal estate as agreed upon by these three appraisers. I recognize only the middle name, that of Conrad Dintelmann. He was born on 11/??/1836 in Darmstadt, Germany so he is one generation younger than Margaret Reiss Ebert. Conrad's sister Eva Dintelmann married Margaret Reiss Ebert's son Charles Reiss on 11/15/1866 and Conrad's son George married Margaret's granddaughter Eva Reiss on 4/22/2008. So the Dintelmanns and the Eberts were neighbors and close friends. They were a big help for Margaret with the loss of her husband Conrad.

Here are the header of page one and the footer of page two of the appraisal list which follows. I separated those parts of those two pages so I could blow up the list for better viewing. Check out Conrad's estate items and values. His top three possessions were 340 bushels of wheat and two horses. I wonder if any of these household items passed to Margaret's children and are still family treasures 135 years later. There are five quilts and lots of furniture pieces. Fascinating!!!

		ARTICLES	VALUE	
			Dollars	Cents
1	1/3	1/3 of a Woods reaper more combined	8	00
2	3	acres of corn growing in field	15	00
3	1/2	acres of corn growing in field	3	00
4	3	Stacks hay	2	00
5	1 1/2	acres corn growing	20	00
6	1	red cow	15	00
7	1	heifer	1	50
8	1	lot apples on trees	1	00
9	1	patch corn	2	00
10	2	Stacks hay	4	00
11	1	lot potatoes growing	8	00
12	1	Wagon		50
13	2	ladders	1	50
14	1	Old wagon		50
15	1	hay rack	1	00
16	1	Roller	3	00
17	1	Square harrow		10
18	1	Grindstone and shaving horse		50
19	2	old plows and shares	2	00
20	1	lot lumber	1	00
21	4	forks		25
22	2	Rakes		15
23	3	hoes		50
24	3	shovels		50
25	2	Sythes		10
26	4	measures		25
27	2	axes and a hatched		50
28	1	lot old iron		50
29	4	augers		25
30	3	Saws		5
31	1	Sickle		5
32	1	Corn knife		10
33	2	Sifters		25
34	1	Saddle		25
35	1	Ladies saddle		25
36	1	barrel with salt	1	00
37	1	lot oats	5	00
38	1	log chain		25
39	4	All grouping hoes		10
40	1	Cutting box	2	00
41	1	bundle shingles		50
42	1	lot corn		50
43	3	hogs	12	00
44	100	barn yard chickens	8	00
45	1	colt	20	00
46	1	brown mare	60	00
47	1	white horse	70	00
48	2	sets harns	6	00

all bought by wife or widow

237

49	1	double tree		10
50	1	cradle		50
51	1	cross cut saw		75
52	1	spring seat	1	50
53	23	sacks	2	00
54	340	bushels of wheat	204	00
55	1	iron kettle and fixture	1	00
56	1	old stove		25
57	1	butter churn		10
58	20	pounds pork	1	00
59	1	stove	1	00
60	2	cans with fat	6	50
61	2	brass kettles	3	00
62	1	sausage stuffer	1	00
63	7	baskets	1	00
64	1	funnel		25
65	1	lot chairs		25
66	1	bed & bed-stead	2	00
67	5	quilts	7	00
68	2	barrels & 2 kegs	2	00
69	1	keg with vinegar		50
70	3	tubs		50
71	1	lot of crokery		50
72	1	cooking stove, pipes and some pictures	35	00
73	2	tables	2	00
74	1	lounch	1	50
75	6	chairs		35
76	2	beds and bedsteads	10	00
77	1	bureau & chest	2	00
78	1	bed & bed-stead	2	00
79	1	chest & old clothes	1	25
80	1	table & 2 benches	1	00
81	1	kitchenashrine & 1 shelf	1	00
82	1	lot kitchen furniture	5	00
83	1	clock & 2 mirrors	1	50
		TOTAL	594	45

I mentioned above that ownership of the original 120-acre Adam Reiss farm was transitioning to his son Frank Reiss. Adam's wife Margaret inherited one-third of that farm per his will and his five children split the remaining two-thirds equally. On 12/2/1861 Frank's half-brother John Reiss and his bride Maria of 41 days sold their share to Frank for $200. They were living in Belleville and apparently had no interest in farming.

On 12/18/1869 Frank's brother Charles Reiss sold his share to him for $1,000. On 11/4/1872 Frank's brother Martin Reiss sold his share to him for $670. On 5/12/1884 Frank's sister Kate Reiss Wittig sold her share to him for $725. At this point the original Adam Reiss farm of 120 acres is owned 1/3 by Margaret Reiss Ebert and 2/3s by Frank Reiss.

Even seven years after Conrad Ebert died, his widow Margaret is still settling various ownership and debt issues. Perhaps he died without a will which made his estate more complicated. Anyway in late 1887 his heirs decided to sell the 20 acres Conrad had purchased in 1868. Perhaps the heirs simply didn't want that tract because it is hilly and only partially tillable. Even today we have it in CRP grass instead of row crops.

Charles Reiss was helping his mother with the paperwork and legal affairs. Here are the sale bill announcing the upcoming auction and a handwritten note by Frank Reiss listing where he had posted the sale bill.

Charles Reiss was the successful bidder with $550 at this auction. He then resold this 20 acres to his brother Frank Reiss. Maybe Frank simply wanted more of an arms length deal because everyone knew he wanted it so he could continue his ownership transition.

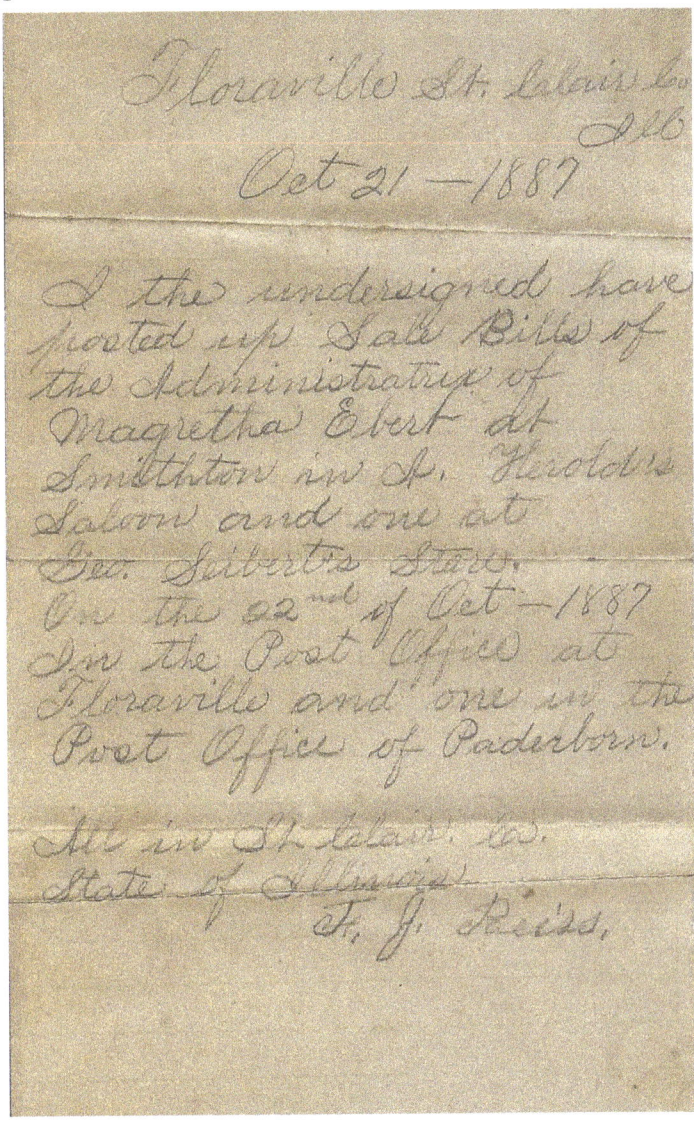

ADMINISTRATRIX'
Sale of Real Estate

By virtue of an order and decree of the County Court of St. Clair County, Illinois, made on the petition of the undersigned, Margaretha Ebert, administratrix of the estate of Conrad Ebert, deceased, for leave to sell the real estate of said deceased, at the August Term, A. D. 1887, I shall, on

Saturday, November 19, 1887,

between the hours of 10 o'clock in the forenoon and 5 o'clock in the afternoon of said day, sell at public sale, at the premises to be sold, in said County, the real estate described as follows, to-wit:

The north half of the southeast quarter of the northeast quarter of Section seven (7), in Township two (2) South, Range eight (8) West, containing twenty (20) acres, situated in the County of St. Clair and State of Illinois, including the dower of said Margaretha Ebert,

on the following terms, to-wit: On a credit of six months, the purchaser to give approved security and a mortgage on the premises sold, to secure the payment of the purchase money.

Somewhere along this ownership transition process, Frank Reiss bought his mother's 1/3 share of the original 120-acre farm before she died on 6/23/1902. I don't have that legal document. On 8/11/1906 the remaining 40-acre tract which Conrad Ebert had purchased in 1854 was sold by his heirs for $500 to Frank Reiss' oldest surviving son, George W. Reiss who is my grandfather.

Will, Kayla, and Ava, this whole estate and land ownership transition process is pretty complicated as you can see. Frank Reiss started buying out his siblings in late 1861 and it took another 44 years before his son George would complete the process. That's pretty amazing. Equally amazing is the 1880 snapshot of farm and household inventory belonging to your great great great great step-grandfather Conrad Ebert.

Love, Granddad

"Ask now about the former days, long before your time."

(Deuteronomy 4:32)

George Reiss Penmanship Lessons

Dear Will, Kayla, and Ava,   September 16, 2013

Your great great grandfather, George Reiss, was an intelligent man and a very successful farmer in St. Clair County, Illinois. He doubled the size of the Reiss Family Farm and was an astute businessman and community leader. You would be impressed and proud if you met him today.

George accomplished much even though he had only four years of public education. That was at the one-room school in Floraville, about 1.7 miles west of where he was born in a log cabin on the family farm on April 22, 1873. He was the fourth of eleven children but the oldest to reach adulthood.

Here are two of 109 pages where young George practiced penmanship by carefully writing 21 copies of the first line which had been written by his teacher. He would have used a quill pen possibly made from a turkey feather and liquid ink. The year was about 1883 when George was age 10. He would have officially been in the fourth grade but since it was a one-room school he probably eavesdroped on the higher grades. I'm sure he was "smarter than a fifth grader" to quote that popular television show.

His pages were 7" by 9.5" but I shrunk two of them for this story. It looks like they were also practicing capital "M's" on both pages because that letter is repeated at the end of each line.

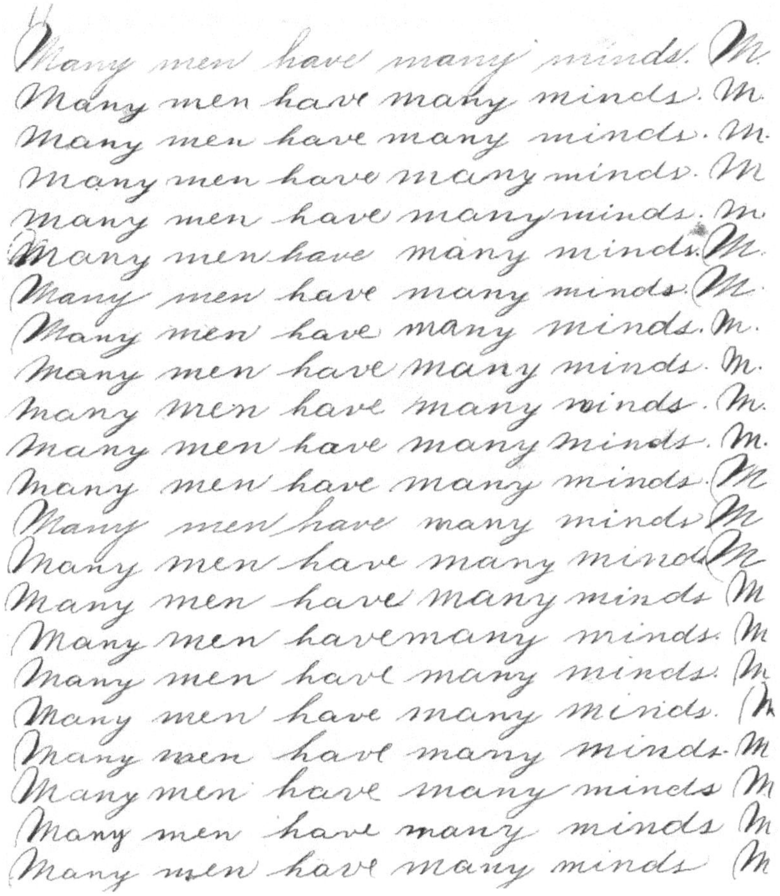

Some of the other phrases which were copied appear below. They were used to teach young minds about more than just penmanship.

Many men have many minds,
Today will never be tomorrow,
Strike while the iron is hot,
Penmanship is an art,
Contentment leads to happiness,
We live in the state of Illinois,
St. Clair is the name of our county,
Reading makes a versed man,
Always have a plan to work by,
Never go to extremes in anything,
Floraville is a small village,
Do not lose nor sell your books,
A good son will help his father,
Never come tardy to school,
Aim at improvement in writing,
From nothing, nothing comes,
Good manners procure respect,
Kindness comes from the heart,

Make hay while the sun shines M.
Make hay while the sun shines M.
Make hay while the sun shines M.
Make hay while the sun shines M.
Make hay while the sun shines M.
Make hay while the sun shines M.
Make hay while the sun shines M.
Make hay while the sun shines M.
Make hay while the sun shines M.
Make hay while the sun shines M.
Make hay while the sun shines M.
Make hay while the sun shines M.
Make hay while the sun shines M.
Make hay while the sun shines M.
Make hay while the sun shines M.
Make hay while the sun shines M.
Make hay while the sun shines M.
Make hay while the sun shines m.
Make hay while the sun shines M.
Make hay while the sun shines M.
Make hay while the sun shines M.
Make hay while the sun sun M.
Make hay while the sun shines M.

Much depends upon promptness,
Nothing venture, nothing have,
Occupation prevents temptation,
Sell not virtue to purchase riches,
The honest man need not repent,
Ches. Arthur is president of the US,
Washington was our first president,
Daniel Webster was a great orator,
Today will never dawn again,
Christmas will soon be here,
Tomorrow may be never,
May is the month of roses,
Our earth is a great sphere,
Every beginning is different,
We do not like to see our own sins,
Live coals of fire glow with heat,
Never stop trying to improve,
Our time is worth a good deal,
Use one kind of ink for writing,
Tea is the leaf of a bush,
Gentle means are often best,
Children should not whisper in school

Grand DD and I were in Scotland last year and visited the Highland Folk Museum near Kingussie and Newtonmore. It was a series of buildings that had been moved to a 40-acre site. My favorite was a one-room school which was full of visiting fourth-graders like your grandfather George above.

We paid very special attention to what the teacher was saying and to what the students were doing. We even did the same penmanship lesson ourselves with a quill pen. Here are the pictures. Notice the old school desks and the small slates the children are writing on. The blackboard behind the teacher has the plans for the day. Notice there is both a recess and a physical education lesson.

The last picture below is my penmanship lesson where the teacher gave me a grade of 7.5 out of a possible 10. He didn't like that ink smudge in

the upper left which was caused when Grand DD tried to write on my paper. I told the teacher it wasn't my mistake so he wrote in red – "blames wife!"

Will, Kayla, and Ava, we already have old school desks for you in our basement and in our log cabin. I even have a real turkey feather found in our yard which we'll make into a quill pen. Grand DD used to teach fourth grade so someday soon you two will have your own authentic penmanship lessons here. Be aware that you'll have to do it without spell check, texting, and Google. Your great great grandfather George would have been very proud!!!

Love, Granddad

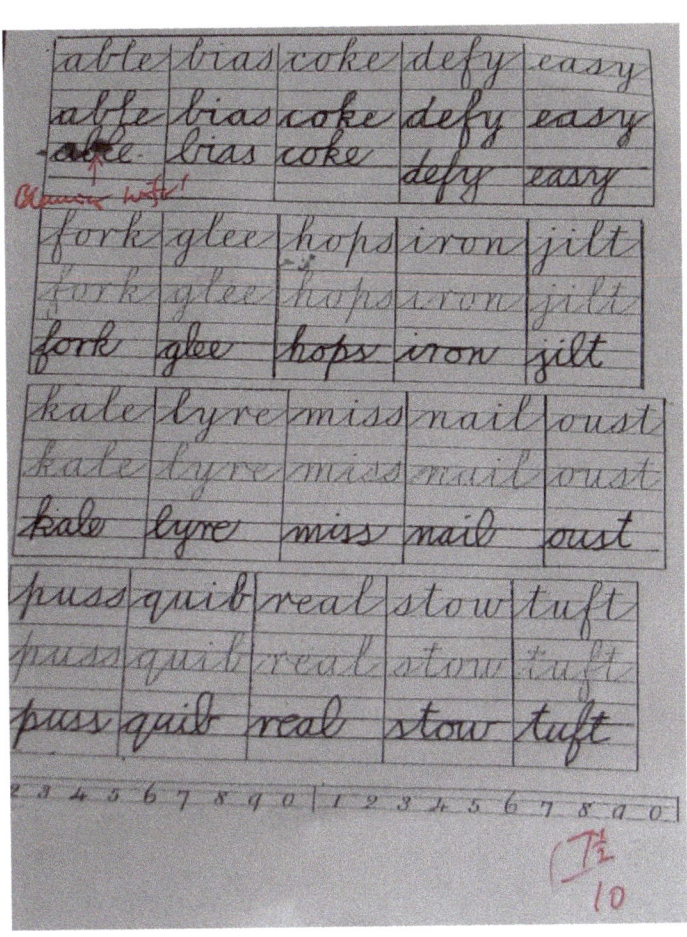

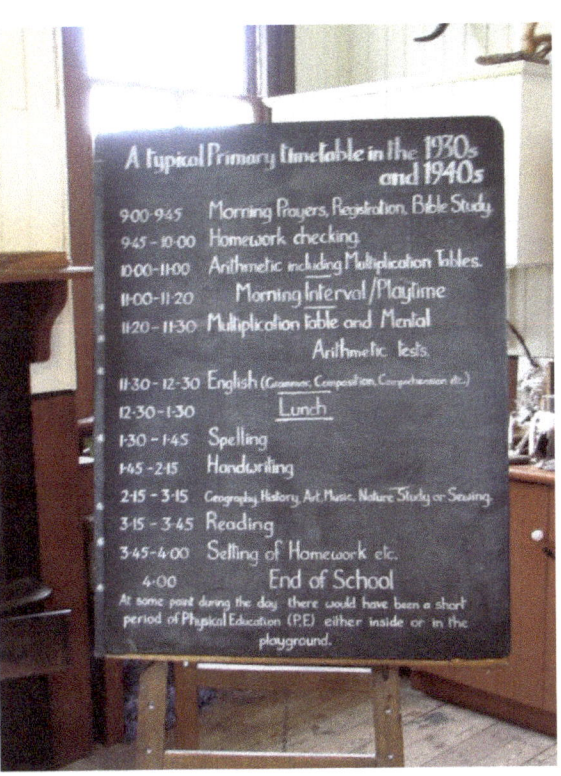

Shelling Corn

Dear Will, Kayla, and Ava,   November 24, 2014

Do you recognize this young farmer? He's having fun shelling ear corn the old fashioned way. He is turning the large flywheel which is a lot easier than turning the small hand crank on this side. The words read, Burrall's Corn-Sheller, W. D. Burrall, Geneva, NY, Patent Extended 1859. Patent dates normally reveal the earliest something can be made, not the latest. However, the Burrall Company was awarded another patent on this machine on March 14, 1863. So it's safe to conclude this particular sheller was made between 1859 and early 1863. Half of that four-year window was occupied by the raging Civil War.

This sheller is quite significant for another reason. In the 1840s, most shellers did not separate the cob from the loose corn. Thomas D. Burrall was perhaps the first to invent a sheller that did. Shellers of the 1840s simply deposited cobs and kernels in a pile on the ground. The working mechanisms of most shellers were fully exposed and made no accommodation for a bucket to catch the corn.

Patented in 1845, the Burrall sheller was an important improvement in corn shellers. As you can see there is room underneath for a bucket to catch the corn as it exits that spout. You can also see that a bucket was not this farmer's concern because his corn is all over the floor. Cobs exit near the left legs. The Burrall sheller was popular for decades. It appeared after 1900 in farm implement guides. Replacement parts were still available in 1948.

Below is our young farmer operating a newer corn sheller in my garage attic museum. It was made by Marseilles Manufacturing Company which was organized in 1870 with A. Adams as its president. He had established a machine shop in Elgin, Illinois in 1840 and began to make corn

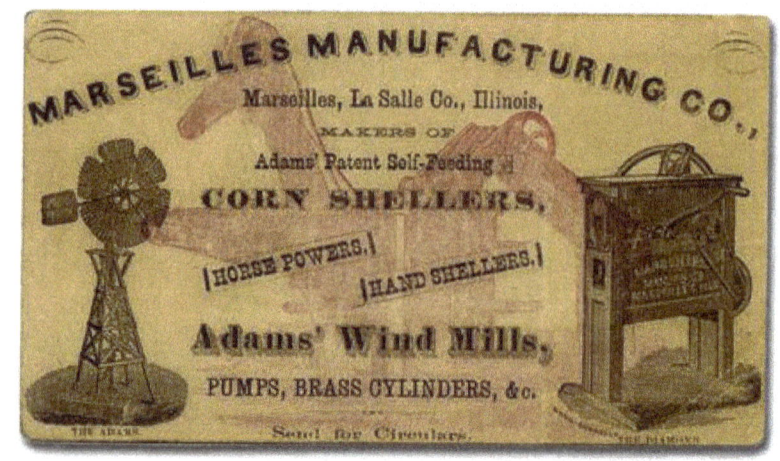

shellers in 1855. That business relocated to Marseilles, Illinois where this wooden model was made. Some years later a selling arrangement was made with Deere and Company, whereby they took charge of the sales of the entire production of that factory. In 1908 a part of the stock of the company was acquired by the Deere interests, and soon after the plant was moved to East Moline, where better facilities were available.

Once again our young farmer is turning the flywheel instead of the side crank because it's easier even though it requires more arm movement. And once again, you can see corn on the floor since the bucket is missing.

I remember my grandfather George "Pop" Reiss using a wooden corn sheller like this. I can't recall his brand name but it very well may have been a Marseilles model. He let me crank it to shell corn which was then ground for chicken feed. I enjoyed "helping" Pop every chance I could. He was a neat guy and a very hard worker.

Pop also showed me how to use his small box corn sheller like the next picture below. It was smaller and less expensive so the farmer chose the machine that best suited his needs. I have five different box shellers but my favorite by far is this one called Black Hawk made by A. H. Patch in Clarksville, Tennessee. It's has very elaborate cast parts and to me, it's a work of art. Those springs allow it to shell small ears like popcorn and much larger ears of field corn. It also works wonders on shelling walnuts in case anyone living in Springfield is interested.

Here's our young farmer tending his flower garden. These are called resurrection lilies. First the green leaves come up in April and die back in July. Then the single stalks of flowers come up in August with nice flowers as you can see – hence the name. This young man is wearing the souvenir shirt his grandparents brought back from their July trip to five countries in southern Africa including Botswana.

Will, Kayla, and Ava, modern farming can be hard work but it also gives you a huge appreciation for how much much harder it used to be. But farm technology from 150 years ago was clever, artful, fascinating, and made in the Midwest. Equipment colors were green, red, yellow, or black.

The next time you enjoy a Big Mac and fries at McDonalds, thank a farmer and the companies that made his labor-saving equipment.

Love, Granddad

Harvesting Wheat on the Reiss Family Farm

Dear Will, Kayla, and Ava,   July 15, 2013

Exactly 130 years ago yesterday on July 14, 1883 your great great great grandfather Frank Reiss received 46 pounds of binder twine that he had ordered the previous month. Price was $0.20 per pound.

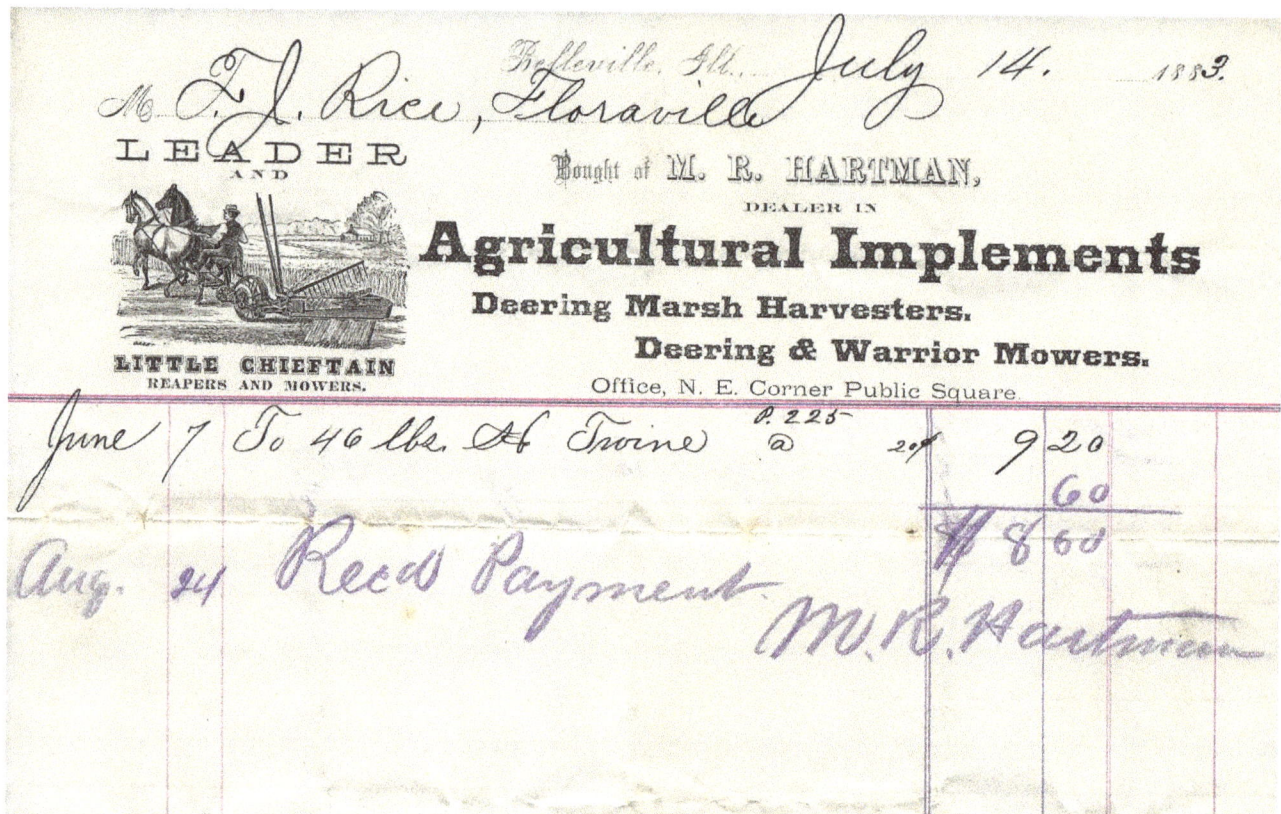

The **reaper-binder**, or **binder**, was a farm implement that improved upon the reaper. The binder was invented in 1872 by Charles Withington. In addition to cutting the small-grain crop, it would also tie the stems into small bundles, or sheaves. These sheaves were then 'shocked' into conical stooks, resembling small tipis, to allow the grain to dry for several days before being threshed. Refer to my Granddad's Mondays of 4/29/2013 about "bringing in the sheaves."

Withington's original binder used wire to tie the bundles. There were various problems with using wire and it was not long before William Deering invented a binder that used twine and a knotter (invented in 1858 by John Appleby).

Early binders were horse-drawn and powered by a bull wheel. Later models were tractor-drawn. The implement had a reel and a sickle bar, like a modern grain head for a combine harvester, or combine. The cut stems would fall onto a canvas, which conveyed the crop to the binding mechanism. This mechanism bundled the stems of grain and tied a piece of twine around the bundle. Once tied, it was discharged from the back of the binder.

With the replacement of the threshing machine by the combine harvester, the binder became almost obsolete. Some grain crops such as oats are now cut and formed into windrows with a swather. With other grain crops such as wheat, the grain is now mostly cut and threshed by a combine in a single operation, while the binder is still in use at small fields or outskirts of mountain areas.

Here's Frank Reiss and his son George harvesting wheat with a reaper-binder about 1910. My grandfather George is walking with a sheave of cut and bound wheat in his hands. He is piling a dozen or so sheaves into stooks or shocks. Below is what the fully harvested field might look like while waiting for the wheat to dry before it is hauled to the threshing floor in a barn.

Frank Reiss and son George harvesting wheat on Reiss Farm about 1910

Below are the Reiss brothers, Frank on the left and my dad Irwin on the right, after a hard day in the wheat field stacking sheaves into shocks behind them. The picture dates from about 1927. Notice the bib overalls and straw hats to create a little shade.

Franklin and Irwin Reiss about 1927

Below are two modern binders. The one on the right is pulled by a tractor instead of horses. There is a sickle bar cutter along the front edge of those white canvas panels. The cut wheat falls backward and the canvas belt rotates toward the binder operator where it is automatically tied into bundles or sheaves which fall out the right side.

That binder operator is probably not actually needed since the whole machine should be automatic. Here is one old farmer's interesting story - About 1905 an Illinois farmer commented that when he first began farming, "It took ten men with cradle scythes to cut and bind my grain. Now our hired girl gets on the seat of a self-binder and does the whole business." Will and Kayla, refer back to my Granddad's Mondays of April 29, 2013 to learn about cradle scythes.

Will, Kayla, and Ava, the binder below is used in small rice paddies in Asia. It harvests one row of rice at a time. The operator walks behind the machine and the bound sheaves are ejected along his right side.

Oh, and binder twine – today you can buy it from Shenzhen, China at $2.00 for a 2.5 kilogram spool FOB the US. That's $.36/lb instead of the $.20/lb it was 130 years ago. Just click on "add to cart" and buy it with Paypal. How times have changed!!!

Fanning Mill in 1955

Dear Will, Kayla, and Ava,   March 11, 2013

Here is a 58-year old photo of my first cousins, Richard and George, at the Reiss family farm in St. Clair County, Illinois. You can see that Richard is straining to turn that crank which causes a large internal fan to rotate which creates a big wind that will blow out the right hand end of this fanning mill. The idea is to fill the hopper on top with oats, wheat, or other cereal grains which were contaminated with dirt, weed seeds, chaff, debris, broken grain seeds, bits of straw, etc. during harvest. The seeds you want to keep are heavier and/or smaller than the rest of the mix and will end up being collected in one or two drawers underneath the mill. All the lighter weight undesirables blow out the right end with the strong wind made by the fan.

Here's a cross-sectional drawing of a fanning mill. The hand crank is attached to the larger gear which meshes with the smaller gear which is attached to four fan blades. The larger gear has about twice as many teeth as the smaller gear which means it will cause the fan to rotate at twice the speed of the hand crank. The fan makes the wind which blows to the left across a series of screens or sieves with different size openings. Larger bits stay on top and exit while smaller heavier bits fall toward the bottom depending on their size and weight. The two angled boards near the bottom direct oat seeds into one drawer and the other one directs wheat seeds to a second drawer which are not shown.

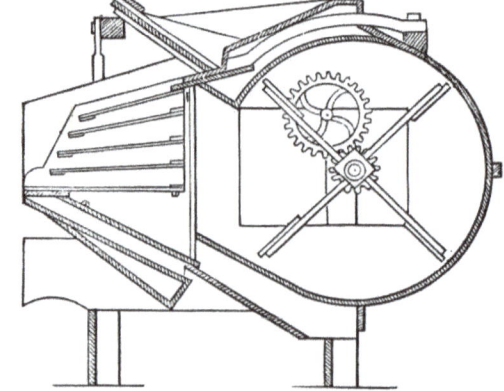

Fanning mills removed straw, chaff, stones, dirt and dust, weed seeds, and light immature seeds from wheat, oats, rye, barley, and other cereal grains. It was important to remove contaminants for better preservation during storage, to have mold and grit free flour, and for securing viable seed for spring planting that was free of weed seeds that would compete with a growing cereal crop. Fanning mills were a great technical advance over winnowing, the hand-process of pouring grain from one container to another in a breeze to blow away the lighter matter.

In many ways, fanning mills resemble a miniature threshing machine. Both machines have shaking sieves over which the threshed grain kernels mixed with bits of straw, chaff, stones and soil particles rattle. The smaller pieces fall through holes to a lower sieve where smaller particles are separated. Both machines have fans that move air across and upward through the sieves to float off the light straw, chaff, and dust. The big difference is that threshing machines have a mechanism for knocking the grain kernels free of their attachment to the grain stalk.

Before the introduction of threshing machines, grain was removed from the stalk heads by trampling or flailing. This operation was done usually on a wooden floor in a barn. Threshing barns were built for the purpose of storing grain sheaves from harvest time until the slack winter season when the fully mature grain could be separated from the dry straw. These barns were built around a central threshing floor where the bundles of ripened grain could be spread to a uniform thickness and treaded upon by hooves of horses or oxen or pounded by farm hands using wooden flails to loosen grain kernels from heads of the cereal plant stalks. Here are grain heads of wheat on the left and oats on the right.

When most of the kernels had been loosened from the grain heads, the straw was lifted off with forks and stored for use as bedding for livestock. The remaining material on the threshing floor was scooped up to be winnowed when there was a breeze. Threshing barns usually had wide doors which could be opened at either end of the center section to allow a favorable wind to waft through the building. The chaff, bits of straw, and the loose grain from the threshing floor were put in a winnowing basket or tray and tossed upward into a breeze where currents of air carried the straw pieces, lighter chaff and dust farther away, as the heavier kernels of grain fell more directly downward into a basket or onto a blanket.

Flailing and winnowing are strenuous tasks. It has been estimated that, using a flail, one person could separate only seven bushels of grain per day. Separating kernels of grain from chaff and stalks was a labor-intensive manual procedure, and careful attention was required to extract the maximum amount of good grain from the material left on the threshing floor after flailing and trampling. To ease the arduous work and relieve the monotony, threshing became a shared neighborly work project and a social activity that continued on when farmers went from farm to farm with their wagons to help each other gather shocks to feed into a threshing machine. Commonly called "a separator" and mounted on wheels, it was moved from farm to farm. All the cooperating farmers in a circuit made up a "threshing ring."

Fanning mills did a much more efficient job than winnowing, and they cleaned grain more thoroughly than a threshing machine. Mills were kept around farms for a long time to reclean oats and wheat in the spring for planting.

Our fanning mill kinda looks like this advertisement by the E. H. Pease Manufacturing Company of Racine, Wisconsin. I Googled fanning mills and Racine and I looked on eBay to learn more details which appear below. There is even a cute "granddad's story" below by a different granddad.

THE "PEASE" FANNING MILLS
FOR FARM AND WAREHOUSE USE.

These Mills Clean, Screen, SEPARATE and GRADE all kinds of Grain and Seed.

The ONLY MILLS in the United States that will SEPARATE OATS FROM WHEAT successfully.

We also manufacture Horse Powers, Flax Reels, Oat Clippers, Dustless Grain Separators, Grain Elevator Machinery and outfits complete.

Full Descriptive Catalogues Free. Address

E. H. PEASE MFG. CO., RACINE, WIS.

[The above Company is "ALL RIGHT."—Editor.]

Fanning mill technology goes back to the early 1800s. There were 15 different patents issued between 1808 and 1829. But significant quantities of fanning mills weren't made until the Civil War ended in 1865 when farming and farm lands became national priorities with the westward expansion.

Fanning mill production centered on Racine, Wisconsin because it was near the middle of the cereal grain belt and had adequate sources of wood and foundries for cast iron gears. Racine was to fanning mills what Detroit was to automobiles. Here is a history of Racine County written in 1879 that mentions various producers, some with biographies:

Racine is headquarters for fanning-mills with more goods of this kind being manufactured here than at any other point in the United States. In fact, it is claimed that Racine sends out more fanning mills than the total amount manufactured elsewhere in our Union. Prominent among the firms in the business are:

The Blake-Beebe Company, formerly Blake, Beebe & Co., manufacturer of the Champion Warehouse and Farm Fanning-Mills. Mr. Lucius S. Blake, the founder of the house, started in the fanning-mill business in 1844, and has become so identified with this specialty that he is often called "Fanning-mill Blake." The first year, he built 100 fanning-mills, and continued to manufacture from 100 to 300 for about ten years. In 1854, the business began to increase, until, in 1858, he associated himself with James T. Elliott. They made from 500 to 1,000 mills per year, until, in the year 1872, they manufactured 2,000 mills.

The Racine Agricultural Foundry and Machine Works of A. P. Dickey have been in continuous operation, where now located, for thirty-three years. The capital employed is $75,000, and the sales aggregate 5,000 farm and warehouse fans annually, the market for which has rapidly increased of late. Mr. Dickey received the highest award at the Philadelphia Centennial Exposition, in 1876, and at the Paris Exposition, in 1867. Sales are made throughout the United States, in Europe, Australia, and India.

Daniel Bull, fanning-mill manufacturer, started in 1867. The factory is a four-story brick building, occupying five lots. Some twenty men are employed. Twenty-five hundred fanning mills are turned out annually.

E. P. Dickey, manufacturer of the American Sifter and Pacific Fanning-Mills also Badger State Milk Safe and Star Feed Cutter, commenced business in 1854. His factory was formerly located where Black's livery-stable now stands, corner of Fourth and Wisconsin streets. Five hundred mills, 300 milk safes, and 100 feed cutters are turned out annually, and the business amounts to over $15,000 per year.

C. & N. Altringer, manufacturer of the Excelsior Fanning-Mills, located corner of Fourteenth and Villa streets, commenced business in 1869, making about 250 mills the first year, since then from 500 to 600, until within the last three years. They now manufacture from 800 to 1,000 mills, which are mostly sold in the West. Their average working force is six men.

Hughes & Williams, manufacturers of the Badger State Fanning-Mills, commenced business in the fall of 1877 at Racine Junction. They manufacture about 400 mills per year, which are sold through the Western States.

Tostevin & Le Ray, manufacturers of the Union Sifter Fanning-Mills, commenced business in 1869, making 500 mills. The firm now averages about 900 mills per year, and employs eight men. Their sales are confined to the West.

Johnson & Field, manufacturers of the Racine Fanning-Mills, located at Racine Junction, started in 1867. They employ on an average twelve men, and manufacture about 1,000 mills per year. Their sales are made in the West and South.

Freeman & Evans, manufacturers of the Centennial Fanning-Mills, located at Racine Junction, commenced business in 1876, and have built up an extensive trade.

E. H. Pease Manufacturing Company

Racine Implement Company

S. Freeman & Sons Manufacturing Company

Will, Kayla, and Ava, here's a granddad story about a fanning mill that I found on the internet which you will enjoy. . . . . . . Spring was coming one year back in the 1920s and oats in the overhead bin needed cleaning so they could be used for seed.

Before breakfast one morning, Granddad went out to 'check' the bin. Arriving in the kitchen for his bacon and eggs, he remarked loudly enough to be heard by his sons, Ed (my dad) and Charles, that he must have lost his $20 gold piece in the oats bin. Granddad then finished his breakfast and headed off to his real estate office.

Buoyed by the prospect of finding real money, the boys spent most of the day hand-cranking oats through a small fanning mill, constantly on watch for the coin, which never appeared. Granddad came home that night and remarked to Grandma at the dinner table that he'd 'found' his coin, in his desk drawer at work.

Here's more from that same source – Like the first mills introduced, these also were hand powered, because most farms did not have the luxury of electricity until the middle 1940s. When electricity did come to rural America, fanning mills got motors, mostly 1/4- or 1/3-hp machines, which kept the speed constant, allowing for better adjustment of the mill and a better cleaning job in the end. They also eliminated much of the labor-intensive aspect of cleaning grain.

Early fanning mills were usually made of furniture-quality hardwood and nicely finished with joints similar to those used in furniture. They often had rounded corners and pinstriping or stenciling too. Twin City Manufacturing, out of Minneapolis and Winnipeg, Canada, made mills of both high and low quality. The company's Competition model was cheaply constructed out of pine; the New No. 1, constructed by Twin City for Deere & Company, had an all-oak frame, mortised joints, a threaded feed adjustment and an adjustable damper on the fan.

Will, Kayla, and Ava, now you know a lot about fanning mills, something the average person today has never even heard of, let alone understood why they were developed and how they fit into farm life. Our farm fanning mill no longer exists so we'll have to find one at some hands-on museum so you can try your hand at cranking. That will become a story that you can pass on to your grandchildren. In the meantime, ask your mom to make oatmeal or porridge all winter long using debris-free oats.

Love, Granddad

Grand Army of the Republic

Dear Will, Kayla, and Ava,   November 11, 2013

Your great great great grandfather, Frank Reiss, was one of the 30 charter members of Post 684 of the Grand Army of the Republic (GAR) in Millstadt, Illinois which was formed on September 22, 1889. Their first post commander was William Hartmann. These are the buttons with the GAR logo that were intended for his uniform but since they're still attached to a cardboard sheet, I don't think he had a uniform made. Plus it had been 23 years since he had worn a Union Army uniform in the Civil War. Millstadt is about five miles northwest of the Reiss Family Farm.

The Illinois Adjutant General's Report published in 1902 mentions that Frank Reiss was drafted on December 2, 1864 as a private into Company G of the Illinois 31st Infantry Regiment and was mustered out of service on July 19, 1865 in Louisville, Kentucky. His first day of service was December 9, 1864 at Camp Butler northeast of Springfield after which he probably joined his Company in Savannah, Georgia in January 1865. A letter dated January 5, 1865 from Frank's brother Martin Reiss to another brother Charles Reiss mentions Frank recently going off to war. Frank participated in the May 24, 1865 Grand Review parade in Washington, D. C. which passed in review before President Andrew Johnson who had succeeded Abraham Lincoln as president just 39 days earlier. Frank's regiment was part of the 1st Brigade, 3rd Division, of the 17th Army Corps.

After the end of Civil War, organizations were formed for veterans to network and maintain connections with each other. Many of the veterans used their shared experiences as a basis for fellowship. Groups of men began joining together, first for camaraderie and later for political power. Emerging as most influential among the various organizations was the Grand Army of the Republic, founded on April 6, 1866, on the principles of "Fraternity, Charity and Loyalty," in Decatur, Illinois, by Benjamin F. Stephenson.

The GAR was organized into "Departments" at the state level and "Posts" at the community level, and military-style uniforms were worn by its members. There were posts in every state in the US, and several posts overseas. The pattern of establishing departments and local posts was later used by other veterans' organizations including the American Legion after World War I and the Veterans of Foreign Wars after World War II.

In 1868, the GAR Commander-in-Chief General John A. Logan (right) established May 30 as Decoration Day, later known as Memorial Day. In its first celebrations, people used this day to commemorate the dead of the Civil War by decorating their graves with flowers and flags.

The GAR's political power grew during the latter part of the 19th century, and it helped elect several Republican US presidents, beginning with Ulysses S. Grant and ending with William McKinley. Five members were elected president of the US. For a time, candidates could not get nominated to the Republican ticket without the endorsement of the GAR voting bloc. Membership peaked at 490,000 veterans in 1890.

John Alexander Logan (2/9/1826 – 12/26/1886) was quite a guy. Our Frank Reiss probably met/saw him several times. Logan was a military officer and political leader. He served in the Mexican-American War and in the Union Army as a general during the Civil War. He served the state of Illinois as a state senator, congressman, and senator and was an unsuccessful candidate for Vice-President of the United States with James G. Blaine in the election of 1884. For this campaign, he commissioned the painting of the Atlanta Cyclorama, which emphasized his heroism in the Battle of Atlanta.

Logan fought at Bull Run as an unattached volunteer to a Michigan regiment, and then returned to Washington, resigned his congressional seat, and entered the Union Army as Colonel of the 31st Illinois Volunteers, which he organized. My great grandfather Frank Reiss was part of the 31st Illinois. Logan served in the army of Ulysses S. Grant in the Western Theater and was present at the Battle of Belmont where my great great great uncle George Basler was wounded. Logan commanded the Union Army during the May 1865 Grand Review in Washington which included Frank Reiss.

When Logan died in 1886, his body lay in state in the United States

Capitol. Several states have honored Logan including Illinois with a statue in Grant Park (above right), monument in Logan Square, and Logan Boulevard, all in Chicago. Logan is one of only three people mentioned by name in the Illinois state song. He is the father of U.S. Army officer and Medal of Honor recipient John Alexander Logan, Jr. Here is part of the Illinois state song:

> *On the record of thy years,*
> *Abraham Lincoln's name appears,*
> *Grant and Logan, and our tears,*
> *Illinois, Illinois,*
> *Grant and Logan, and our tears,*

Here is the GAR Hall in downtown Peoria. Inside is the marble bust of Gen. John Logan, the Union general who after the Civil War helped organize the Grand Army of the Republic. Logan is also credited with naming May 30, 1868, as the first Memorial Day. The hall was dedicated in 1909 and was listed on the National Register of Historic Places in 1976.

We had a large family reunion in 1984 to celebrate the 150th anniversary of the Reiss Family Farm. My dad was one of the main speakers. He wore a red plaid vest where he had replaced the original buttons with the smaller GAR buttons that belonged to his grandfather Frank Reiss. It's in my closet now so I'll be sure and show it to you some day.

Will, Kayla, and Ava, today is Veterans Day which is a national holiday when we honor the men and women who served in our country's armed forces whether it was during peace times or during war times. Please remember your great great great grandfather Frank Reiss for his contribution during the Civil War. He is one of four relatives on my dad's side who fought with four different Illinois infantry regiments. On my mom's side were about thirty-five relatives who fought with various Confederate infantry and cavalry regiments plus one who fought with yet another Illinois regiment.

Love, Granddad

A New House in 1889

Dear Will, Kayla, Ava, and Blake,   December 14, 2015

My great grandparents Frank and Anna Sybilla Reiss built this modern house in 1889. Their first ten children were born in the nearby log cabin that Frank's father, Adam Reiss, had built in 1838. Their eleventh and last child, William Martin, was born in this house in 1890. Sadly the first child Charles Martin died at age 7, the second child Adam Joseph died at age 5, third child Catherine died at age 7 months, and the tenth child Elizabetha (Lizza) died at age 9 months.

Frank and Anna are sitting on the porch with young William between in a gown as was the custom then. He looks about two years old so this picture would date from 1892. The names and approximate ages of the other six children from the left are Henry William 12, George William 19, John Jacob 15, Anna Margaret 17, Louis Phillip 10, and Louisa Kathryn 8 on the right end of the porch. They must have liked "William" because they used it three times just like two generations in our Springfield family.

Check out the picture on the next page and notice how the porch was closed-in, right up to the angled basement access doors behind George. My guess is that was done prior to 1900 when the house was still full of kids. Notice also that a second porch was added on the south side with lots of windows to let in sunlight for warmth and for potted flowers. The roofline was changed significantly in two directions to extend over these additions. Access to the house became through the front left door which leads to the south porch, followed by a right turn from there into the kitchen. The cornerstone, marked 1889, is just right of the new entrance step.

Here's more on the children:

- George married Katie Luetzelschwab. Nine years later on 5/21/1920 they paid his parents $7,700 to buy this house and their original 180 acres. They lived in this house until building a newer one next door in 1940 at which time this house became a rental for farm tenants. George and Katie's three sons were born upstairs in that south bedroom. Those sons inherited the farm in 1986 when Katie died and it's now in the hands of the two following generations.

- Anna Margaretta married George Dintelmann and had two sons.

- John Jacob married Mary Etta Sellards and had two daughters. They founded the Reiss Dairy in Sikeston, Missouri.

- Henry William married Emma Caroline and then Bertha Rischert. He was a pharmacist in St. Louis. No children.

- Louis Phillip married Harriet Wright and had a daughter and two sons. He was a refrigeration engineer in Texas.

- Louisa Kathryn married Philip Petry and had a son who died as an infant and then three daughters.

- William Martin married Mabel Golden and then Rose Freant. He owned a photography studio in Alton, IL. No children.

Will, Kayla, Ava, and Blake, your great great great grandparents lived a long time. Frank died on 11/21/1921 at age 80 and Anna on 5/14/1930 at age 95. They were married for 55 years. Here's a family picture from 1925 but without Katie Petry. You can tell the farmer George by his tan.

Love, Granddad

Back: William, Louie, Henry, John Reiss. Front: George, Anna Reiss, Margaret Reiss Dintelmann 1925

1890 – 1899

1890 Population of St. Clair County is 66,571.

1890 States total 42, national population is 62.98 million. Idaho and Wyoming are added in 1890 and Utah in 1896.

1890 President is Benjamin Harrison. Grover Cleveland is inaugurated in 1893 and William McKinley in 1897.

1890 The United States census begin using an automated tabulating machine with punch cards invented by Herman Hollerith. His company eventually became IBM.

1891 The Wrigley Company was founded in Chicago, originally selling soap, baking powder, and the next year, chewing gum.

1891 Carnegie Hall opened in New York with its first public performance under the guest conductor, Tchaikovsky.

1892 Ellis Island opened as the main east coast immigration center. It closed in 1954 after 12 million immigrants had been processed.

1892 James Naismith published the rules of basketball and the first official game was held five days later at the YMCA in Springfield, Massachusetts.

1892 The first recital of the Pledge of Allegiance in U.S. public schools is done to mark the 400th anniversary of Columbus Day.

1893 The Chicago World Columbian Exposition which included the world's first Ferris Wheel. It could hold 2,160 riders.

1895 The first professional football game is played in Latrobe, Pennsylvania.

1895 The first US patent for the automobile, #549160, was granted to George B. Selden for his two stroke automobile engine.

1895 First graduating class from Stanford University includes Herbert Hoover. Later alumni include 19 senators, 35 congressmen, 12 governors, 23 ambassadors, 5 supreme court justices, 21 Nobel laureates, and 18 astronauts.

1897 The first Boston Marathon is run with fifteen runners.

1897 First underground subway opened in North America in Boston.

1898 Treaty signed ending the Spanish-American War. The Spanish grant independence to Cuba and cede Puerto Rico, Guam, and the Philippines to the US.

The Lang Family Farm

Dear Will, Kayla, and Ava,   June 2, 2014

The extended Lang family has been very special for the extended Reiss family for over 85 years thanks to several connections:

- Edna Luetzelschwab was born on 10/16/1905 as the youngest sister of my grandmother Katie Luetzelschwab Reiss. She married Henry G. Lang born 1/2/1900 on 8/14/1927 with that union lasting for a little over 50 years. They had four children – Lavern born on 6/6/1928, Harold born on 12/11/1930, Vera born on 11/11/1932, and Myrtle born on 12/13/1933. Notice all those unique month/day numbers.

- Henry Lang was one of several crop share tenants on the Reiss family farm from 1942 to 1954. He rented the field east of the barn and the fields west and north of the mailbox. His primary crop was wheat.

- Lavern Lang was the lone crop share tenant on the family farm from 1954 to 2006.

There was Henry Lang and his son Henry G. Lang. That "G" didn't stand for anything. Young Henry just added it on his own name because he didn't want to be called "Junior." Our relative was "the son" because he married my grandmother's sister Edna. But you need to know about "the father" because that's the farmland connection.

Henry Lang was born on 3/26/1865. His parents were Philipp Lang (born 6/9/1830) and Philipina Krieger Lang (born 1/24/1840). Maybe they called each other "Phil." Henry Lang married Elizabeth (Lizzy) Becker Eckert on 11/20/1895. She had previously married William Eckert on 11/8/1885 and had two sons, Arthur and Walter Eckert. When William died intestate

on 1/28/1892, Lizzy ended up with his 141 acres in Sections 28 and 33 of Millstadt Township. See the email from my professional genealogist, Diane Walsh, at the end of this story.

Anyway, that auction step gave Lizzy the legal ownership to bring this farm into her second marriage which was to Henry Lang. He apparently outlived her such that her farm became the Lang family farm.

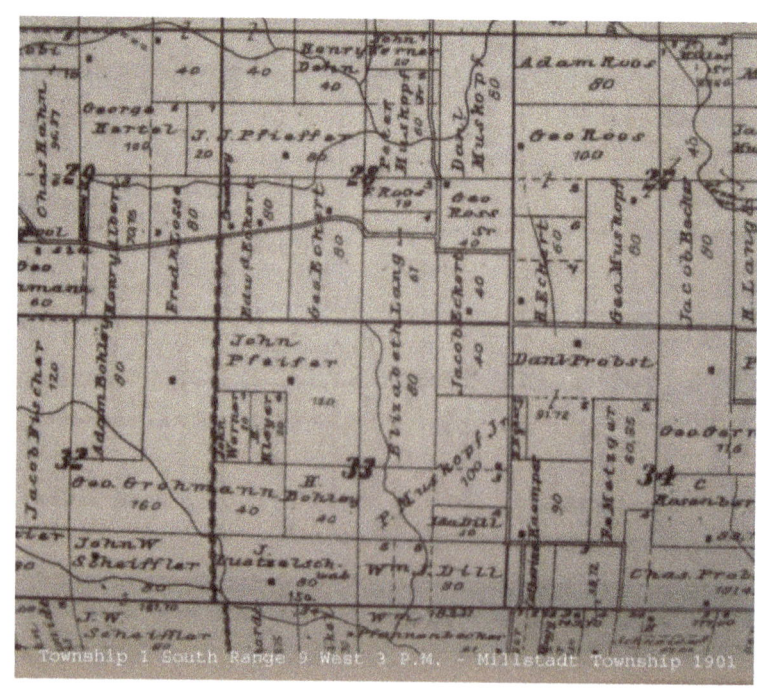

Henry and Lizzy Lang had two more children, a daughter Alma born on 1/9/1897 and a son Henry G. born on 1/2/1900. This plat book map from 1901 shows Elizabeth Lang owning

141 acres in Sections 28 and 33. The Langs established a homestead on their 141 acres at 5338 Bohleysville Road by building a barn in 1904 and a house in 1905. The carpenter for both was George Probst of Floraville. Henry Lang died in October 1927 of an apparent heart attack while hand cranking his truck's engine.

Look closely at the south half of the southwest quarter of Section 33 and you'll see the John Luetzelschwab farm. That's where Edna Luetzelschwab and her ten siblings grew up. John and two of his sons later purchased the north half of that SW quarter to square out the Luetzelschwab farm at 160 acres. That farm history will be a separate Granddad's Mondays story.

That common corner between the Luetzelschwab and Lang farms made it easy for Edna Luetzelschwab and Henry G. Lang to be an item. They were neighbors and best buds which led to their wedding on 8/14/1927. Here's their family photo from November 1952 (left to right) with Myrtle (now Metter), Harold, Lavern, and Vera (now Stumpf). Beautiful family!!!

Henry G. Lang died suddenly on 1/12/1978 in St. Elizabeth Hospital in Belleville. He is buried in Freivogel Cemetery in Millstadt. Edna died at a nursing center in Waterloo on 11/25/1990. Their sons Lavern and Harold bought their sisters' shares of the Lang family farm a few years before Edna passed away.

Within the last ten years Leon and Joan Lang bought three acres of the north end of the Lang family farm from his dad Lavern and uncle Harold. Leon and Joan then built a modern barn which was the site of the 2009 Luetzelschwab Family Reunion. Here are census snapshots.

1900 Census shows Henry Lang age 35, Lizzie Lang age 38, Alma Lang 3, Henry Lang 4/12, Arthur Eckert 11, and Walter Eckert 9.

1910 Census shows Henry Lang 45, Lizzie 47 both married 15 years but his first and her second with 4 of 4 children still living, Alma 13, Henry G. 10, Arthur Eckert stepson 21. Neighbors are Henry Eckert on one side and widowed Catharine Eckert on the other side.

1930 Census shows Henry Lang age 30 first married at 23, Edna 24 first married at 18, Lavern 1 10/12, mother Lizzie Lang 67 widowed and first married at 27.

Will, Kayla, and Ava, on 4/1/2014 Grand DD and I stopped at Schubert's Packing Company in Millstadt to buy pork sausage. Maybe you remember that name from my Granddad's Mondays story of 7/8/2013. After paying for our sausage, I asked the lady behind the counter for directions to Freivogel Cemetery. She gave good directions and asked who I was looking for. I said, "Lang and Luetzelschwab." At that point she said, "I am both!!!" Her name was Patti Metter Kern and she is the daughter of Myrtle Lang Metter and granddaughter of Henry and Edna Luetzelschwab Lang. That means that Patti and I are second cousins. Small world and neat story, right! I probably met her at the 2009 Luetzelschwab Reunion and look forward to reconnecting at the 2015 Luetzelschwab Reunion on the Lang Family Farm on June 6. You three are invited as well. That reunion will be the sesquicentennial celebration (150 years) of the Luetzelschwabs immigrating to the US from Magden, Switzerland. Here are photos from Freivogel Cemetery southwest of Millstadt.

Enterprise Sausage Press

Dear Will, Kayla, and Ava,   January 27, 2014

Here is my first cousin, Richard Reiss, demonstrating how to use an Enterprise sausage/fruit press in a 1960 photograph by his father Frank at the Reiss family farm. His right hand turns a crank which causes a round disc to squeeze down inside the cast iron cylinder. There is a spout facing Richard where fruit juice would run out into a bowl. That same spout could also connect to a sausage casing such that ground and seasoned pork meat would be pushed into it. Making sausage is one of the finishing operations of butchering a hog, something that happened on the Reiss farm almost every winter. The press and basic attachments appear on the next page.

The Enterprise Manufacturing Company was founded in 1864 by T. Henry Asbury (1840-1907) in Philadelphia. In 1866, they incorporated and moved to 3rd and Dauphin Streets, where they operated very successfully as a maker of home and store equipment for grinding, chopping and slicing meats, coffee, and fruits. They also patented a detachable sad iron and handle. This permitted reheating one iron while another was in use. This iron proved to be a bonanza and by the turn of the century, Enterprise employed 1,200 people, including 160 foundry molders who poured 15,000 pounds of iron per day. They shipped $6 million of product per year. Charles W. Asbury (1870-1935) continued the business which included a large number of catalog items, millers, grinders, a lard press, and a sausage stuffer like ours which was introduced in 1899.

Their most famous product was a line of those large red and black coffee mills you see in antique shops. This Model 12-1/2 was made between 1886 and 1898, stood 42" high, had 25" diameter

wheels, and weighed about 140 pounds. Such mills, when they could be afforded, were status symbols in general stores around the nation.

My basement museum has many Enterprise products including a bottle capper, two cherry pitters, a coffee grinder, a cork compressor, three food choppers, four ice shavers, two juicers, a nutcracker, two raisin seeders, a sausage stuffer, a tobacco cutter, a trivet, and

a shoe last. Here's the complete sausage press with attachments. Notice the perforated liner and plate which would be used for juicing various fruits. The tube and lock ring at right connect to the spout and then into the sausage casing. The words on the press say, "This cylinder is bored true" meaning there was a secondary machining operation to precise dimensions rather than leaving it "as cast."

Before the Reiss farm had electricity and a home freezer, my grandma would "fry-in" their homemade sausage as the first step in preserving it for the winter. That cooked sausage was packed into earthenware crocks and totally covered with hot liquid lard to seal out the air. After the crocks cooled, they were placed in the cool basement cellar for storage and periodic use during the winter. The lard was rendered at the time of the initial butchering by melting all the pork fat trimmings.

Since the liquid lard was about 400 degrees when poured into the sausage-filled crocks, that meat would continue to cook. That meant grandma had to allow for that secondary cooking by not "frying-in" the sausage too much.

During the winter months Grandma would remove preserved pork sausage for major meals. She had to be careful to "reseal" the larded crocks by using a wooden ladle to re-smooth the lard or pour in more liquid lard so no air could reach the sausage.

Will, Kayla, and Ava, this whole process of making, frying-in, and larding pork sausage sounds like a lot of work, doesn't it. If you wanted winter sausage today, we would bundle you three into heavy coats, strap you into three child safety seats, drive to McDonalds, undo the safety seats, stand in line at the counter, buy high sugar sodas, pay too much, remove your heavy coats so you could play in their gym, bus our own table after eating, and worry about chemicals and trans-fats in our fast food. I don't know, maybe Grandma's way was better!!!

Love, Granddad

1900 – 1909

1900 Population of St. Clair County is 86,685.

1900 States total 45, national population is 76.09 million. Oklahoma was added in 1907.

1900 President is William McKinley. Theodore Roosevelt is inaugurated in 1901 and William Howard Taft in 1909.

1900 A hurricane in Galveston, Texas kills 8,000 people and remains the most deadly natural disaster in American history.

1901 Charles R. Walgreen opened his first drug store in Chicago.

1902 The first Rose Bowl where Michigan defeated Stanford 49 – 0.

1902 The first movie theatre in the United States opened in Los Angeles.

1902 Willis Haviland Carrier invented the air conditioner.

1903 The first trans-US automobile trip from San Francisco to New York is completed in 70 days.

1903 The modern baseball World Series (9 games) with the Boston Americans defeating the Pittsburgh Pirates.

1903 First manned airplane flight by the Wright Brothers, 852 feet in 59 seconds.

1904 Summer Olympics held in St. Louis, first time in the Western Hemisphere.

1904 The first successful field tractor is invented by American Benjamin Holt, using a caterpillar track to spread the weight in heavy agricultural machinery.

1905 The city of Las Vegas, Nevada is formed with the sale of 110 acres in the downtown area.

1906 San Francisco earthquake, estimated at 7.8 on the Richter scale, killed 3,000 and did $375 million in property damage.

Raising Hogs

Dear Will and Kayla,   February 11, 2013

Your great great grandfather, George William Reiss, holds the record for living the longest on our family farm in St. Clair County, Illinois. He was born on the farm on April 22, 1873 and died there on 8/19/1964 at age 91.3 years. We called him Pop. He worked all of his life on that farm growing crops with his parents and raising hogs, probably on his own. He and his wife also raised chickens for eggs and for meat. The rest of this Granddad's Mondays is about his hog history except for the next paragraph.

George married the family's domestic helper, Catherine Luetzelschwab, on April 16, 1911. She was born on March 25, 1890 so she had just turned 21 and he was almost 38 when they got married. She was already living in the family home because the 1910 Census shows her there as Katie Lueteelschwab. George and Katie bought 140 acres of land north of Klein Road on April 12, 1917 and what is now the Sportsman's 40 acres on April 20, 1917. Then they bought the original home farm of 180 acres from his parents for $7,700 on May 21, 1920 which created the overall family farm of 360 acres as we know it today. I remember my Grandma Katie telling me that she cried many times about how much money she and Pop owed.

Here is a picture of George with his hogs in 1905. Notice the split rail fence behind him which separated the hogs in front from the sheep beyond. This picture is looking north from the log granary. The tall barn was not there yet because George built it about 1920. The hogs look like a variety called Chester White including the two darker ones which are probably reddish brown in color. Here's what I found on Chester Whites.

George W. Reiss in 1905 at the Reiss Family Farm

270

The **Chester White** is a breed of domestic pig which originated in Chester County, Pennsylvania. It was formerly known as the Chester County White. The Chester White was first developed around 1815-1818, using strains of large, white pigs common to the northeastern U.S. and a white boar imported from Bedfordshire, England.

Today the Chester White is a versatile breed suited to both intensive and extensive husbandry. Though not as popular as the Duroc, Yorkshire, or Hampshire, the Chester White is actively used in commercial crossbreeding operations for pork. The Chester White is the most durable of the white breeds; it can gain as much as 1.36 pounds a day and gain 1 pound for every 3 pounds of grain it is fed.

You'll see in George's sales history below that he sold his hogs at an average weight of 242 pounds. So if that breed gained as much as 1.36 pounds per day, their age at market was at least 178 days or 6 months. If they gained 1 pound for every 3 pounds they ate, each pig would have consumed 726 pounds of corn and other food. Since a bushel of corn weighs 56 pounds as loose kernels, each pig would have consumed about 13 bushels of corn seeds. It looks like George had from 10 to 18 hogs at any given time. So for 15 hogs, total corn demand would have been about 195 bushels of seeds or about 5 acres of corn averaging 40 bushels per acre. He sold his hogs for about $.07 per pound which means his corn could not have cost any more than 1/3 of that figure or about $.0233 per pound or $1.31 per bushel. The oldest corn price I could find on Google was 1970 at $1.50 so I'm sure it was way under George's breakeven point of $1.31 some 60 years earlier. I'm sure George did very well financially with his hog business even though it was very labor intensive and included the challenge of driving a horse-drawn wagonload of pigs to market in East St. Louis. More on that later. Here is his production and sales history over 18 years.

Livestock Commission Agent	Date	Number of Hogs	Total Weight	Price per CWT	Total $
C. E. White & Co.	April 3, 1902	8	1,910	6.90	131.79
Stewart, Son & McCormack	April 23, 1903	5	1,330	7.05	93.76
C. E. White & Co.	July 2, 1903	5	1,450	5.75	83.37
C. E. White & Co.	April 11, 1904	7	1,400	5.25	73.50
Stewart, Son & McCormack	Sept. 7, 1905	5	1,520	5.70	86.64
Stewart, Son & McCormack	Sept. 13, 1905	6	1,420	5.30	75.26
C. E. White & Co.	Mar. 23, 1907	8	1,580	6.35	100.33
Barse	Sept. 4, 1907	5	1,080	6.50	70.20
Barse	Sept. 16, 1907	5	1,020	6.50	66.30
C. E. White & Co.	Sept. 29, 1908	7	1,690	6.70	113.23
C. E. White & Co.	June 1, 1909	7	1,710	7.25	123.97
C. E. White & Co.	July 19, 1909	8	2,170	8.25	179.02
C. E. White & Co.	July 13, 1911	6	1,720	6.80	116.96
C. E. White & Co.	Aug. 2, 1911	6	1,740	7.25	126.15
C. E. White & Co.	Sept 2, 1911	6	1,870	7.50	136.50
Fry, Hanna & Harrison	April 11, 1916	11	2,450	9.65	236.42
Hanna & Harrison	April 11, 1917	20	4,600	16.50	742.90
Hanna & Harrison	Jan. 11, 1918	4	1,370	16.25	222.62
Hanna & Harrison	Feb. 28, 1918	5	1,910	16.40	313.24
Hanna & Harrison	Mar. 21, 1918	5	1,740	17.00	295.80

Hanna & Harrison	April 9, 1918	7	1,580	17.70	279.66
Hanna & Harrison	June 4, 1918	6	1,460	16.75	238.34
Hanna & Harrison	July 31, 1918	8	1,620	19.22	311.85
Hanna & Harrison	Sept. 10, 1918	8	2,000	20.00	400.00
Milton – Marshall	June 14, 1919	8	2,200	21.15	465.30

Here is George's sale record for 8 hogs on April 3, 1902. The commission agent who handled the deal charged a $1.00 fee and the stockyard charged $.48 which was probably a flat fee of $.06 per hog.

Here is a paragraph from The History of Southern Illinois written in 1912 by George Washington Smith – East St. Louis is the third largest city in the state, with a population of 58,547. Its interests are varied. It is a real city. Meat packing is a great industry. Railroading absorbs the interests of thousands. The greatest mule market in the world is here. The school system is modern and the church and social life is upon a high plane. There are three bridges across the great river and a fourth one nearing completion. They are in order of age The Eads, The Merchants, The McKinley, and what is sometimes called The Free Bridge; it is not complete.

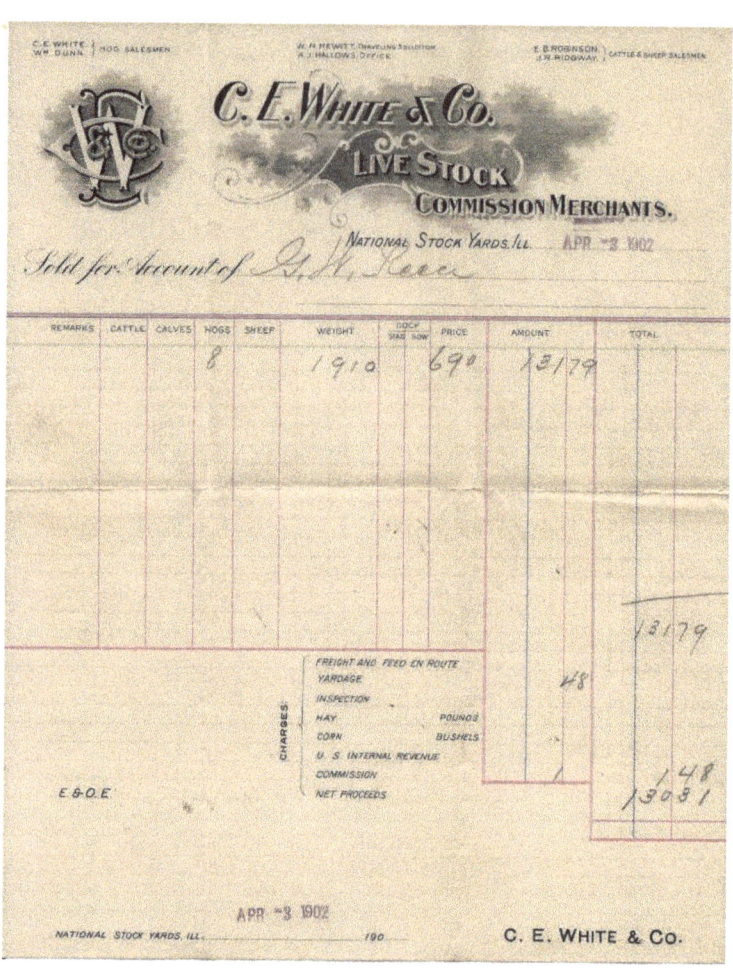

The St. Louis National Stockyards Company is formed in East St. Louis in 1873 – National City had its beginnings as a business investment by East-Coast venture capitalists in the early 1870s. East St. Louis mayor John Bowman had envisioned a new stockyard operation in East St. Louis that would rival the famous Union Stock Yards in Chicago and make the stockyards in nearby St. Louis minor by comparison, and he approached a group of wealthy investors about establishing it. Most of these investors were railroad men, and virtually all of them were from the East. The man who led this group of investors was Archibald M. Allerton, a New York attorney, who also was one of the owners of New York's National Drove Yard. Allerton and his fellow investors believed such an operation would be a successful venture, but had several conditions they wanted met before they would invest in East St. Louis: 1) they wanted to build their operation on land not incorporated into any existing city, so as to avoid strict regulations, with a promise that East St. Louis would never attempt annexation of their property, 2) they wanted to build their own infrastructure independently of East St. Louis, and 3) they wanted

East St. Louis to provide their property with city services such as fire protection. Mayor Bowman acquiesced to these conditions, and the agreement was made official on July 17, 1872, at the East St. Louis city council meeting. The investors had purchased 656 acres of land known as Gallagher Pastures on the northeast edge of East St. Louis upon which to build their new stockyard operation, and construction had begun on May 30, 1871. Ultimately, they would spend $1.5 million to construct the complex. It included 100 acres of animal pens and 60 acres for sheds, as well as the Allerton House (later known as the National Hotel, at which Theodore Roosevelt once stayed) – one of the finest hotels in the area – and a new Exchange Building. On October 31, 1872, the original 17 stockholders who had invested in the new stockyard operation met in Mayor Bowman's office and elected the first Board of Directors for the operation, with Archibald Allerton as its first President. The St. Louis National Stockyards Company was incorporated in Illinois four days later on November 4 and officially opened for business on November 19, 1873.

The early years (1873-1907) -- Once established, the St. Louis National Stockyards did not take long to become a major player in the livestock and meatpacking industries. The first shipment of cattle had arrived at the complex in June 1873, almost five months before the yards officially opened, and many more shipments would follow. The National Stockyards had been built to accommodate up to 15,000 head of cattle, 10,000 sheep, 20,000 hogs, in addition to a large quantity of non-meat animals such as horses and mules. This large capacity did not go unnoticed by the meatpacking firms in the East, who very shortly after the Stockyards' inception began to build plants here – which the Stockyards' board had anticipated by purchasing enough land to accommodate packinghouse operations alongside the yards. The centralization of stockyard operations along railroad terminals had led the major meatpacking companies to follow suit, locating their major operations near the stockyard operations to trim shipping costs connected to transporting whole animals by killing and processing their meat in a single location and shipping only the finished product. The first packinghouse operation to build a plant at the National Stockyards was the White House Provision Company. It was followed soon after by Richardson and Company's East St. Louis Packing and Provision Company, which opened on November 13, 1873. Richardson's was able to process 2,000 hogs per day at its beginning, and by the end of 1874 was processing 6,000 per day. Other packing companies began to arrive right on their heels. The St. Louis Beef Canning Company relocated to the Stockyards in 1879, and was followed closely by plants owned by the big-name meatpacking firms. Nelson Morris began operations at the Stockyards in 1889, Gustavus Swift arrived in 1893, and Philip Armour commenced production in 1903. There were also many other smaller firms who built plants near the yards, who along with the big operations helped to make the St. Louis area – and specifically the St. Louis National Stockyards – one of the nation's premier meatpacking centers, with the Stockyards directly employing 1,200 workers and processing approximately 50,000 animals weekly and boasting sales of more than $2 million each year at the turn of the 20th century.

National City, Illinois incorporates in 1907 – As the St. Louis National Stockyards and its related industries grew and became established, they returned major dividends for their investors and provided large profits for both livestock owners and meatpacking firms. However, things quickly became more complicated for the yards. In order to counter the increasing intervention of government into its affairs, the St. Louis National Stockyards and its related commercial interests incorporated as National City, Illinois, in July 1907. National City was in all respects a company town, as the St. Louis National Stockyards Company owned all the property in the town. The town consisted of two streets a block long, with about 40 houses arranged in four rows on them, a building that served as a church and school, a police/fire station and a store. The village had a population at its height of 300, all of whom were employees of the stockyards. Everything in the town was under the direct control of the company, from the mayor (handpicked by the company, the town only saw three changes of mayor between 1907 and 1982) to the tax assessments. This control enabled the St. Louis National Stockyards Company to efficiently run its own affairs with minimal outside governmental interference such as taxation and regulation. National City was the first industrial suburb outside East St. Louis, and it would set an example to be followed by other major industries in the St. Louis area, establishing such other company towns on the Illinois side of the Mississippi as Granite City (steel), Alorton (aluminum), Sauget (chemicals) and Wood River and Roxana (oil refinery).

From incorporation through World War II (1907-1947) -- Following its incorporation as National City, the St. Louis National Stockyards continued to grow as a livestock and meat processing center. World War I in particular expedited this growth. The Stockyards had numerous government contracts, both for supplying meat and providing horses and mules for use as pack animals. By 1920, National City had 14,000 people working there, and the St. Louis National Stockyards had the largest horse and mule market in the world, which would continue until shortly after the end of World War II. In addition, it placed third among American cattle markets and second among hog markets. In 1919, the total money received by the Stockyards was $8.25 million, illustrating the success of the yards during this time. However, World War I and its immediate aftermath would also cause the beginnings of dramatic changes for the Stockyards and its related operations – changes that would ultimately be the beginning of the end for National City.

Here are Pop's Chester White hogs in 1947 in a lot north of the old granary and barn. He retired from farming in 1948 at age 75. Various farm tenants kept hogs after Pop retired but this is one of the last photos of his porkers.

Decline (1947-1997) – The peak year for the National City Stockyards came in 1947, with 1,860,000 cattle – in addition to other animals -- being unloaded there. The Stockyards continued to do well through the 1950s. Receipts of cattle vacillated during this decade, but National City competed for first in the nation in hog receipts, eventually surpassing Chicago and **Omaha** to become the largest hog market in the world in 1954 and earning East St. Louis the epithet "Hog Capital of the Nation." However, though National City would continue to dominate the hog market for the next decade, its fortunes were changing with the market. The advent of the truck – and later, the **interstate highway system** – coupled with rising labor costs connected to **unionization** and the antiquation of outdated factories was causing the **meatpacking industry** to decentralize and relocate away from centralized **terminal markets** such as National City to rural areas, where it could find cheaper, nonunion labor, build new factories close to the livestock

274

producers and buy directly from them, thus eliminating the middleman of the stockyard industry and cutting costs.

In 1959, National City placed fourth among major stockyards in the nation. However, as the 1960s began, its gradual decline had begun in earnest. The Armour packinghouse in National City was the first plant owned by a major national firm to close in 1959, laying off 1,400 employees. In 1965, the St. Louis Metro-East region, of which National City was a part, had 43 packing plants processing 100,000 animals weekly; by 1970, just five years later, there were 32. In National City, Hunter Packing Company closed its doors in 1980, laying off 1,100 workers; Royal Packing Company followed closely behind in January 1981. They were followed by others, until Swift Independent Packing Company, the last packinghouse located in National City, shut down for good in 1986. The Chicago Union Stock Yards, long the industry leader, had already closed in 1971.

As this process of decentralization was underway, the Stockyards themselves continued to gradually diminish in importance to the livestock industry as well. By 1963, National City had slipped to fifth in stockyard production, losing its place atop the hog market in 1967 to Omaha, and it dropped to third place just a year later as St. Paul overtook it. This was evidence not just of National City's decline, but also that of terminal livestock markets as a whole across the country. In 1970, St. Louis National Stockyards Company President Gilbert Novotny stated that 30% of livestock sold in the U.S. was sold through terminal markets, a dramatic decline from the 90% sales terminal markets boasted in the 1920s. This precipitous decline mirrored the loss of packinghouse operations to the rural countryside.

Present – Today, National City, Illinois is essentially a ghost town. There are no residents living there, and much of the land is a post-industrial wasteland, with the remains of dilapidated factories – many overgrown with vegetation and covered in graffiti – standing as empty, crumbling shells, testifying to the one-time greatness of the St. Louis National Stockyards as a national meatpacking and livestock center. Nevertheless, National City has not been completely abandoned. Several industries have located there, including a major rendering company, a recycling plant, one of America's largest manufacturers of Asian foods, several warehouse, and trucking operations. National City was annexed by Fairmont City.

Will and Kayla, now you know how your grandfather's grandfather played a small part in feeding American soldiers and sailors during World Wars I and II. You can also see where Pop's retirement from the hog business in 1948 was the beginning of the end for the St. Louis National Stockyards. Now it's time for some scrumptious BBQ ribs at Texas Roadhouse!!!

Love, Granddad

Reiss Farm in Lamb County Texas (1907)

Dear Will and Kayla,   October 22, 2012

Your great great grandfather, George W. Reiss, bought 160 acres of ranch land in Lamb County in the southwest corner of the Texas panhandle 105 years ago this past Thursday on October 18, 1907. He paid $15 per acre for it, <u>site-unseen</u>. In fact he saw it for the first time 40 years later in 1947. That land is 3.0 miles north and 1.5 miles east of a small town called Earth whose current population 1,065.

Earth was established by William E. Halsell, who laid out the townsite in 1924. Originally Halsell named the town Fairlawn, but in 1925 it was renamed Earth when it was learned that there was already a town in Texas named Fairlawn. In order to find a new name the townspeople sent in suggestions, and the agreed-upon best name was chosen. Here's what Earth and our farm look like from Texas aerial photographs.

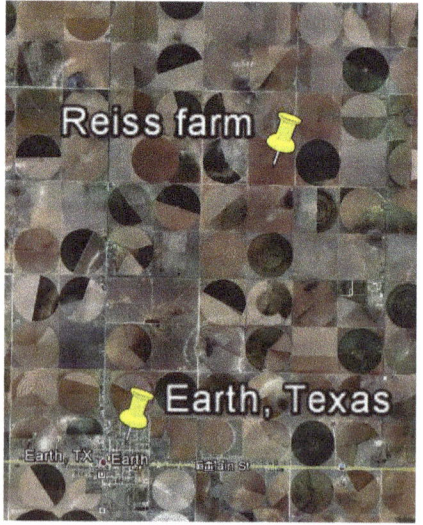

All those round circles are made by center-pivot irrigation systems. That technology was invented in 1949 by farmer Frank Zybach, who lived in the dry Texas panhandle near the town of Dalhart which is 142 miles due north of Earth. Each circle is centered on a 160-acre field measuring a half mile on each side which makes that square field one-fourth of a square mile. Since there are 640 acres in a square mile (or section), one-fourth of 640 is 160 acres. So center-pivot irrigation systems allowed ranch land to be converted to farm land since necessary moisture for crops was virtually guaranteed.

You can do the math and learn that these half-mile diameter circles cover 78.5% of these half-mile long squares. More expensive center-pivots with hinged ends can sweep about half those corners to thereby irrigate about 89% of these squares. But most farmers plant the corners to wheat or crops requiring less water.

Our farm has a center-pivot irrigation system but it's only barely visible because nothing was planted when this picture was taken. Our well is under the second "s" in our last name. It is powered by electricity from a public utility line running along our south line. Even though it's not obvious, our northwest corner is somewhat inclined and too steep to farm. So our 160-acre farm is 125 acres of irrigation, 26 acres of dry land farming, and 9 fallow acres Notice there are no trees and very few farmsteads.

Back up to 1907. Why would my grandfather George Reiss buy 160 acres of Texas ranch/farm land, site unseen, some 863 miles southwest of his parent's conventional farm near Floraville, Illinois? Good question! Pivot irrigation had not been invented and the village of Earth had not been established. Well, in October 1907 George was 34.5 years old, single, and probably aware of how successful the 1893 Oklahoma land rush had been on 2.0 million acres of ranch/farm land. He was probably a reader of one or two farming magazines and had seen advertisements offering parts of the famous XIT Ranch for sale at $15 per acre. Why not take a chance!!!

I can appreciate my grandfather's thought process and optimism because GrandDD and I did the same thing a year ago buying 120 acres of reclaimed coal mine farmland, site unseen, near my home town of Sullivan, Indiana. We paid $3,000 per acre and are confident our return on investment will be about three times the interest rate on our loan.

History of the XIT Ranch

The **XIT Ranch** was a cattle ranch in the Texas Panhandle which operated from 1885 to 1912. Comprising over 3,000,000 acres of land, it ran for two hundred miles along the border with New Mexico, varying in width from 20 to 30 miles. The ranch stretched across all or portions of Dallam, Hartley, Oldham, Deaf Smith, Parmer, Castro, Bailey, Lamb, Cochran, and Hockley Counties.

In 1879, the Sixteenth Texas Legislature appropriated 3,000,000 acres of state-owned land to finance a new state capitol. In 1882 in a special legislative session, the Seventeenth Texas Legislature struck a bargain with Charles B. and John V. Farwell of Chicago, Illinois, under which a syndicate led by the Farwells, with mostly British investors, agreed to build a new

$3,000,000 Texas State Capitol in Austin and to accept the 3,000,000 acres of Panhandle land as payment.

The ranch started operations in 1885 and at its peak averaged handling 150,000 head of cattle within its 1,500 miles of fencing. That was about one cow per 20 acres of land so you can see there wasn't much water. So the ranch erected 325 windmills and 100 dams across its land.

According to the XIT Ranch Museum, the ranch covered portions of ten counties which apparently helped perpetuate the misbelief that the brand, XIT, stands for "Ten In Texas." The brand, in fact, was originated to thwart rustlers.

However timing was bad for the XIT as cattle prices crashed in 1886 and 1887. By the fall of 1888, the ranch was unable to sell its cattle and make a profit. The cattle were constantly plagued by rustlers and predators, especially wolves leading to further losses for the syndicate. In 1901, the syndicate that owned the ranch began selling off the land to pay foreign investors as the bonds became due. By 1905, most of the land was subdivided, with large tracts being sold to other cattlemen and small amounts of land being sold to farmers. The last of the XIT cattle were sold on November 1, 1912, and land sales subsequently increased.

The XIT Ranch had a number of rules including the following:

- No employee was allowed to carry any weapons for offense or self-defense.
- Gambling or card playing of any description was strictly prohibited.
- No liquor or intoxicating beverages were allowed to employees during their time of service.
- No employees were allowed to hunt wild game on any of the XIT horses.
- Employees were not allowed to own any of the horses or cattle on the ranch.

History of William Halsell from whom George Reiss bought his 160 acres in 1907

There were two ranching operations in Texas which, by mere coincidence, had a "Mashed O" brand. In both cases, the reasoning behind the use of this brand was that it was easy to see, it would not blot, and it could not be made upside down or altered easily.

The Mashed O, or Spring Lake Ranch, in Lamb and Bailey Counties, is part of the ranching empire owned by the Halsell Cattle Company of San Antonio, which also had holdings near Vinita, Oklahoma, where the company offices were located before 1945. The brand was started in 1889 by the brothers J. Glenn and William E. Halsell in the Cherokee Nation Indian Territory. The story goes that when the Halsells dissolved their partnership, William took one of the circles from their old Three O (linked) brand and flattened it slightly with a hammer on the anvil in their blacksmith shop; the Mashed O resulted. From 1895 to 1898 William Halsell used that brand on 20,000 head of cattle on his Oklahoma ranch properties, which totaled some 150,000 acres.

In 1901 William Halsell purchased 184,155 acres of the old Spring Lake Division of the XIT Ranch at $2 an acre. This tract consisted of two large pastures separated by a stretch of shinnery (a dense growth of small trees). The south pasture was centered around the old Sod House

278

Camp, so named because the Estes brothers, who were hunting buffalo, had set up camp there in 1885. The north pasture was centered around the old Spring Lake Division headquarters, which Halsell utilized as his own. The headquarters, located in a grove of trees near a spring-fed lake (hence the name), gradually grew to include the main house, an office building, a bunkhouse, and the dining hall with a basement that was used as a commissary. His son, Ewing Halsell, was made general manager of the Spring Lake interests about that time and held that position for the remainder of his life.

In 1923, after the Santa Fe Railroad had built across the Sod House pasture and platted the town of Amherst, the Halsells decided to sell that area as farmland at $25 an acre. Two years later land in the ranch's northeastern portion, on which the town of Earth was subsequently located, was likewise parceled off. Will Rogers, a longtime friend of the Halsells, visited them at the Spring Lake headquarters in 1935, shortly before his death with Wiley Post in an airplane crash near Point Barrow, Alaska.

History of Lamb County

The South Plains of Texas was long the domain of Apache Indians until they were pushed out of the region by the more warlike Comanche around 1700. The Comanche ruled the Panhandle-Plains until the Red River War of 1873–74, when they were crushed by the United States Army. In 1875 the Comanche left the Panhandle-Plains for reservations in Indian Territory, leaving the region to the buffalo hunters. Between 1876 and 1880 the huge buffalo herds on the Texas Plains were almost exterminated, leaving the area open for occupation by cattlemen. Lamb County was established by the Texas legislature in 1876 from lands previously assigned to Bexar County.

Ranching arrived in the area when the huge XIT Ranch, occupying 3,050,000 acres of land, was established in 1885. Most of the eastern and northern part of the county was XIT land. C. C. Slaughter's Running Water Ranch occupied land in Lamb, Hale, Swisher, and Castro counties. The county's economy developed slowly as large-scale ranching completely dominated the area during the late nineteenth century and into the first years of the twentieth. Only four people lived in the county in 1890, and as late as 1900 there were only thirty-one people there. That year five ranches, encompassing 529,000 acres, had been established, and 10,908 cattle were reported. No crops were reported in the agricultural census taken in 1899. In the early 1900s the large ranches began to break up, and farmers began to establish themselves. In 1901 the XIT decided to sell its holdings. George W. Littlefield purchased most of the Yellowhouse Division of the XIT, 300,000 acres, and established the LFD Ranch in 1901. The Halsell family, led by William E. Halsell, purchased 185,000 acres of the old XIT Ranch's Springlake and Yellowhouse Divisions to be operated as the Mashed O Ranch. These two new ranches joined an older ranch that occupied parts of Hockley, Lubbock, Lamb, and Hale counties. In 1908 Slaughter sold much of his Running Water Ranch to land speculator William P. Soash. These lands lay around the tiny community of Olton. Soash sold the land to incoming farmers and stock farmers, and on June 20, 1908, Lamb County was organized with Olton as the seat of government. By 1910 there were ninety-two ranches and farms, and the population had risen to 540. The county was primarily a ranching area with a small number of merchants, farmers, and stockfarmers; in 1910,

40,355 cattle were reported in the county, while only 489 acres were planted in corn, the county's most important crop that year.

Immigration into the area was encouraged in the early 1910s when the Santa Fe Railroad made plans to build a branch line from Lubbock to Clovis, New Mexico, bisecting Lamb County from southeast to northwest and crossing George Littlefield's LFD Ranch. Littlefield cooperated with the railroad in bringing the line to fruition and helped to establish a townsite, ultimately known as Littlefield, on the railroad. Preliminary work on the Lubbock-Clovis line began as early as 1909, and by 1912 the townsite of Littlefield had been laid out. George Littlefield initiated land sales of major ranches in 1912 when he began to sell off parts of the LFD Ranch. Once the railroad was finished in March 1913 and the town of Littlefield established, farmers began to move into the area in larger numbers. By 1920 the county had 172 farms and ranches, and the population had increased to 1,175. Cropland expanded while the number of cattle declined. About 28,000 cattle were counted that year, and 8,517 acres were planted in sorghum, 2,551 acres in wheat, and 400 acres in cotton. During the 1920s the old ranchers realized great profits from land sales to thousands of newly arriving farmers; all three of the county's large ranches began to market their acreages. Littlefield accelerated his sales in the 1920s, the Halsells initiated land sales in 1923, and the Ellwoods began to sell out in 1925. As land sales progressed, small farming communities cropped up: Sudan was established in 1917 and was followed by Pep (1923), Amherst (1923), Earth (1924), Witharral (1924), Spade (1924), and Rocky Ford (1926). The number of farms increased to 632 by 1925 and to 2,381 by 1930. Most of the new farmers came to grow cotton, which during the 1920s moved from a relatively minor crop to the center of the area's economy. By 1930 cotton occupied 100,700 acres in Lamb County. Many local farmers also began to raise poultry during the 1920s; by 1930, 135,000 chickens were reported on farms, and farmers sold 487,000 dozens of eggs. The population grew during the 1920s, and by 1930 the census listed 17,452 residents. The county's emerging agricultural economy held through the Great Depression. Though the number of farms decreased slightly (to 2,167), cropland acres harvested increased from 316,214 in 1930 to 350,344 in 1940; cotton land increased to 119,000 acres. The population also grew slightly during the 1930s to reach 17,606 by 1940.

The county's rapid economic development also shaped its political geography. In the years after 1920 Littlefield developed into the county's leading community, and by 1930 it had about three times the population of Olton. After three attempts to change the county seat from Olton to Littlefield (in 1929, 1932, and 1937), Littlefield residents finally succeeded in 1946. As Lamb County evolved in the years after World War I a transportation system slowly emerged. A major route, State Highway 7 (now U.S. Highway 84), from Lubbock to Farwell and Clovis, was fully operational by the mid-1920s. A dirt road linked Littlefield to Hale Center, and another dirt lane ran westward from Littlefield to the county line. During the 1930s and 1940s the county built a network of farm-to-market roads, which were paved in the 1950s and 1960s. After World War II Littlefield developed into a trade center; meanwhile, oil discoveries in the very southern part of the county in 1945 also boosted Littlefield's economy. This production, although relatively small, was a welcome addition to the local economy. Over 326,000 barrels of oil were produced in the county in 1948; 419,000 barrels in 1956; 721,000 barrels in 1974; 1,096,000 barrels in 1978; and 1,103,000 in 1982. In 1990 519,000 barrels were produced. The population of the county increased after World War II to reach 20,015 in 1950 and 21,896 in 1960. Mechanization of agriculture and consolidation of farming operations pushed the population down somewhat in the 1960s, but it grew again during the 1970s, partly because of expanding oil operations in the area. The number of residents was 17,770 in 1970, 18,669 in 1980, and 15,072 in 1990. By the 1980s U.S. Highway 70, from Plainview to Muleshoe, had been built across the northern part of the county, U.S. 84 angled across the southwestern half, and a network of farm-to-market roads linked the county's many rural communities to Littlefield and to both U.S. 70 and U.S. 84.

In the 1980s Lamb County had a diversified economy based on agriculture but enhanced by commercial, industrial, and petroleum production. The county averaged $130 million a year in agricultural production with half coming from cotton, corn, wheat, grain sorghum, and soybean farming and the other half from cattle, hog, and sheep feedlot operations. By 1980, 447,000 acres (70 percent) were under cultivation for farm crops. About 210,000 acres were irrigated. Littlefield had agribusinesses, retail facilities, a textile mill, a fertilizer plant, and an irrigation-systems factory, as well as a hospital and nursing homes. Oil production averaged $3.5 million a year, while manufacturing added another $9.2 million a year. The county's primary towns were Littlefield (1990 population, 4,489), Olton (2,116), Earth (1,228), Sudan (983), Amherst (724), and Springlake (132).

So, Will and Kayla, that's far more than you wanted to know about the history of the Texas Panhandle and our little family involvement in that scenario. But at least when your teacher asks, "Where on earth is Earth?" you can correctly answer.

Love, Granddad

Was the Reiss Family Farm Ever Larger?

Dear Will, Kayla, and Ava,   May 26, 2014

Here is a plat book map from 1901 showing parts of Section 7 and 8 of Prairie du Long Township of St. Clair County, IL. Right in the middle of Section 7 you see Frank Reiss owning three 40-acre parcels totaling 118.42 acres which were originally purchased by his father, Adam Reiss, in 1838, 1839, and 1842. To the right of those are two parcels bought by Adam Reiss' widow Margaret and her second husband Conrad Ebert – 40 acres in 1852 and 20 acres in 1868. You can see the dotted lines representing the farm lanes from the west and from the north through the woods. In the upper center are 120 acres and then to the right another 20 acres belonging to Jacob Schaefer which my grandfather Geo. W. Reiss purchased in 1917. Also in Section 8 is 40 acres owned by Eva Mueth which Geo. W. Reiss also bought in 1917 which is now the Smithton Sportsmen's Club. Those 1917 purchases exactly doubled the size of the Reiss family farm which continues to this date as 360 acres.

Now look in the upper left corner and you'll see 79 acres owned by Geo. W. Reiss. This is not part of our current family farm. Its southeast corner is where our mailbox is today at the end of the woods lane. Is this my grandfather? When did he buy? When did he sell? Did he need his money out of this field so he could buy the 160 acres that he bought in Lamb County, Texas in 1907? What's the real deal?

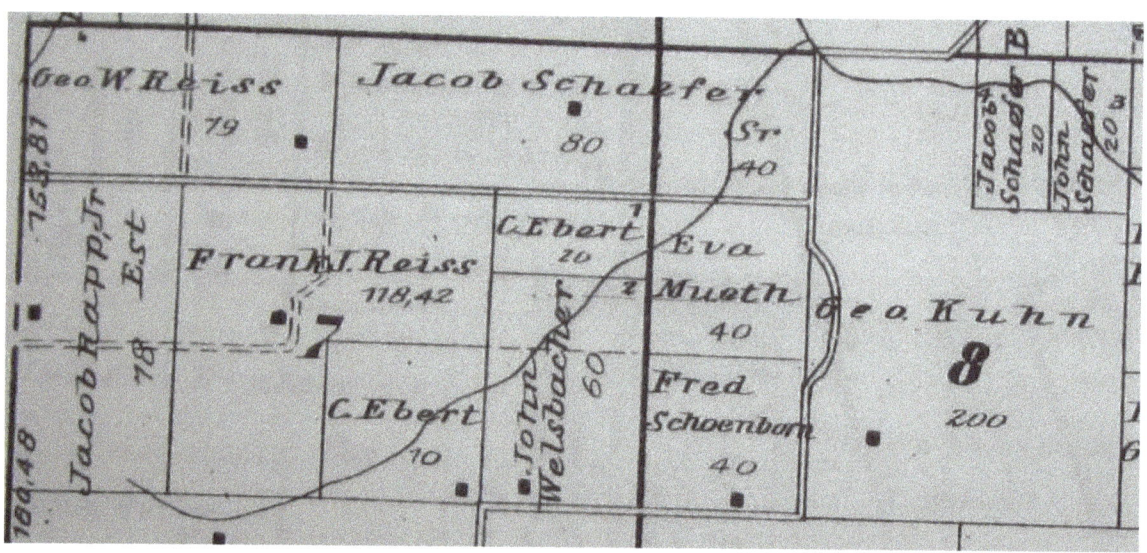

Turns out this Geo. W. Reiss bought this 79 acres in 1889 when our George W. Reiss would have been only 16 and not of legal age to buy land. Turns out also that this Geo. W. Reiss died in 1916 and left this land to his wife, Lena, and her sisters. They quickly sold it to the Metzger family on 9/12/1916 who still owns it. That indenture appears on the next page.

Will, Kayla, and Ava, the answer to the title question above is: NO! The Geo W. Reiss on the plat book IS NOT our George W. Reiss. Nevertheless, isn't it really strange how two different people with the same fairly unique name could be neighbors. Small world!!!

Love, Granddad

THIS INDENTURE WITNESSETH, That the Grantors, LENA REIS, a widow, of the City of Belleville, County of St. Clair and State of Illinois, SISTER ILLUMINATA, formerly LAURA REIS, a spinster, of the City of St. Louis and State of Missouri, ADDIE C. WULLER (nee REIS) and EDGAR J. WULLER, her husband, ELIZABETH REIS, a spinster and JOSEPHINE REIS, a spinster, of the City of Belleville, County of St. Clair and State of Illinois, for and in consideration of the sum of THIRTY FOUR HUNDRED DOLLARS, in hand paid, CONVEY AND WARRANT TO JOHN C. METZGER, of the County of St. Clair and State of Illinois, the following described Real Estate, to wit:

The North one half ($\frac{1}{2}$) of the Northwest quarter ($\frac{1}{4}$) of Section numbered Seven (7) in Township Two (2) South, Range Eight (8) West of the Third Principal Meridian, excepting a strip of land Twenty (20) feet wide off of the West side from North to South, of the North east quarter ($\frac{1}{4}$) of the Northwest quarter ($\frac{1}{4}$) of said Section numbered Seven (7).

Situated in the County of St. Clair and State of Illinois, hereby releasing and waiving all rights under and by virtue of the Homestead Exemption Laws of the State of Illinois.

Said Lena Reis being the widow, and said Sister Illuminata formerly Laura Reis, Addie C. Wuller (nee Reis), Elizabeth Reis and Josephine Reis, being the children, and only surviving heirs of George Reis, deceased.

Grantee herein assumes the payment of the General Taxes for the year 1916, now a lien on said premises.

Dated this Twelfth day of September, A.D. 1916.

Wheat Harvest

Dear Will, Kayla, and Ava,   June 30, 2014

My favorite time of the year is harvest – harvesting anything. That's when you enjoy and appreciate the fruits of your labor. Summer harvest involves wheat, apricots, blackberries, raspberries, strawberries, etc. Fall harvest involves corn, soybeans, rice, apples, etc. Those farm seed crops historically involved clever old-time equipment, lots of community hand labor, and small farms of a few hundred acres. Today those seed harvests require large and expensive machinery, very little hand labor, and farms of a few thousand acres.

My favorite aspect of all those farm harvests is the equipment, especially the iron and technology that's more than a hundred years old. Some of that is mentioned in my Granddad's Mondays of 4/29/2013 about "Bringing in the Sheaves" and 7/15/2013 about "Harvesting Wheat on the Reiss Family Farm." Both of those stories were about cutting mature wheat by hand with a scythe or with a mechanical reaper-binder to create shocks of wheat for drying the grain before threshing.

My story today will take that wheat harvest from the shock stage on through threshing. Here's a photo from about 1905 of threshing wheat on the Reiss Family Farm. This field is northeast of the old barn. Out of the picture to the right is a steam powered tractor with a large flywheel which turns the long belt that supplies rotational energy to the threshing machine. You can see that foot-wide belt in line with that empty wagon to the right. The upper level is at that man's knees and the lower level is at his feet. This tractor-thresher equipment combination and crew would go from farm to farm to farm and be shared among area farmers. Our Reiss ancestor farmers never owned either machine.

Wheat shocks throughout the field were loaded onto horse-drawn wagons and then brought to this stationary tractor-thresher location. Individual wheat sheaves were pitchforked from the wagons into the threshing machine which chugs and churns such that wheat seeds come out one place and wheat straw is shot out that long tube. The grain is put in gunny sacks and then stacked for eventual transport. You can see such a stack left of the huge stack of straw. You can also see four men in this picture and there are probably a few more men and boys out of the scene. The air was usually heavy with lots of dust and coal smoke from the tractor so during hot and humid weather, these would be a very challenging days. Threshing crews would check the wind direction and try to place their equipment so any wind helped clear the air.

Here's a photo from a 2010 Central States Threshermen's Reunion where old-timers and new-timers get together to operate and demonstrate traditional harvesting. It's the same technology as the first picture on the Reiss farm except here you get a better view of the coal-fired steam tractor turning a large flywheel which uses a long belt to transfer that energy to a threshing machine. My favorite steam show is at Pontiac, Illinois over the five-day Labor Day weekend, August 28 through September 1.

The combine harvester, or simply combine, was invented in the US by Hiram Moore in 1834 to harvest grain crops. The name derives from its combining three separate operations comprising harvesting – reaping, threshing, and winnowing – into a single process. Among the crops harvested with a combine are wheat, oats, rye, barley, corn, soybeans, and flax (linseed). The waste straw left behind was either spread on the field or baled for feed and bedding for livestock. Combine harvesters are one of the most economically important labor saving inventions, enabling a small fraction of the population to be engaged in agriculture.

Early versions of combine harvesters were pulled by horse or mule teams like this 1902 photo with 33 horses. This combine was made by Holt Manufacturing, one of the two companies which merged in 1925 to create ==Caterpillar Tractor Co==. Of course later combine models were pulled by diesel tractors made by Caterpillar and other manufacturers.

Here are entries from the July 1944 diary of my grandma Katie Reiss. She is cooking lunch for the threshing crew in the next photo at their neighbor's farm, the Koerbers.

Sat 8 – I was at Koerber's. They want to thresh, but it rained too much.

Mon 10 – I helped cook for threshers at Koerber's.

Tues 11 – Hot again, still threshing at Koerber's.

Sat 15 – 90 degrees at noon. We finished thresher cooking at Koerber's.

Wed 19 – 88 degrees at noon. I helped cook at Alma's for the thresher. This was the last job.

Fri 21 – Schilling boys helped us put up straw for litter.

Here's a postcard from Rose Somebody in Freeburg to Bertha Somebody in Belleville on 7/19/1909. It shows "haying" rather than threshing which is gathering a crop like alfalfa, clover, or even wheat straw with grasses. This is before the days of hay balers.

The photo below from July 1945 shows wheat being combined on the south field of the Reiss Family Farm. You can see the DC wind charger in the back right corner which was installed in late 1940. But you cannot see the AC electric service pole that was installed in that same corner on 11/17/1945 so that helps date this picture. Maybe you remember both of those electrical Granddad's Mondays stories from 12/9/2013.

I think the man driving the tractor and small combine is Henry Lang who is the brother-in-law of my grandparents who owned the farm. His son Lavern Lang became the farm tenant in 1954.

The photo on the next page from July 1956 shows our Reiss farm tenant, Lavern Lang, combining wheat in the pond field between the two rows of cedar trees. He bought that Allis Chalmers combine new in 1953. Rotational energy is transferred by a power take off from the back of the tractor to the combine. Some larger combines had their own engine. Lavern's combine cut a six foot swath of wheat. Years later Lavern sold that combine to the Gerald Zacheis Antique Tractor Museum in Sparta, Illinois. That business also auctions used farm equipment so we'll just have to visit some day to see if Lavern's combine is still there. There are several hundred restored farm machines on display in their air-conditioned building. Sparta is 32 miles southeast of our family farm. The museum phone number is 618 521 7757.

Below is another field of wheat just west of the 1940 home on the Reiss Family Farm.

Will, Kayla, and Ava, here are two photos of large modern combines. The upper photo shows how just two men could easily harvest a farm of 1,000 acres or more. The lower photo was probably created on a computer to show 23 combines with no dust making fast work of a large wheat field. What do you think our relatives in the 1905 photo on page 1 would say if they could see how harvesting technology has radically changed in just 100 years? Let's plan on visiting the Zacheis Museum in Sparta and the Threshermen's Reunion in Pontiac. Whaduyasay?

Love, Granddad

Last Will of Margaret Basler Reiss Ebert

Dear Will, Kayla, Ava, and Blake,   June 22, 2015

Your great great great great grandmother Margaret was an extraordinary woman. She was 22 years as a single person mostly in Switzerland, then 9 years married to Adam Reiss bearing 5 children, then 30 years married to Conrad Ebert bearing 3 or 4 children, then her final 22 years as a single person.

Her cover girl picture from our letters book was probably taken on 4/9/1866 at the double wedding of her children Frank Reiss to Anna Sybilla Feder and Kate Reiss to Charles Max Wittig. Her next photo was probably taken in the early 1880s during her periodic visits to her daughter Kate Wittig in Davenport, Iowa.

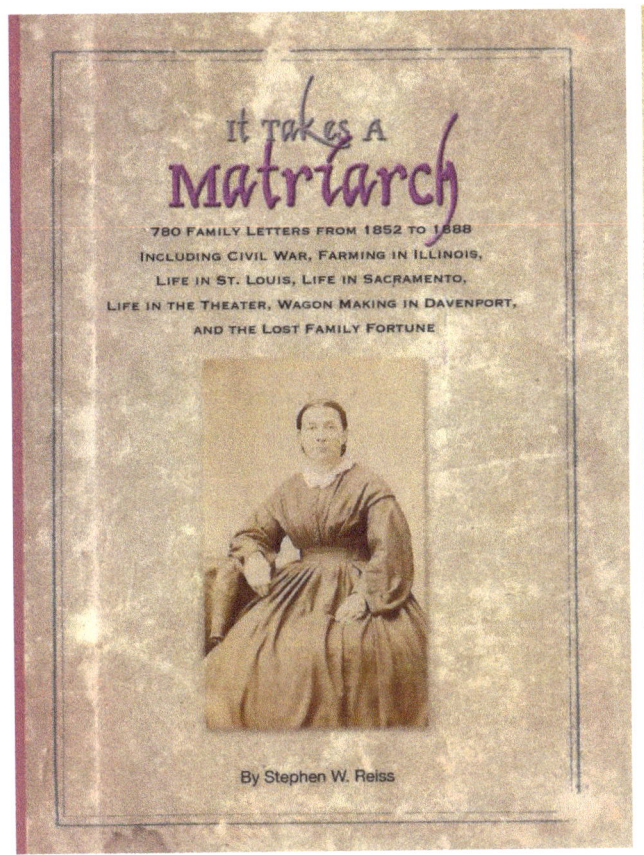

Below is her third photo taken about 1890. With it is her obituary from late June 1902 which was published in German before her funeral in Hecker, Illinois and burial a mile west of town in rural St. Augustine Cemetery.

Margaretha Ebert.

In Prairie du Long Township starb onsag Morgen im Alter von 84 Jahren und 9 Monaten Frau Margaretha Ebert, geborene Basler, Wittwe von Herrn Conrad Ebert. Sie starb auf der Farm ihrer Tochter, Frau Conrad Neff, 2 Meilen nördlich von Hecker.

Die Verstorbene wurde in der Schweiz geboren und kam im Jahre 1840 nach den Ver. Staaten. Ihr erster Gatte Herr Reiß starb im Jahre 1848. Ihr zweiter Gatte, Herr Conrad Ebert, starb im Jahre 1852. Sie hinterläßt folgende Kinder: John Reiß in Belleville, Frank Reiß in Floraville, Charles auf der Ridge Prairie, Martin in Missouri, Frau Max Wittig in Davenport, Ja., Frau Conrad Neff, sowie 31 Enkel und 3 Urenkel; ferner hinterläßt sie ihre Schwestern Frau Charles Krone und Frau Perew.

Das Leichenbegängniß fand statt am Mittwoch Morgen 8 Uhr nach der katholischen Kirche in Hecker und dem dortigen Friedhofe.

Translation – In the Prairie du Long Township died on Sunday morning Mrs. Margaretha Ebert at an age of 83 years and 9 months. Mrs. Ebert's maiden name was Margaretha Basler. She was the widow of Mr. Conrad Ebert. At the time of her death, Mrs. Ebert was living on the farm of her daughter, Mrs. Conrad Neff, two miles north of Hecker. Mrs. Ebert was born in Switzerland and came to the United States in the year 1839. Her first husband Mr. Reiss died in 1848 (correct date was 5/23/1849). Her second husband Mr. Conrad Ebert died in the year 1852 (correct date was 7/23/1880).

Mrs. Ebert is survived by her children: John Reiss in Belleville, Frank Reiss in Floraville, Charles Reiss in the Ridge Prairie, Martin Rice in Missouri, Mrs. Max Wittig in Davenport, Ia, and Mrs. Conrad Neff as well as 31 grandchildren and 3 great grandchildren. Also her sisters Mrs. Charles Krone and Mrs. Perrow. The funeral service has been on Wednesday morning at 8:00 o'clock in the Catholic Church in Hecker and the burial took place right after the service at the local cemetery.

Will, Kayla, Ava, and Blake, the next page is Grandma Margaret's will where she gives 20 acres to her daughter Margaret and grandson by her deceased daughter Louisa and the balance of her estate to her Reiss children. These papers were filed by Margaret's oldest son Frank Reiss a week after his mother died. We were so blessed to have Grandma Margaret in our historic midst for 83 years. Life moves on. Maybe some day we can all meet Grandma Margaret in heaven.

Love, Granddad

In the name of God, Amen: I Margaretha Ebert, of the Township of Prairie Du Long in the County of St. Clair and State of Illinois of the age of seventy nine years and being of sound mind and memory, do make, publish and declare this my last will and testament, in the manner following that is to say:

First: I give and bequeath to my grandson George Neff Jr. son of my deceased daughter Louisa Neff wife of George Neff Sr. and to my daughter Margaretha Neff, wife of Conrad Neff the following piece of land being the north half (1/2) of the south East quarter (1/4) of the North East quarter (1/4) of the North East one quarter (1/4) of Section Number Seven (7) Town two (2) South of Range Eight west being twenty (20) acres situated in Prairie Du Long Township in the County of St. Clair and State of Illinois, said lands to be sold and from the proceeds therefrom obtained Margaretha Neff is to receive One hundred dollars more than George Neff Jr.

Second: I order that all my debts be paid first out of the sale of the above described piece of land.

Third and lastly I give and bequeath all the rest, residue and remainder of my personal estate goods and chattels, of what nature or kind soever to my children by my former husband John Adam Reiss namely to Franz Joseph Reiss, Charles J. Reiss, Martin C. Reiss and Katherina Wittig to be divided equally between them share and share alike and I hereby appoint my son Frank Joseph Reiss sole executor of this my last will and testament, hereby revoking all former wills by me made.

In witness whereof I have hereunto set my hand and seal this second day of November in the year of our Lord one thousand eight hundred and ninety seven.

Margaretha Ebert (Seal.)

The above instrument consisting of one sheet was at the date thereof signed, sealed, published and declared by the said Margaretha Ebert as and for her last will and testament, in presence of us who at her request and in her presence and in the presence of each other have subscribed our names as witnesses thereto.

George Schaaf.

A. F. Seibert.

Endorsed:

Filed _June 30"_ , A. D. 19 0 _2_

Proved and admitted to Record _July 23"_ A. D. 19 0 _2_

A true Record of the Last Will and Testament of _Margaret Ebert_ deceased, and the endorsements thereon.

293

Twelve Family Farms in St. Clair County, Illinois

Dear Will, Kayla, Ava, and Blake,   June 22, 2015

Let me tell you how your relatives established twelve farms in this county just east of St. Louis, Missouri. Here is a map of Illinois showing St. Clair County in red. The farms were established in five different townships – near the bottom are New Athens, Prairie du Long, and both parts of Millstadt. Near the top center are St. Clair and Caseyville. Plats of the three lower townships are included in this story because they show multiple farms. Actually two of these farms are barely over the southwest border in Monroe County to the west but I included them in this summary on St. Clair County.

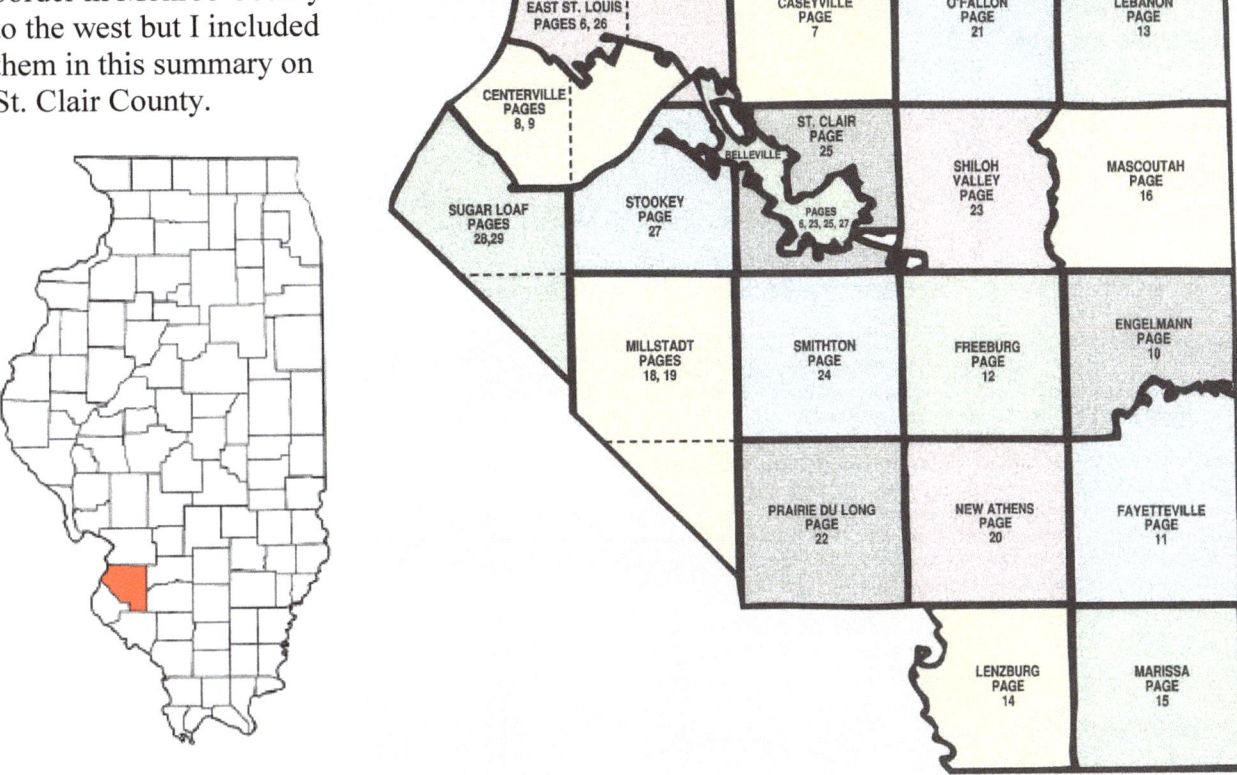

Farm #1 – Your **great great great great grandfather Adam Reiss** arrived in New Orleans from Germany in 1833. He spent that winter in Natchez, Mississippi and then moved to St. Clair County in the spring. He bought 40 acres in Section 7 of New Athens Township on 4/1/1834. It was perfectly flat with no trees. It was 100% tillable but John Deere did not invent his steel plow until later that decade. Adam sold this farm in 1837 maybe because his fiancée, Anna Marie "Mary" Schuessler, had arrived in 1836 from their hometown of Obernau, Germany. They married in 1838 but sadly she died on 12/11/1838 in the birth of their son John who survived. This Farm #1 was later purchased by another relative, Conrad Dintelmann, in 1883.

Farm #2 – Adam Reiss bought four more 40-acre farms. This third one was in 1839 in Section 23 of Monroe County just west of that triangular part of lower Millstadt Township. It stayed in the family after Adam's passing and was eventually sold as two 20-acre farms in 1875 and 1882.

Farm #3 – You know this as our current Reiss family farm. Adam bought his second, fourth, and fifth 40-acre adjacent farms in Section 7 of Prairie du Long Township. They are exactly six miles west of his Farm #1. He bought the second one in 1838 before his wife died and the fourth in 1839. Adam married Margaret Basler on 9/10/1840. They bought the fifth farm in 1842.

Here's the New Athens plat showing Adam Reiss' Farm #1 and three of the six Farm #8 parts bought by Conrad Dintelmann whose sister Ava married Adam's son Charles and whose son George married Adam's granddaughter Margaret. Small world!

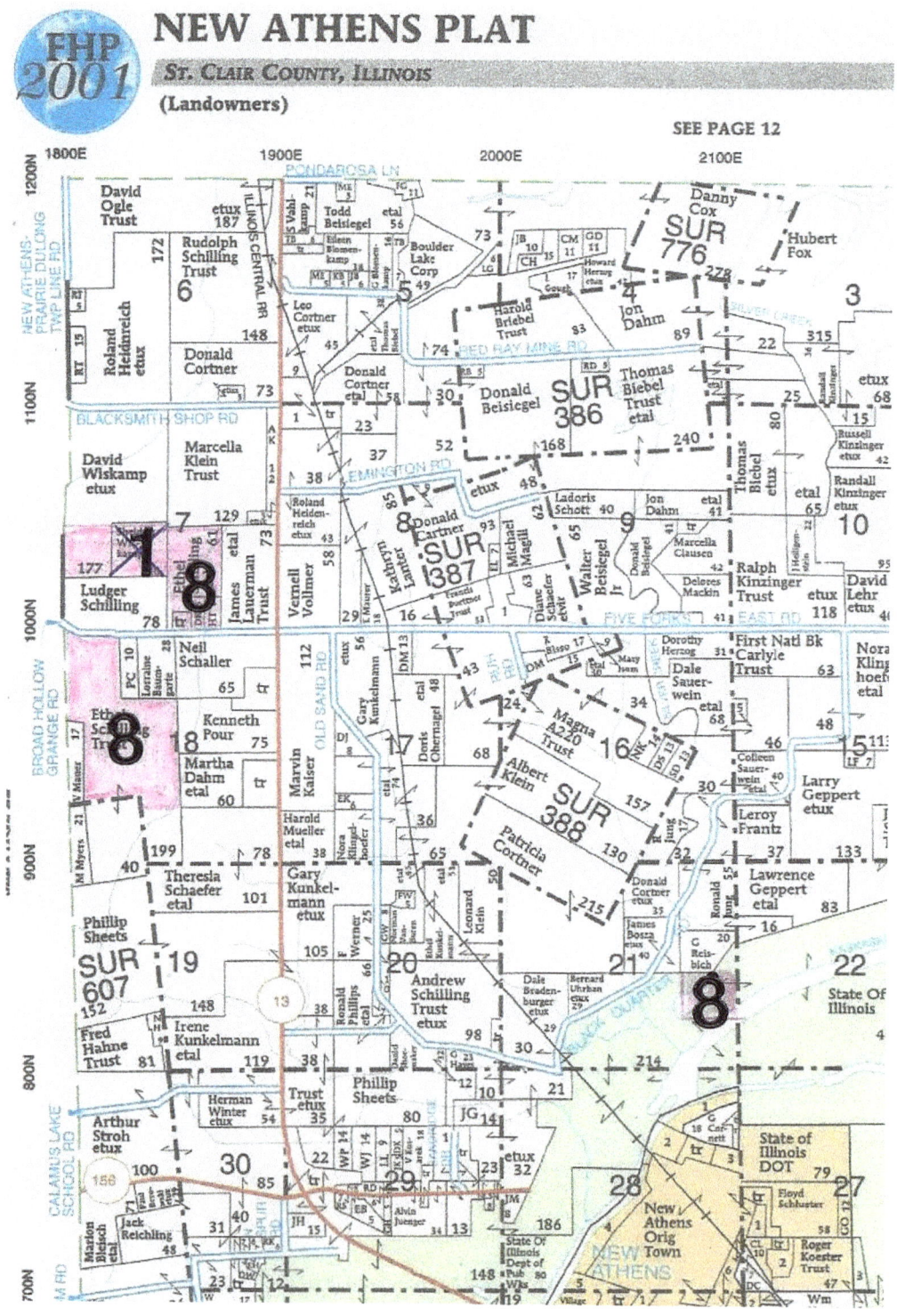

Here's the Prairie du Long plat showing the second, fourth, and fifth 40-acre farms that Adam Reiss bought in Section 7. He and Margaret had grown their homestead to 120 acres which became the nucleus for the expanding Reiss family farm. Sadly, Adam died on 5/23/1849. Margaret then married Conrad Ebert on 4/2/1850. He had emigrated from Germany in 1847. Margaret and Conrad bought an adjacent 40 acres in 1854 and an adjacent 20 acres in 1868.

Those 180 acres eventually passed to Adam's son, Frank Reiss, years after he married Anna Sybilla Feder in 1866. **They are your great great great grandparents**. Her parents bought Farm #11 that you'll read about below. Farm #3 passed to their son George who had married Katie Luetzelschwab in 1911. **They are your great great grandparents**. They bought 30 acres in 1914 as Farm #4 below and another 180 acres in 1917 to enlarge Farm #3 to 360 acres.

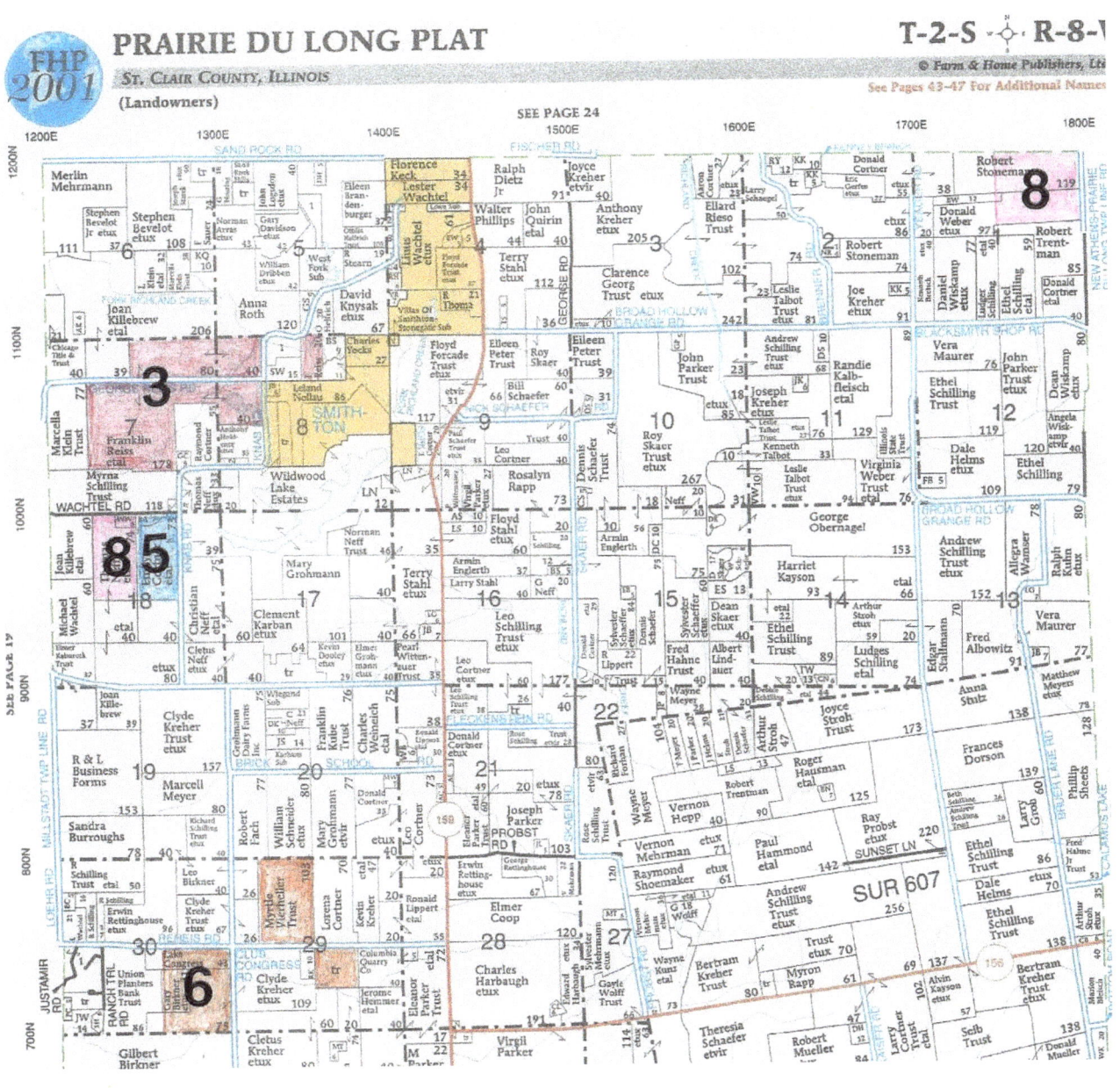

Farm #4 – George and Katie Reiss bought these 30 acres in 1914. It straddles the line between Monroe County and South Millstadt Township. The seller was the Crook family so we always referred to it as the Crook's farm.

Here's the Millstadt South plat showing Adam Reiss' Farm #2 in Monroe County and George Reiss' Farm #4 straddling the county line. You can also see the last of the six parts of Conrad Dintelmann's Farm #8 just west of Paderborn.

Farm #5 – Frantz Stauder arrived from Germany in 1836 and bought 40 acres in 1840 in Section 18 of Prairie du Long. That's just half a mile south of the Adam Reiss farm where Frantz would have met the younger sister, Sophia Basler, of Adam's second wife Margaret. Frantz and Sophia married on 3/28/1842. They bought an adjacent 40 acres in 1844. Frantz and Adam were best buddies. He was present when Adam died in 1849, witnessed his will, and appraised his estate.

Farm #6 – Go back to Farm #3 in the 1850s where Conrad and Margaret Reiss Ebert had two daughters who eventually married the two Neff brothers. They were sons of Conrad Neff who had immigrated in 1837. He bought three farms in Sections 29 and 30 of Prairie du Long Township. The Neff descendents are your "half" cousins since you are related to Margaret Reiss Ebert but not to her husband Conrad.

Farm #7 – Finally we get to **Johann and Katharina Basler who are your great great great great great grandparents**. They and eight of their nine children arrived in 1839 from Switzerland and settled in the Paderborn area. We've already mentioned that their oldest daughter Margaret married Adam Reiss and the second oldest daughter married Frantz Stauder. Sadly Katharina died on 3/5/1841. Nine months later Johann bought 40 acres in December at northeast corner of Paderborn. In January 1843, Johann donated two acres off his south line to St. Michael's for a new Catholic church and cemetery. In November 1843 he sold his remaining 38 acres and moved with his younger children to Louisville, Kentucky to live with his oldest son Nicholaus.

Farm #8 – By now you know that Conrad Dintelmann bought six farms in three different townships. His total of 603 acres makes him the largest landowner of all these family farms. It was Conrad's sister Ava and his son George who married into the Reiss family so Conrad is

MILLSTADT SOUTH PLAT

St. Clair County, Illinois
(Landowners)

technically not one of our relatives. There have been two additional Reiss – Dintelmann marriages in the last 30 years. Conrad's DNA is well connected with ours and that's good.

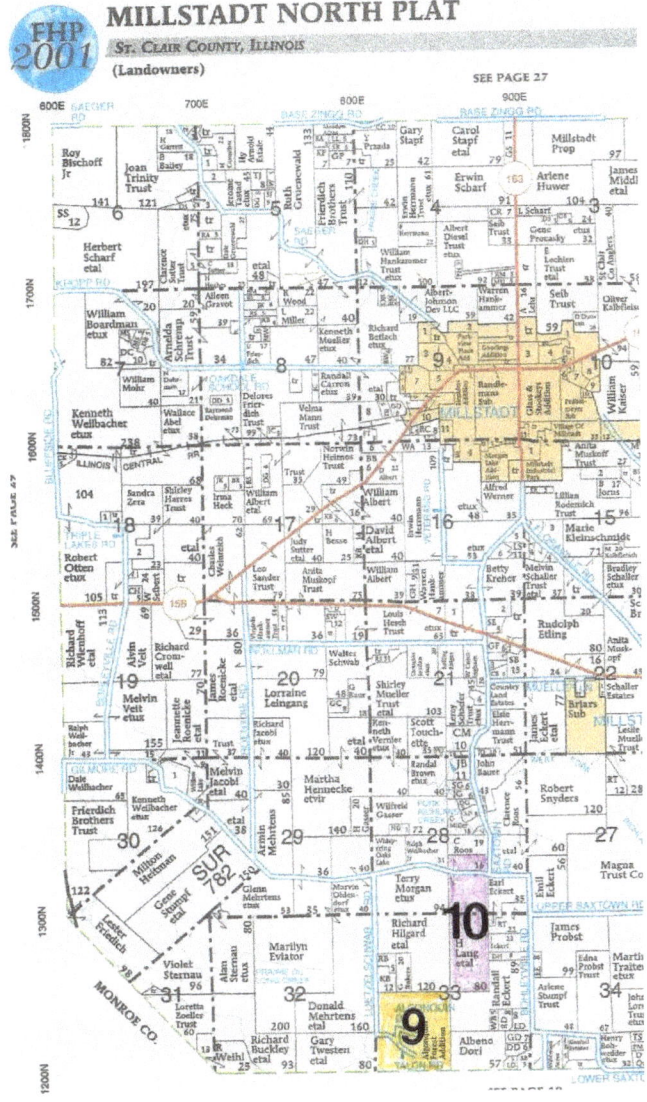

Farm #9 – John Baptiste and Maria Anna Luetzelschwab and their four children emigrated from Switzerland to Madison County, Illinois in 1865. **They are your great great great great grandparents**. Their son John Jacob married Charlotta Hoelscher in 1881 and started their family which would eventually total eleven children, all of whom reached adulthood. In 1883 they bought 80 acres in Section 9 of Millstadt North Township. Their daughter Katy married George Reiss in 1911 to become the third matriarch of Farm #3. Their son Jacob bought an adjacent 80 acres in 1938 to bring Farm #9 to 160 acres. It was eventually sold in 1977 and developed into a rural subdivision.

Farm #10 – Henry Lang married Elizabeth Becker Eckert in 1895 whose first husband William Eckert had died in 1892. They owned 61 acres in Section 28 and an adjacent 80 acres in Section 33 of Millstadt North Township so those 141 acres was brought to her second marriage. The Langs had two more children, one of whom was Henry G. Lang who eventually married Edna Luetzelschwab which makes them **your great great great aunt and uncle.** Henry G. and Edna ended up with Farm #10 and had four children. Their son Lavern was the tenant farmer for Reiss Farm #3 for almost 50 years.

Farm #11 – Adam Reiss' son, Frank Reiss, married Anna Sybilla Feder in 1866. **They are your great great great grandparents** and the owners of Farm #3 for about 40 years. Her parents were **George and Anna Sybilla Feder who are your great great great great grandparents**. They emigrated from Germany in 1845 and worked as farmers. They finally bought their 140 acres in Section 15 of St. Clair Township in 1867. That plat is not included in this story because they were the only family farm in that township.

Farm #12 – Charles Reiss is the next younger brother of Frank Reiss who owned Farm #3 for about 40 years. Charles married Ava Dintelmann in 1866 and then relocated to O'Fallon Township. They rented several farms for years before buying their own 80 acres in 1891 in Caseyville Township to the west. That plat is not included in this story because they were the only family farm in that township. Charles and Ava would be **your great great great great aunt and uncle**. Here's an overall summary of the twelve family farms in St. Clair County.

Name	Arrival	Township	Farm No.	Section No.	Buy Acres	Buy Date	Sold Acres	Sold Date
Adam Reiss	1833	New Athens	1	7	40	1834	40	1837
		Monroe County	2	23	40	1839	20+20	1875+1882
		Prairie du Long	3	7	40	1838		
		Prairie du Long	3	7	40	1839		
		Prairie du Long	3	7	40	1842		
Conrad Ebert	1847	Prairie du Long	3	7	40	1854		
		Prairie du Long	3	7	20	1868		
George Reiss		Prairie du Long	3	7+8	180	1917		
		Monroe County	4	25	15	1914		
		Millstadt South	4	25	15	1914		
Frantz Stauder	1836	Prairie du Long	5	18	40	1840	40	1866
		Prairie du Long	5	18	40	1844	40	1866
Conrad Neff	1837	Prairie du Long	6	29	147	1855		
		Prairie du Long	6	30	160	1874		
Johann Basler	1839	Millstadt South	7	13	40	1841	40	1843
Conrad Dintelmann	1848	New Athens	8	7	160	1883		
		New Athens	8	18	170			
		New Athens	8	21	40	1883		
		Prairie du Long	8	18	80	1863		
		Prairie du Long	8	1	133			
		Millstadt South	8	14	20	1863		
John Luetzelschwab	1865	Millstadt North	9	33	80	1882	80	1977
Jacob Luetzelschwab	1865	Millstadt North	9	33	80	1938	80	1977
Henry Lang		Millstadt North	10	28	61	1892		
		Millstadt North	10	33	80	1892		
George Feder	1845	Belleville	11	15	140	1867		
Charles Reiss		Caseyville	12	27	80	1891		

Will, Kayla, Ava, and Blake, all this may sound like TMI but at last it's all together in one place. It's really cool that Adam Reiss' Farm #1 was later part of Conrad Dintelmann's Farm #8. These farm owners from well over 100 years ago were very hard workers and awesome stewards of their land. You are very blessed to come from such good stock.

Love, Granddad

300

1910 – 1919

1910 Population of St. Clair County is 119,870.

1910 States total 46, national population is 92.41 million. New Mexico and Arizona were added in 1907.

1910 President is William Howard Taft. Woodrow Wilson is inaugurated in 1913.

1910 The Boy Scouts of America was founded.

1911 The Indianapolis 500 was run for the first time and won by Ray Harroun.

1911 The first transcontinental airline flight was completed after numerous stops and 82 hours in the air.

1913 The American Girl Guides was founded and renamed the Girl Scouts a year later.

1913 The 16th Amendment to the US Constitution is ratified, allowing the Federal government to impose an income tax.

1913 Ford Motor Company introduces the first moving assembly line.

1914 Ford Motor Company begins paying workers $5 for an 8-hour day, up from $2.40 for a 9-hour day.

1915 US Coast Guard is established.

1916 US National Park Service is created.

1917 US Congress declares war on Germany and joins its allies in World War I.

1918 Airmail services is begun by the US Postal Service.

1919 The Treaty of Versailles is signed, ending World War I.

1919 The Green Bay Packers franchise was founded. Today it is the only non-profit, community-owned major league professional sports team in the US. There are more owners than seats in their stadium.

1919 The Chicago Bears franchise was founded in Decatur, Illinois but moved to Chicago in 1921. They hold the NFL record for the most enshrinees in the Pro Football Hall of Fame and the most retired jersey numbers. The Bears have more regular season and overall victories than any other NFL franchise.

Matriarch #3 – Catherine Charlotte Luetzelschwab Reiss

Dear Will, Kayla, and Ava,   August 25, 2014

Last Monday you learned about Matriarch #1 who was my great great grandmother Margaret Basler Reiss Ebert and about Matriarch #2 who was my great grandmother Anna Antonia Sybilla Feder Reiss. Today you can learn about Matriarch #3 who is my grandmother Catherine Charlotte Luetzelschwab Reiss. She is the only one of these three women that I actually knew because our times on earth overlapped by 42 years with about 37 of those years being on the Reiss family farm.

Grandma Katie was born on 3/25/1890 on the Luetzelschwab family farm in St. Clair County. She was baptized at Zion United Church of Christ in Millstadt (renamed Zion Evangelical in 2005) on 5/8/1890 and confirmed there on Palm Sunday 4/5/1903. She married George William Reiss at St. Paul's United Church of Christ in Floraville on 4/16/1911. All three sacraments and the local church documents were in German. The St. Clair County wedding document was in English. Three of those four documents are framed and displayed in our home.

Catherine Luetzelschwab Reiss wedding Picture

One of the wedding gifts which Katie and George received was this porcelain bowl which is also on display in our home. It probably had a pitcher with it originally and was a bedroom set for washing faces and hands before the times of indoor bathrooms and running water. There is a note on the bottom of this bowl from my Aunt Gerry Reiss saying it was a wedding gift to Katie and George that was given by her mother Catherine Hoelscher who had received it as a wedding gift when she married Jacob Luetzelschwab on 5/26/1881. So as a double wedding gift, this bowl is really very special.

When Katie married George in 1911, he was living with his parents, Frank age 70 and Anna Sybilla ages 67, on the family farm. He was farming those 180 acres and was doing quite well. He farmed with horses and raised crops, hogs, sheep, and chickens. He also owned 160 acres of farmland in Lamb County, Texas which he had bought sight-unseen on 10/18/1907 for $15 per acre or a total of $2,400.

Katie's first ten years of marriage were exciting to say the least. Here are the major details –

- Son William George was born on 5/6/1912.

- Son Franklin Jacob was born on Halloween night 10/31/1915. Trick or treat!!!

- Katie and George bought 140 adjacent acres on 4/12/1917 from the Schaefer family for $4,000. They paid $1,000 down and signed two $500 mortgages and a $2,000 mortgage held by the Schaefers, all with different due dates.

- Katie and George bought 40 acres on 10/20/1917 from the Chamberlin family for $800. That corner has been leased to the Smithton Sportsman's Club since 7/20/1951. Initial rent was $25 per year which is only a 3.1% return on investment.

- Son Irwin Henry was born on 9/18/1918.

- Katie and George bought the 180-acre family farm from his parents on 4/12/1920 for $7,700. Parts of that deed appear on the next page. George's father died 1.5 years later on 11/21/1921.

I remember Grandma Katie telling me several times how she cried and cried over how much debt they were accumulating in buying 160 acres in Texas and 360 acres in Illinois. They did all this while raising three very young sons which meant all the farm labor fell on her husband with occasional help from hired hands. To further underscore the challenge, their farm did not get electricity until 11/17/1945 and George did all his field work by hand or with horses. He never owned a tractor. ==I find the first 30 years of their married life absolutely amazing.==

WARRANTY DEED.—Statutory Form.

This Indenture Witnesseth, That the Grantors Frank J. Reiss and Anna S. Reiss his wife of the Prairie du Long Township County of St. Clair and State of Illinois, for and in consideration of the sum of Seventy seven Hundred (7700⁰⁰/₁₀₀) DOLLARS, in hand paid, Convey and Warrant to George W. Reiss and Catherine Charlotte Reiss his wife of the Prairie du Long Township County of St. Clair and State of Illinois

Dated this 12th day of April A. D. 1920.

Frank J. Reiss   (SEAL)
Anna S. Reiss   (SEAL)
                   (SEAL)

Here's Katie with her handsome family about 1935.

On the next page is a photo from about 1943 of all eleven Luetzelschwab siblings and one niece. From left to right in back are Lena Becker, Mary Weihl, Katie Reiss, Herman, Lottie Sander, John, Jacob, and Frank. Minnie Sponemann is in the wheelchair. Front row is Edna Lang, niece Janet Pauketat, and Caroline Gummersheimer. Brother John is the carpenter-contractor who built Katie and George's new home in 1940.

George and Katie Reiss with sons Irwin, Bill, and Franklin

Grandma Katie kept two five-year daily diaries – 1944 through 1948 and 1949 through 1953. I transcribed both diaries, added old photos, inserted elaborations in italics where needed, and submitted both galleys to Author House for publishing. Both books appear below.

Katie's entries for ten days in July 1949 made me laugh out loud as she recounts babysitting for us three grandchildren. I was six months older than you, Will. My brother Ken was six months older than you, Kayla, and my sister Mickey was a year older than you, Ava. It was fun to draw comparisons between 1949 and the three five-day babysits we just finished with you three. Will and Ava, your folks enjoyed a July vacation in Las Vegas and an August vacation in New York. Kayla, your mom had a business trip to Rhode Island and your dad was working second shift.

Here are Katie's words from July 1949 –

Fri 1 – 85 degrees at 8 o'clock a.m., fair. I had my work with the children. Pop mixed feed. We mailed 3 dollars to the Successful Farmers paper for renewal for 3 years.

Sat 2 – Fair hot. I couldn't do more than take care of the children.

Sun 3 – Fair hot. Bill, Anita, and June came in the evening. They brought fireworks. June stayed here for the week.

Mon 4 – Fair hot. We did only our cooking and cared for the children. Irwin called up in the evening from Montana.

Tues 5 – Fair hot. We washed and ironed. Taxes for 1948 were $280.31 for our land and everything.

Wed 6 – Fair hot. We canned apple sauce and took care of the children.

Thurs 7 – Partly cloudy, hot. I washed and peeled apples. By five o'clock we got the hardest rain ever. Creeks were out.

Fri 8 – Hot. We baked cookies and washed and picked blackberries, and took care of the children.

Sat 9 – Fair. June Ann & I canned apple sauce and made jelly. Bill & Anita came and took June along home.

Sun 10 – Fair cooler. Mary & Irv came back from their trip to Montana. We all went to the Turner picnic in the evening.

As the titles of these two books suggest, Katie was an avid quilter and Grange member. She and George were even co-founders of the Floraville Grange in 1948. They were also active in their church in Floraville. These two books will thoroughly amaze and impress all readers.

Here's Katie with her first great granddaughter, Tammy McBrayer, who was born on 9/28/1968.

Will, Kayla, and Ava, you can see that quilting, Grange, church, farming, family, and friends all combined very well for Katie and George Reiss. You have to also include hugs, smiles, walks through the woods to the mailbox, gathering eggs, making pies, playing with kittens, and many other fun farm activities in that list. It's obvious to me that grandmas always know best.

Grandma Katie lived to age 96 and George to age 91. But now all their siblings and spouses, their three sons and spouses, a grandchild, and a great grandchild have passed on to a greater reward. That's the way life works. The challenge is to create, shape, and foster what we leave behind for others.

Love, Granddad

Golden Weddings

Dear Will, Kayla, Ava, and Blake,   September 15, 2014

I recently did a mental exercise of naming the descendents of Adam and Margaret Basler Reiss who had celebrated golden wedding anniversaries by being married 50 years or longer. I came up with half a dozen names. Thinking I had missed a few and wondering what couple was the longest married, I consulted our family tree and put together the list below. I was missing a few wedding and death dates so my list may be short or long by one or two couples. The colors identify generations with grey as first, green as second, blue as third, and none as fourth.

John Reiss branch – 76 adults born before 1990 with 4% making gold

John R. Reiss (12/11/1838 – 6/18/1919) married Maria Josephine Gass (2/6/1844 – 12/2/1920) on 10/22/1861 in Paderborn. Married for 57 years, 7 months, 27 days.

> Margaret Jane Meehling (10/9/1927 – 10/27/1995) married Arthur R. Engquist (10/1/1924 – 4/22/2002) on 5/5/?? Married over 50 years.

Mary Reiss (12/23/1863 – 8/9/1945) married Jacob Ferkel (7/1/1862 – 4/17/1938) on 12/23/1887. Married 50 years, 3 months, 25 days.

Frank Reiss branch – 127 adults born before 1990 with 10% making gold

Frank Joseph Reiss (9/27/1841 – 11/21/1921) married Anna Antonia Syvilla Feder (9/26/1844 – 5/14/1930) on 4/9/1866 in a double ceremony with his sister Kate and Max Wittig. Married 55 years, 7 months, 12 days.

> George William Reiss (4/22/1873 – 8/19/1964) married Catharine Charlotte Luetzelschwab (3/25/1890 – 10/17/1986) on 4/16/1911 at St. Paul's Church in Floraville. Married 53 years, 4 months, 3 days.

> > June Ann Reiss (12/2/1936 --) married James McBrayer (7/7/1936 --) on 8/2/1958 in Belleville, Illinois. Married 56 years, 1 month, 13 days and counting.

> > Franklin Jacob Reiss (10/31/1915 – 7/8/2002) married Geraldine Hulet (6/1/1916 – 9/10/2008) on 8/22/1940. Married 61 years, 10 months, 16 days.

> > Irwin Reiss (9/18/1917 – 4/11/2007) married Mary Leone Stephenson (3/15/1921 – 5/16/2010) on 11/8/1942 in Atascadero, California. Married 64 years, 5 months, 3 days.

Lillian Zola Reiss (11/25/1911 – 5/30/2002) married Lonnie Maurice Standley (12/16/1907 – 7/31/2007) on 5/13/1934 in Sikeston, Missouri. Married 68 years, 17 days.

Linda Lee Reiss (6/19/1935 --) married David Freeman (6/24/1931 --) on 6/17/1956 in Darien, Connecticut. Married 58 years, 2 months, 29 days and counting.

Lewis Philip Reiss (1/28/1937 --) married Sally Strangman Quicke (10/23/1936 --) on 8/9/1958 in Darien, Connecticut. Married 56 years, 1 month, 6 days and counting.

Roya Ann Reiss (11/27/1936 --) married Edward Earl Singleton (5/13/1931 --) on 3/24/1956 in Newport, Rhode Island. Married 58 years, 5 months, 22 days and counting.

Earl L. Quirin (5/9/1934 --) married Carol Lemons (4/3/1936 --) on 1/27/1954. Married 60 years, 7 months, 19 days and counting.

Arthur F. Quirin (10/14/1936 --) married Betty Landleff (7/14/1938 --) on 10/28/1961. Married 52 years, 10 months, 18 days and counting.

Viola Petry (3/11/1916 – 7/26/2008) married Ralph William Bald (9/17/1914 – 3/17/1992) on 11/30/1939 in Smithton. Married 52 years, 3 months, 17 days.

Eugenia Petry (10/3/1917 – 8/21/1993) married Franklin Dwight Teel (8/24/1918 –) on 3/14/1942. Married 51 years, 5 months, 7 days.

Charles Reiss branch – 72 adults born before 1990 with 10% making gold

Rolland Charles Reiss (7/27/1931 – 8/28/2004) married Selda Brendel (2/28/1934 --) on 10/17/1953. Married 50 years, 10 months, 11 days.

Lucille Reiss (7/21/1908 – 4/13/1982) married Henry Dietz (2/29/1904 – 1/??/1985) on 10/12/1931. Married 50 years, 6 months, 1 day.

Barbara Ann Dietz (2/23/1935 --) married Dr. Richard Paul Peters (10/12/1931 --) on 5/30/1962. Married 52 years, 3 months, 16 days.

Charles Frederick "Tinker" Reiss Jr. (7/26/1873 – 10/28/1958) married Rose Schilling (5/10/1884 – 1/18/1972) on 6/3/1903 in St. Louis. Married 55 years 4 months, 25 days.

Jessie M. Reiss (1/5/1904 – 12/14/1996) married John Delbert Schau (10/25/1890 – 11/18/1973) on 5/5/1920. Married 53 years, 6 months, 13 days.

Earl William Reiss (7/3/1901 – 6/29/1990) married Helen Hughes (8/1/1913 – 6/9/2006) on 4/12/1930. Married 60 years, 2 months, 17 days.

Eva (Evelyn) Julia Reiss (6/18/1918 – 3/21/2008) married Kenneth C. Bevirt (2/27/1915 – 9/30/2000) on 6/4/1938. Married 62 years, 3 months, 26 days.

Martin Reiss branch – 10 adults born before 1990 with 10% making gold

Nancy Louise Rice (12/27/1919 – 3/8/2005) married Robert Earl Stepp Jr. (5/28/1918 – 5/24/2005) in 1936. Married over 61 years.

Kate Reiss Wittig branch – 29 adults born before 1990 with 24% making gold

Catharine (Kate) Reiss (3/23/1847 – 4/2/1916) married Charles Max Wittig (1/16/1838 – 1/30/1918) on 4/9/1866 in a double ceremony with her brother Frank and Anna Feder. She actually died one week short of their 50th anniversary but I included them anyway.

Georgia Elizabeth Keener (8/25/1910 --) married Kenneth Stolp (3/2/1907 – 12/26/1992) on 3/29/1942 in Chico, California. Married 50 years, 8 months, 27 days.

Frida Catherine Wittig (9/28/1878 – 1961) married Ernest Fred Colville (3/1/1876 – 4/??/1964) on 8/19/1903 in Davenport, Iowa. Married over 57 years.

Jean Catherine Colville (7/22/1908 – 9/26/1997) married Caldwell Buck (12/7/1903 – 5/24/1985) on 2/20/1932 in New York City. Married 53 years, 3 months, 4 days.

Roger Colville Buck (4/13/1936 --) married Adale Elias Tannous (3/8/1940 --) on 7/13/1963. Married 51 years, 2 months, 2 days and counting.

Fred Charles Buck (8/28/1939 --) married Betty Darlene Owen (12/5/1938 --) on 6/22/1964 in Covina, California. Married 50 years 2 months, 24 days and counting.

Patricia Louise Colville (11/1/1920 --) married Gerald Waldsmith Giard (9/11/1914 – 5/19/1995) on 2/22/1941 in Yakama, Washington. Married 54 years, 2 months, 27 days.

Instead of half a dozen golden weddings, I found 31. The yellow highlights identify 7 couples who were married 60 years or more, one of which is still counting. Lillian and Lonnie Standley hold the record at 68 years. Must be something about decades of drinking Reiss Dairy milk!!!

These weddings were celebrated every month of the year except September. April, May, June, August, and October were the most popular with four weddings each.

Here is a very faint invitation to our first golden wedding celebration, that of John and Maria Reiss held on 11/3/1911 in Belleville. The stationery belongs to their unmarried daughter Barbara Reiss who lived with them at 322 South Church Street.

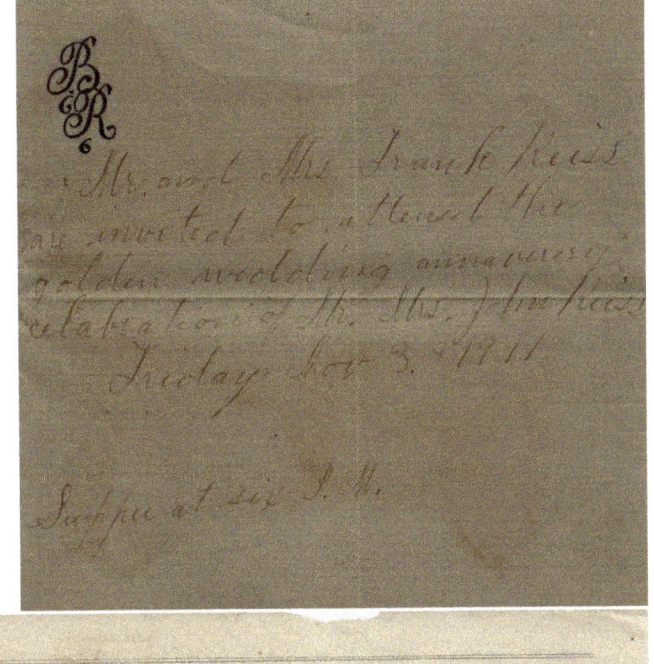

Here is a certificate of record dated 4/15/1915 confirming that Frank Reiss and Anna Sevilla Feder were married on 4/9/1866.

Will, Kayla, Ava, and Blake you four come from a long line of relatives who celebrated 50 and more years of marriage. Grand DD and I are at 43 years, my parents had 64 years, and Dad's parents had 53 years. Your parents are on track for long marriages of their own.

Love, Granddad

Grandma Katie's Gold Pocket Watch

Dear Will, Kayla, Ava, and Blake,   April 13, 2015

This is my grandmother Catherine Charlotte Luetzelschwab who became Mrs. George Reiss on April 16, 1911. That's 104 years ago this Thursday. She went by Katie but we all just called her Grandma. Notice the gold watch which was an engagement gift from her future husband. It was made by Elgin. Here are views of the inside, front, and back.

The watch serial number is 8068031 on the inside of the cover. The front cover has two love birds, some flowers with leaves, a crest where initials could have been added, and fancy edging. The back is the same two love birds plus a small village with five cottages near a small lake. It's on a long chain with a tiny heart. Both the watch and its original box are in good condition.

Elgin National Watch Company – In the spring of 1864 half a dozen ambitious Chicago businessmen decided that if Massachusetts could build a factory that built watches, Illinois could do the same. Harper's magazine summed their sentiment perfectly: "It was the genuine, audacious, self-reliant Western spirit." By August of that year this consortium, including then-Chicago mayor Benjamin W. Raymond, purchased an abandoned farm 30 miles north of Chicago and built a watch factory there. After a year of designing and building the lathes and machines to achieve seemingly impossible levels of precision, a team of watchmakers and mechanical engineers produced their first pocket watch movement, named for mayor "B.W. Raymond." The watch was exquisite and the Elgin National Watch Company was born.

By 1910, word of Elgin's obsession with precision had spread around the world. Elgin engineers built their own observatory to maintain scientifically precise times in their watches. Later, their accurate "wristlet" watches proved to be vital to the WWI war effort, helping to fuel a craze back in the states for something called "The Wrist Watch." By the opulent Jazz Age, if you weren't displaying the exuberant symmetry of an Elgin wristwatch or carrying a svelte, distinctive Elgin pocket watch, then who were you? Elgin had helped define the American pocket watch as unsurpassed in "Railroad Accuracy." By 1930, the post-Civil War dream factory imagined by a handful of American entrepreneurs had produced 32 million "time machines."

During World War II, all civilian manufacturing was halted and the company moved into the defense industry, manufacturing military watches, chronometers, fuses for artillery shells, altimeters, and other aircraft instruments and sapphire bearings used for aiming cannons. While their altruism was vital to the war effort, Elgin's patriotism ironically opened an opportunity for the Swiss to enter the market. By 1964, after a Mid-Century decade that saw the rise of the elite "Lord and Lady Elgin" series, the original Elgin factory closed. Over the course of a century, the dream factory just north of Chicago had produced half of all jeweled pocket and wristwatches manufactured in the United States. The legendary Elgin watch has become woven into the fabric of America.

Here's more on that serial number 8068031:

Production Year: 1900
Size: 18s
Jewels: 7 jewels
Grade: 208
Model: 5
Class: 63
Run Quantity: 5000
Production Date: 1898 to 1903
Total Grade Production: 294,000
Movement Configuration: Open Face
Movement Setting: Pendant Wind and Set
Movement Finish: Nickel Damaskeening
Plate: Full Plate
Barrel: Going Barrel
Adjusted: No

Pocket watch Cases – Elgin never made pocket watch cases. Until well into the 1920s, it was a common practice for a retail shop to offer a selection of watch movements and a selection of watch cases. A customer would pick out a movement and a case separately and the watchmaker or jeweler would assemble them together. This is true of most early American watch makes. Vintage American makes are remarkably standardized in their form factors, so as to fit a great variety of likewise standardized watch cases made by many case manufacturers.

Jewels – Jewels in a watch are typically synthetic garnets, rubies, or sapphires. They are not of significant value and are not there for decorative purposes. The jewels in a watch are there because they are very hard material that does not wear. They are used as bearings for the pivots of gears and wheels. The hardened steel of each pivot inside a donut-shaped synthetic jewel is extremely long-lived and mechanically reliable, so long as the pivot points are clean and lightly lubricated. Jewels in the shape of pins and posts are also used in the escapement.

Jewel counts in the vast majority of vintage watches work fairly simply. There are two jewels used as pallet stones, one roller jewel in the escapement, two for the balance wheel pivots, and two cap jewels to cover each balance pivot for a minimum of seven jewels. Other wheels in the train may also have jeweled pivots, upper and lower, so as to increase the jewel count in pairs. In high grade watches, additional faster moving wheels, such as the escape wheel, may also have cap jewels added in pairs. Twenty-three jewels are the most you will find in a vintage Elgin, railroad grade, pocket watch.

Will, Kayla, Ava, and Blake, I typed "Elgin 7 jewels" into eBay and got 139 hits. There were a dozen watches comparable to Grandma's with starting prices from $200 to $1300 to $3000. It's a good thing this Reiss family heirloom is not for sale. It's beautiful.

Love, Granddad

Gold Coins (1873 and 1890)

Dear Will and Kayla,   April 16, 2012

Here are two $20 gold coins dated 1873 and 1890, the years that your great great grandparents, George and Katie Reiss, were born. George William Reiss was born on April 22, 1873 (139 years ago this week) and Catharina "Katie" Charlotte Luetzelschwab was born on March 25, 1890. He was almost 17 years older than her. They were married on Easter Sunday, April 16, 1911 (101 years ago today) at St. Paul's Church in Floraville, Illinois. I have their marriage certificate in a beautiful frame in our upstairs hallway.

I think George's parents were afraid their oldest surviving son, who was quite handsome, was never going to get married. So in 1910 when George was 37 years old, they hired attractive, young Katie Luetzelschwab to be their domestic worker to help with laundry, cooking, and light duty chores around the home farm south of Belleville, Illinois. Well, George was no dummy and he soon took proper notice of their live-in worker. He got over any bashfulness that might have existed and I'm sure Katie did her best to impress him with her cooking, darning socks, making quilts, and all that domestic stuff. It all worked and they were married about a year later. I'm sure many of their "dates" were long slow walks in the woods. Keep that domestic worker trick in mind as the ultimate matchmaker tool if your children are slow about spreading their wings. George gave this 1890 coin to his bride, Katie, as a wedding gift. I don't know where or when

he got the 1873 coin but I do know they gave it to their third son (my dad), Irwin Henry Reiss, and his bride, Mary Leone Stephenson, as a wedding gift on November 8, 1942. It was a real big hit with the wedding crowd in Atascadero, California. Irv's parents could not make the trip from Illinois for the wedding since the United States was in the middle of World War II and gasoline, batteries, car tires, and many other items were rationed or simply not available.

George and Katie were married for 53 years and 4 months. I remember going to their golden wedding anniversary celebration in 1961 at the Smithton Sportsmens Club on the Reiss Family

Farm. We six grandchildren always called them Grandma and Pop. They were outstanding grandparents and taught us how to play pinochle cards, find mushrooms in the woods, pick dewberries along the country lanes, fish in the farm pond, take care of baby kittens which were all over their farmstead, play in the hay mow in the old barn, go to the "fish place" in Smithton for weekend suppers, decorate a cedar tree cut from their pasture as our Christmas tree, sleep upstairs under feather blankets, take baths in a wash tub of cistern water warmed by the sun, feed the chickens and gather eggs, pick apricots in the orchard, eat Grandma's fruit pies where she used custard instead of corn starch for filling, cook with a kitchen stove that burned corn cobs or kindling, play with clay marbles and Lincoln logs on the living room carpet, butcher hogs, dig a cistern, look for arrowheads on their Indian mound, dismantle a 1932 Model A pickup truck, feed Pop's two horses that he farmed with until 1948, and do lots of other really cool things.

Will and Kayla, here is their picture from 1959. Pop died in August 1964 at age 91 when our family was on vacation in Europe. Dad flew back ahead of Mom and us three kids to go to his funeral. We had left our car in New York with Mom's brother so the rest of us drove back to our home in Sullivan, Indiana. Grandma died in October 1986 at age 96 two months before Caterpillar moved us to South Korea. I remember going to her funeral which was really sad for me because I don't do funerals very well and because I had so many fond memories of my grandparents. They are buried side by side in Franklin Cemetery in Smithton, Illinois. Their two gold coins are also side by side now in a plastic case in a safe in our home. They should stay in our family forever.

Love, Granddad

Old Washbowl (1881)

Dear Will and Kayla,   May 28, 2012

There is an old pitcher and bowl set in our back bedroom which we call our Heritage Room. These were typically used in bedrooms and hotel rooms in the 1800s and earlier when the nearest bathroom was outdoors or down the hall from your hotel room. These pitcher and bowl sets allowed folks to wash their face and hands or maybe take a light sponge bath before going to bed. This photo is just the bowl part of that set – kinda pretty, don't you think?

If you turn the pitcher over, there is a note written by your great great aunt Gerry Reiss that reads: "The pitcher is not of the set, but purchased in 1965, same style, not rose pattern." If you turn this bowl over, there is another note by Gerry that reads: "This washing bowl was once a wedding gift to Catherine Luetzelschwab when she married Geo. W. Reiss on 4/16/1911. It had been a wedding gift to Catherine Hoelscher when she married Jacob Luetzelschwab on 5/26/1881." (131 years ago last Saturday). Now what do you think of this bowl? Pretty awesome isn't it – a double wedding gift and significant family piece. See what a huge difference that note made. Great idea on Gerry's part. This edition of Granddad's Mondays is an expansion on Gerry's original note to help make sure the importance of this bowl is preserved.

Catherine and George Reiss were your great great grandparents and the third owners of the Reiss family farm in St. Clair County, Illinois. Catherine and Jacob Luetzelschwab were your great great great grandparents. His heritage is Swiss and hers is German. Notes about them from our family tree appear below but first I want to tell you how the Luetzelschwab name has been misspelled over the years in federal census records. Here are eleven different incorrect spellings of Luetzelschwab by professional census takers. And you thought "Reiss" was difficult for folks to spell and pronounce – just be thankful your last name isn't even more unique.

1870 Litzilshaw

1880 Litxelschaup

1900 Litzelschwaab, Litzetschwaab

1910 Lueteelschwab

1920 Suetzelschuab, Luetzelschwa

1930 Ludzetschcoab, Lustzetichwab, Lutzelichwab, Lutzelschwah

Will and Kayla, here are 50 years of details about your great great great grandparents. The yellow highlight is your great great grandmother Katie. The grey highlight is her brother John who built the 1940 house on the Reiss Family Farm and was paid $.50 per hour. . . . . John Jacob Luetzelschwab, Sr. (7/14/1858 – 10/28/1940) was born in Magden, Switzerland and married Charlotta Hoelscher (11/15/1862 – 4/23/1925) on 5/26/1881 in Nameoki, Illinois. She was born in Madison County, Illinois. About 1883 they moved with baby daughter Mary to a farm about 3.5 miles south of Millstadt, Illinois in Section 33, Township 1, Range 9 West. His father John joined them in 1892 and lived with them until his death in 1916. Her grave is in Evergreen Cemetery in Millstadt. The **1900 Census** shows Jacob Litzetschwaab age 41 working as a farmer, Charlotte age 37, married 19 years with 9 of 9 children still living, John C. age 17 working as a farmer, Minnie age 14, Herman age 12, Katy age 12, Charlotte age 7, Lena age 5, Jacob age 4, Frank age 2, and his widowed father John B age 75. The **1910 Census** shows Jacob age 51 working as a farmer, Charlotte H. age 47 born in Illinois married 28 years with 11 of 11 children still living, John C. age 26 working as a carpenter, Herman F. age 22 working as a carpenter, Charlotte H. age 17, Lena J age 15, Jacob age 14 working on the home farm, Frank age 12, Carolina G age 7, Edna L. age 4, and his widowed father John B. age 85. Daughter Catherine Charlotte Lueteelschwab age 20 was enumerated with the George Reiss household working there as a servant. The **1920 Census** shows Jacob Suetzelschuab age 61 working as a farmer, Charlotte age 57, Herman age 32 working as a farmer, Jacob Jr. age 24 working as a carpenter, Frank age 22 working as a farmer, Caroline age 19, and Edna age 14 all living on a farm on Columbia Road. The **1930 Census** shows widowed Jacob Ludzetschcoab age 71 working as a farmer, Herman age 41 working as a farmer, and Frank age 29 working as a farmer living on their home farm. Living next door is daughter Lena Speichinger and her family

Well, we started talking about a washbowl and now we're talking about preserving family history with paper notes (and Granddad's Mondays)!!! Have a great week.

Love, Granddad

Cedar Row Farm

Dear Will, Kayla, Ava, and Blake,   October 13, 2014

Your great great grandfather George "Pop" Reiss planted two rows of cedar trees about 1900 on the Reiss family farm. This Illinois aerial photo was taken late in the morning because the shadows angle off to the north northwest which makes the trees appear much taller. Kinda neat photo effect, don't you think?

The north row was probably intended as a windbreak to knock down storms coming from the northwest. The south row was planted right along the west farm lane probably as an accent effect. My guess is that trees for both rows were volunteer saplings which Pop simply transplanted from croplands where they would be destroyed by farming. These trees were planted well before the second homestead was built on the south side of the farm lane in 1940. Pop was really proud of his cedar trees and eventually named his farm "Cedar Row Farm" which was part of his mailing address with the Post Office. I remember writing letters to my grandparents in the 1950s and my dad always made sure I included "Cedar Row Farm" as a separate line of the envelope address.

The first picture below is the north cedar row in 1955. It looks like Pop kept the lower branches trimmed. The second picture is the south cedar row in 2015 so you can kinda see how much these trees have grown in 60 years. The field betweent the cedar rows was cow pasture at various times which required barbed wire strands be nailed to the cedars. Those wires eventually grew into the trees such that there is no commercial value now for lumber, shingles, or pulp.

Will, Kayla, Ava, and Blake, I'm proud to say your great great grandfather was a "tree guy." Not only did he plant these two rows of cedar trees but Pop also planted about an acre of pine trees in 1940 which is mentioned in my story on 10/15/2012. Seeds from one of these south row cedars grew up to become the Christmas tree in my story on 12/17/2012. It will be a little difficult to collect a cedar "leaf" for your seventh grade science project, but we'll do our best since there is a long family connection.

Love, Granddad

George Reiss Buys the Crook's Farm

Dear Will, Kayla, Ava, and Blake,   December 29, 2014

It was 100 years ago tomorrow that your great great grandfather George "Pop" Reiss bought this 30-acre farm in the southeast quarter of the southeast quarter of Section 25, Township 2 South and Range 9 West. The purchase was made on December 30, 1914 by George W Reiss (no mention of his wife Catherine) for $1,000 from Albert Crook and his wife Mary, and Joseph Crook, a single man. It included a "road or right of way" which the deed indicated Albert Crook et al acquired in a partition suit against Sarah Weber et al citing St Clair County Chancery Book K: 554.2. A. Weber owned the 10 acres in St Clair circa 1901.

The 1920 census shows Albert Crook and Joseph Crook as neighbors in a village called New Design in Monroe County, Illinois. Albert was age 43 and Joseph was age 31. Their wives are both named Mary. Their father was Alexander Crook who emigrated from England. He appears as A. Crook in the southern tip of this 1880 atlas of St. Clair Co.

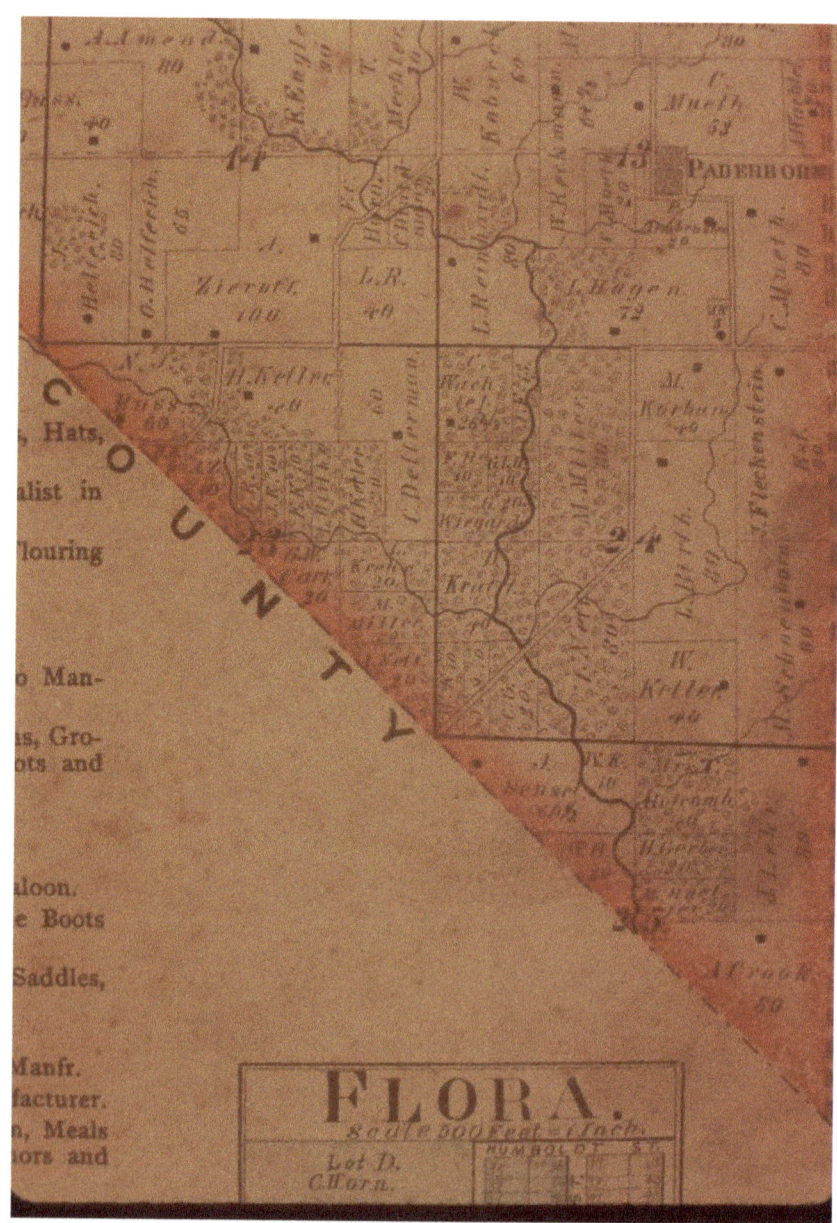

Thomas Winstanley was the first purchaser of the southeast quarter of Section 25 on 4/8/1818 which was eight months before Illinois became a state on 12/3/1818. That means that Thomas Houghan was not involved like he was later on three 40-acre sales to Adam Reiss and other of our relatives in the 1830s and 1840s.

You can see in the maps which follow that 20 of these 30 acres are in Section 25 of Fountain Township in Monroe County and the remaining 10 acres are in Section 25 of Millstadt Township in St. Clair County. The bordering section numbers are the same when two counties touch along a 45-degree northwest – southeast line.

Our family always referred to these 30 acres as the "Crook's Farm." Likewise we also referred to the 180 acres that Pop and Katie bought in 1917 from the Schaefer family as the "Schaefer Farm." It's just handy. Most of the farms my parents bought later in Sullivan County, Indiana were named after the previous owners.

Dad and his two brothers Bill and Frank inherited these 30 acres when their father died on 8/19/1964. Then on 3/10/1983 Bill sold his third to his brothers and Irwin's wife Mary. The Monroe County plat book only has enough space to show "Franklin Reiss" and the St. Clair County plat book has even less space and shows just "FR." Had there been enough space, both plat books would have shown "Franklin Reiss et al."

Bill also sold his one-third of 20 acres in Section 8 of St. Clair County to his brothers on that March 10, 1983 date. Most documents will show both the 30 acres and the 20 acres together because it was one overall transaction on that date. Today those 50 acres are called "The Reiss Brothers Farm." Here are parts of two descriptions:

Lawyers Title Insurance Policy #85-81-160628 for $18,000 transferring two tracts from William Reiss to Franklin Reiss and to Irwin and Mary Reiss as joint tenants. Tract 2 as 10 acres is the south part of the east half of the southeast quarter of Section 25 in Township 2 South, Range 9 west plus the survey commencing at the southwest corner of the southeast quarter of the southeast quarter of said Section 25, thence north 15 chains and 15 links, thence west 19 chains and 80 links to the place of beginning situated partly in Monroe and partly in St. Clair County. Also a right of way running along the east side of land given and set off to Alexander Crook

Here's Frank's son George in 1955 hunting for elephants in a wheat field on the Crook's Farm. The crop looks good but not all the 30 acres was tillable. Today it's all in CRP and feeding wildlife. It is included when the main part of the Reiss Family Farm is leased for hunting.

Here are plats showing 20 acres of Monroe County contiguous with 10 acres of St. Clair County.

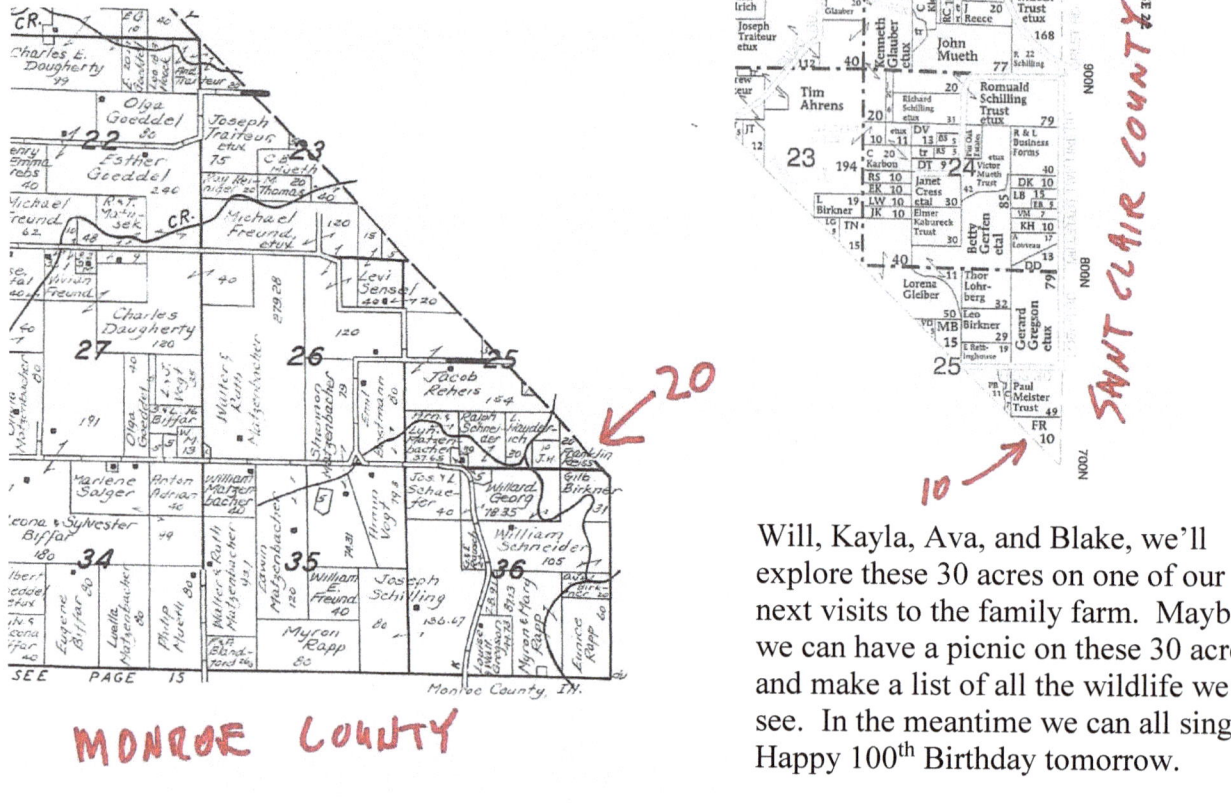

MONROE COUNTY

SAINT CLAIR COUNTY

Will, Kayla, Ava, and Blake, we'll explore these 30 acres on one of our next visits to the family farm. Maybe we can have a picnic on these 30 acres and make a list of all the wildlife we see. In the meantime we can all sing Happy 100th Birthday tomorrow.

Love, Granddad

World War I – Jacob Luetzelschwab Jr.

Dear Will, Kayla, Ava, and Blake,   April 6, 2015

This man was my Grandma Katie Reiss' second youngest brother which makes him my great uncle. He's also the only man I'm aware of in our extended family who fought in World War I. They called it the Great War back then because World War II didn't happen until 20 years later such that this one could be called War I. This war started on 7/28/1914 when Austria-Hungary declared war on Serbia and then it quickly escalated with Great Britain, France, the Russian Empire on one side and Austria-Hungary, Germany, the Ottoman Empire, and Bulgaria on the other. The United States joined with their allies when Congress declared war on Germany on **April 6, 1917 which was 98 years ago today.** Congress declared war on Austria-Hungary on December 7, 1917. Italy and Japan joined with the Allies on later dates.

On 5/18/1917, Congress adopted the Selective Service Act for ages 21 to 31 and in August 1918, raised the ages to 18 to 45. Before the war ended, 24 million men had registered; 2 million were drafted. The government raised $21 billion for the war by selling Liberty Bonds. President Wilson appointed John J. Pershing Commander-in-Chief of American Expeditionary Forces, with the first landing in France June 1917. By November 11, 1918 when the war ended, there were 2.1 million American soldiers in France.

Here is Jacob's draft registration from 6/5/1917 when he was age 21. He comments in a letter which follows about the possibilities of his brothers also being drafted.

Jacob was drafted into the **132nd Illinois Infantry Regiment**. Here's his journal of personal events – "Left for army from home to Camp Taylor, Louisville, Kentucky Sept. 22, 1917. Left Camp Taylor April 7, 1918. Arrived at Camp Logan, Houston, Texas April 12 and left May 7. Going over to France left from Houston, Texas to Oklahoma to Kansas to Missouri to Illinois to Indiana to Ohio to Pennsylvania to Buffalo, New York to New York City. Arrived at Camp Upton, Long Island, New York May 12 and left May 15 for Hoboken, New Jersey. Arrived on boat and sailed May 16. Arrived Brest, France May 24, unloaded May 26, and left May 30. Arrived in Osmont May 31 and left June 1. Arrived in Metignay June 4 and left June 10. Arrived Monsho June 11. Went to Bayehoille June 12 and left June 20. Arrived in Mollenwoods June 20."

"First night in trenches. Went in trenches near Mollenwoods June 30, over the top July 4 Kammel Wood Drive. Back to Mollenwoods July 12. Went to trenches Albert Front July 21 and returned July 23. Went in trenches Ethel on Albert Front over the top July 31. Returned from trenches to Mollenwoods August 5. Went to Bound Woods August 6. Went in trenches right of Albert Front August 7 and the British went over the top. Returned to Guarenwoods August 12. Went to Amiens Front August 15. Returned to Longview August 19. Started on train August 24, arrived in Ressons August 25 and left Sept. 6. Arrived at Verdun Sept. 7 and left Sept. 7. Arrived in Deloline Sept. 8. Arrived in trenches Sept 9 called Dead Man's Hill. Over the top Sept 26. Went through Forges Woods, over the top Argonne Woods October 12. Returned to Bethercort Oct. 14. Left the trenches Oct. 18. Arrived in Genecourt Oct. 20. Arrived in woods near Metz Oct. 22, went to outpost November 1. Back to Woule Nov. 6. Went to camp on hill Nov. 9. Went to Loransville Nov. 10. Went to Dancourt, ceased firing Nov. 11 which was 11th day, 11th month and the 11th hour."

"Went to St. Delere Nov. 11. Arrived in Dancourt Nov. 17 and left Nov. 23. Arrived in Woll Nov. 23 and left December 9 for Germany. Arrived in Conflans Dec. 10 and left Dec. 11. Arrived in Lominger Dec. 11, arrived in east Luxemburg Dec. 12. Left East Luxemburg Dec. 13, arrived in Remich, Luxemburg Dec. 14. Left Remich Dec. 15 for Weiten, Germany. Went through Fredenburg and five kilometers to Saarbruk. Arrived in Weiten, Germany Dec. 15. Left Germany Dec. 18. Arrived in Remich, Luxemburg Dec. 18 and left Dec. 20. Arrived in Bouglinster, Luxemburg Dec. 21. Here's where we are now for a couple weeks or a month's stay in Bouglinster, Luxemburg till the 24th of April 1919. That was four months and 3 days. Left for home the 25th of April and reached Brest, France the 29th of April. Was on the train 85 hours. We are in a big camp in tents till the ships come in to take us home. Left Brest the 8th of May 1919. At four o'clock we sailed from Brest and landed in U.S. May 17 and went to Camp Miles, Long Island. Left Camp Miles May 25 for Chicago, Ill. Went to Hoboken, New Jersey, to New York, to Philadelphia, to West Virginia, to Maryland, to Pittsburgh, to Pennsylvania, to Ohio, to Indianapolis, Indiana, to Chicago, Illinois where we were in the Parade the 27th of May 1919. Then to Camp Grant Rockford, Ill. There's where we got discharged May 30. Left for home from Rockford Camp Grant to Springfield, Ill, to St. Louis, Mo. and home to Millstadt, Ill. on June 2, 1919."

Below is the official insignia of the 132nd Infantry Regiment. The green oak tree at the top is for the Forges Wood battle and the stars represent the five major operations in which the Regiment

326

took part in France which are in the <mark>yellow highlights above</mark>. The last three are back   to back to back. The two lower triangles represent other wars.

- Amiens, 17 July - 5 August 1918
- Somme Offensive, 8–20 August 1918
- Verdun-Frommerville, 8–25 September 1918
- Meuse-Argonne Offensive, 26 September - 21 October 1918
- Troyon, 25 October 2011 - 11 November 1918

Here is a French map showing the five battles where Jacob was in combat. They are north and northeast of Paris so the battles were quite concentrated for the 132nd. Below is Jacob's letter to his sister and other relatives on 8/13/1918.

On Active Service with the
American Expeditionary Force

Mrs. Jacob Weihl   August 13, 1918
R. R. No. 3
Waterloo, Illinois

Dear Sister Mary, Brother Jacob, and children,
Well, I received your letter some time ago but didn't get to answer right away, didn't have no time, was in the trenches most of the time. So I want to write you's a few lines to let you's no that I am well yet and hope the same of you's all.

I received Elsie's letter shortly and was very glad to hear from you's, I always like to hear from you's how everything is getting along, maybe you's got more time to write than I have, you's mite think I have lot of time to write but we are in fighting some now, we go in the trenches for about 4 or 6 days, then we go out for one day to clean up a little bit and then right back in the trenches, and there I don't feel like writing a letter when them big shells come flying over and drop pretty close to you, they shake the ground, some days it's quiet in the trenches but then days there is a hole lot of shelling coming over and gas shells too.

Well they are pretty strong at him now, got him on a run, he don't get no chance no more, they don't let him get ready no more. That's the quickest way to get the war to a end, keep a going right at him, in three day's fighting the Kaiser lost thirteen thousand men, three hundred officers, and a couple hundred guns, big guns that was them days when we was up in the trenches too, but we didn't go over the top that time. I guess we are going over this time we go in the trenches, well I always was lucky and I hope I will be lucky this time too, and get through again, hope God will stay with me all the time so that I can go back home again to you's all, and the war will be over soon. I think it will be over by next spring, lot of them say we will be going back by Christmas. I hope it's true.

Well, what kind of news do you's read in the papers over there?, that it's going to end pretty soon. Say, sister, the next time you send me a letter, cut some news out of the papers and send them to me, all kinds news, war or any kinds a good news. I like to hear what the paper says about it over there. I guess there ain't very many young fellows around out there no more. They all have to go to the training camps and I guess lot of farmers are in a bad business getting help this summer. It sure makes it bad but they could help it, they have to go.

Brother Frankie, he can stay home a year yet till next registration fifth June then he has to go too but he don't have to come over here. I don't think that Herman has to go, he might have to go but he will get out of it, well I hope they both don't have to go and stay home helping Papa and Mamma along so they don't have to be alone. I have a letter wrote for home but I didn't send it yet with you's.

Well, how is everything over there. I guess you are done threshing by now. How many hundred bushels did you's get, over here they just started to harvest on 4th Aug. They got a full strong wheat but no help. Most old men and women do the work and then they got one kinder for about five or six farmers and then it's a five foot cutter but it's the same kind of binder we got at home. They raise everything over here except corn. That's one thing they don't raise over here but there's thousands and thousands acres of land all shot up from them big heavy shells, they make holes in the ground from 6 to 8 feet deep and about every 8 or 10 feet apart is a hole. Then you can think how that land looks and besides the trenches dug yet. Well, I just got two letters now, one from Smithton and one from St. Louis. I think they are from Sister Katie (*my grandma*) and Minnie. I am all well, glad when I get letters from any place.

Excuse my paper, it looks so dirty. I always have it in my packet then I can keep it clean and writing with a lead pencil. Well I want to open the letters to see what news they now before I finish this letter. I see that they are all well yet. I am glad too, they wrote it's awful dry for the crops, we got nice weather now too but for a couple days ago it rained for two weeks and we was out in the trenches. You can think how it was there in the mud till over your shoes, if you wanted to sleep, lay down on the wet ground. Well I guess that's all I know of for this time, I have to hurry up and get my letter done to turn it in before night. So I hope this letter will reach you's all well as it leaves here and hope to see you's all soon. Well I write the address on this side in case you lost my address. So good luck to you's from your loving brother.

Pvt. Jacob Luetzelschwab Jr.
132 Inf. Co. M
Via New York

Our Trip to Germany by Jacob Luetzelschwab

We spent six months in the trenches
And done our share real kind
And every one was satisfied
When the armistice was signed.

Then we started working
Tho we enjoyed it no doubt,
Shooting off shells and grenades
Which were lying abut.

We picked up all the tin cans
As the colonel had wished,
And then went off to Woll
When everything was finished.

We were then with our Battalion
Captain Yagle in the lead,
And a lonely hike indeed,
We started out for Conflans.

That was on the 9th of December
If I remember right,
After hiking 30 kilos
We reached late that night.

We rested over Sunday
Everything went fine,
And early Monday morning
Again we fell in line.

We hiked to mance before dinner
And stayed over night,
Then we started out for Lominger
The march was sure a fright.

The next morning it was raining
But the boys were feeling gay,
And after climbing many hills
We arrived into Earl that day.

There was boo-hoo beer and wine
And the boys were feeling great,
The town sure was a wonder
For some of them got in quite late.

Next day we hiked to Abinger
Where we lined up for our pay,
And after inspection
We were free for half a day.

But the boys were not satisfied
Off to Luxemburg City they went,
And when the M.P. found them there
Back to Abinger they were sent.

Then we started for another town
Just a few kilos was our wish,
But we hiked sixteen kilos
To reach the town of Remich.

Early Sunday morning we crossed
The Remich Bridge the Moselle River,
And on our hike that afternoon
We climbed one awful ridge.

We reached the town of Weiten
And we rested for a day,
Which gave us a lot of time
To spend some of our money.

It seems we had gone far enough
So we started hiking back,
We reached the town of Remich
And again unrolled our packs.

Some Woodbine smokes (cigs) were issued
The kind the boys dislike,
Then to the town of Flaxwieler
We made another hike.

Bouglinster was our next stop
Just twelve kilos away,
Where we ate our cans dinner
And spent New Year's day.

This is a grand old army
And all the boys will say,
They say the next move that we make
Will be back to the good old U.S.A.

Jacob made it home safely. Here's the entire family with parents and eleven children. It looks like a special gathering to welcome Jacob home since he is still in uniform in the lower right.

Jacob Luetzelschwab family, 1919
Mary, Minnie, Catherine, Lottie, Lena, Caroline, Edna

John, Herman, Jacob and Charlotte, Jacob Jr., and Frank

Jacob married Cora Rosine Muskopf on 2/12/1925 in Millstadt. He went by Jakie where the "a" is long. They had one daughter, Janet Marie on 11/24/1930. Jakie and Cora lived to welcome four grandchildren into the world.

Below is Jakie in 1954 adding an "I" beam support and piers in the cellar of Grandma Katie's 1889 house at the home farm. He's also working on a chimney upgrade. Jakie and Cora are buried in Evergreen Cemetery in Millstadt.

Will, Kayla, Ava, and Blake, isn't this an impressive story about Uncle Jakie? I'm glad he made it home safely with no wounds. He saw a lot of the world thanks to his service in the U. S. Army but there were probably many sights he would just as soon forget. Even after nearly two year's service and at age 46, Jakie still had to register for the draft again as World War II approached. His signature did not change much in those 24 intervening years. His merit award, his dog tags, and both sides of his Verdun Medal appear below.

Love, Granddad

REGISTRATION CARD—(Men born on or after April 28, 1877 and on or before February 16, 1897)

SERIAL NUMBER	1. NAME (Print)			ORDER NUMBER
U 1233	JACOB (First)	— (Middle)	LUETZELSCHWAB (Last)	

2. PLACE OF RESIDENCE (Print)

MILLSTADT TWP.   ST. CLAIR   ILL.
(Number and street)   (Town, township, village, or city)   (County)   (State)

[THE PLACE OF RESIDENCE GIVEN ON THE LINE ABOVE WILL DETERMINE LOCAL BOARD JURISDICTION; LINE 2 OF REGISTRATION CERTIFICATE WILL BE IDENTICAL]

3. MAILING ADDRESS
R.F.D. #1   Millstadt   Illinois
[Mailing address if other than place indicated on line 2. If same insert word same]

4. TELEPHONE	5. AGE IN YEARS 46	6. PLACE OF BIRTH St. Clair (Town or county)
14-F-1 (Exchange) (Number)	DATE OF BIRTH 11 - 9 - 1895 (Mo.) (Day) (Yr.)	Illinois (State or country)

7. NAME AND ADDRESS OF PERSON WHO WILL ALWAYS KNOW YOUR ADDRESS
Mrs. Cora Luetzelschwab, R.F.D. #1, Millstadt, Ill

8. EMPLOYER'S NAME AND ADDRESS
Self-employed

9. PLACE OF EMPLOYMENT OR BUSINESS
Millstadt Twp.   St. Clair   Ill.
(Number and street or R.F.D. number)   (Town)   (County)   (State)

I AFFIRM THAT I HAVE VERIFIED ABOVE ANSWERS AND THAT THEY ARE TRUE.

Jacob Luetzelschwab
(Registrant's signature)

D. S. S. Form 1
(Revised 4-1-42)   (over)   16—21630-2

On the next page is a certificate acknowledging Jacob's **gallantry and splendid performance** at Bois de Fays, France on October 8, 1918. It was signed by Major General George Bell who commanded the 33rd Infantry Division and the United States VI Corps during World War I. At the start of the war Bell was promoted to Major General and assigned to command the Illinois National Guard's 33rd Division. He commanded throughout the war, with the 33rd attaining distinction as the only American division to fight while organized with both French and British forces as well as fighting under its own flag.

The
THIRTY-THIRD DIVISION
AMERICAN EXPEDITIONARY FORCES

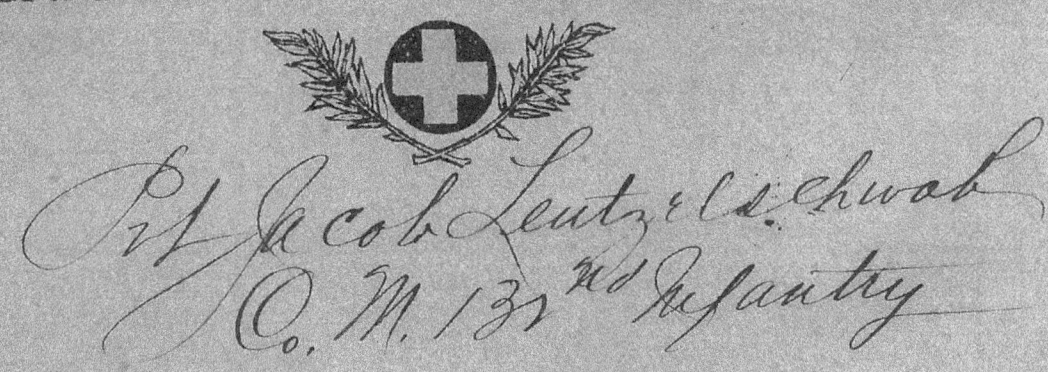

Pvt Jacob Leutzel Schwab
Co. M. 132nd Infantry

The reports of your Regimental Commander and of the Commanding General of the 66th Brigade testify to your gallantry and splendid performance of duty at *Bois de Fays* on *Oct 9th 1918*

Your conduct on that occasion has afforded me genuine gratification, and I have accordingly directed that your name and action be inscribed on the ROLL OF HONOR of the "Prairie Division."

Geo. Bell Jr.
Major General
Commanding 33rd Division

The Verdun Medal

On 20th November 1916, right in the middle of the war and in the heat of the battle, the Conseil Municipal de Verdun (Verdun Municipal Council) which was, at the time, located on the Rue de Bellechasse in Paris, now the headquarters of the Department of Veterans Affairs, decided to introduce the Verdun Medal, awarded to *'great leaders, officers, soldiers, everyone, hero or unknown soldier, living or deceased…'*. The City of Verdun, *'inviolated and now standing on its ruins, dedicated the medal as a token of its recognition'*.

A few weeks previously, Head of State Raymond Poincaré, had visited the underground citadel to award the City of Verdun the Légion d'Honneur and the Croix de Guerre, along with various decorations from foreign powers. In a now historic speech, he acknowledged Germany's defeat at Verdun a few months ahead of time with the words, 'These are the walls against which the supreme hopes of Imperial Germany were shattered. This is where they sought to achieve a resounding a dramatic victory. This is where, with a quiet firmness, France told them 'you shall not pass'. The expression *"Verdun, on ne passe pas"* (Verdun, they shall not pass) became the motto inscribed on the Verdun Medal.

On 26th April 1922, the Conseil Municipal decided that the medal would be awarded to 'soldiers of the French and allied armies who served between 31st July 1914 and 11th November 1918 in the Army of Verdun, the sector spanning the area between Argonne and the St. Mihiel hernia, in the area that came under gunfire (excluding air bombings)'. As part of the same movement, the 'Livre d'or des Soldats de Verdun' (Gold Book of the Soldiers of Verdun) was created and a Livre d'Or commission set up to review the cases put forward by servicemen and their families who wished to apply for it. Even today, almost a hundred years after the battle, descendants of former servicemen request copies of pages of the Livre d'Or featuring the names of family members who fought in the war.

Reiss Farm Income and Expenses in 1919

Dear Will, Kayla, Ava, and Blake,   January 19, 2015

The year of 1919 is one of only two years where we have handwritten income and expense statements for the Reiss farm. The other year is probably 1918 or 1920 since the handwriting and format are the same as this dated summary for 1919.

Let's look at the big picture before we zoom in on the family farm. The **post–World War I recession** was an economic recession that hit much of the world in the aftermath of World War I. In many nations, especially in North America, this growth continued during the war as nations mobilized their economies to fight the war in Europe. After the war ended, the global economy began to decline.

In North America the recession immediately following World War I was extremely brief, lasting for only 7 months from August 1918 to March 1919. A second, much more severe recession, sometimes labeled a depression, began in January 1920. Several indexes of economic activity suggest the recession was moderately severe.

The Reiss farm was supporting two families in 1919. **Generation Two** was Frank who was born on the family farm on 9/27/1841 and his wife Anna Sybilla who was born a day earlier but three years later on 9/26/1844. They were married on 4/9/1866. In 1919 they were ages 78 and 75, married 63 years, debt free, and enjoying the senior life with 7 of 11 children surviving and 13 of 14 grandchildren surviving.

Generation Three was their son George who was born on the family farm on 4/22/1873 and his wife Katie who was born 3/25/1890. They were married on 4/16/1911 and had three young sons born in 1912, 1915, and 1917. In 1919 they were ages 46 and 29, married 8 years, and heavily in debt from buying the Texas farm in 1907, the Crook farm in 1914, and the Schaefer farm in 1917. George and Katie had to watch every penny which would only get worse when they bought the home farm in 1921.

We can analyze the income numbers above and see that 52% of their income came from raising hogs, 29% from selling eggs, 12% from growing wheat, 8% from selling milk and cream, and 3% from butchering chickens. I had not known until seeing this summary that my grandparents were even in the dairy business which required milking cows twice a day and handling 4.5 tons of liquid that year. Those guys on Shark Tank would have said to get out of the dairy and chicken butchering business because the time required versus the income was out of balance.

Here are their expenses for 1919. The first seven lines with the bracket are animal feed which totals $2,364.09 or 87% of all expenses. Shipstuff is the byproduct of milling wheat into flour. It is fed to hogs where four pounds of shipstuff will generate one pound of weight gain. Screenings are largely small and broken kernels of corn, bits of cob, and weed seeds. Linseed meal is the solids from processing flaxseed into linseed oil. It is fed to cattle to improve their coats. That last item of molasses is a sweetener to make all this other stuff more appealing to animals. Kinda like Honey Nut Cheerios versus regular Cheerios!

Will, Kayla, Ava, and Blake, in summary for the year 1919, the two Reiss families generated $2,108.21 in profit on $4,831.12 in sales or an impressive 43.6%. That does not reflect their own pay or all the very healthy veggies, fruit, eggs, chickens, milk, and maybe a hog they grew and raised for their own needs. No wonder they all lived so long.

Love, Granddad

Expences in 1919

466 sacks Shipstuff	$1350.75	
16430 lbs Screenings	410.75	
6300 lbs Linseed Meal	233.25	
144 bu Barley	190.57	
2000 lbs Meat Scraps & Tank	107.11	
4 loads Clover Hay	35.00	
4 Bbls. Molasses	36.46	
Labor	54.25	
Taxes	85.36	
Interest	99.90	
Thrashing	51.80	
Insurance	18.41	
Gasoline Oil Grease	29.55	
License	4.75	
boarding	15.00	
	2722.91	

1920 – 1929

1920 Population of St. Clair County is 136,520.

1920 States total 48, national population is 106.46 million.

1920 President is Woodrow Wilson. Warren Harding is inaugurated in 1921, Calvin Coolidge in 1923, and Herbert Hoover in 1929.

1920 The 19th Amendment was ratified giving women the right to vote.

1920 The American Professional Football League is formed with eleven teams. It changed its name to the National Football League in 1922.

1922 *Readers Digest* magazine was founded.

1922 The Lincoln Memorial was dedicated in Washington, DC.

1923 *Time* magazine was founded.

1924 The first Winter Olympic Games were held in Chamonix, France with 16 nations participating.

1925 The Scopes Monkey Trial found John T. Scopes guilty of teaching evolution which violated Tennessee law.

1926 The NBC Radio Network is formed by Westinghouse, General Electric, and RCA, opening with twenty-four stations.

1927 Charles Lindbergh flied non-stop across the Atlantic Ocean in 33.5 hours.

1927 Sculptor Gutzon Borglum begins work on Mount Rushmore. It would be completed 14 years later.

1927 First television developed by inventor Philo T. Farnsworth.

1929 Stock market crashed and started the worst depression in US history.

Primitive Walnut Furniture (1915)

Dear Will and Kayla,   September 3, 2012

Here are two more family furniture pieces at our lake house in Sullivan, Indiana. Both are made of walnut wood and both are called "primitive" because they were handmade instead of factory-made. Both pieces came from the Reiss Family Farm south of Belleville, Illinois and were used by your great great grandparents, George and Katie Reiss.

My guess is that both were made by Katie's oldest brother, John Luetzelschwab, who lived less than ten miles away and who was both a carpenter and a building contractor. He definitely had the skills, supplies, and equipment to make furniture like this from scratch. John built a new home for George and Katie in 1940 and charged them for materials and his labor at $0.50 per hour. That new house is just south of the 1889 home where these two furniture pieces probably first appeared.

John C. and Katie Luetzelschwab, about 1940

This first piece is called a "dry" sink because there was no attached water faucet or drain like modern sinks. The grey lining that you see is zinc plated sheet metal which does not rust. A "dry" sink could be used for slightly "wet" jobs like cleaning and cutting fruit and vegetables, mixing cake batter or cookie dough, cutting up chickens, stuffing sausage, and maybe even changing baby diapers.

There are 79 dry sinks listed on eBay at the moment but only 3 are made from walnut wood. Prices range from $300 to $2,250. I think ours is cool because it's been in the Reiss family for at least 75 years and because it was probably made by one of our Luetzelschwab relatives.

Will and Kayla, the other furniture piece is a farm desk below. All the drawers are dovetailed. There are vertical dividers behind the upper doors for storing files and farm records. This desk is quite heavy and it takes two men and a boy to move it any distance. There is nothing like it on eBay. It's a good place to do your school homework during family gatherings at the lake house.

Love, Granddad

Farming with Horses

Dear Will, Kayla, Ava, and Blake,   July 14, 2014

I think you know by now that your great great grandfather, George Reiss, farmed the home farm in St. Clair County with horses. Pop never owned a tractor. He used only horses until 1948 when he retired at age 75. His horses also retired then but they were probably only 20 years old. I remember feeding them handfuls of grass through the fence boards. They liked that.

I am totally totally totally blown away by how labor intensive it is to farm with horses. We know from Grandma Katie's two diaries which covered 1944 through 1953 how hard her husband worked to first plow his fields, then smooth the ground with a disk or harrow, then plant his crop, then cultivate for weeds, and finally harvest with horse-drawn equipment or a wagon he loaded with hand-picked corn.

Grand DD and I wanted Will to see what's involved in plowing with horses, so we traveled 20 miles north of Springfield in the spring of 2013 to see lots of demonstrations in a 40-acre field. There were about 30 teams of horses, mules, and ponies. All pulled one-bottom plows which would make furrows about two feet of width and five inches of depth. You can do the math and see that a one-acre field that was only two feet wide would be four miles long. So plowing one full acre of any shape was considered a full day's work for one horse and operator whether that man was walking or riding. Plowing a 40-acre field would take a month so no wonder farms were much smaller than they are now. Check out our photos below.

Here's are three paragraphs I found on the internet – The question of how many horses to keep was tied closely to the value of the tractor when the farmer considered the most hectic stage of production: springtime plowing. Without a tractor, plowing created a temporary large demand for horses. After the ground thawed, farmers had only a few weeks available to break and disk their fields. Plowing was a time-consuming job: a single horse took a full ten-hour day to break one acre.

A single draught horse can normally pull a single-furrow plow in clean light soil, but in heavier soils two horses are needed, one walking on the land and one in the furrow. For plows with two or more furrows more than two horses are needed and, usually, one or more horses have to walk on the loose plowed sod – and that makes hard going for them, and the horse treads the newly plowed land down. It is usual to rest such horses every half hour for about ten minutes.

Amish farmers tend to use a team of about seven horses or mules when spring plowing and as Amish farmers often help each other plow, teams are sometimes changed at noon. Using this method about 10 acres can be plowed per day in light soils and about 2 acres in heavy soils.

Will, Kayla, Ava, and Blake, the letter on the next page was written 145 years ago by your great great great great uncle Charles Reiss. He was the third son of Adam Reiss who established our family farm in 1838. Charles loaned his team of mules to a neighbor near his farm in O'Fallon,

Illinois who severely overworked and underfed them. Charles was not happy and minced no words. His phonetic English is a challenge at times. German was his first language. Enjoy.

Love, Granddad

Jan the 7th, 1869
O'Fallon

Brother Frank,

I am giting consarn for not hearing anney news of Brother Martin or of anney one of yours. Martin I gas is not com & you I expected to com Chrismas or New Years but you dit not so, how ever the weder (*weather*) dus not alweys alou satch as travling wit familay.

Frank I will let you know to bee careful next time in loning your team. That fallow of corse went out the Collinsville Road. At least he was at his broter in laws & I think or have heard so that tha had a fallin out togater & so he come up to me yet after we hat spoken & he told me storey that tha hat been at the graveyard at her Faters so long. We knot (*knowed*) in the first quarter of an hour that the men drove them. The poor mules was awful hukray (*hungry*) and tursday (*thirsty*), but don't you tell him about it at least not of me. I gave him corn along & told him partickler to feed tham in Balleville. But it is doutful if he has dun it. I du dispice the fallow now. Some how I think he had to much back at home alltho that she is nothing but a little shiting liing bitch & dumhead.

Frank I wish you talk C. Armbruster. See wen my note is du, what day & month. I will send the interest, but see if I can have the money six monts or a year longer. Trey so if you can. We have a good prospect for next year. Our wheat looks splandant yet. Let me know in time of all quasttions. I think my mother in law is out there now. Have you seen one hurt of her? Are their anney thing new? News of Martin or Crone?

Come over hear some time yet if you can. If there should bee more satch nice weter, Mother & Ebert could come even too. I have my cyder tabt (*tapped*) now. Tell tham so & give my love to Mother & children. I also give my complaments to you & famlay and hope that this will find you all in good heald. My selve & famley have been pradey well ever sins William began to walk a little sins three days. He is very slow about it. Your Brother,

C. J. Reiss

PS: How dit Chrismas & Newyears pa of? Our Chrismas a friend of ours paid for a gallon of bear witch we drink in the eavning & lunsht (*lunch*) sassach (*sausage*) to it. A happy & lucke new year to you all in dat famley.

One-Room School in Floraville, Illinois

Dear Will and Kayla,   September 16, 2013

This coming Wednesday would have been the 95th birthday of your great grandfather, Irwin H. Reiss. He and his two older brothers, Bill and Frank, were all very smart young men thanks in large part to their outstanding teacher, Oscar Probst. Irwin and Frank had Mr. Probst as a teacher for all eight years but their older brother Bill who started school in the fall of 1918 had a different teacher for the first two years. All three boys walked 1.7 miles from the Reiss family farm west to Floraville for instruction in a one-room school. My dad used to boast that it was uphill both directions and really cold in the winters.

OSCAR J. PROBST

There was a celebration honoring Mr. Probst on 9/18/1955. He was a highly regarded public servant having taught at the Floraville School from 1920 to 1937 and earlier from 1910 to 1911. He had many two-generation students who fondly remember him. Several of his former students including my Uncle Frank Reiss formed a committee to honor Mr. Probst. Frank was part of the program.

This Floraville School is also where your great great grandfather, George Reiss, was educated as a youngster as were six of his ten siblings. The other four died before they reached school age. My grandfather served as the clerk of the Floraville school board for over 20 years so you know that education was a big priority in his family.

The photo below was taken by Frank Reiss in 1962. A few years later the building was sold to a family who converted it into a private home. Several rooms were added in the front and along one side but the original structure still survives.

Here's a story from 12/14/1964 about the closing of this one-room school in Floraville.

The school bell has tolled for the last time in Floraville. Residents of the Illinois community will no longer hear the sonorous

summons to study nor see the students scurrying from the playground into the brick building. The bell will be replaced next fall by the toot of a horn as school busses transport the youngsters to a consolidated school at nearby Smithton.

The children were generally happy about the change as they look forward to the newness and excitement of a larger school. One girl, however, who had attended several large and small schools, said she preferred the smallest of them all – Floraville. She enjoyed being able to know all the other students and to study under a "real ding dong teacher – the best."

One-room schools were once the backbone of rural education in the United States. In them, one teacher had to work long and hard to teach 20, 30, or more pupils in all eight grades. In past decades, before the push for consolidation, the county and state fortified the country schools with roving specialists – county nurses, music and art teachers, audio-visual specialists – and with radio programs directed at the one-room schools. As the number of these schools dwindled, however, these services were dropped.

In Floraville, local sentiment backed by the fear of higher taxes in the consolidated districts helped the one-room country school to survive as long as it did. In 1963, however, the state did not issue its usual certificate of recognition to Floraville, thus posing the threat of the end of state aid. Floraville residents decided it was time to give up their school, which had flourished for over 50 years.

The one-room school has its disadvantages. Small classes eliminate much of the competition between students that educators feel is important. Classes are necessarily short and study projects limited because of the many demands on the lone teacher. Yet, an inquisitive youngster could obtain an excellent education in a one-room school. There was always the intriguing opportunity to eavesdrop on class discussions of the upper grades or to browse among the histories, novels, and anthologies meant for the older students.

There were fifteen of one-room schools in the area of our family farm. The school in Floraville is #4 near the bottom center.

Undoubtedly, much has been gained by the consolidation of rural schools, but just as certainly something has been lost. A one-room school was always a family affair – especially during the Christmas programs, the Arbor Day outings, the spring picnics. The big disadvantage of a one-room school – its smallness – was also its charm.

The last recess of the last day of school is a joyous occasion for the boys, girls, and a tag-along dog at the Floraville School, 10 miles southwest of Belleville. It was a sad day, however, for the lone teacher who had worked for 15 years in the little brick building and the many alumni of the school who still live in the tiny Illinois community. Floraville, the last of the one-room schools in St. Clair County (once there were about 100), will not re-open in the fall. Its 17 pupils will ride busses to a nearby consolidated school. As elsewhere in rural America, the one-room school will become merely a nostalgic memory. In 1945, before the push towards consolidated districts began, there were 8,045 one-room schools in Illinois. In the 1963-64 term, there were only 15.

So, Will and Kayla, one-room schoolhouses had their place in history. They were effective and practical for small and somewhat isolated communities before the days of school buses. Some parents today choose to home school their children which is kinda like a modern version of a one-room school but without all the friendships and memories from recess and special programs.

Love, Granddad

Shucking the Down Row

Dear Will, Kayla, Ava, and Blake,   September 15, 2014

This is one of the phrases my dad used frequently with older friends who had grown up on a farm. It refers to hand picking or shucking individual ears of field corn from rows that had been knocked down during old time harvests by horses, wagons, tractors pulling early combines, etc. That job usually fell to the farm children since they could bend over more easily than adults and were already closer to the ground. Here's a recent photo of Amish farmers harvesting corn with two teams of horses, one pulling a two-row corn picker and the other a wagon. You can see how the first pass around a field of corn to "open it up" for harvesting would result in at least four rows of corn being knocked down which then required hand shucking.

In this photo, the horses have been replaced by a tractor which was powerful enough to pull the two-row corn picker and a wagon. The tractor is not as wide as four horses, so it would knock down only two or three rows of corn in opening up a field.

Farmers shucking the down rows used a curved husking knife or a peg strapped to the palm of a heavy glove. The person walked down each row, picking corn from stalks on the right and left, twisting each ear from the stalk and tossing it into a

wagon pulled by horses or a tractor. He had a peg on his hand and would open the shucks, pull the ear out, and throw it in the wagon. Here are three different husking peg designs for sale on eBay for $26.

For about ten years I was a member of the International Society of Apple Parer Enthusiasts (APES) and Kollectors of Old Kitchen Stuff (KOOKS). Kinda fits my personality, don't ya think? Those are associations of serious collectors of old cast iron kitchen contraptions like the 350 pieces in my basement museum. One of the founders of APES was Jim Moffett of Modesto, Illinois which is 40 miles southwest of Springfield. Grand DD and I visited Jim and Phyllis about five years ago to get acquainted and to see his premium collection of apple devices. It was awesome and really put my collection to shame. Anyway, Jim had written a book, American Corn Huskers, which I purchased from them with autographs. We also gave them a pint of our homemade maple syrup.

Husking pegs were Jim's special interest because he grew up harvesting entire fields of corn by hand and not just the down rows. The 1938 Illinois State Corn Husking Contest was held on his family farm near Modesto. Total crowd for that event was 85,000 so it was a super huge deal. Jim's book is a summary with drawings of 262 patents for huskers dating from 1856 to 1938.

The next corn harvesting invention was to mount the corn picker on the front sides of the tractor. The farmer is still harvesting two rows but there is no offset and no knocked down corn requiring hand shucking. In all three corn

picking methods, the crop was harvested as ear corn which was then transferred to a wooden or metal corn crib for further drying and storage. Ear corn could be fed directly to hogs and cattle but it had to be ground for chickens.

Combines with greatly increased capacity and sophistication are available today. Here is the largest one in North America with 16 rows and a powerful Caterpillar diesel engine with 462 horsepower. It can harvest 80 bushels of corn per minute and stores it as loose seeds rather than as ear corn. Its grain tank on top holds 360 bushels so in a record crop year like 2014, that tank will fill on less than two acres or five minutes. That's why the takeaway wagon drives along side so the harvest can be offloaded on the go through that black auger on top that swings out.

Will, Kayla, Ava, and Blake, the days of "shucking the down row" are over but the idea of hardworking farmers being judicious stewards of their crop, their equipment, their land, and the environment in general are just as strong as when my dad Irv, his dad George, his dad Frank, and his dad Adam were doing all this by hand on the Reiss family farm since 1838.

Today, in one minute farmers can harvest what it took farmers 100 years ago to do in one day!!! Modern machines are radically more productive and expensive. That why farmers need 2,000 or more acres to support those larger capital investments to make all the numbers work out.

This Thursday would have been my dad's 97th birthday. So, Happy Birthday, Dad. I'm sure your great grandchildren enjoyed learning something more about your childhood – and just in time to watch record corn and soybean crops being harvested this month and next.

Love, Granddad

PS: I sent this story on August 28 to some of my farmer friends. Here is what I got back from Velma Peterson whose family is crop share tenants on six of our farms including YOUR DOUBLE R and my latest reclaim farm called Peabody.

Fred & Velma Peterson

Great, Steve, I remember some of these things all too well. One winter we had a picker much like the one in the picture with the Farmall, however it was mounted on to the tractor, a Farmall H, as I recall. But the ground didn't freeze and we had had too many fall rains and my dad and Fred's dad purchased a team of horses each to go back to the old days of picking corn by hand, shucking pegs and all. The wagon always had one side taller than the other so when you tossed the corn into the wagon it would keep you from overthrowing the ear. My dad kept that team of horses for many years--just in case we had another wet fall. Some times the farmer would shuck the rows to open the field so they didn't have any down corn. Do remember one year my sister and I gleaned corn over the Thanksgiving vacation from school in shorts and short sleeved blouses for it was so warm. The early varieties didn't have some of the traits to keep it standing and we would glean most fields. Research has come a long way in helping in this matter.

As far as soybeans, my dad was one of the first farmers in the area to plant soybeans. The beans, themselves, were black in color and made great hay for the dairy cattle. They weren't worth anything at the elevator, but he had read that they were extremely good feed for dairy cattle. Boy was that hay itchy when it was bailed, but the cows loved it. Suppose that was a form of feed similar to soybean meal.

Sorry Steve, didn't intend to go on so long, but it was a happy time. Lunch hour was always an hour for the horses needed the rest and time to eat their grain. Consequently the farmer rested too. Loved those days and the great meals that the ladies of the neighborhood would compile.

Would love to sit at that table again for just a little while. No cells or ipads too, only the talk.

Velma

Hoistin' Hay

Dear Will, Kayla, Ava, and Blake,   June 8, 2015

Here's a picture from about 1920 of my grandfather "Pop" Reiss using a hay trolley system to load hay into his new barn on the family farm. Looks pretty clever and maybe even a little fun with horses and the smell of fresh hay. All that hay was grown, cut, and cured in two or three such cycles during the summer and fall. Then it's loaded as loose hay like this or as bales onto a hayrack and brought under the pointy end (hay hood) way up high on the barn. Then a work crew moved it up and into the haymow or loft where it was stored for use during the winter as food for cows and horses which were fed in the lower half of the barn. That single horse in the middle of this picture does all the work by pulling a rope to raise the hay and pull it inside the barn.

The barn hay carrier or trolley must be a very reliable device due to its location. The peak of the barn juts out, extending the track, so the lift pulley can go up and down outside the barn. Under the peak, a large barn door was needed to not limit the amount of hay carried up and in with each load. A "trip block" is bolted to the track under the peak that locks the carrier position and releases the lift pulley to drop down to the hayrack or wagon on the ground where it is loaded with loose or baled hay. A large pull rope, typically 1" diameter which can lift 7000 pounds, threads through the carrier and lift pulley, through several pulleys at the other end of the mow, and then through outside pulleys where it can be pulled by horses or a tractor. Hanging from the lift pulley is a hay fork or a sling, which has a trip rope attached to release the hay and to pull the

351

carrier back out to the peak for the next load. This mechanization made filling large barns with hay and bedding a manageable task.

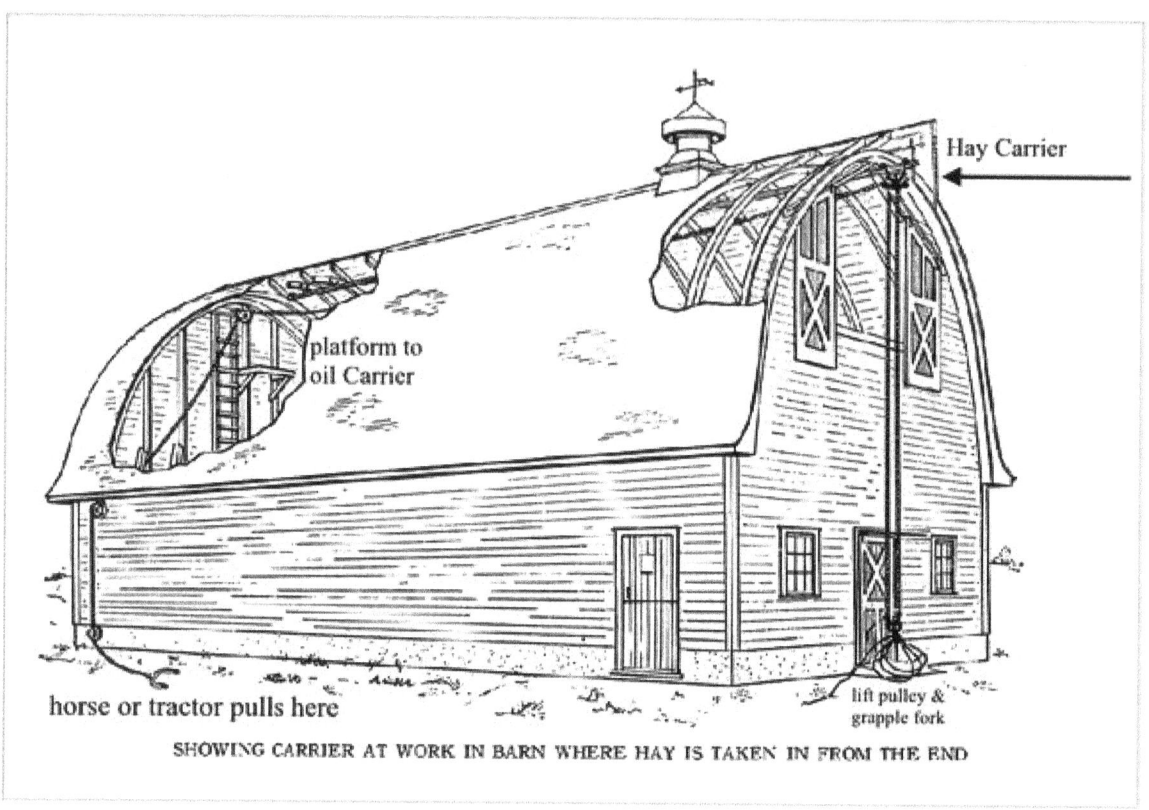

platform to oil Carrier

Hay Carrier

horse or tractor pulls here

lift pulley & grapple fork

SHOWING CARRIER AT WORK IN BARN WHERE HAY IS TAKEN IN FROM THE END

I wrote to our crop share tenant, Shaun Drake, on our Turman Creek farm near Sullivan to ask about any hay trolley that might still be in that barn. Here is is reply:

Hello Steve. That was a very good article. It was truly an amazing system back in the day. Our grandparents had an old barn with a trolley that us kids used to play on like that. We would swing across the barn and fall into the hay. That old barn burnt a few years back. It was kinda sad.

As far as the Turman Creek barn track goes, it appears it was a double track. It is metal. The trolley is missing. I tried navigating in the old barn yesterday, but it is in such poor shape I couldn't get very far. The track is all mangled and bent apart. The old barn has just given up. Do you happen to know what year that barn was constructed? It looks like it was built with wooden pegs. Thanks, Shaun

Here's an advertisement from 1940 which shows carriers that run on metal rails or on wooden beams. It also shows hay forks for grabbing a large bundle of loose hay. There is also a sketch showing carriers unloading hay in a one-story barn. Note the three directional pulleys between the carrier and the horse pulling the rope.

HAYING TOOLS AND ACCESSORIES

DIRECTIONS FOR ERECTING MYERS' PATENT STEEL TRACK

Scaffold by placing ropes from rafter to rafter, say 6 feet from ridge pole or peak and about 10 feet apart. Then place extension ladder across the ropes with board to stand on. Now nail one rafter bracket temporarily at each end of barn and drawn a line from one end to the other and stretch tight.

Then nail all rafter brackets even with this line. You are now ready to put up the track, which can be done in sections. Hoist near to rafter brackets by ropes. Then place hanging hook over rafter bracket and down through track, attach lower clamp and tighten lock nut.

MATERIAL REQUIRED FOR A STEEL TRACK OUTFIT FOR DIFFERENT LENGTH BARNS

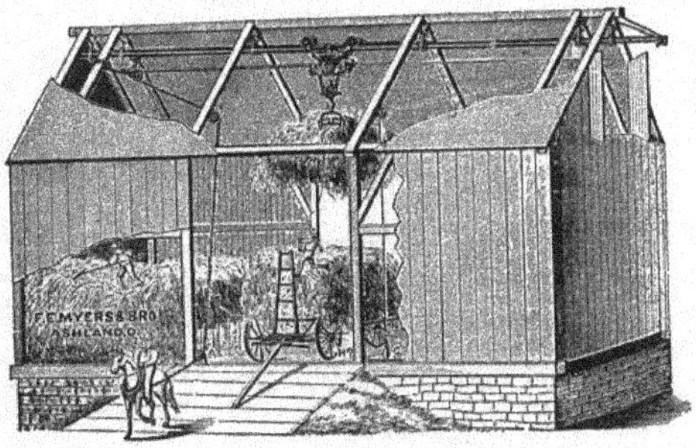

For a 40 Foot Barn—One Hay Unloader. 36 ft. Steel Track. 19 Hanging Hooks. 19 Rafter Brackets. 5 Knot Passing Pulleys. 1 Fork or 3 Slings. 6 Floor Hooks. 110 ft. ¾ in. Manila Rope. 50 ft. ⅝ in. Trip Rope. 40 ft. ⅝ in. Reverse Rope.

For a 50 Foot Barn—One Hay Unloader. 48 ft. Steel Track. 25 Hanging Hooks. 25 Rafter Brackets. 5 Knot Passing Pulleys. 1 Fork or 3 Slings. 6 Floor Hooks. 130 ft. ¾ in. Manila Rope. 55 ft. ⅝ in. Trip Rope. 50 ft. ⅝ in. Reverse Rope.

For a 60 Foot Barn—One Hay Unloader. 54 ft. Steel Track. 28 Hanging Hooks. 28 Rafter Brackets. 5 Knot Passing Pulleys. 1 Fork or 3 Slings. 6 Floor Hooks. 160 ft. ¾ in. Manila Rope. 60 ft. ⅝ in. Trip Rope. 60 ft. ⅝ in. Reverse Rope.

For a 70 Foot Barn—One Hay Unloader. 66 ft. of Track. 34 Hanging Hooks. 3½ lbs. Bracket Nails. 5 Fig. 1120 Pulleys. 1 Fork or 3 Slings. 6 Floor Hooks. 190 ft. ¾ in. Draft Rope. 70 ft. ⅝ in. Trip Rope. 70 ft. ⅝ in. Reverse Rope.

For an 80 Foot Barn—One Hay Unloader. 78 ft. of Track. 40 Hanging Hooks. 40 Rafter Brackets. 4 lbs. Bracket Nails. 5 Fig. 1120 Pulleys. 1 Fork or 3 Slings. 6 Floor Hooks. 210 ft. ¾ in. Draft Rope. 80 ft. ⅝ in. Trip Rope. 80 ft. ⅝ in. Reverse Rope.

Different lengths of barns will use track, hanging hook and rope in same ratio as above.

If required to take hay in at end of barn and have rope pass down at far end to horse, same amount of draft rope. If draft rope be returned to same end of barn and then down, this requires about one-fourth more draft rope.

How to Reverse Carrier—Set fork in hay. Tie ends of rope together, to which horse and weight are attached. Pull on small rope until knot comes to the floor, then untie ropes. Fasten weight G on small rope, change pulley A to floor hook H. This reverses carrier for opposite direction without leaving the floor or climbing up. Use all knot passing pulleys. For taking in hay at end of barn use V-shaped brace for track support, as shown in cut.

HAY CARRIERS

MYERS' CLOVER LEAF UNLOADER

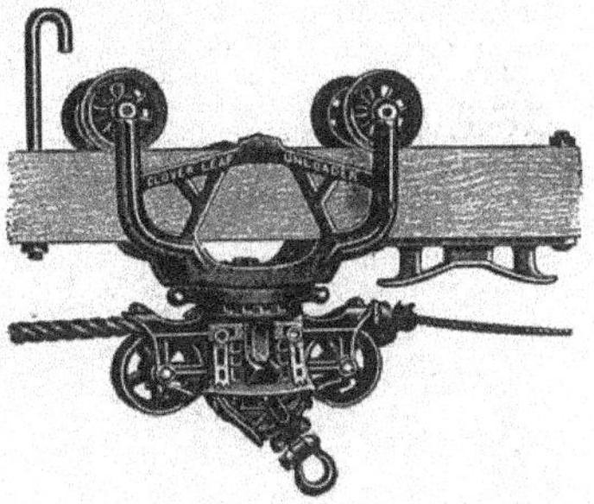

For Wood Track; Rope Draft; Reversible and Swivel

Built for using rope for draft. Malleable iron throughout. Fitted with wide open mouth to receive the fork pulley when approaching in any direction. Swinging fork pulley relieves the carrier from all strain when drawing hay over high beam or into well filled mow.

The track wheels revolve on turned steel axles. Rope sheaves and track wheels are fitted with large turned bearings. Rope sheaves have long hubs.

By the swivel and reversible device the machine can be reversed by reversing the swivel or by drawing the rope through from end to end.

Each

No. 120—12 in. truck; ¾ in. turned steel axles; 4 in. sheaves; wt. each 32 lbs. $12.00

Open stock.

HAY CARRIERS

MYERS' CLOVER LEAF UNLOADER

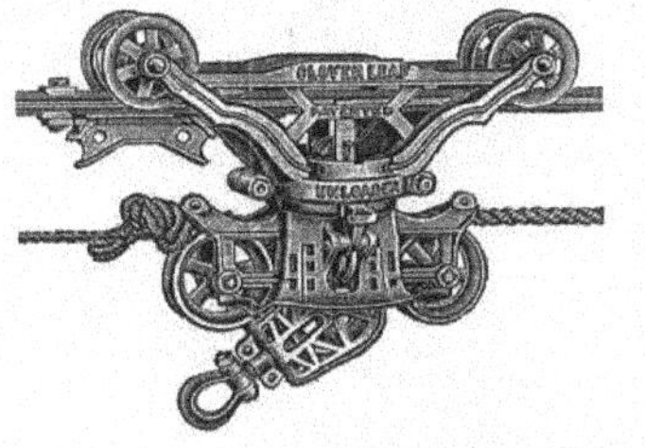

For Double Steel Track; Adjustable to Fit All Makes of Steel Track; Rope Draft; Reversible and Swivel

Built for using rope for draft. Malleable iron throughout. It is heavy and substantially built. Fitted with wide open mouth to receive the fork pulley when approaching in any direction. Swinging fork pulley relieves the carrier from all strain when drawing hay over high beam or into well filled mow.

The track wheels revolve on turned steel axles. The rope sheaves have longer hubs than any other make of carrier. Lock is composed of three parts and has no springs. It grasps the fork pulley on either side.

Complete with fork pulley and knocker.

Each

No. 118—16 in. truck, 4 in. sheaves, 3¼ in. track wheels; wt. each 30 lbs. $12.00

Open stock.

HAY FORKS

MYERS' ADJUSTABLE COMPRESSION GRAPPLE

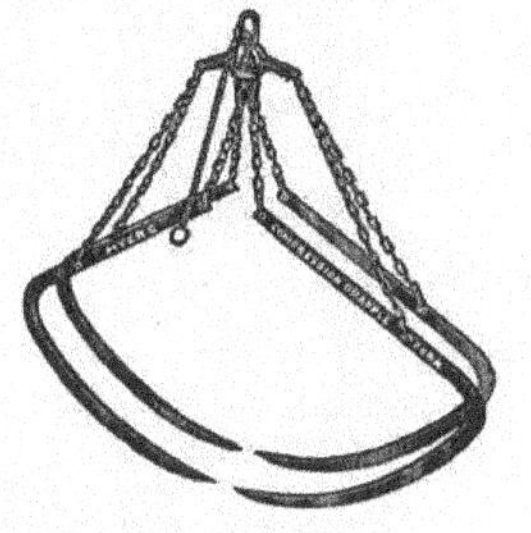

Hardened spring steel tines, carefully oil tempered.

Handles any kind of hay straw; beans or corn fodder. Lifts an unusually large load. Easy to handle and set as it returns to the load closed and locked. To set the fork, grasp two of the tines, one in each hand, and force them into the hay as far apart as desired. Then set the others in the same manner. When the load is lifted each tine draws toward the center, compressing the load which permits handling short or loose material.

Drops the hay in the mow in the same position as on the wagon, making it easy to spread in the mow.

Each

No. 1A—4-tine; 26 in. tines; 77 in. spread when open; wt. each 38 lbs. $12.50

Open stock.

Here is an assortment of different carrier designs. All of them have wheels at the top which allow them to run along a horizontal steel track. All of these carriers have a central drop down pulley that does the vertical work. All of them have a knot to secure one end of the rope to the carrier. Sometimes there is a hole in the cast iron carrier body for that knot and sometimes that knot is against a wheel that does not rotate. I prefer those with the extra wheel like the two on top and the two on the right just because they are more symmetrical and look a lot more artsy. I would like to make one into a chandelier in my log cabin. Read on.

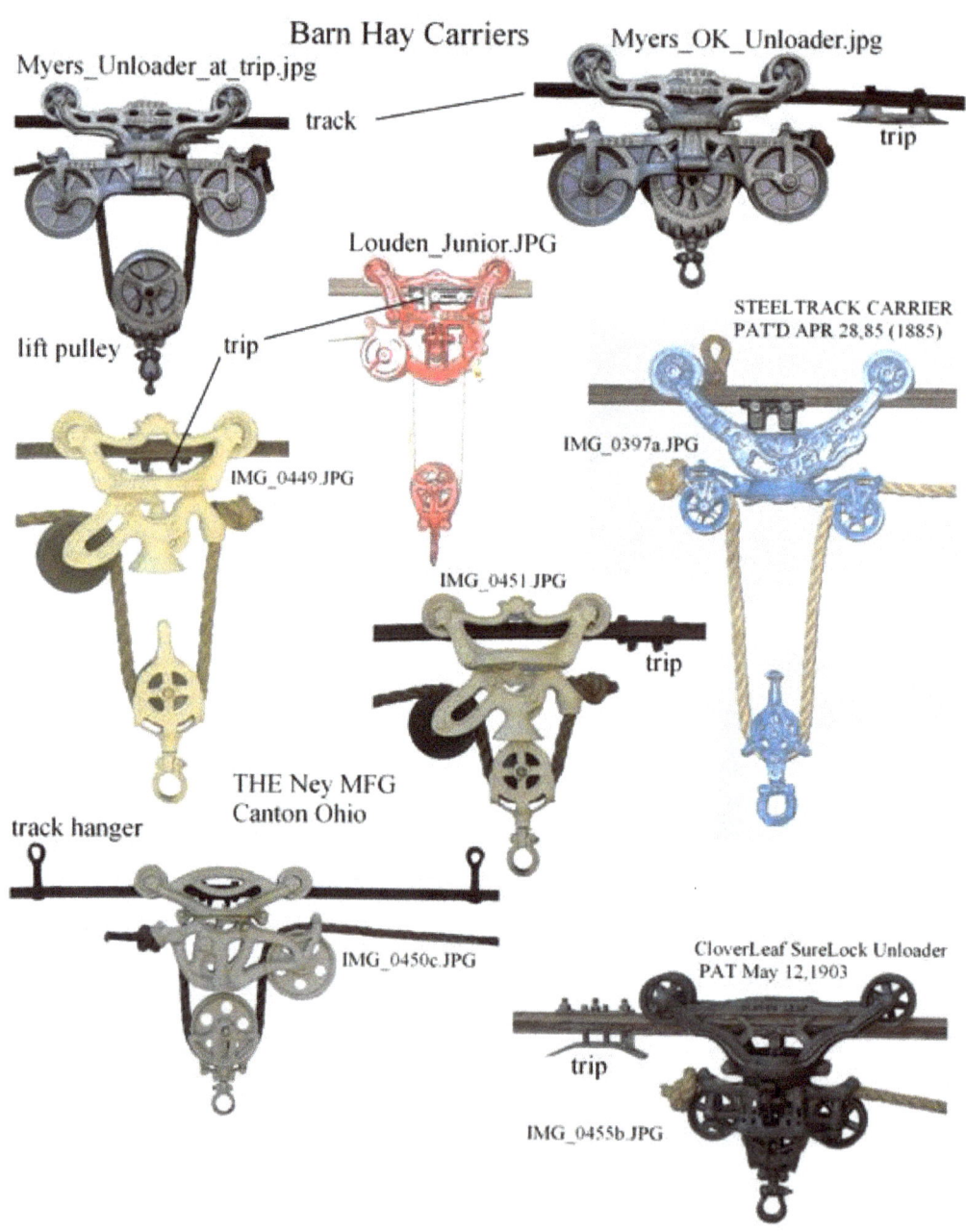

Barn Hay Carriers

Myers_Unloader_at_trip.jpg

Myers_OK_Unloader.jpg

track

trip

lift pulley

trip

Louden_Junior.JPG

STEEL TRACK CARRIER
PAT'D APR 28,85 (1885)

IMG_0397a.JPG

IMG_0449.JPG

IMG_0451.JPG

trip

track hanger

THE Ney MFG
Canton Ohio

IMG_0450c.JPG

CloverLeaf SureLock Unloader
PAT May 12,1903

trip

IMG_0455b.JPG

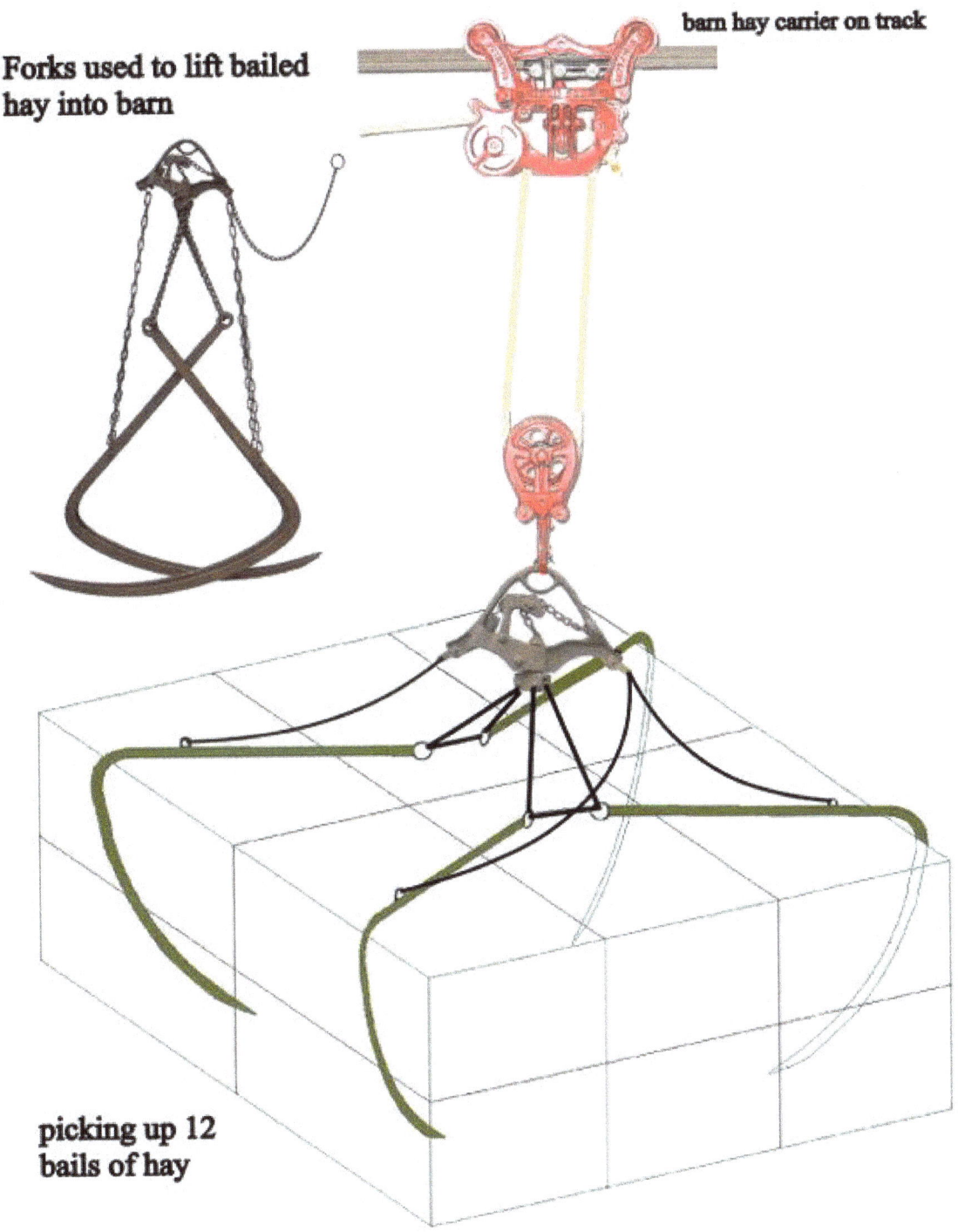

Forks used to lift bailed hay into barn

barn hay carrier on track

picking up 12 bails of hay

Hay trolley history can be divided into two distinct but overlapping phases. The period between 1860 and 1920 was the era of invention and experimentation for trolley makers, when numerous small-scale "cottage" manufacturers drew designs and filed for patents. There were three such producers in Illinois, two in Indiana, and one each in Iowa, Ohio, and Wisconsin.

The years between 1900 and 1945 marked the peak of hay trolley manufacture. Like many companies of that era, most small, independent makers were consolidated into just a few large companies, which in turn dominated the trolley market. Even at the peak of business before World War II, only a few companies boasted total earnings of more than $100,000 per year. There were three in Illinois, three in Wisconsin, two in Ohio, and one in Iowa.

Eight manufacturers produced 400 different trolley designs over the years. The largest segment of the trolleys was made by one manufacturer, F.E. Myers Bro., of Ashland, Ohio. Myers produced about 58 different trolley types through the years. The company is still in business and has an extensive collection of sales literature/catalogs. They also make hardware for sliding barn doors, rolling library shelf ladders, etc.

Farmers used hay trolleys to move square bales into barns well into the 1980s, but that system lost importance with the introduction of large round bales which were simply too heavy for the trolleys. Haymows and two story barns are now obsolete as a result.

Here is the 100-year old hay trolley I bought from Bob Anderson on eBay last spring to make into a chandelier for our log cabin. I'm going to add low-heat LED light bulbs inside half a dozen old Ball Mason canning jars to hang down from the lower pulleys. I later salvaged the hay trolley and track when the old barn on the Reiss family farm was demolished in September 2015. Both trolleys are Clover Leaf designs but ours from the home farm is slightly smaller. ==Now one track will have two hay trolley carrier chandeliers in stereo!!!==

Dear Will, Kayla, Ava, and Blake, isn't all this mechanical stuff fascinating? Can you imagine getting all that hay up into a mow by just manual labor? You've seen the 350 cast iron kitchen contraptions in my basement museum. If I had stayed as an unsupervised single man, I would have probably built two or three more log cabins and a large post and beam barn to display even larger collections of guy stuff. Fortunately, I am supervised (that would be Grand DD) and as such, censor my quirky interests to smaller and fewer items to thus keep that "uniqueness" down to a dull roar. The workings of a hay trolley are at one time simple enough for a young person to understand, yet can make an engineer pause and appreciate their genius.

Love, Granddad

Grandma's Sewing Machine

Dear Will, Kayla, Ava, and Blake,   June 29, 2015

This is the sewing machine that my grandma Katie Reiss used for many years. Maybe you remember seeing it in our log cabin. It was made by White Sewing Machine Company which is now part of the Husavarna Viking Company. Its serial number is 1665378.

The first White patent date was March 11, 1890 which is exactly two weeks before Grandma was born in March 25, 1890. Hers is a Family Rotary (FR) model.

I called Husqvarna Viking at 800 446 2333 and was told her machine was made on 6/18/1911 if it has a round bobbin case or it was made on 2/26/1909 if it has a bullet style shuttle. I checked and it has a bullet type shuttle so it was made two years before Grandma and Pop were married on 4/16/1911.

This machine does not need electricity but instead was powered by the operator pedaling on the foot treadle. It's hard to see in the picture below but there is a narrow leather belt that wraps around top of the machine just left of the hand wheel and then wraps around a pulley to the right of the foot treadle. The operator would first push start the large wheel on top to get the machine in motion and then keep it going by foot power. These were called "treadle" sewing machines regardless of the actual brand name.

White was, next to Singer, perhaps the largest and best known of the US sewing machine companies. Unlike Singer, they did not offer many different models, or change models very often. Their engineering was extremely good, and their products stood the test of time. They introduced their VS machine in the late 1870's and manufactured it with minor improvements into the early 1900's. They introduced a new model, the Family Rotary, or FR, which was a very well designed and strong machine, in the late 1890's and manufactured this design, with some variations, up until World War II.

The company was founded by Thomas White, who had some prior experience in sewing machine manufacturing. He located in Cleveland, Ohio. The company was formed in 1876. White was a large and prosperous company, giving Singer a run for their money. White took over the Domestic and King sewing machine companies and eventually became White Consolidated Industries. They ceased manufacturing in the United States sometime after WWII, probably the late 60's or early 70's. After that their machines were made in Japan.

The White machines found today are very usable. There is one serious consideration as to the VS machines ... the shuttle and bobbin are very unique. The shuttle has a post in it, and the bobbin has a hollow core.

The White Family Rotary is the most common White. They are a truly outstanding machine. One caution on this model ... Everything about the White is the reverse of the Singer ... the hand wheel rotates away from you instead of toward you, and the thread rolls off of the bobbin in the favored, or easy, direction, not cutting back over a lip as on Singer round bobbins.

358

White owned their own forests and operated their own cabinet factories, rather than contracting this out. They were noted for having the highest quality of cabinets. Their library table and Martha Washington sewing cabinet model electrics are classics, as is the Mission or Arts and Crafts treadle.

Grandma's sewing machine included this attachment kit made by The Greist Manufacturing Company of New Haven, CN. It is used on ruffler, tucker, and hemmer operations. Patent date on some pieces is 7/7/1891.

Grand DD and I saw dozens of old treadle sewing machines in daily use in Nepal while we were there for three weeks in May 2013 building houses with Habitat for Humanity. You already know these machines were very well made but the reason they are still so popular is that they do not need electricity. That allows every small shop or home to have a treadle machine to earn a living or at least make clothes for themselves. We saw several portable machines where there is a small peg on the hand wheel so it can be cranked by hand. There is no treadle or cabinet with drawers.

Two years ago your dad/uncle Adam and I had a tour of the Methodist Midwest Mission Distribution Center in Chatham, Illinois just southeast of Springfield. They specialize in refurbishing old treadle sewing machines for the third world, particularly Africa. These non-electric machines allow young women to make a living by sewing rather than by prostitution like so many historically resorted to. So now I look for old treadle machines at garage sales and flea markets so we can donate them to the MMDC for another life. Here's an ad by the MMDC.

MMDC is also in need of treadle sewing machines.

Machines do not need to be in working order– although that is a plus; MMDC has volunteers who repair machines. Questions? call 217-483-7911 or email office@midwestmissiondc.org

Will, Kayla, Ava, and Blake, I bought a replacement leather belt from the MMDC to hopefully put my Grandma's sewing machine back in operation. Maybe we can make handkerchiefs or something similar some day. Maybe we can also donate time to the MMDC to help those who are less fortunate. They also refurbish bicycles and stuff goody bags with household goods.

Love, Granddad

Sickle Bar Mower

Dear Will and Kayla,   August 13, 2012

Maybe you remember seeing this sickle-bar mower in our front yard. It's the result of a little joke I played on Grand DD. She had been asking for years that I buy her a riding mower so she could help with mowing the grass and keeping our yard looking nice. I had thought that a riding mower was simply not practical given the number of trees it would have to mow around. You can see some of those trees in the background.

So one day I was browsing at Dewey Egen's outdoor antique shop on the south side of Peoria. He has a lot of neat iron junk at reasonable prices. So I bought this riding mower and your dad/uncle Adam helped me load it into our truck, bring it to our home, and place it in southeast corner of our front yard.

I went inside and happily told Grand DD that I had finally gotten a good deal on a one-horsepower riding mower to answer her long time request. I brought her outside and showed her our purchase. Well, to say the least, Grand DD was not too impressed. But we all had a good laugh and it fits well with our woodsy urban setting. I think she is used to my goofiness.

Go to http://www.youtube.com/watch?v=z2Y9Re8j2ak and you can see this mower in operation cutting weeds. Ironically it is being pulled by the kind of riding mower that Grand DD really had in mind. But that demonstration makes a huge point and emphasizes the reason that sickle bar mowers were invented in the first place. They cut off weeds, alfalfa, wheat stubble, etc. at ground level so the farmer can rake the cuttings into windrows to bail and eventually feed to his livestock. Modern riding lawnmowers leave weeds and grass in tiny bits that are simply too small to bail and feed to animals. So still today there are ongoing needs for both kinds of mowers.

Here's a paragraph in engineer-speak about our McCormick-Deering No. 7 sickle bar mower. This one applies to both one- and two-horsepower models. *The mover converts the curvilinear motion of the ground wheels into the rectilinear motion of the knife. Transmission by gears alone is the most common method. The large gear is keyed to the main axle, and meshes with the small spur gear on the secondary shaft. The large bevel gear on this shaft in turn meshes with the bevel pinion on the counter shaft. The left wheel drives a gear box which powers the cutting. The left back pedal engages the drive shaft. The power is transmitted down the shaft to a flywheel. A piece of wood, which is no longer there, connected the flywheel to the mower blade. The right handle swings the mower vertical to allow for going to and from the field. The right back handle controls the angle of the mower to the ground. The hitch pole is setup for two horses that would be walking to the left of the rows now to be mowed.*

In 1902, J.P. Morgan merged the **McCormick Harvesting Machine Company** and Deering Harvester Company, along with three smaller agricultural equipment firms, to create International Harvester. IH over the years used a number of brand names to market its tractor and harvesting products. The McCormick-Deering brand name was used from 1923 to 1947 so that's the age range of our riding mower. In 1985 IH sold its agricultural division to J. I. Case which was renamed as Case IH. The remainder of IH was renamed as Navistar International in 1986.

So anyway, Will and Kayla, that's probably more than you really wanted to know about Grand DD's riding mower which is now a yard ornament. But for what it's worth, I'm aware of three other No. 7 mowers that are also used as yard ornaments. Let me know if you would like one for your yard.

Love, Granddad

Corn Shocks

Dear Will, Kayla, Ava, and Blake,   November 24, 2014

Have your dads sing <u>and dance</u> **"The Twelve Days of Christmas"** when December finally arrives and Santa Claus is just around the corner. It was one of their favorite and fun Christmas activities when they were your ages and a bit older. "The Twelve Days of Christmas" is an English Christmas carol that enumerates a series of increasingly grand gifts given on each of the twelve days of Christmas in the manner of a cumulative song. The song, first published in England in 1780 without music as a chant or rhyme, is thought to be French in origin.

Here's a more modern farmers' version of that folk song. Notice that the grandest gift is a dozen corn shocks. So <u>corn shocks</u> are the subject of this story because they are my favorite symbol of old time farming. Corn shocks are extremely rare now and I haven't seen one for many years, let alone a whole field full of them like this Amish farm with long shadows in the setting sun.

On the twelfth day of Christmas, the farmer gave to me...

12 corn shocks standing
11 sweets for topping
10 exhibits for learning
9 chairs a-rocking
8 guests for dinner
7 buildings to explore
6 tractors plowing
5 special events,
4 barn cats,
3 tasty cheeses,
2 draft horses
and a sparrow in a fruit tree.

My favorite artist is Grant Wood. He was born in east central Iowa on 2/13/1891 and died a day before his 51st birthday on 2/12/1942. Grand DD and I toured his studio last year in Grand Rapids, Iowa. It was the carriage house to a

large mansion in the front which is now a funeral home. He lived and painted in that studio from 1924 to 1935 when he did many of his most important works. The most popular of course is "American Gothic" at right which is probably the second most famous painting in the world after the "Mona Lisa" by Leonardo da Vinci. The "gothic" part of that title comes from the window in the background. The woman is Wood's sister and the man is his dentist.

Wood is best known for his paintings depicting the rural American Midwest. The next page shows all four of his paintings which included corn shocks in the artwork. The first two were painted in the studio we visited as was American Gothic in 1930. Here is "The Cornfield" on the left from 1927 and "Fall Plowing" from 1931.

Here is "January" on the left from 1937 and "Iowa Cornfield" from 1941.

Notice the animal tracks in "January" which were made by a rabbit. That's their pattern of front feet side by side and back feet in line. They are easy to identify because I don't know any other critter that makes that pattern. This rabbit's tracks are leading out of the corn shock which means he must have weathered the snowstorm inside before venturing outside the next morning.

About January of 1957 (maybe 20 years to the day after Wood painted "January"!) my brother Ken, neighbor chum Dennis, and I were walking in a harvested cornfield north of the golf course in our hometown of Sullivan, Indiana. There was about four inches of snow on the ground. We noticed that rabbit tracks went into a foot tall heap of corn plant trash and that the tracks did not come out. That meant the rabbit was still inside. We slowly and quietly surrounded that heap and put all six of our gloved hands down on top of it. We slowly pulled out individual pieces of corn plants until we had that live wild rabbit in our hands. It was awesome to catch such a quick and elusive wild creature by hand. Ever since that experience, I have wondered whether Indians,

364

early farmers, hunters, and other curious kids like us had done the same thing with similar logic and similar success.

Here's another corn shock picture. It was taken by my Uncle Frank Reiss in 1944 and shows his young son George beside a huge corn shock on the Reiss family farm. The house in the background was built by my grandparents in 1940 and is what we called the "new house." This shock is in the field to the south. It may have been one of the last shocks my grandfather "Pop" Reiss made since later pictures show him husking individual ears of corn by hand rather than shocking entire plants. He retired from farming four years later in 1948 at age 75.

It was important to allow the ears of corn to dry on their stalks in the field for as long as possible, but still harvest them before wind, rain, or snow might blow down the mature plants. Corn that had fallen on the ground was difficult to harvest and could easily begin to rot. The farmer had two harvesting options. He could hand pick or husk individual ears from the standing corn, throw them into a slow moving horse-drawn wagon, and transfer it to a corncrib at his homestead where it would continue to air-dry naturally. Husking two wagonloads of ear corn by hand per day was considered good progress.

The farmer's other harvesting option was to cut individual plants off near the ground either by hand or with a horse-drawn binder and stack them as shocks of 60 to 200 complete corn plants. Those shocks would eventually be dismantled after further drying and ears of corn removed for transfer to a corncrib. The plant residue may or may not have then been hauled in to feed livestock. So shocking was a temporary or intermediate field storage option depending on available labor, weather, corncrib capacity, livestock feeding needs, etc. A percentage of the harvest also had to be saved as the next year's seed corn.

In early years on the prairie, settlers built small cribs from hewn logs and rough sawn boards for storing ear corn to feed livestock and to make their own cornmeal. Because it was important to keep the corn dry, these structures were built with simple roofs and raised wooden or fieldstone foundations. Pop had a corncrib like that just south of his barn. Its foundation was similar to what you can see on the old log granary which stored loose seeds of wheat, barley, rye, corn, etc.

Ear corn storage in cribs eventually gave way to shelled corn storage in round steel drying bins like those four north of the "old house." Today corn shocks are obsolete and made only for harvest festivals or by farming groups like the Amish who prefer older farming technologies.

Will, Kayla, Ava, and Blake, let's plan several trips around Illinois so we can learn more about corn shocks and corn husking. Three possibilities appear on the next page.

Love, Granddad

- Arthur, Illinois is about 130 miles southeast of Dunlap. That's where we can watch the Amish use horses to plow, plant, cultivate, harvest, and transport corn, both with or without that intermediate step of shocks. All of that was standard practice for your great great grandfather George "Pop" Reiss on the home farm. He never owned a tractor. We need to appreciate that history and realize how challenging it was in pre-electricity, pre-tractor days.

- Roseville, Illinois is about 75 miles west of Dunlap. That's where the Illinois State Corn Husking Contest has been held in late September for the past 33 years. There are eight age categories for boys, girls, men, and women. The top three finishers in each category go to the National Corn Husking Contest in Ohio.

- Kewanee, Illinois is about 40 miles northwest of Dunlap. That's where National Cornhuskers Hall of Fame is located. Seventy-five years ago, some of the most admired Midwestern athletes were not football or basketball players, but cornhuskers. Today, the National Cornhuskers' Hall of Fame in Kewanee, pays tribute to those men who had the physical strength and stamina to out-husk their competitors. For many years, a Kewanee business, Boss Manufacturing Company, produced corn husking wristbands, hooks and pegs. Some of those items, as well as company advertisements, are on display. Exhibits also feature patents for corn husking equipment, newspaper clippings, and an ear of corn from the 1932 national corn husking contest. The 1936 Corn husking Championship in Licking County, Ohio, attracted 160,000 spectators. At that time, the record crowd at a U.S. sporting event was 168,000 at the Memorial Day auto race in Indianapolis, making the corn husking competition the second largest event of the era.